DEVELOPING
APPLICATIONS
WITH
MICROSOFT OFFICE

Strategies for Designing, Developing, and Delivering
Custom Business Solutions Using Microsoft Office

CHRISTINE SOLOMON

PUBLISHED BY
Microsoft Press
A Division of Microsoft Corporation
One Microsoft Way
Redmond, Washington 98052-6399

Library of Congress Cataloging-in-Publication Data
Solomon, Christine, 1962–
    Developing applications with Microsoft office / by Christine
Solomon.
        p.   cm.
    Includes index.
    1. Microsoft Windows (Computer file). 2. Microsoft Word for
Windows. 3. Microsoft Excel for Windows. 4. Microsoft PowerPoint
for Windows. 5. Microsoft Mail for Windows. 6. Microsoft Access.
I. Title.
HF5548.2.S648 1995
650'.0285'5369--dc20   94-24466
                                                          CIP

Printed and bound in the United States of America.

1 2 3 4 5 6 7 8 9 QMQM 9 8 7 6 5 4

Distributed to the book trade in Canada by Macmillan of Canada, a division of Canada Publishing Corporation.

A CIP catalogue record for this book is available from the British Library.

Microsoft Press books are available through booksellers and distributors worldwide. For further information about
international editions, contact your local Microsoft Corporation office. Or contact Microsoft Press International
directly at fax (206) 936-7329.

Acquisitions Editor: Lucinda Rowley
Project Editor: Alix Krakowski
Manuscript Editor: Ina Chang
Technical Editor: Marc Young

For M. Votl

CONTENTS SUMMARY

TABLE OF CONTENTS

PART THREE   The Professional's Handbook

FOREWORD

I first met Christine Solomon when the firm she is with, Micro Modeling Associates, was involved in creating Bankers Trust's first graphical user interface standards. I was struck by her team's ability to make Microsoft Windows–based application development practical for both developers and end users. Since that time, we have worked with Christine and her firm on several projects, ranging from updates to the GUI standards to implementation of complex spreadsheet engines for our financial services businesses.

At Bankers Trust, we feel that it's important to broadly utilize a limited set of technologies. By successfully implementing our core technologies, we have proven over the years that we can deliver technological solutions faster, at lower cost, and with much higher quality than our competitors. When we first began experimenting with Windows several years ago, we found the beginnings of a technological solution that would carry us into the 1990s. Today, we use Windows, Microsoft Windows NT, and Microsoft Office throughout our organization—and we are realizing the benefits from this strategy.

As early adopters of this technology, we didn't have the benefit of a road map such as the one presented in this book. Learning by trial and error, with some help from outside firms, we were able to successfully implement Office solutions in our organization. We felt that a practical, well-thought-out book would save others the effort we expended to make appropriate use of this technology. When Christine first mentioned the possibility of a book on Office development, I was excited. Finally we would have something that put all the pieces together without burying us in every detail.

This book is the outcome of Christine's experience with Office development as well as that of Micro Modeling and many corporations. While the technology can often be complex, this book provides a path through that complexity. For new developers, it provides a great introduction. For managers like me it offers advice on what can be done with the technology without hyping it. And for all readers, it provides fun and interesting anecdotes on real-life experiences.

Lyle C. Anderson, Managing Director
Bankers Trust Information Services

PREFACE

A colleague of mine who started his career as a financial analyst likes to show a slide he created that features two pie charts. The first chart shows the percentage of the workday that financial analysts plan to devote to such tasks as typing data into spreadsheets (a small slice of the pie—just a sliver, really) and analyzing financial data (three-quarters of the pie). The second chart shows the actual time spent on these same tasks: Typing data into spreadsheets accounts for one-third of the pie, and analyzing financial data accounts for just over half of the pie.

You could create a similar pair of charts for many professional jobs because such jobs tend to present a similar problem: They require a great deal of time-consuming, PC-related labor, from manual formatting to data entry.

This book presents a solution to this problem: a Microsoft Office–based development strategy that decreases the amount of time people spend on such activities as data entry and manual formatting so that they can spend more time on productive business tasks. By developing custom applications with Office, you can deliver timesaving tools to the desktop—in Microsoft Excel and Microsoft Word.

Why I Wrote This Book

When Microsoft introduced Excel for Windows in the late 1980s, a few people immediately recognized the potential business value of a spreadsheet that included a full programming language. I built my first Excel application in 1989—a cash accounting and inventory system for a gourmet health food restaurant in New York City. Around the same time, Andy Mehring and Roy Wetterstrom founded the firm I now work for, Micro Modeling Associates, and dedicated the firm to building highly sophisticated Excel-based applications.

To date, Micro Modeling has built more than 500 custom business applications (from publishing systems to accounting systems) in Excel, Word, Microsoft Access, and Visual Basic.

Still, too few people understand that they can build powerful, elegant applications—even mission-critical applications—using Office development tools. Even those people who use Office products and write a lot of macros often don't understand that they can use these tools to develop *applications*.

This book, which summarizes the experience of many who pioneered Office development, explains how to build applications with Access, Excel, and Word. I don't emphasize use of Visual Basic, but I include two applications built with Visual Basic to give a sense of how this tool can fit into an Office-based development strategy.

Who Should Read This Book

Although this book includes over a dozen fully functional sample applications built with Office products and Visual Basic, it does *not* assume that you are a programmer. Instead, it's written for everyone interested in using Office products to develop business applications:

- Information system (IS) professionals interested in incorporating Office into their development strategies to improve how their companies do business

- Managers who want to know how other companies are using Office to solve common business problems

- Power users who are experts in using one or more Office products and who are interested in replacing manual labor with automated solutions for getting their jobs done

- Developers who want sample code and ideas for developing business applications using Office products and who want to understand what other developers are doing with these tools

What This Book Is About

This book contains a great deal of code, but it isn't a primer on how to code applications in Access Basic, VBA for Excel, or WordBasic. And even though it provides a few "how-tos" for key tasks (such as how to set up the ODBC driver manager), by and large it focuses on integrating a large body of technical information and experience to deliver a broad range of business functionality using Office development tools. I comment the sample code heavily (and provide it on disk, alongside working demos), but I don't take you step by step through coding an application. I assume that you know the mechanics of coding in each language or are learning it elsewhere.

This book combines three large bodies of knowledge. Part 1, "An Office Development Strategy," provides an overview of how to take advantage of the main technologies at your disposal as you develop business applications with Office products and Visual Basic, including the following:

- A discussion of how end-user development tools such as Excel and Word fit into corporate development strategies

- A comparison of all the Microsoft BASICs—Access Basic, VBA for Excel, WordBasic, and Visual Basic—and how they contribute to corporate development

- An overview of how to increase productivity by reengineering both the process that developers use to build applications *and* the business processes that applications automate

- A discussion of how to make custom business applications easier to use by adhering to graphical standards when designing user interfaces

- An introduction to Open Database Connectivity (ODBC) and how it simplifies the process of delivering corporate data to the desktop

- An overview of the Windows API, which enables developers to significantly extend and expand the capabilities of business applications developed with Office tools

Part 2, "The Integrated Office," is a survey of building applications with Office products, including the following:

- An overview of how to structure Office-based business applications that look and feel like commercial Windows-based products rather than a bunch of macros

- An up close look at a variety of business applications developed with Office tools

- A discussion of how to use OLE and DDE to develop business applications that use more than one Office product

Part 3, "The Professional's Handbook," covers three general topics that provide the finishing touches for delivering custom business applications to end users:

- Windows Help, which, in addition to enabling you to deliver context-sensitive Help for business applications, lets you turn policy manuals and other corporate materials into online publications.

- Documentation and training, which are more than good ideas: They're key elements for ensuring that the development process produces applications that are used productively.

- Managing application rollouts, whether of shrink-wrapped products or custom business applications.

I hope that the information provided here—which is adapted from the experience of those who have pioneered business-application development using Office products—makes your own experience more productive.

Christine Solomon
Internet: csolomon@panix.com
CompuServe: 74720,3446

ACKNOWLEDGMENTS

Many people contributed their experiences, suggestions, research, and programming expertise to this book. I have learned a great deal from them and am grateful for their time, their effort, and their candor.

Thank you to:

Andy Mehring and Roy Wetterstrom, the founding partners of Micro Modeling Associates, Inc., for their support and for the use of Micro Modeling resources and materials. Their participation in this project added a depth to this book that it would not have had otherwise;

Lyle Anderson, who wrote the foreword and who lent me both his copy of *Paradigm Shift* and his time;

Rick Bullen, who provided materials and insights into Microsoft Excel–based development specifically and end-user development tools generally;

Chuck Chace, who contributed sidebar materials and a wide variety of sample code;

Mary Chipman, who contributed the sample application TimeNtry, provided information about Microsoft Access security, and introduced me to her fine network of Access developers;

Mike Gunderloy, who contributed MenuBldR.MDA and reviewed the chapters on Access, OLE, and DDE;

Lenore Michaels, who contributed case studies and material on how to manage application rollouts;

Brian Stanton, who provided a code review;

Ken Getz and Adrian Baer, who contributed to the chapter on Access;

Steve Harshbarger, Eric Birnbaum, Ellen Huber, Jason Harper, and all those at Micro Modeling who contributed their wide variety of technical expertise and experience;

Steve Koeppel, Marc Prensky, Stanley Rose, Glenn Shimamoto, Leon Smith, Anish Mathai, Robert Berkley, and Rick Hopfer at Bankers Trust, who provided important historical information and glimpses into the future;

Vince DeGiaimo, James Oliverio, and Miriam Anderson in the investment banking group at Donaldson, Lufkin & Jenrette, who provided information and insights based on their rich experience in integrating data at the desktop;

Susan Warzek, Bill DiChristina, Bill Faulkner, and Michael Oeth at FactSet, who provided a frank appraisal of the messy process of redeveloping commercial products to run under Microsoft Windows;

Candy Schwartz at PaineWebber, who has a cutting-edge vision for converting traditional publishing systems into Microsoft Office–based publishing systems;

Tony Sorrell at Philip Morris, who shared insights garnered from his broad experience with IS (information systems) in corporate America;

Virginia Howlett at Microsoft, who gave me permission to use her palette of "sexy" application icons;

and

Claudette Moore, who helped shape the original *idea* of this book.

It's traditional for authors to thank their publishers, but this is more than a bow to tradition: Ina Chang, the manuscript editor, turned my draft manuscript into the book you're holding in your hands; Marc Young, the technical editor, contributed his technical knowledge and testing skills and shaped the BASIC primer; Richard Gold, assistant managing editor, provided thoughtful guidance; Lucinda Rowley, acquisitions editor, helped to focus the content with pointed suggestions and encouragement; and many others at Microsoft Press designed, scheduled, composed, proofread, and in other ways added their creativity and common sense.

Thank you all.

PART ONE

An Office Development Strategy

The biggest hurdle facing organizations that decide to develop business applications using end-user development tools is a misconception: that Microsoft Excel and Microsoft Word are easy to use.

The truth is that Excel and Word are easy to *start* using, but they're not easy to use well. As a consultant who develops business applications for Fortune 1000 companies, I inevitably meet the Excel and Word gurus at each company I work with. In talking to them about the automation and productivity issues they face, I find out what they *don't* know about Excel and Word. The local Excel guru doesn't understand functions and has never heard of arrays. Or the local Word guru doesn't understand styles and has never heard of field codes.

The problem is that management, IS professionals, developers, and end users alike have believed the advertising. As a result, people who use Excel and Word rarely use them as productively as they could.

I've been using Excel and Word since they were first released for the Macintosh in the mid-1980s, and every day I learn a little more about them. They are big, sophisticated products. They are big, sophisticated development tools. There's a lot to learn. Part 1 of this book provides a solid foundation for this learning.

Chapter 1 makes the case for end-user development tools—what they are, why companies are starting to use them, and where they fit into the development process. The question of "fit" is an important one. Although some companies have been developing business applications using end-user development tools for a few years, to most companies it's a new idea. Even companies that are doing development using Microsoft Office products and Visual Basic are working out the appropriate place for each tool in their overall development strategy.

Chapter 2 explains the essentials of business-application development using Microsoft's BASICs (Access Basic, VBA for Excel, WordBasic, and Visual Basic) and compares these versions of the BASIC language. (Appendix B contains a BASIC programming primer.)

Chapter 3 provides a brief guide to an application-development methodology that is appropriate for fast-paced business environments. It also addresses the need to reengineer the business process itself in many cases, to improve productivity.

Chapters 4 through 6 cover general topics that all IS professionals and developers should factor into their application-development strategy. Chapter 4 explains how to create good user interfaces by adhering to Office standards and a "common" user interface. Chapter 5 offers advice on getting data to the desktop where businesspeople can use it to do business better. Chapter 6 deals with using the Windows application programming interface (and even C/C++) to do things that Access Basic, VBA for Excel, WordBasic, and Visual Basic can't do otherwise.

1

Do Real Developers Use End-User Development Tools?

A typing cart.

That's how an IS professional in the investment banking group at Donaldson, Lufkin & Jenrette (DLJ) described the company's first desktop PC. The cart held one PC (two floppy drives, no hard disk), which ran Lotus 1-2-3. When bankers needed to analyze a company's financials, they'd wheel the PC over and get to work. Before long, enough bankers were using the system to warrant an additional PC and cart. Within three years, the company had a PC on every desk.

Today, DLJ's investment banking group has 500 people networked nationwide.

To compete in today's changing marketplace, more companies are converting from *system islands*—stand-alone PCs, stand-alone applications, and older mainframe-based systems—to *integrated desktops* that provide point-and-click access to enterprise-wide data and communications. This in turn is changing business-application development.

This chapter answers three common questions about using end-user development tools to create business applications:

- What role do end-user development tools play in business-application development?

- How do end-user development tools enhance productivity for both end users *and* developers?

- How do companies incorporate end-user development tools into a traditional development environment?

This chapter also includes a roundtable discussion among members of the Technology Strategic Planning Group at Bankers Trust, who describe how end-user development tools fit into their overall development strategy.

The Push-Button Business

Here's how an IS professional at one of the world's largest commercial banks summarized the company's experience with PCs during the past decade:

> We were originally a MultiMate, then a WordPerfect organization. We were running Lotus 1-2-3 and a lot of stand-alone applications, but up until about four years ago, the most common PC program was V-TERM or CO-TERM or everyone's favorite terminal emulator. A PC was basically a terminal emulator.
>
> For years now, we've called technology "the enabling factor," but it really wasn't. It was still just a record-keeping system. Today, with the easier-to-use Windows environment and the ability to integrate data at the desktop, technology is finally enabling people to do business in a way that they couldn't before.

Although the idea of integrating information at users' desktops isn't new, it's increasingly possible. John Sculley, when he was CEO of Apple Computer, originally publicized this vision in a video called *The Knowledge Navigator*. Today Microsoft calls it "information at your fingertips." Some IS professionals call it the "push-button business"—all the information you need, a mouse click or a keystroke away.

Eliminating the Middleman

Companies once used computers primarily for record keeping. Computers kept those records well, but *retrieving* the records was another story: You had to tell programmers—sometimes months in advance—what information you wanted, and then they had to write a program to find it.

Today's customers won't wait that long—they can turn to companies that will deliver information faster. As a result, businesses are reengineering information flow and eliminating the programmer-middleman. As one IS professional put it, "Instead of focusing on processing reports, we're focusing on bringing information to the people who use it and making sure they *can* use it."

Technical advances in hardware and software are converging to make desktop integration a reality. Figure 1-1 provides a look at some of the milestones in the development of the integrated desktop. But for desktop integration to help people do their jobs better, it has to be easy: Users must be able to retrieve and use all the information they need by pushing a button or two. To get to this point, you can either hire an army of programmers to develop specific business tools *or* reduce your reliance on traditional programming languages (such as COBOL and C/C++) in favor of end-user development tools.

1957	**FORTRAN**: One of the first high-level programming languages.
1960	**COBOL**: COmmon Business-Oriented Language.
1964	John Kemeny and Thomas Kurtz at Dartmouth develop **BASIC**: Beginners All-Purpose Symbolic Instruction Code.
1968	**Simula**: The first object-oriented programming language.
1972	Bell Labs develops **C**, which is now the primary language in systems programming. Also, Xerox develops the **first desktop computer** (called Alto), which it later sells as the Xerox 850 dedicated word processor.
1977	Steve Jobs and Steve Wozniak incorporate **Apple Computer** and start producing the **Apple II**. Bill Gates and Paul Allen start **Microsoft Corporation** and release the first PC programming language—a BASIC interpreter that needs only 4 KB.
1978	Dan Bricklin and Bob Frankston develop **VisiCalc**, the first electronic spreadsheet.
1980	DEC, Intel, and Xerox release the spec for the **Ethernet** networks. The first generation of **Local Area Networks** (LANs) transmit data at 4 to 10 megabits per second.
1981	IBM introduces its first **PC**, which runs on **MS-DOS**. Also, IBM introduces its first **relational database management system**, **SQL/DS**.
1983	Lotus releases **1-2-3**, the first integrated spreadsheet, which includes database functions, charting, and a macro language. Also, **Smalltalk** becomes the first object-oriented programming language for the PC.
1984	Apple introduces the **Macintosh**, and **desktop publishing** is born.
1987	Microsoft introduces **Windows** and **Excel**. Even in its first release, Excel has a highly programmable macro language and is the first Windows development environment. Also, Bjarne Stroustrup develops **C++**, an object-oriented extension of C. (The "++" is a pun since it's C's own increment operator.)
1990	Microsoft releases **Windows version 3**, **Excel version 3**, and **Word for Windows/WordBasic**. Also, companies start to release the second generation of LAN products, which can transmit data at 100 megabits per second.
1992	Microsoft releases **Visual Basic** and **Access/Access Basic**.
1993	Microsoft releases **Visual C++**.
1994	Microsoft releases **Visual Basic for Applications** with Excel version 5, Project version 4, ODBC, and OLE2.

In the early to mid-1970s, IBM coined the term "word processor" to market Selectric typewriters that store words on tape.

During the same period, DEC, Wang, IBM, and others started marketing minicomputer-based office automation systems, primarily for business word processing.

The configuration of the first IBM PC:

CPU	8088
RAM	64 KB
Floppy drive	160 KB
Monitor	Monochrome

Word for Windows was the first application to use a traditional programming language—BASIC—as a macro language.

Figure 1-1. *Milestones in the development of the integrated desktop.*

Using Shrink-Wrapped Products as Development Tools

Microsoft Access, Microsoft Excel, and Microsoft Word are not only good applications, they're strong development tools. Their programmable macro languages let you customize the base application to meet specific business needs. In fact, instead of adding software as new products come out and new projects come up, many firms are choosing to customize their existing shrink-wrapped products. For example, instead of buying a dedicated forms-generator, the Philip Morris human resources department developed an application in Word that automates and simplifies the process of filling in personnel review and evaluation forms. A shrink-wrapped product that is used to build a custom business application is an *end-user development tool*.

Two broad categories of applications lend themselves to this development style:

- Business applications used by business people who spend a lot of time in Excel or in Word

- Business applications that do what Excel or Word do well (for example, budgeting systems or publishing)

As companies standardize on a suite of products (such as Microsoft Office) and use it as the starting point for application development, they speed up both the decision-making and the development process. A fair percentage of business-application development delivers solutions to particular groups of people with specific business needs: financial analysts who need to value companies; researchers, artists, and editors who need to produce publications; human resources personnel who need to distribute policies; and customer service departments that need to respond to inquiries. In many cases, automated solutions built with end-user development tools—which are on the desktop already and which business people use every day—are the fastest, most flexible, and most cost-efficient solutions available.

End-User Development Tools: Ready for Prime Time

In 1987, Microsoft shipped two applications that changed PC computing dramatically: Microsoft Windows version 2 and Excel version 1. Although neither product caught on until the version 3 release, a few pioneers, including Merrill Lynch and Bankers Trust, started their first Windows development projects in Excel version 1. And several major financial institutions and Big Six accounting firms decided to reengineer their business applications for the spreadsheet. It was only natural: Bankers and accountants live in spreadsheets, so the most effective tools for them are those that are spreadsheet based.

Although several firms started this reengineering effort with Lotus 1-2-3, they were stymied by the fact that 1-2-3 didn't have a full-fledged programming language. Those that started with Excel fared much better. Excel has the distinction of being the first application to run under Windows as well as being the first Windows-based development environment. In fact, for a couple of years Excel's macro language was the *only* Windows-based programming language. The first programmers to develop business applications under Windows often supplemented Excel's macro language with custom-built scripting languages.

Although all versions of Excel had the same core macro language, version 3 added important structural elements—such as the ability to indent code, multiline If...Then statements, and the use of Else If—that qualified it as a fully programmable macro language. It provided a more structured, airtight environment and a level of control that went far beyond keystroke emulation or basic navigation, enabling developers to build custom applications not even recognizable as Excel.

FYI

Spreadsheets and Business: Perfect Together

Since 1978, when VisiCalc (the first electronic spreadsheet) spurred sales of the Apple II, spreadsheets have provided the business rationale for buying PCs. The reason this is the case—despite the fact that word processing is the most common use of PCs today—is that many large companies used minicomputer-based word processing systems from Wang, IBM, and DEC since the mid-1970s. Spreadsheets, on the other hand, are pure PC tools.

Over the years, there have been two major improvements on the original VisiCalc design. Both have provided needed business functionality, and both have been bestsellers. Lotus 1-2-3 made the first improvement by integrating the spreadsheet with database capabilities, charting, and a simple macro language. Excel's contribution was to expand the macro capability into a full-featured programming language, which made it possible to program a spreadsheet in much the same way that dBASE made it possible to program a database.

FYI

Is Access an End-User Development Tool?

Excel and Word are classic end-user development tools because spreadsheets and word processors are classic end-user tools—people who don't know anything about programming use them every day. Databases are *not* classic end-user tools—they're programmer tools. This makes Access an unusual hybrid.

Microsoft markets Access as an end-user tool, and in some ways it is. It's certainly easier to use than other relational databases, but it nonetheless requires some knowledge of relational databases, which most people don't have...yet. But as companies convert their stand-alone PCs into integrated desktops that access enterprise-wide data, more people are using relational databases. Who knows? Relational databases may be *turning into* end-user tools.

FYI

About Macros

The first macros, written in the mid-1940s, were referred to as "macroinstructions" and were either built into the assembly language or provided by a separate piece of software. Assembly-language programmers used macroinstructions to bundle together a sequence of frequently used commands into a single instruction. The compiler later expanded the macro—in other words, replaced it with the actual sequence of commands. The main benefits of macros are their simplicity and their speed (relative to the speed of subroutines). The tradeoff is in program size: Each time a macro is run, it repeats its instruction sequence, often increasing the length of the program. Today, many traditional programming languages (including the various flavors of C) have a macro capability.

In the 1980s, shrink-wrapped PC applications borrowed the term "macro" to describe their ability to record a sequence of keystrokes, assign it a single keystroke, and then play it back. Microsoft redeveloped and extended this early concept of macros to create fully programmable macro languages for its Office suite—complete with control structures, subroutines, functions, and the ability to access the Windows API. Microsoft later merged the idea of programmable macro languages with a bona fide programming language—BASIC—and Access Basic, Visual Basic for Applications (VBA), and WordBasic were born.

The following features distinguish fully programmable macro languages (such as VBA for Excel and WordBasic) from keystroke emulators:

■ Complete access to the shrink-wrapped application's commands

■ Use of a function-based language

■ Use of the programmer's standard palette of control structures (If...Then...Else, Do...Loops, For...Next, and so on)

■ Use of built-in text editors for writing code

■ Ability to indent, remark, and structure code so that it's easy to maintain.

■ Ability to debug

■ Ability to create tamperproof code

■ Ability to create a professional interface (in Windows, the ability to assign macros to menus, toolbars, command buttons, and so on; launch a business application from an icon in Program Manager; create custom dialog boxes; and add custom Help)

■ Ability to customize the shrink-wrapped application's standard interface by adding or eliminating commands, menu items, scroll bars, and so on

■ Use of the Windows application programming interface (API) and custom dynamic-link libraries (DLLs)

Although end-user development tools with their programmable macro languages can never take the place of C (in any of its flavors) for hard-core systems programming, many business applications are not hard-core systems. A lot of business applications are "mission critical" for particular groups of people (departments, teams, or workgroups) rather than for the company as a whole. In these cases, end-user development tools are often ideal for two reasons:

■ They help get sound business applications up and running quickly because they let developers use, repackage, and extend existing shrink-wrapped functionality.

■ They let users stay in an environment they're already familiar with, such as Excel or Word.

The Advantages of End-User Development Tools

Consider some of the following advantages of using end-user development tools to develop business applications.

End-user development tools speed up the development process. Because these tools enhance and extend existing functionality (rather than require that you start from scratch), you can build applications more quickly.

End-user development tools encourage need-driven development. Instead of rushing out to buy the software market's latest darling, you focus on automating existing tools to improve productivity.

Business applications built with end-user development tools are easy to use. Because they're based on applications that are already familiar, applications designed with these tools can be rolled out to large populations with little training and support. For example, PaineWebber rolled out publishing templates to all 250 people in the equity research department—from clerical staff familiar with Word to analysts who were much less familiar with it—with minimal training and support.

End-user development tools are less costly. IS professionals are beginning to understand that the development cycle consists of continuous refinement. End-user development tools, which don't require as large an up-front investment, make that cycle smoother and less costly and let businesses adapt quickly to changing trends and advances in technology. For example, a Fortune 1000 clothing manufacturer built a prototype system in Access for its customer service department and used it for several months—tweaking it continuously—before committing it to Sybase and a PowerBuilder front end.

End-user development tools enhance business flexibility. Business changes continuously, and so do end-user development tools. The tools are easy to move to and *up to* as upgrades come out.

End-user development tools running in a networked environment help ensure that the benefits of technology make it to users' desktops. They let users retrieve, analyze, and publish data themselves. Research analysts in Merrill Lynch's mutual funds department use Excel not only to analyze data but to deliver camera-ready copy for their publications.

Choosing the Right Tool for the Job

While the Office products are good tools for both end users and developers, you still have to choose the right tool for the job.

Some people believe that they need only one software package—an understandable conceit in these days when nearly every product has a spelling checker and drawing tools. I know a man who believes that the only shrink-wrapped application anyone needs is Excel. He builds business applications in Excel, he draws diagrams in Excel, and he writes reports in Excel.

While it's true that you can write a simple report in Excel, Excel isn't a writer's tool. So if you're using Excel to develop text-oriented and document-oriented applications, you're complicating the task—not only for yourself but for the end user.

The key to choosing the right end-user development tool for the job is to determine not only which tool is most familiar to the developer and to the users but which tool is naturally suited to the task at hand. Here's a list of business applications that I've seen built with Office products and Visual Basic:

Microsoft Access

- Accounting/bookkeeping

- Data consolidation from databases

- Data storage

- Executive information systems

- Information tracking

- Forms for data entry, editing, and viewing

- Data publishing

Microsoft Excel

- Financial models, including corporate valuation and tax models

- Reporting against any database

- Statistical publishing

- Executive information systems

- Presentation systems

- Forms for data entry, editing, and viewing

Microsoft Word

- Automated letter generation and mail merge for any database

- Publishing and reporting

- Document generation

- Plan tracking, archiving, and updating

- Business forms for individual entry

Visual Basic

■ Data entry for any database

■ Any front end

■ Computer-based training (CBT) systems

■ Executive information systems

■ Presentation systems

■ Forms for data entry, editing, and viewing

■ Time tracking (to automate billing)

■ A wide variety of applications that aren't Office-product specific

Third-generation end-user development tools

Although many companies are just beginning to develop business applications using end-user development tools, these tools are actually in their third generation. (Figure 1-2 provides a generational overview of Access, Excel, and Word.) These tools are not only more powerful development environments in their own right, but through OLE automation they let you assemble business applications by using objects from shrink-wrapped products.

	1st Generation	**2nd Generation**	**3rd Generation**
Applications	• Excel version 3 (Excel macro language)	• Excel version 4 (Excel macro language)	• Excel version 5 (Visual Basic for Applications)
	• Word version 1 (WordBasic)	• Word version 2 (WordBasic)	• Word version 6 (WordBasic)
		• Access version 1 (Access Basic)	• Access version 2 (Access Basic)
Key features	• programmable macro language	• programmable macro language	• programmable macro language
	• DDE	• DDE	• DDE
		• ability to share information across applications with OLE1	• ability to share information across applications with OLE2
			• basic object orientation
			• OLE automation

Figure 1-2. *Three generations of end-user development tools.*

Word: No developer's darling, but a solid development tool nonetheless

Recently I heard two comments about Word that are worth repeating here. One manager was confused by my reference to Word as an end-user development tool because "it's only a word processor." A trainer characterized Word as "something that you give to secretaries, and they learn to use it in a few hours."

Even IS professionals who immediately recognize the value of developing business applications in Excel sometimes have trouble recognizing Word's value as a development tool. I've seen a developer waste days jury-rigging a mail merge between Access and Excel because he "couldn't deal with Word." He should have spent those days learning Word and doing it right. Not only would he have delivered a better mail merge system, but he would have been prepared for the inevitable next time when Word was the right tool for the job.

This reluctance to use Word as a development tool reflects ignorance of the importance of word processing in business. IS professionals in a variety of companies (from banks to manufacturers) have mentioned to me that their company's first mass use of PCs was for word processing. The U.S. Bureau of Labor Statistics reports that 41 percent of all business computing is word processing—nearly a third more than the next largest category, databases. In addition, the bureau found that better-educated people (such as managers) spend the most time using word processors—a fact that certainly jibes with experience. Just as the work of accountants, bankers, and financial analysts generally boils down to a spreadsheet, most business activity boils down to a document, whether it's a letter, a report, a proposal, or a contract.

Unfortunately, IS professionals who dismiss word processing's business importance miss important opportunities in business-application development. Most word processing tasks (which tend to be time-consuming and labor intensive) can be sped up and improved with automation. For example, Donaldson, Lufkin & Jenrette's investment banking group decided to develop highly automated templates for word processing. Not only did they end up with a new, more sophisticated look for their pitch books without adding processing time, but they eliminated a great deal of manual formatting.

Of course, word processing isn't just for word processors. When the Philip Morris human resources department decided to automate their midyear and end-of-year personnel review forms, they chose Word as the development tool for two reasons: First, Word was the only piece of software that all managers used; second, it seemed the appropriate choice given that the review form *is* a form. They duplicated the printed form in a Word template, added three commands and a DDE link to Visual Basic for functionality that Word couldn't provide, and rolled it out. It took approximately seven person-days to automate the system, and zero training.

Compare this to the company that decided to automate a review form using Visual Basic. They couldn't articulate why Visual Basic was the right tool, except to say that they wanted an easy-to-use interface with a form that took only a few moments to fill out. (And they doubted that Word could satisfy those requirements.) Because Visual Basic was the current developer's darling, it seemed easier to go with VB than to determine which tool was best suited to the job.

Three months and many sleepless nights later, they rolled out version 1. And now they're not so sure that Visual Basic is such a hot tool. Not even a darling can replace the right tool for the job.

Business Systems Developed by Businesspeople

After a sales meeting with a prospective client, I scribbled this note for the file: *Not a decision maker for computer stuff.* She was responsible for producing several weekly and monthly publications, but the computers she used to produce them fell into another person's domain. Even though she looked to me for advice, she couldn't have taken it. IS had to make the decision—and they had other priorities. A year or so later—after two directors of computing came and went—she managed to solve *one* of the problems that she had talked to me about originally.

This contrasts strikingly with another client, a publications director who had full authority over the technology in her area and who could independently obtain the resources and expertise she needed. Although I spent a fair amount of time with the department's IS professionals (to whom she looked for information), the decision and the budget were hers. She built a complete publishing solution in Excel and Word in far less time than it took the other client to solve a single problem.

Companies that make integrated desktops a strategic part of their business technology often have to juggle some reorganization between IS and the business units. In their book *Paradigm Shift*, Don Tapscott and Art Caston note the importance of reorganization in the new era of computing.

The stereotypical IS model—in which business units queue up at the IS department's door and IS doles out resources—doesn't work in today's highly competitive environment. Instead, companies are integrating IS functions into the business as a whole.

The successful company mentioned above has clearly done this. In fact, the company borrowed from several of the models that Tapscott and Caston mention. In addition to creating a centralized IS department responsible for the mainframe and the corporate network, the company also dispersed IS expertise throughout the organization and put business users in control of it. Plus, they used outsourcing to build specific components.

No matter what organizational model companies use, there's no doubt that businesspeople work better (that is, more closely and more productively) with technology people who understand their business. And the more the technologists understand, the better.

Marrying technical expertise to business expertise is becoming increasingly valuable as companies start developing applications with end-user development tools. As growing numbers of businesspeople become power users of these tools, they—not developers—become the force driving the application development process. This is changing the development process in fundamental ways—including, in some cases, *who* does the development.

You Want *Me* to Use *What?*

It's hard to recruit for end-user development. This isn't so surprising when you remember that although BASIC is the most popular programming language in the world, C is the primary language for systems programming. This is the "great divide" between traditional and end-user development: Historically, BASIC has been used by beginners and for development of small applications, while C has been reserved for "real application" development.

But times are changing. The BASIC found in Access Basic, VBA for Excel, WordBasic, and Visual Basic has matured into a programming language with enough structure and speed to support several thousand lines of code. In other words, these flavors of BASIC have enough programming power to support a mission-critical business application for a specific department, team, or workgroup.

The old stereotype persists, however, and people from traditional development backgrounds still tend to pooh-pooh jobs for developing business applications with VBA for Excel, WordBasic, and even (though to a lesser extent) Access Basic and Visual Basic. They want to develop with C++ and Oracle.

People with business backgrounds and technical interests, on the other hand—people who have used end-user development tools as end users and who are aware of their programming power—usually jump at the chance to develop with these tools.

My experience has been that it's somewhat easier to recruit from the ranks of power users than from the ranks of developers, and companies that create new positions for end-user development frequently have the same experience. On the other hand, companies with existing development staffs have retrained traditional programmers to use end-user development tools.

There are advantages and disadvantages either way.

Traditional programmers

■ PROS: Traditional programmers who are committed to learning the business and to improving business operations have the experience and methodological framework for producing robust business applications no matter what development tool they use. They can pick up any BASIC-style language very quickly. If they have experience with Windows and C++ development, they understand how to use the Windows API to expand the capabilities of end-user development tools.

■ CONS: Traditional programmers don't use end-user applications, and too many don't understand the business activities that these applications support. When dealing with end-user development tools, programmers who don't know anything besides computers are a business liability. The communications gap between business people and programmers is a heavy drag on productivity.

Power users

■ PROS: Power users understand both the business and the end-user tool with which they develop applications. They know the workflow and can spot opportunities for combining steps and automating tasks. They know the application and its shortcuts, which create cleaner code for controlling applications programmatically.

■ CONS: Power users tend to be fans of the applications they know best, and their enthusiasm colors their decision-making about which tool is right for the job. They also have to learn how to program, and they have to learn the methodological framework for developing robust applications.

Turning Programmers into Power Users

Programming in traditional development environments differs from programming with end-user development tools. Both require knowledge of the programming language and methodology, but the latter also requires knowledge of the end-user tool itself.

I've met developers who are embarrassed to admit that they have to *learn* an end-user tool. Part of their discomfort stems from the fact that management doesn't understand how rich these tools are and trivializes the learning process. But learning to use Excel and Word at the level of sophistication necessary to develop robust business applications is not a trivial exercise. And even though Excel and Word are easy to use, they're by no means easy to use *well*. Give users one application and one week, and they'll probably figure out how to perform a variety of tasks. But they probably won't figure out how to perform these tasks most efficiently or how to tap the true power of the application.

To work effectively with end-user development tools, programmers must first become power users of shrink-wrapped products.

FYI

When Good Programming Skills Aren't Enough

When you develop applications with end-user development tools, it's not enough to know the programming language. You also have to know the best, most efficient practices for using the shrink-wrapped product. Here's an example from Excel that illustrates why this is so important.

Let's say you're writing code that controls a worksheet and retrieves data from it. Column A in your worksheet contains a list of companies. You need to calculate the number of times that "IBM" appears in this list.

Casual Excel users do this by entering functions in column B that indicate "if the cell in the previous column = IBM, display 1; otherwise use 0." (The actual formula is =IF(A1="IBM",1,0).) At the bottom of column B, users then sum the 1s to calculate how many times "IBM" appears (see Figure 1-3).

Power users (and good Excel developers), on the other hand, use an *array* to perform the entire calculation in a single cell. With an array, you say in effect, "if an item in this collection of company names = IBM, then add 1; otherwise add 0." Excel values each item in the array separately. Does the first item equal IBM? Does the second? And so on. (The formula is {=SUM(IF(A1:A11="IBM",1,0))}, where {} indicates the array.)

When you use arrays to handle these sorts of calculations, your code runs faster.

B1	▼	=IF(A1="IBM",1,0)		
	A	B	C	D
1	IBM	1		
2	CON ED	0		
3	MACY'S	0		
4	ZABAR'S	0		
5	AT&T	0		
6	IBM	1		
7	GM	0		
8	NYNEX	0		
9	EXXON	0		
10	FORD	0		
11	IBM	1		
12		3		

B1	▼	{=SUM(IF(A1:A11="IBM",1,0))}		
	A	B	C	D	E
1	IBM	3			
2	CON ED				
3	MACY'S				
4	ZABAR'S				
5	AT&T				
6	IBM				
7	GM				
8	NYNEX				
9	EXXON				
10	FORD				
11	IBM				

Figure 1-3. *The example on the left shows a common, but inefficient, way to determine the number of times a particular name appears in column A. The example on the right uses a single-cell array formula to calculate the result more efficiently.*

One of the worst business applications I've ever seen was built by a developer who didn't know Word. He *thought* he knew Word—after all, he knew how to type, change fonts, and make things boldface. But he didn't know that you could establish basic formatting in templates (including headers and footers) and use bookmarks to manipulate specific elements of the document under macro control. As a result, he wrote 40 pages of WordBasic code to format a presentation. The application was dead slow, and it bombed if any other program was running. Knowing how to program is no substitute for knowing the shrink-wrapped product that you're programming with.

Turning Power Users into Programmers

Traditional programmers aren't the only ones who are too quick to assume that developing with end-user development tools is simple. Power users have the same problem, but it sneaks up on them from the opposite direction. While traditional programmers tend to be cavalier about the shrink-wrapped application (because it's less familiar), power users tend to be cavalier about programming. They use the macro recorder, paste the recorded macros together, and before long they have an application. Or so they think.

Too often, business systems developed by business people are jerry-built. One of the most glaring examples I've seen was a business application built by a banker who didn't know anything about programming. It was a financial model that relied on several hundred lines of Excel code. It was entirely hard coded. It was entirely unreadable. There were no variables, no code structure, and no comments.

Astonishingly, business people relied on this program when making business decisions—or, rather, they did until the creator of the "program" left the company. Once that happened, no one could get the model to work. The reason? They didn't know the secret—that you had to enter the interest rate in cell IV16384 before you ran the macro (or some similar bit of nonsense).

To become solid developers, power users must learn standard development methodology and zealously employ good programming practices.

Roundtable Discussion at Bankers Trust: Microsoft Office Development

In an effort to reengineer its technical architecture, Bankers Trust (BT) is moving approximately 700 of its 1200 developers to Windows. BT's business-application development strategy for Windows emphasizes end-user development tools and Visual Basic. Here's a discussion among members of the Technology Strategic Planning Group on Windows development at the bank—its genesis, its challenges, and its potential.

Author: What was the first business application that Bankers Trust developed in Windows?

Stanley Rose (vice president): The first Windows application that we developed was BT World, which gives customers access to account information. BT World got started in '84. At that time it was a DOS-based application, so we had to write another application—BTPC—to provide background data transfer.

The big demo of BT World—the big rollout—was October 19, 1987. BT held it at a conference center in North Carolina, and all the investment managers were there. The people who were giving the demo explained how the BT World application lets you look at your portfolios real time, so you can check how the market's doing. Then they demonstrated how easy it is to do. They dialed in and looked at some portfolios, which showed that the market was down 350 points. You can imagine the uproar. The investment managers all said, "This is the quality of the thing you built? It shows 350 points down for the Dow? That's ridiculous." Then they realized it was true.

So that was the big BT World rollout. At that point it was still DOS based. They started to convert it to Windows under the first versions of Windows and Excel.

Steve Koeppel (vice president): There were a couple of things BT World needed that Windows provided. First, the application had to let people continue to work while it pulled data from host systems. Second, the application needed a flexible output format so that the developers weren't trapped programming every report a customer wanted. The best way to do this was to dump data into a spreadsheet. The only environment that provided both things was Windows and Excel. So for years now, BT World has been doing mass custom reporting through the Excel macro language, as opposed to mainframe programming.

Author: The developers for the BT World application clearly saw the value of using end-user programming tools very early on. Are you now pushing other developers toward developing with these tools?

Lyle Anderson (managing director): Yes. These applications—Excel, Word, Access—*are* development tools as well as end-user tools. We look at them as developer *components*. One of the reasons we chose to go with a site license for these tools was to create a standard environment that application developers can add to and integrate, instead of starting every application from scratch.

One of our goals is to move developers up a few notches in the development process and to move them away from having to build all the components themselves and make them all consistent.

Stanley Rose: That's right. When we bought the Office site license, we weren't just looking for a word processor or a spreadsheet, because we had those. We were looking for the ability to build macro-based applications. I think one of the mistakes we've made over the years is that we've *built* vs. *bought*—and we've paid a lot for that. We've ended up having to support our infrastructure instead of supporting our business applications.

Author: Is Windows and Windows-based development making end users as a whole more productive?

Leon Smith (managing director): The answer is very solidly "yes" and very solidly "no"—you have to recognize both phenomena. I think, by and large, the simple answer is "yes." Users are, in fact, exchanging more information, asking more questions, getting more use out of data, developing more databases of their own. They're doing all the good stuff you'd intuit that they'd do with these tools.

Are they more productive? If you look at overall productivity, I think it's probably down or flat because of the time they're investing learning how to do that stuff, or supporting the software, or supporting the PC, or whatever. I think support costs are offsetting other gains.

Stanley Rose: There's a tremendous amount of hidden support that occurs, where Leon has a problem and I help him, and I have a problem so Lyle helps me.

Lyle Anderson: Industry analysts are saying that up to 70 percent of total PC support costs are hidden. So our cost studies capture only a fraction of what we're really spending.

If you look at the aggregate, though—let's say revenue per employee at the bank or across the U.S.—it has increased over the last four or five years. Whether it's attributable to PCs, I don't know. It probably isn't. I think Leon's suspicion is correct, but we don't have a lot of data one way or the other.

Robert Berkley (vice president): Something else is happening, too. People are doing work that they never did before. This morning I fine-tuned my presentation until minutes before I gave it. In the past I would have had to release it a day or so early to have slides made. But now, people are producing their own slides in PowerPoint, and they're producing documents in Word that are camera ready.

Lyle Anderson: I'll give you another example. I don't think we would be able to run our derivatives business without spreadsheets. You need the speed, flexibility, and sheer calculation power of electronic spreadsheets to spot the opportunities that let us create derivative products.

Leon Smith: But could you run that business without Windows?

Lyle Anderson: I think Windows helps. It certainly helps for camera-ready copy, and it lets users visualize complex data much more quickly.

Author: Are end-user development tools making developers more productive?

Steve Koeppel: I think that a large percentage of our development community—perhaps more than half—is still doing things pretty much the way they've always done them. Even if they're developing in Windows, integrating off-the-shelf packages is still a big cultural shift for most developers. Probably less than a third of our Windows developers accept shrink-wrapped software as a viable method of delivery.

Leon Smith: And not all of our developers are *in* Windows. There are a certain number of legacy systems, and the people who maintain them probably haven't touched Windows yet. I'd say that less than half of our total development staff is working in Windows now.

Steve Koeppel: Office development has great potential for improving productivity. It used to be that we couldn't move data from one application to another application easily. It meant a whole other development cycle, and as a result it didn't get done. We have examples today of business people using these tools to integrate data in a way that they couldn't before, and to develop new financial products. These users now have to push the technology people.

The thing that never would have happened before is users asking, "Can you deliver this application in Excel or in Word?" Now that's going to happen more and more. Some developers are already delivering Office applications. However, I think a lot of developers are less productive at the moment because of the learning curve. There are a lot of new tools, and developers are just learning which ones to use, how to put them together, etc.

Stanley Rose: On the other hand, look at reports. Developers would spend hours hard-coding reports, and then the user would want one thing changed....

Lyle Anderson: That's a good point. I think a couple of things are happening here. One is that we're integrating more around the person. We're providing more information, more functionality directly to an individual—which is something we've never done before. If you look at some of the goals of reengineering, one is to eliminate steps, and these tools are giving us the ability to do that.

The other thing that's happening (and this supports Steve's point) is that we're integrating much more data at the desktop. It used to be that data integration was primarily a lot of host applications that talked to each other. Today we're bringing it all down to the individual desktop and integrating there.

Robert Berkley: We're bringing the development process right down to the decision maker.

Lyle Anderson: Yes. One stop. Do it once, do it right, and turn it over to the users.

Another issue that we're dealing with today is that the world of developers is changing dramatically. Historically, we've been responsible for delivering business applications. We've generally viewed these applications end-to-end: input, process, output.

I think that, going forward, our role as developers is increasingly going to be to acquire information, control it, ensure its integrity, and provide it to the internal and/or external consumer in some kind of manageable format or repository. Right now, developers are in the data publishing business. I think that we're going to get out of that business and that the end users are going to take it over. They already have, to some extent. We'll give end users the data, and we'll give them the tools to use that data, and then we'll let them do their own thing. Users will take our "information warehouse" (or whatever we're going to call it), retrieve the information that they want, massage it, build their own queries, and publish their own reports.

Anish Mathai (managing director): I'd like to add to that. I think that the Office tools are providing a value-added component in terms of the *type* of data that's liable to be entered into the database for publishing. Historically, the applications we've built all tended to be transaction oriented. There was little "qualitative" about them. But today we're moving toward applications with qualitative components—for instance, where credit analysts add opinion pieces that are linked to the hard transactions. The technology is enabling this integration. So when I look at it, I see us moving from a purely input-process-output *transaction* orientation to additional information that is around the transaction but isn't the transaction itself. And all of this information is linked—both to internal sources and to external sources.

Lyle Anderson: I've always thought that technology professionals have two views of the world. There is the inter*actor* view, which focuses on people, and the inter*action* view. Historically the interaction, or transaction, view of the world has been driving our design of systems and information. Part of what's happening now is that our primary view is shifting toward actors—toward customers, bank employees, etc. We're starting to focus on bringing to the desktop any and all information—quantitative and qualitative—that particular people need.

Anish Mathai: That's right. Typically, in an organization—and certainly at Bankers Trust—most of our systems were oriented toward back-office processing. As people moved up in management—and they didn't have to go very high—they started to rely on nonsystem data to make decisions. They hired consultants to do reports and studies and analyses. At the chairman's level, almost all of the information was either a synopsis of transactions or external data—with the weight being on external data. The new technologies are now allowing us to build systems that meet the needs of higher levels of management.

Stanley Rose: Another thing happened at the same time: People at that level are more interested in becoming involved in the use of the technology. Six, seven, eight years ago our senior management didn't have PCs in their office, they didn't have PCs at home, and they didn't want PCs. They wouldn't even use a dumb terminal for e-mail because they looked down on it.

Leon Smith: I think that Windows graphical presentation has gone a long way toward making PCs more acceptable to people higher up in the organization—to people who would not have dealt with them otherwise. Actually, it's a combination of more professional, more usable, and more acceptable. Windows is certainly easier to use—particularly by someone who doesn't spend all day using it. If you spend all day using it, it's not so hard to remember the keywords and the commands at the DOS prompt because you do it all the time. But if you're a casual user—which senior managers are, by definition—it's much easier to remember an icon.

Lyle Anderson: And that's reflected in training. I don't know the costs for MultiMate and WordPerfect training at the bank—I suspect it was significant in the '80s—but now we spend very little money on Word training. We basically have one trainer that subcontracts out, and that's it.

Author: You're the people responsible for reengineering the bank's technical architecture. What are some of the issues that you're wrestling with?

Lyle Anderson: One issue is integration. One of the reasons that we chose a site license for Office was to create a standard desktop, but another reason was to move the integration problem, as much as possible, away from BT and onto Microsoft. I want it to be *their* problem to glue together a desktop, not ours. I want them to be responsible for making sure it all works together. *We'll* focus on building outstanding business applications.

Leon Smith: Traditionally that's been our approach—to try to move the integration problem to the vendor. I think it took a long time to figure out what that meant in the PC world—for a while we got really lost there. But our traditional model with IBM and DEC was to take all products from the same vendor and to leave the vendor with the problem of making sure they worked together.

Lyle Anderson: I don't think we expect to get as far with PCs as we got with DEC or IBM. My interpretation of history is that we basically chose a DEC approach or an IBM approach to solving a given problem. We chose an architecture that was defined by either of these vendors and pretty much chose the product line with it. There wasn't the degree of openness that we have in the PC world. Microsoft accounts for only 5 percent of the total PC market, including hardware and software. We have Office as the application base, we have a variety of hardware underneath, then we have other stuff that we use, such as Lotus Notes.

We can give Microsoft the problem of gluing Office together to provide integrated development components, but that still leaves us with a lot of work to do on the overall architecture. Especially when business applications use a combination of all our platforms: Microsoft, DEC, and IBM.

Steve Koeppel: Exactly. All of these workstations and the goal of desktop integration rely entirely on networks, which isn't part of the Microsoft delivery. There are servers and boxes and wiring and all kinds of things that have to be in place—and working dependably—in order for us to make use of the software.

Stanley Rose: These machines—PCs and servers—are as important as the traditional host environments. But we've put in a lot more moving parts, and even if every part were as reliable as the host (and none are), we'd have a less reliable environment just because of the multiplication factor.

Lyle Anderson: That's right if you're assuming single points of failure. That's part of the architecture—you have to build redundancy into the architecture to prevent that from occurring. We have to look at solutions that will create real architectural security and reliability, equal to that of the host. We have some pieces of that solution now, but there's still a lot more to do.

Rick Hopfer (vice president): We want to have the same level of security and reliability and uptime that we've had with mainframes, *and* we want to have the same personal motivation and end-user creativity that we have with PCs. We want to combine the two of them.

Author: And will you be including that recipe as part of the bank's technical architecture?

Lyle Anderson: Yes. As soon as we can figure it out.

2

Application Development: The BASICs

All languages change and expand in response to changing needs, and computer languages are no exception. Words, functions, and new syntax are constantly being added. In some cases, markedly different languages develop from a common ancestor, just as Microsoft's family of BASICs evolved from the original Dartmouth BASIC.

This chapter provides an overview of the Microsoft BASICs—Access Basic, VBA for Excel, WordBasic, and Visual Basic—and shows how similar they really are.

BASIC, My Dear Watson

BASIC was invented in the mid-1960s by two professors at Dartmouth College as a way to teach programming to beginners. Although its name (an acronym for Beginner's All-Purpose Symbolic Instruction Code) might imply otherwise, BASIC is actually far less symbolic than other programming languages, such as C. In fact, BASIC commands are essentially English commands. For example, compare the following equivalent lines of BASIC code and C code. (Both produce a beep when you type *Eeyore*.)

BASIC

```
If MyName$ = "Eeyore" Then Beep
```

C

```
If (strcmp(MyName, "Eeyore") == 0)
  putchar('\a');
```

When Bill Gates and Paul Allen founded Microsoft in 1975, their first product was a full-featured BASIC language interpreter that needed only 4 KB of memory. Today, although BASIC is the most popular programming language, it isn't as popular for systems programming.

The Problems with BASIC

From the start, BASIC suffered from certain drawbacks that kept it from being taken seriously by "real" programmers. Not only was it primitive in the way it handled and organized code, but its interpreters were designed primarily for low-end machines. Added to these shortcomings was the fact that BASIC is an *interpreted* (rather than *compiled*) language. Interpreted languages provide a faster development environment, but they result in applications with drawbacks of their own:

- The resulting applications are inherently slower because they require that an interpreter translate the code into a machine-executable form. (Applications developed with compiled languages such as C/C++ are slower to develop, but they run faster because they're in machine-executable form already.)

- Interpreted applications require an interpreter, which means that they take up more space. (For example, the Visual Basic interpreter, VBRUN*.DLL, requires 400 KB.)

BASIC and Office Make Beautiful Macros Together

Since its introduction, BASIC has grown up. In 1990, Microsoft added a whole new dimension to BASIC with Microsoft Word version 1, which included a programmable macro language dubbed "WordBasic"—the first version of BASIC to be incorporated into an application as a macro language. By adding a powerful version of BASIC to a macro language, Microsoft transformed a "mere" macro language into a solid programming tool. Today the family of BASIC-based macro languages has expanded to include Access Basic (for Microsoft Access), Visual Basic, and Visual Basic for Applications (VBA)—a macro-language version of Visual Basic that Microsoft Excel has been the first to use.

Closing In on a Common Macro Language

During the past few years, Microsoft has been developing a *common macro language* called Visual Basic for Applications (VBA). A common macro language offers a number of advantages:

- Because the language obstacle is eliminated, business applications can be developed more easily with a wider range of products. Developers don't have to relearn common statements, procedures, functions, control structures, or syntax.

- A common macro language facilitates cross-application programmability (which lets developers use OLE automation to assemble business applications from shrink-wrapped products) by making it easier to control the OLE automation server using the client application's programming language.

■ A common macro language increases code reuse by making code reusable among applications. For example, with slight modifications (and sometimes no modifications), developers can use Access Basic code in Visual Basic.

Excel is the only Microsoft Office product that currently uses VBA. (Access and Word might not use it until their 1996–97 releases.) However, you don't have to wait for VBA to take advantage of a common macro language. To a large extent, the Microsoft BASICs—Access Basic, VBA for Excel, WordBasic, and Visual Basic—already have a common language: BASIC.

**Bridging the Gap Between a Common
Macro Language and the Push-Button Business**

VBA is both a superset and a subset of Visual Basic version 3. One way to think about VBA is that eventually it will be the core language, and each Office product—and Visual Basic—will extend that language to cover its own specialized features. (VBA version 2 serves as the language engine of Visual Basic version 4.) These "application-specific extensions" are where the "A" comes into VBA.

But that "A" requires more of developers than learning a new batch of commands. It requires that they become "Renaissance developers"—people who understand not only databases (which have long been standard fare in computer science departments) but also spreadsheet-based business analysis, financial modeling, and desktop publishing. For many companies, finding developers with such a broad skill set is the hardest part of integrating data at the desktop.

One company I work with is attempting to "grow" these developers. It is piloting a yearlong training program to turn computer science majors just out of college into Windows developers—not into C/C++ programmers, but into developers who can build sophisticated applications using Office products and Visual Basic. The company is also exploring the possibility of making a version of this training program available to traditional developers who want to "re-tool" their skills.

The company's goal is to provide developers with all the knowledge they need to build the push-button business—to create the applications that will enable people to use enterprise-wide data from their PCs.

The Basics of the BASICs

The Microsoft BASICs are similar languages with similar development environments. The rest of this chapter compares the following features of these languages:

- Standard BASIC
- Procedural vs. event-driven programming
- Syntax
- Dialog boxes
- Message boxes
- Input boxes
- Control structures
- Code editor
- Intrinsic constants

NOTE   Because WordBasic requires—and all of the Microsoft BASICs can use—the type declaration character $ for string variables, I use this character for string variables in sample code in this chapter.

Standard BASIC

Roughly 60 statements and functions are common to both traditional BASIC and the Microsoft BASICs. (See Appendix B for a BASIC primer.) Some of these are relics of the old days, or should be—for example, Call, GoSub...Return, Let, On...GoTo, and On...Sub. Others still form the core language—for example, If...Then and string manipulation functions such as Str$() and Left$(). Still others, such as While...Wend, are giving way to more flexible control structures—for example, Do...Loop.

Procedural vs. Event-Driven Programming

The major difference among the various flavors of BASIC is a structural one: WordBasic is a *procedural* programming language, while the other BASICs are *event-driven* programming languages.

In procedural languages, the program is in control. The program—not the user—determines what happens next, and it asks for user input, when necessary, by displaying a dialog box. WordBasic is a procedural programming language: It runs a macro from beginning to end, retaining complete control and allowing the user to choose from a limited set of options (dictated by the macro). For example, the macro might display a dialog box prompting the user to select an item from a list box.

In event-driven languages, the user—not the program—is in control. The user controls the application by clicking a button or pressing a key. Applications developed with event-driven languages also respond to system events (such as timer functions) and to events triggered indirectly by the code (such as Load events, which occur whenever Access Basic or Visual Basic opens a form). Access Basic, VBA for Excel, and Visual Basic are all event-driven programming languages.

Syntax

Access, Excel, and Visual Basic are built from *objects*—essentially, bundles of functionality—that you can manipulate through code. You do this in two ways:

- By setting or retrieving their *properties* (or characteristics)
- By using their *methods* (or procedures)

For example, Excel worksheets are objects. When you change a worksheet's name in code, you change its Name property. When you activate it in code, you use its Activate method. The general syntax for manipulating objects is:

```
object.property or object.method
```

Figure 2-1 shows a diagram of the syntax.

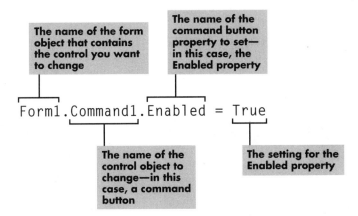

Figure 2-1. *Because objects can be "nested," you might have to drill down to pinpoint the one you want to work with. For example, the Visual Basic code shown here sets the Enabled property of a command button on Form1 to True. In any given line of code, you can either set a property or perform a method—you can't do both at once.*

Although Access Basic, VBA for Excel, and Visual Basic use an object-centric syntax, WordBasic doesn't. Rather, it has a *.arguments* syntax based on the options available in Word's dialog boxes. You can see the difference between WordBasic's *.arguments* syntax and the *object.property* syntax of the other BASICs by comparing the following pieces of code:

WordBasic

```
Sub MAIN
  ViewToolbars .Toolbar = "Drawing", .Show
End Sub
```

VBA for Excel

```
Sub DrawingToolbarOn()
  Toolbars("Drawing").Visible = True
End Sub
```

FYI

Where Does Visual Basic Fit into Office Development?

Microsoft's Office products, in conjunction with Visual Basic, provide a solid set of tools for building mission-critical business applications for departments, teams, or workgroups. Since each of Microsoft's BASIC-based development tools has its own strengths, many companies use the entire suite, plus C/C++ for DLLs. (See Chapter 6 for more information on how C/C++ enhances BASIC-based development.) Such companies can then match a business application to the most suitable development environment: Access for departmental databases; Excel for spreadsheet functionality; Word for text processing and desktop publishing functions; and Visual Basic for "stand-alone," non–product-specific applications and interfaces.

This strategy offers three advantages:

■ It provides targeted development tools for most business tasks.

■ It provides a small, closely related set of development tools with a common language: BASIC.

■ It provides a development environment that simplifies the process of building an application that uses data from other applications and/or integrates functionality from different shrink-wrapped products. (See Chapter 5 for information on ODBC; see Chapter 11 for information on OLE automation; see Chapter 12 for information on DDE.)

The WordBasic code corresponds directly to the Toolbars command on Word's View menu and to the options in the Toolbars dialog box. The .Show/.Hide argument corresponds to the status of the check box next to the Drawing toolbar.

By contrast, VBA for Excel syntax does not mimic the Excel interface. (Nor does Access Basic syntax mimic the Access interface.) Toolbars are among the many objects that VBA for Excel and Access Basic can manipulate. Drawing is a specific toolbar, and one of its properties is Visible. (Other properties are Position—such as floating—and BuiltIn, which enables you to distinguish between custom and built-in toolbars.) The clear separation between the programming language and the application's interface is one of the features that gives VBA for Excel and Access Basic the object-centric look and feel of the programming language on which they're modeled: Visual Basic.

Positional vs. named arguments

Another syntactical difference among the BASICs is in their support of positional or named arguments. *Positional arguments* are those that must appear in a specific order within a list of arguments. If you choose not to specify an available argument, you must still leave space for it (using commas), unless it's an optional argument at the end of the list. Access Basic and Visual Basic both use positional arguments. For example, the following code omits the third argument, which sets the default text for an input box:

```
Answer$ = InputBox$("Type your name, last name first:", "Who Are→
    You", , 100, 100)
```

> **NOTE** For ease of reading, the → character represents a line break that does not appear in the actual code.

Although you can express arguments in VBA for Excel as positional arguments, Excel also supports *named arguments*. This feature lets you specify arguments without reference to their position. For example, the following line of code uses a named argument to go to the range "SalesSummary." (The named argument is in bold.)

```
Application.Goto Reference:="SalesSummary"
```

WordBasic uses *only* named arguments, and its syntax is slightly different from that used in VBA for Excel. For example, the following line of code goes to the bookmarked range "SalesSummary." (Again, the named argument is in bold.)

```
EditGoTo .Destination = "SalesSummary"
```

Dialog Boxes

As you'd expect, all of the Microsoft BASICs can create a standard Windows interface, but each uses a unique interface to do so. Dialog boxes are a perfect illustration of the differences:

■ In Access Basic and Visual Basic, you use forms to create main screens and dialog boxes.

■ In WordBasic, you use a separate dialog editor (similar to the one provided with the Windows Software Development Kit [SDK]) to create dialog boxes.

■ In VBA for Excel, you use dialog sheets to create dialog boxes.

NOTE Excel and Word, which provide a much more limited selection of dialog box controls than either Access Basic or Visual Basic, also let you create forms-based applications by adding controls to documents and worksheets.

Message Boxes

The MsgBox function is a standard feature of the Windows interface and of the Microsoft BASICs (see Figure 2-2). For example, the following code displays a message box with the title *Just Checking*, the question *Anybody home?*, Yes and No buttons (code = 4), and a question mark icon (code = 32). The variable *jc* stores the value of the button that the user clicks. The message type (36) is the sum of the codes for the button type and the icon. The first example shows the code for Access Basic, VBA for Excel, and Visual Basic. The second shows WordBasic's version of the message box function. Notice that WordBasic switches the order of the last two arguments.

```
jc = MsgBox("Anybody home?", 36, "Just Checking")

jc = MsgBox("Anybody home?", "Just Checking", 36)
```

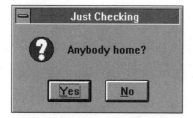

Figure 2-2. *The Microsoft BASICs display the same message boxes.*

Input Boxes

All of the Microsoft BASICs have InputBox functions. For example, all of them can use the following code, which displays an input box with the title *Who Are You* that displays the default text *Last, First* and prompts the user for a name (see Figure 2-3).

```
Answer$ = InputBox$("Type your name, last name first:", "Who Are↴
    You", "Last, First")
```

The last two arguments for this function (specifying the title and default text) are optional. The InputBox functions for Access Basic and Visual Basic version 3 have two additional arguments (also optional) that position the input box on the screen. VBA for Excel goes one step further and lets you add a Help button. The following VBA for Excel code displays an input box that makes two refinements to the previous example: It positions the input box 100 twips (a twip is $^{1}/_{1440}$ of an inch) from the upper left corner of the screen and adds a Help button that calls the Help topic with the context number 10 in INPUT.HLP. (See Chapter 13 for information on context-sensitive Help.)

```
Answer$ = InputBox$("Type your name, last name first:", "Who Are↴
    You", "Last, First", 100, 100, "INPUT.HLP", 10)
```

NOTE   Access Basic and Visual Basic also let you return a variant rather than a string.

Figure 2-3. *The Microsoft BASICs display the same input boxes.*

Control Structures

Although the Microsoft BASICs support the same core control structures— If...Then...Else, Select Case, For...Next, and While...Wend—Access Basic,

VBA for Excel, and Visual Basic support an additional control structure: Do…Loop (a more flexible version of While…Wend).

VBA for Excel and Visual Basic version 4 also support two new control structures:

- With…End With lets you use multiple properties and methods of an object without having to reference the object each time. For example, the following two VBA code examples do the same thing: format the selected range in a worksheet with a 14-point Arial font. The second example uses the With…End With control structure to avoid referencing the Selection.Font object for each property (Name and Size).

```
Sub FormatFontI()
  Selection.Font.Name = "Arial"
  Selection.Font.Size = 14
End Sub

Sub FormatFontII()
  With Selection.Font
    .Name = "Arial"
    .Size = 14
  End With
End Sub
```

- For Each…Next simplifies the process of cycling through all the objects in a *collection*. (A collection is a list of the current members that a given type of object contains—for example, in VBA for Excel the Worksheets collection is a list of Worksheet objects.) The following code loops through the worksheets in a Worksheets collection and writes their names to a new worksheet:

```
Sub GetEachName()
'Insert a new sheet.
  Worksheets.Add

'Store each sheet's name as x.
  Dim x As String

'Use a counter to select the range for entering a name.
  Dim i As Integer
  i = 1
  For Each Worksheet In Worksheets
    x = Worksheet.Name
    Range("A" & i).Formula = x
    i = i + 1
  Next
End Sub
```

Code Editor

Access Basic and Visual Basic also organize code within modules in much the same way: by object and procedure (see Figure 2-4). Both VBA for Excel and WordBasic use a more traditional format, listing subroutines and functions one after the other in module sheets (Excel) or in macro-editing windows (Word).

The main difference between Excel's module sheets and Word's macro-editing windows is that Excel lets you call the individual subroutines and functions within a module using the Macro command on the Tools menu. Word, however, lets you call only the main WordBasic procedures (those that start with *Sub MAIN*) using the Tools Macro command. Although you can call individual subroutines and functions stored in Word's macros, you have to do this through code.

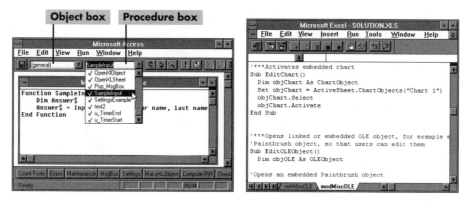

Figure 2-4. *The figure on the left shows the Access code editor (which displays a single procedure at a time). The figure on the right shows the Excel code editor (which lists all procedures in a module sequentially).*

Intrinsic Constants

Access Basic, VBA for Excel, and Visual Basic version 4 use *intrinsic constants*—constants whose names are provided by the language itself (i.e., the developer doesn't need to declare them). They use these intrinsic constants as follows:

- As arguments to functions
- As return values for functions
- As property settings for objects
- As arguments to methods

All VBA for Excel constants are intrinsic. (They use the naming convention *xlNameOfConstant* for Excel functionality and *vbNameOfConstant* for general VBA statements and functions.) To find the values for the Excel constants, use the file XLCONST.TXT on the *Office Solutions* disk included with this book. (This file is also available through the *Office Developer's Kit* as XLCONST.BAS.)

Access Basic provides intrinsic constants for such things as data access, macro actions, security, and variant types. (Search under "Constants" in the Access Help file.)

FYI

The Ideal of a Common Macro Language vs. the Reality of Shrink-Wrapped Products

No matter how quickly Microsoft moves toward a common macro language, most of the capabilities of the Microsoft BASICs reflect those of the underlying shrink-wrapped product. Most Access Basic commands manipulate databases, and most VBA for Excel commands manipulate spreadsheets.

The following code samples demonstrate how to count the fonts installed under Windows in Access Basic, VBA for Excel, WordBasic, and Visual Basic version 3.

I originally conceived this example as a way to prove how similar the BASICs already are. I knew I could determine the number of installed printer fonts and their names in both WordBasic and Visual Basic, and I figured that I could do the same in Access Basic and VBA for Excel. And, of course, I could—after declaring a Windows API function (GetProfileString) and writing a routine. Access Basic and VBA for Excel don't have as many commands devoted to fonts as either WordBasic (whose desktop publishing features make extensive use of fonts) or Visual Basic (whose status as a general development tool requires the ability to manage input/output generally).

The lesson here is that if the development tool you're using doesn't provide commands to access a capability that you need, use Microsoft's other common macro language—the Windows API. (See Chapter 6.)

NOTE The code in the first sample is identical for Access Basic and VBA for Excel.

Access Basic and VBA for Excel

```
Option Explicit
Declare Function GetProfileString Lib "KERNEL"↴
  (ByVal lpAppName As String, lpKeyName As Any,↴
  ByVal lpDefault As String, ByVal lpReturnedString↴
  As String, ByVal nSize As Integer) As Integer

'Displays result of the NumberOfFonts function.
Sub CountingFonts()
  Dim strMsg
  strMsg = "The number of fonts listed in the [fonts] "
  strMsg = strMsg & "section of your WIN.INI file is "
  MsgBox strMsg & NumberOfFonts()
End Sub


'This function returns the number of fonts listed in the
'fonts section of WIN.INI. To get only the printer fonts, you
'might also have to read the printer's section of WIN.INI.
Function NumberOfFonts() As Integer

'Return value of GetProfileString.
  Dim iLength As Integer

'Buffer to hold string retrieved by GetProfileString.
  Dim sBuffer As String

'Stores null character (ANSI code 0), which marks end of string.
  Dim NullChar As String

'Null character's position in string.
  Dim iNullPosition As Integer

'Counter.
  Dim iFontCount As Integer

'Maximum string length that function retrieves.
  Const MAX_LENGTH = 3000

  NullChar = Chr$(0)
  sBuffer = String$(MAX_LENGTH, 0)

'The argument ByVal 0& retrieves the entire [fonts] section.
  iLength = GetProfileString("fonts", ByVal 0&, "", sBuffer,↴
    Len(sBuffer))
  sBuffer = Left$(sBuffer, iLength)
```

```
'Counts null characters; each indicates end of a font entry.
  iNullPosition = 0
  Do
    iNullPosition = InStr(iNullPosition + 1, sBuffer, NullChar)
    If iNullPosition = 0 Then Exit Do
    iFontCount = iFontCount + 1
  Loop
  NumberOfFonts = iFontCount
End Function
```

WordBasic

```
Sub MAIN
'Returns the number of fonts available for the current printer.
'This is the number of fonts listed in the font dialog box,
'including printer fonts, TrueType fonts, and Windows system fonts.
  A = CountFonts()
  MsgBox "There are" + Str$(A) + " fonts installed for the current⟶
    printer."
End Sub
```

Visual Basic

```
Sub Form_Load ()
'Returns the number of fonts available for the current printer.
  Dim A As Integer
  Dim strMsg As String

  A = Printer.FontCount
  strMsg = "There are" & Str$(A) & " printer fonts "
  strMsg = strMsg & "installed for the current printer."
  MsgBox strMsg
End Sub
```

3

Reengineering the Process

A business application has two aspects: the process that developers use to build the application and the business process that the application automates. To improve the quality of business applications, you may need to reengineer the application development process. To improve business productivity through these applications, you may need to reengineer the business process itself. This chapter addresses these issues.

Who Cares About the Method, as Long as It's Done Tomorrow?

No matter what development tools you use, you'll develop better business applications if you use a development methodology. Not many developers like to hear this. Of the developers I know, I can name fewer than a dozen who have any interest in methodology. Here are some representative observations on the subject:

- The director of engineering at a commercial software company explained why they don't need a methodology: "We hire smart people and let them be creative."

- A developer at a bank told me that they "don't have time for methods." They just "find out what an application should do, then start coding."

- Another developer said that in her organization, methodology is irrelevant. The point is to "get projects done by the deadline." If this means that the code isn't well-documented or particularly fast, they worry about it later.

Come to think of it, most of the developers I know who are interested in methodology aren't even developers anymore—they're managers. Developers don't have time for methodology. They're too busy coding to bother with paperwork. And unfortunately, that's how a lot of them view methodology—as paperwork.

In many developers' minds, methodology equals technical documentation—which tends to be something that they work on after all the "real" work is done. First you write an application; then you document it. But this historical approach to methodology defeats its purpose—which is not to fill out this form or jump through that hoop, but to produce a solid application that's easy to maintain.

> **NOTE** Throughout this section, "documentation" refers to technical documentation used by developers, not by end users.

1001 Steps, and *Then* You Start to Code

Back in the 1960s, people didn't develop applications: They wrote programs. It wasn't until the early 1970s that software development gained recognition as an engineering-style profession in which developers planned projects and built applications, just as civil engineers plan transportation networks and build roads. With this recognition came the practice of using methodologies to develop applications.

Those early methodologies—typically, thousands of pages of step-by-step instructions stored in huge three-ring binders—included checklists of hundreds of things for developers to think about, do, and document *before* starting to build the applications. This was exactly the sort of thing that gave methodology a bad name.

But these methodologies made sense at the time. They were linear approaches to application development that mirrored the procedural programs that developers were coding. The idea was that if developers did a good job of planning a project and analyzing the requirements, they could produce a big, thick book (known as the *functional spec*) containing everything there was to know about the application. The developers would then take the book and disappear into a room to write COBOL programs and DB2 tables. Six months or nine months or three years later, they'd emerge from the room and say, "Here it is. What do you think?"

This approach also made sense because of the hardware limitations of the time. Programming on a mainframe was a slow, cumbersome process. A single compile might take hours and then fail because of a syntactical error. As a result, it could take days or weeks to modify a program. The goal of the early methodologies was to avoid these time-consuming modifications by delivering a complete system.

The PC revolution

The PC revolution brought several changes that had a dramatic effect on the development process:

- Applications got smaller. Most PC-based business applications are geared toward a handful of specific functions—they don't store and organize corporate databases containing millions of records. A developer at one large company I have worked with says that the company prefers PC projects that are no more than "three by three" from start to beta—in other words, projects that require no more than nine staff-months (three developers times three months) of effort.

- Application development became faster and easier.

- Faster development simplified the process of modifying applications. Today people *expect* applications to be refined based on user feedback.

For PC developers—especially those who build front-end applications—the "1001 steps" approach to maintainable applications doesn't make sense. However, this doesn't mean that methodology should be thrown out—which is what many developers have done. Rather, it means that methodologies should be scaled in proportion to the project. If you estimate that a project will take three developers three months to finish, you can't spend the first three weeks planning. But you can spend the first three *days* planning—and you should.

FYI

Preventing Flops

It's instructive to talk to developers about PC development projects that have flopped. I've found that failed projects tend to fall into three broad categories:

- Bad programming jobs (applications that were poorly designed)

- Inappropriate programming jobs (applications that didn't do what users expected them to do)

- Obsolete programming jobs (applications that took so long to deliver that they were no longer needed in the originally approved form)

The right methodology can prevent all three types of flops. Glenn Shimamoto heads a project at Bankers Trust that explores methodologies to improve application development. He has identified two practices that increase the likelihood of building successful business applications:

- Constant interaction between developers and users

- An iterative development style that enables developers to make progress in small, controlled leaps that users review and approve

How to Eat an Elephant

The object-oriented literature calls it *use-case analysis*. Microsoft calls it *activity-based planning*. Some of the commercial methodologies call it *task analysis*. All of these terms convey the same idea: Developers must begin the development process by learning everything there is to know about the tasks the application is meant to accomplish.

The following six steps will not only help you learn about those tasks, but they'll serve as the foundation for developing maintainable business applications using Office products and Visual Basic:

1. Identify the tasks.
2. Identify the threads of functionality for each task.
3. Analyze the threads.
4. Group the threads into a series of deliverables.
5. "Beta" each thread.
6. Try again.

Remember that these steps aren't serial, but iterative. Remember too that you can pare them down to fit the size of your project. It's like the old riddle: How do you eat an elephant? Answer: One bite at a time. No matter how large or small the project, the process is pretty much the same. The only thing that changes is the number of bites.

FYI

Application Development Methodology vs. GUI Development

Developers sometimes confuse application development methodology with GUI (graphical user interface) development methodology. This is largely because GUI development is new enough to make headlines. For example, a seasoned developer commented that there are two methods of developing applications: analyzing the tasks that applications must perform *or* talking to users about what they do to perform those tasks. He advocated the first method emphatically and by doing so managed to be both right and wrong. He muddled two separate activities: developing applications and developing GUIs. To develop applications, you have to analyze the tasks they're designed to perform. To develop GUIs, you have to talk to users about what they currently do to perform these tasks.

Chapter 4 presents a GUI development process that's separate and distinct (as it should be) from the application development process.

Step #1. Identify the tasks

This is the "reporter" stage of application development. You must identify the tasks that the application is to perform—both the "obvious" tasks (which users invoke) and those that the application handles behind the scenes. You must identify who, what, when, where, why, and how people will use the application. You must understand the business process so you can map the tasks accurately to a computer application. Like a good reporter, you must take detailed notes. (A tape recorder can come in handy for large applications.)

FYI

A Programmer's Perspective: Walking in the User's Shoes

Ellen Huber, a coworker of mine, described a programming assignment at a Fortune 200 chemicals company that required her to temporarily become a dispatcher in the distribution department. Her job: to act as an end user of an existing application and determine whether the application had to be redesigned (the users' claim) or whether users had to be retrained (management's claim). If the application needed to be redesigned, she would build the prototype.

The department that relied on the application delivered fuel oil, and the application optimized the delivery schedule. The goal was to make as few deliveries as possible while ensuring that customers always had enough fuel. To do this, the application tracked customer usage over time; projected when customers would need a refill; and handled logistics planning, scheduling, and routing. Every morning dispatchers printed out schedules for the drivers, who would—ideally—take the schedule, hop into their trucks, make their deliveries, and come back the next day for the new schedule.

But the application, designed for stable scenarios, floundered when variables arose. Whenever a change occurred—when a customer requested an early delivery or an extra delivery, or rescheduled an existing appointment—users had to start over and reenter all the key information to print out a corrected schedule. Although management was keen on using the application because of the money spent developing it, the application actually generated more work than it saved.

Huber ended up redesigning the system and developing a prototype. She now describes this assignment as one of the most valuable lessons of her programming career:

> It made me realize how important it is to understand the real world that people work in—and the constraints that they work under—as opposed to the theoretical world that people in the IS department think exists. Now I *always* meet the people who are going to be using an application so that I can understand their job. I no longer trust the IS department's system requirements.

Step #2. Identify the threads of functionality for each task

Early methodologies had developers produce a list of application requirements. More recent methodologies describe requirements in terms of task scenarios, or *threads of functionality*. (See the sidebar below.) Each thread of functionality describes—from start to finish—how the user interacts with the PC to perform a task.

Once you describe all of the task scenarios for an application, you have a complete, event-driven requirements statement from which developers can work. You've identified all of the application's elements—forms, commands, message boxes, reports, and so on. You also have a document that users can sign off on.

FYI

A Sample Task Scenario

Here is a sample task scenario for entering data in a database front end:

1. Log on.

2. Double-click the application's icon. The application opens a blank form in which data can be entered immediately.

3. Use the Tab key, the access keys, or the mouse to move from field to field.

4. Either save the record (by clicking the Save button on the toolbar, choosing the Save Record command from the menu, or pressing the shortcut key) or discard it by clicking Cancel.

5. Four fields require data: last name, first name, zip code, and social security number. These fields appear at the top of the form. If users don't enter data for these fields, the application displays a message box explaining that you can't save a record unless these fields have data.

6. If users click Cancel, the application displays a dialog box asking for confirmation. The dialog box contains Yes and No buttons. (No is the default.) Choose Yes to discard the record and display an empty form. Choose No to return to the record you just entered.

7. Click the Save button to update the database.

8. To exit the system, click the Exit button on the toolbar, choose the Exit command from the menu, or press the shortcut key.

This is important because without user sign-off on a detailed description of the application, you risk the "plague of the creeping spec": No matter how clear the tasks and priorities seem today, by tomorrow they'll seem less clear, and by the time you release the first thread of functionality as a beta version, the users may well have an entirely different set of expectations—unless the spec is written down.

Of course, nothing has to be written in stone. The advantage of an iterative methodology is its flexibility: The developers and the users can refine it as the process goes along. On the other hand, you can't hit a moving target, so at some point you have to balance the dynamic list of task scenarios with a firm set of priorities.

Step #3. Analyze the threads

This is the "intelligent hammer" stage of application development. The goal is to break the task scenarios into the components of an application (subroutines, shared subroutines, functions, and so on). For example, in the task scenario described on the previous page, Save and Exit are obviously discrete subroutines. However, the commands that access the database (such as those for updating and retrieving data) might share a connect routine. The more skillful you are at breaking the application into simple components, the easier the application will be to write and maintain. If you document or diagram these design decisions, the development process will be easier still. (As Confucius said, "One great effort, and forever at peace.")

No matter what size application you're developing, comment the code to explain what each component does. If a subroutine or a function is called by several routines, list them. Complete comments are the most useful type of documentation for developers. You might misplace your notebook, but as long as you have commented code you can read it to find out how the procedures work and fit together.

> **NOTE** This chapter doesn't address relational database design, which is a highly specialized field requiring significantly more documentation than other business applications do. (See the sidebar titled "Designing Relational Data" in Chapter 10 for more information.)

Step #4. Group the threads into a series of deliverables

One mainframe tradition that's been passed down to PC development is the "big bang" approach to delivering business applications—the idea that you have to deliver a whole application or nothing. In actuality, businesses often benefit from partial deliveries—whether of applications or pens—as long as they can use whatever they get. That's the powerful side benefit of a task-oriented methodology—it lets you deliver applications in *usable* chunks.

The following are some techniques that can help you "chunk up" a project into deliverables:

- Do the scary things first. That way, as your investment in a project grows, you skate downhill in terms of risk. If you fail, at least you fail small.

- Deliver the most important thread of functionality first.

- Set realistic goals and time frames. My rule of thumb is to double my best estimate. Candy Schwartz, a vice president at PaineWebber, always boosts her best estimate to the next largest unit: If she thinks it will take an hour, she estimates a day; if she thinks it will take a day, she estimates a week.

- Deliver *complete* threads of functionality frequently.

Step #5. "Beta" each thread

Don't deliver applications—deliver alphas, betas, and releases numbered 1.0, 1.1, and so on. Delivering threads of functionality according to a schedule provides a concentrated, official period for people to get back to you regarding what doesn't work at all (bugs to fix ASAP) and what doesn't work as expected (enhancements to incorporate into a future release).

Step #6. Try again

Application development is an iterative process in which applications are not "completed" per se, only improved. This is not an excuse for delivering either bad applications or ones that are functionally incomplete, but a simple acknowledgment that what's "right" evolves naturally over time. The best applications are built with the future in mind: Developers can "grow" them without going back to the drawing board.

PCs Make You More Productive: Fact or Fiction?

Since the late 1970s, hardware and software manufacturers have trumpeted PCs as productivity tools. But are they? Even as hardware becomes faster and software features grow more versatile, studies have consistently found that PCs haven't improved business productivity as a whole. A recent article titled "The Productivity Pit" in the magazine *Across the Board* presented these findings:

- A 1990 study by a professor at Harvard Business School found that the new technology hadn't increased productivity in manufacturing companies.

- A study by the McKinsey Global Institute covering the airline, restaurant, retail, retail banking, and telecommunications industries found that the new technology had made an impact only in telecommunications and retail banking.

- A 1993 survey conducted by *ComputerWorld Magazine* and Anderson Consulting found that most senior executives believed information technology wasn't worth the money spent on it.

No doubt the true value of PCs to business lies somewhere between the computer industry's hype and the researchers' disappointing findings. Today's PC hardware and software are capable of boosting productivity. But maybe it takes a reengineering of the business process as a whole to realize these productivity gains.

FYI

Better Ways to Measure Productivity Gains

When considering PC technology's contributions to business productivity, some who have worked in both the financial services industry (which has realized productivity gains) and manufacturing note that financial services are "ahead of the curve" in PC technology. Tony Sorrell, who manages IS for Philip Morris' New York headquarters, previously worked for American Express. He observed that in financial services, the technology (from mainframes to PCs) is often an important ingredient of the product. For example, you could say that brokerage houses that sell financial products are, in large part, selling the underlying technology that assists in identifying, analyzing, and managing competing investments. Brokers and bankers often use standard PC spreadsheets to analyze these investments.

Although manufacturing has clearly realized productivity gains from automation, it hasn't realized these gains from people working directly with workstations or with PC-based technologies. However, Tony Sorrell pointed out an important issue that all industries face when trying to assess such productivity gains:

> Because the benefits of PC technology can be difficult to quantify, the cost-benefit equation isn't necessarily the best way to measure them. How can we measure, for example, the benefits of directly accessing data from a PC, or being able to analyze that data in a spreadsheet? How can we identify and value the ideas that might come from such analysis? When we can do that, we'll be able to judge the technology better and make better decisions on how to use it.

Another part of the problem may be that companies (and researchers) have believed the advertising. According to the hype, people become more productive just because they use this PC or that software package. In my experience, moving productivity up a notch requires that companies revamp existing business processes, create supporting business applications, and provide job-oriented (as opposed to software-oriented) training. Otherwise, people tend to use PCs just as they used whatever the PC replaced.

For example, a manager in a central accounting office recently assessed the impact on productivity of a new client-server accounting system. He observed dryly, "Before this system was installed, the people working on it tracked information on orange index cards. Now they track it on bigger index cards—workstations." He went on to say that while the office did eke out time savings, it was not the level of savings they'd hoped for. He now understands the importance of reengineering both the process that brings data into accounting and the process by which accounting provides data to management.

Not all automation is reengineering, but IS professionals involved in automation projects might benefit from examining their projects in light of the following three reengineering principles—principles I've seen applied to business applications that provide clear productivity gains. They have a common thrust: to integrate business processes at the desktop.

- **Turn the desktop PC into the Grand Central of business communications.** Distribute data directly to and from the desktop instead of through the standard "print-photocopy-fax-FedEx" route. Donaldson, Lufkin & Jenrette's investment banking group uses this strategy to provide desktop data to its bankers and to integrate information flow and communications among its offices nationwide. (See the sidebar titled "Faster Than FedEx—From NY to LA in 6.77 Seconds" in Chapter 5.)

- **Enter data once, and then reuse it.** Collect data once—as a by-product of work rather than as a business activity in its own right—and then share it. For example, one of the nation's largest insurance companies is reengineering business communications within its corporate offices. The company's new application (which integrates Microsoft Word templates with a multiuser Microsoft Access database and a custom scheduling application) lets them create and use a body of shared data. Whenever users address a letter or create a fax cover sheet for someone *not* in the database, they enter the necessary data (name, address, and so on) as part of that process. In addition, the company is centralizing these communications at the desktop with fax/modem boards and autodialers. (See the section titled "SAMPLE APPLICATION: Business Information Manager [BIM]" in Chapter 10.)

■ **Eliminate redundant activities and extra steps.** One way to eliminate extra steps is to use applications such as Microsoft Excel and Word
to *access* data as well as analyze and publish it. A senior manager I know
is considering replacing paper reports with "live" reports delivered in
Excel. This would give his staff complete control over analysis of the
data, and those who wanted a paper copy could print one.

FYI

Hype, Hype, Hooray

Below are some examples of what software and hardware vendors would
have you believe about their products. All of these examples are from ads in
the June 14, 1994, issue of *PC Magazine*.

■ "Green PCs that put you in the black." (Hewlett Packard)

■ "Project management software that's so powerful, so persuasive, so
insightful, you'll wonder how you lived without it." (Primavera)

■ "General Motors uses Notes to unify Europe. How big is your
problem?" (Lotus)

■ "First you gave us a desk. Now we want to run the whole company."
(Compaq)

■ "This is the end of the paper trail. The end of slow response time. The
end of the search for misfiled papers. The end of the routing game.
The end of the overflowing in-box. The end of sluggish performance.
And sluggish profits." (IBM)

■ "Loosely defined, it's the technological equivalent of having a guardian
angel. It's called IntelliSense™ technology. Simply stated, it watches
over you and even helps you when you need it…. As you're thinking
about your work, your software is too…. What does this mean? You
save time. You're more productive…. Only the Microsoft Office does
so many things to make your job easier to do." (Microsoft)

■ "How fast is an Image™ Series PC? How fast do you think? NEC Image
Series PCs are specifically designed to keep pace with you thought for
thought. Idea for idea. Brainstorm for brainstorm. Whether you're a
graphic designer or a marketing analyst, an engineer or an accountant,
Image Series PCs respond to your ideas as quickly as you can think of
them…. They have everything it takes to put your thoughts into effect
immediately. You'll get more work done. And do it faster, smarter,
more creatively." (NEC)

4

Designing Good GUIs

Back in 1993, I became involved in what's been dubbed "the GUI Standards Project" at Bankers Trust. Our mission was to come up with practical interface standards for Microsoft Windows–based business applications. We interviewed developers, read the relevant literature, experimented with ways of handling various problems, published our findings, created a Visual Basic application shell, and taught workshops.

The project led me to do an about-face. I used to think that the most important element in "graphical user interface" was "graphical," but now I know that it's "user." In fact, when the goal is to make a business application easy to use instead of awesome to look at, the entire interface-design process changes: Developers spend more time learning to take advantage of the Windows skills that users already have—and they spend less time choosing colors and creating 3-D font effects.

When developers use the graphics, modes, and methods that people already know, people will use business applications more productively. And that's the bottom line—better business through better business applications.

This chapter describes how to develop business applications that are easy to use. It promotes a people-oriented approach to GUI development, provides a summary of what you need to know to develop good GUIs, and introduces a GUI development process that results in better applications.

GUI Development: A People-Oriented Approach

In their classic book *In Search of Excellence*, Thomas Peters and Robert Waterman relate one of the lessons they learned from observing some of America's best companies:

> Treat people…as partners; treat them with dignity; treat them with respect. Treat *them*—not capital spending and automation—as the primary source of productivity gains.

The force driving development of business applications is the need to make employees (and business itself) more productive, more competitive, and more profitable. Yet developers frequently think of people—"the primary source of productivity gains," to quote Peters and Waterman—as peripheral. They forget (or simply fail) to treat the users of their applications as partners in the business of boosting productivity.

The stereotype of IS professionals is that they prefer business requirements, system architecture, flow charts, and specifications to users. Users are left out of decisions regarding—of all things—*usability*. One developer told me that in her department, managers are trying to improve productivity by eliminating the need for developers to work with those who use their applications. Developers develop from spec. Period.

I once developed a small system by working from a spec put together by a team of people, only one of whom was a bona fide end user. Although the team liked the product, I had to redesign it completely after the pilot—there were so many use-oriented considerations that never made it into the spec that my interface was awkward to use 25 percent of the time.

We cheat ourselves out of productivity gains when we isolate the people who use business applications from the GUI development process.

FYI

Are GUI Standards Worthwhile?

Don Tapscott and Art Caston make the case bluntly for adhering to GUI standards in their bestselling book *Paradigm Shift*: "Applications that work in similar ways require less training and support.... Experience has shown that the costs can be substantially reduced with a common platform, portable applications across heterogeneous hardware, and a common user interface."

The Principles Behind User-Friendly Interfaces

If PCs are to boost productivity for businesses, IS professionals need to think more about usability. When Microsoft redesigned Word for Windows for the version 2 release, it made a major commitment to testing Word's usability. Microsoft contracted with an independent organization, the National Software Testing Laboratory in Philadelphia, to test the usability of Word against that of WordPerfect for Windows. The test population consisted of WordPerfect for MS-DOS users who had never used a Windows-based word processor. All participants received a brief introduction to using a Windows-based application before they started.

Microsoft produced a video, called *The Microsoft Word Challenge*, and an advertising campaign to publicize the test results, which showed that on average participants finished the test 30 minutes faster using Word and that 79 percent said they preferred Word over WordPerfect. In spite of its promotional nature, the video provides some wonderful insights into how computer users approach an application they've never seen before. I especially like one segment in which a professional word processor compares the process of printing an envelope in Word for Windows version 2 and in WordPerfect for Windows version 5.1. In Word, she clicked the Envelope toolbar button, typed the address, and then printed the envelope. She couldn't figure out how to do it in WordPerfect:

> I couldn't see anything about envelopes in any of the menus....
> I went to Glossary [on the Help menu] and pressed E, but they didn't
> have any envelopes listed, so I went to Index and pressed E and tried
> to select Envelopes, but I still couldn't figure it out.... It was talking
> about paper size, but I still couldn't figure out how to get the enve-
> lope to come up.
>
> I couldn't figure out how to use the Help.

When you encounter a good user interface, you can use it almost intuitively. When developers watch people figure out how to use Windows-based applications, they learn quickly what works and what doesn't. For example, they learn the importance of providing obvious visual clues, such as the envelope icon on the toolbar in Word for Windows version 2. They learn the importance of reducing common multistep tasks (such as printing an envelope) to a single step, such as clicking a button. They learn how important it is that the application's commands (and the associated Help topics) use the same simple words that people use (such as "envelope"). Users shouldn't have to figure out that the way to print an envelope is to change the paper size to $9\frac{1}{2}$ by $4\frac{1}{8}$ inches ("envelope size").

Here are seven principles for developing good, user-friendly interfaces. The following sections cover them in more detail.

- Be consistent.

- Use informative graphics (not sexy ones).

- Easy to read means easy to use.

- Show, don't tell.

- Do, don't ask (unless it's important).

- Hold up your end of the conversation.

- Let the driver drive.

Principle #1. Be Consistent

Business-application developers need to understand what users already know about Windows, and they need to take advantage of this knowledge by using established conventions in their applications.

Unfortunately, most developers would rather be "creative" than consistent. All too often, the result of such creativity is an application that requires users to set aside their hard-won knowledge and start from square one.

The publishing industry as a whole (of which "software publishing" is an important and growing piece) places a high value on consistency. Take newspapers, for example. There are two standard newspaper designs: the "literary" design and the "tabloid" design (see Figure 4-1).

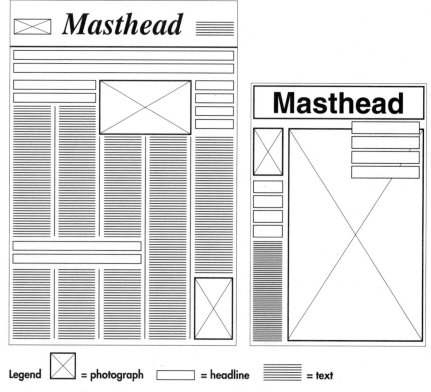

Figure 4-1. *Newspapers are paragons of consistency. There are two standard designs: the "literary" design (left) and the "tabloid" design (right).*

Newspaper editors and layout staff don't redesign their newspaper every day; they simply plug text and photos into the standard look that everyone expects. Likewise, developers should plug into the standard Windows look and feel so that users can plug in too. Users should be able to assume that an application's commands are on the menus and that the commands they use most often can also be executed using toolbar buttons and keyboard shortcuts.

Principle #2. Use Informative Graphics (Not Sexy Ones)

The best example of an informative graphic—a graphic that makes an application easier to use—is the 3-D button. Because people in our culture are used to pushing buttons to make things happen, they push (or "click") on-screen buttons intuitively. And, in response to the user's action, the buttons even appear to be pushed in (see Figure 4-2).

Figure 4-2. *3-D buttons actually seem to "push in" in response to a mouse click.*

User-friendly graphics let people work with an application in the same way that they work in the non-computer world. That means using real-world analogs: buttons to push, boxes to check, magnifying glasses for enlarging text, and so on.

This section describes two categories of informative GUI graphics: buttons (including command buttons, graphic buttons, and toolbar buttons) and standard dialog box controls.

The Great Button Debates

There are three main types of buttons (as shown in Figure 4-3). Button terminology differs, but all buttons fall into one of these categories:

■ Command buttons (also called *text buttons*), such as OK and Cancel

■ Graphic buttons (including those used on toolbars and button bars)

■ Control buttons (such as the buttons to the right and left of the horizontal scroll bar)

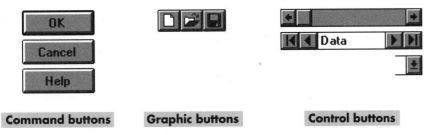

Figure 4-3. *The main button types used in Windows.*

The two biggest button debates are about toolbars vs. button bars and about when to use command buttons.

Toolbars vs. button bars   Toolbar buttons (small, icon-based buttons) and button bar buttons (larger buttons that mix text and graphics) provide single-click mouse access to frequently used commands. The Microsoft Office suite favors the toolbar, while WordPerfect and others favor the button bar. The toolbar's main advantage is its smaller footprint; the button bar's main advantage is that it accommodates text as well as graphics (although Microsoft's recent ToolTips innovation gives toolbars both of these advantages). The *Visual Design Guide*, which comes with Visual Basic version 3 (and predates ToolTips), suggests using button bars when a "product needs the aesthetic benefit of the graphics, but where the graphics alone are not clear, and when…space is not a concern."

When to use command buttons   I once began a presentation about designing business applications with Word for Windows with an anecdote about a Word application I had encountered at a major corporation. It had two dozen fill-in fields and worked just like the old WordPerfect for MS-DOS macros: One-line "dialogs" popped up and asked for a single bit of information at a time. If you skipped a dialog even accidentally, you couldn't go back—nor could you fast-forward to the end. Worst of all, you were trapped in this dialog hell *every time you started a new document.*

The audience's knowing guffaws surprised me: Apparently, throwbacks to this primitive form of Windows programming are still commonplace. A typical example is the "dialog drill-down," which forces users to slog through several dialog boxes to perform a task. To make commands easier to find, developers should use the expanding (or "unfolding") dialog box (see Figure 4-4) for applications built with Microsoft Excel or Word or the tabbed dialog box (a custom control) for applications built with Microsoft Access or Visual Basic.

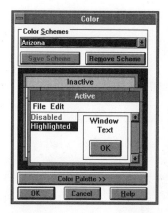 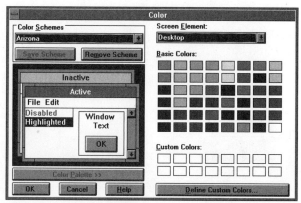

Figure 4-4. *The Color application in Control Panel uses an expanding dialog box when users click Color Palette. This is a good alternative to dialog drill-downs.*

The right control for the job

Windows users know how to handle drop-down menus, list boxes, option buttons, and so on. When business-application developers use these tools correctly (see Figure 4-5), they accelerate learning.

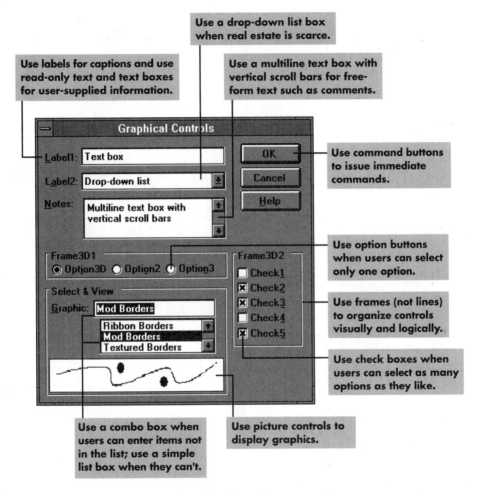

Use a drop-down list box when real estate is scarce.

Use labels for captions and use read-only text and text boxes for user-supplied information.

Use a multiline text box with vertical scroll bars for free-form text such as comments.

Use command buttons to issue immediate commands.

Use option buttons when users can select only one option.

Use frames (not lines) to organize controls visually and logically.

Use check boxes when users can select as many options as they like.

Use a combo box when users can enter items not in the list; use a simple list box when they can't.

Use picture controls to display graphics.

Figure 4-5. *The correct use of standard Windows controls.*

One developer said that she first realized the importance of standard controls when she had to teach a new employee how to use an application she had developed. The employee didn't know much about the business task at hand, but he had used Excel. At several points, when he wasn't sure what to do in a particular dialog box or didn't know how to access a particular command, he mentioned how he would do it in Excel and asked whether it was the same. Because it *was* the same, the lesson turned out to be very short.

This section focuses on the correct use of the following controls: text boxes, labels, scrollable text boxes, list boxes, check boxes, and option buttons.

Text boxes vs. labels I've read that the simplest controls are the most overused (in other words, *misused*) because developers tend to use the controls they know best rather than the right ones for the job. Text boxes (also known as "edit boxes") fall into this category. Developers frequently misuse them for explanatory text when they can prune their code by using labels instead (or the caption property for 3-D panels in Visual Basic). The design of the text box prompts users to type information, and the length of the box suggests how long that information can be. For example, U.S. Immigration forms allow 13 characters each for last and first names, which results in the text boxes shown in Figure 4-6.

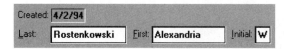

Figure 4-6. *Users respond to visual clues. The smaller the text box, the less text they're likely to type in it. Boxed text on a gray background (see the Created field above) doesn't invite editing, although it does suggest that the text provides relevant business information rather than explanatory information.*

Scrollable text boxes Use scrollable text boxes when users can type free-form text such as notes or comments. You can do this in Access, Excel, and Visual Basic by adding vertical scroll bars to multiline text boxes. I didn't fully realize the power of the vertical scroll bar until I saw an experienced Windows user incorrectly use a multiline text box in Word version 6. (Inexplicably, Word doesn't support scroll bars in text boxes, although you can scroll up and down using the cursor keys.) After typing each line, the user paused, pressed Enter (in case the text didn't wrap automatically), and stopped typing when he got to the end of the box. A good user interface graphic—the vertical scroll bar—would have prevented this misunderstanding.

The family of list boxes The design of the list box suggests that you must select from the list and that the list contains more elements than are visible. The drop-down list box has the same features but is meant for cases in which real estate is scarce. If you have the room, use the simple list box because it's a better graphic—you don't have to open it to see the list—and it needs only one click instead of two. The combo box combines the list box with the text box so users can enter data that's not listed.

Options Check boxes (like text boxes) are clearly adapted from the forms that have become the mainstay of business and government. Use check boxes when the unwritten instructions are "Check all that apply." Use option buttons when users can select only one of the options.

FYI

Read-Only Information

Dialog boxes and forms in business applications include three basic types of information:

- Labels and explanatory text (which users can't edit)

- Business data that users type, edit, or select

- "Read-only" information—data that can't be edited (such as the date on which a record was created or last updated)

Use the following standard techniques (as shown in Figure 4-7) to distinguish read-only text from editable information:

- Use a text box for information that users will type or edit.

- Don't box labels. Let them sit directly on the dialog box.

- When possible, box read-only text to distinguish it from labels and explanatory text. (This is easy to do in Access and Visual Basic, but you can't do it in Word. To do it in Excel, use the Drawing toolbar.)

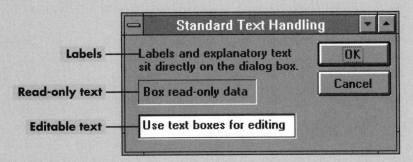

Figure 4-7. *This diagram shows the ideal way to present labels and explanatory text, read-only text, and text that users can edit.*

FYI

Too Much of a Good Thing

Is there a better way to let users select from among 40 options than to provide 40 check boxes? The answer is yes. Use a list box with the multiselect property (see Figure 4-8). The developers at Pepsi International have used this technique to deliver powerful but easy-to-use reporting tools worldwide.

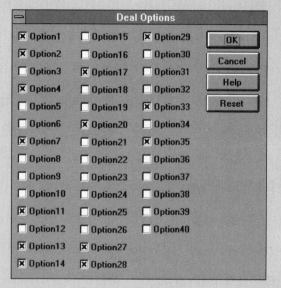

Figure 4-8. *Have more than 10 options? Use a list box.*

If you have more than 10 options in a group, you should use a list box—for two reasons:

- A list box can take up less space.

- Anything with more than 10 items *is* a list—exactly what a list box was designed to handle.

This leads naturally to another question: When is a *list* too long? The best answer I've heard is that a list is too long when its items display slowly as you scroll through it, at which point you should break it up. (For interface display, as opposed to processing operations, I adhere to the more-than-5-seconds-is-too-slow rule.) One way to break it up is to have users select recognizable sections of the list with option buttons and then change the list dynamically.

Sexy Graphics Don't Make Good GUIs

When Microsoft developers clamored for sexier graphics, project designers created a collection of icons, some of which appear in Figure 4-9. This parody was meant to prove a point: GUI graphics should be judged not by their sex appeal but by their ability to convey information.

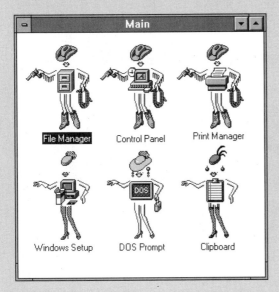

Figure 4-9. *Microsoft designers created these icons to prove a point to developers: Good graphics are informational, not sexy.*

Principle #3. Easy to Read Means Easy to Use

Displaying and using text effectively is one of the biggest challenges facing GUI developers. This section presents some techniques for dealing successfully with five common issues:

- How to select the best font for the job

- What fonts to use in dialog boxes and in forms

- When to use text boxes and when to use labels

- How to present read-only information

- When to use scrollable text boxes

NOTE   In Windows, black is the standard color for text.

Selecting fonts: The Windows standard

Windows-based applications use the System font and three styles of MS Sans Serif, which were designed to be easy to read on the screen. Developers who use TrueType fonts such as Arial for their Access and Visual Basic applications gain nothing by doing so—except the dubious distinction of being different. And TrueType fonts are a headache for users of Windows version 3 (the fonts don't work in that version) and for users who don't have the fonts installed. (The dialog editors in Excel and Word use only MS Sans Serif.)

NOTE   3-D fonts tend to cause headaches too, but for a different reason: They're hard to read.

The following descriptions provide a rationale for using the standard Windows fonts in your applications.

Title bars and menus   Use 10-point System bold for title bars and menus (see Figure 4-10). It ensures that the main elements of the application window are prominent and that the text is still readable when it is grayed out.

Figure 4-10.   *10-point System bold is the standard font for title bars and menus.*

Dialog boxes and forms   Use 8-point MS Sans Serif bold for dialog boxes and forms (see Figure 4-11). The text is easy to read, and you can fit a generous amount of text in a small area. In addition, it takes second place visually to the application's main information—the menu bar and the title bar.

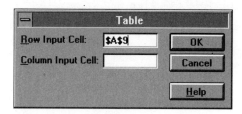

Figure 4-11.   *8-point MS Sans Serif bold is the standard font for dialog boxes and forms.*

FYI

Fonts in Dialog Boxes and Forms

Dialog boxes are a type of nonsizable window used to present data to users and to get data from them. *Forms* are a type of dialog box that lets users enter, edit, and view data stored in databases.

A member of the GUI Standards project at Bankers Trust recommended that fonts be used differently in dialog boxes and forms:

- In dialog boxes, use bold text for labels and for the data that users type, so they can see their options easily.

- In forms, use regular text for field labels and explanations and use bold text for data, so it stands out.

A few of us on the team acknowledged this recommendation with a shrug, until we needed to find a piece of data on a crowded business form and had trouble distinguishing the labels from the information. Figure 4-12 shows how clearly the data stands out when you apply these two rules.

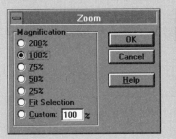 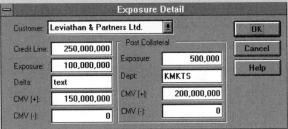

Figure 4-12. *Text in dialog boxes (left) should be in bold. Forms (right) should use bold text only for data entered by users to ensure that it stands out.*

Status bars Use regular 10-point MS Sans Serif for status bars (see Figure 4-13). It accommodates more text than the bold version and takes third place in visual importance.

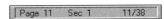

Figure 4-13. *Regular 10-point MS Sans Serif is the standard font for status bar text.*

Icon text Use regular 8-point MS Sans Serif for icon text (see Figure 4-14). It's small enough to accommodate long application names but is still readable.

Mouse

Figure 4-14. *Regular 8-point MS Sans Serif is the standard font for icon text.*

FYI

Yeah, But...

I once suggested to a group of developers that they avoid "dialog drill-down hell" by not having command buttons in dialog boxes open other dialog boxes. Several developers were quick to challenge me. Here are some of the points they raised, along with my answers:

Developer: Yeah, but Microsoft has always used the dialog drill-down approach with its Printer Setup. You have to go through three dialog boxes to get to the Scaling option for PostScript printers and five to get to the Font Substitution Table.

Author: And we probably all wish they hadn't used that approach. Some developers are shocked to discover that the Font Substitution Table exists. More people would know about it—and the Scaling option too—if it weren't buried so deep.

Developer: Developers use dialog drill-downs because there are too many related commands to fit in a single dialog box, no matter how big it is. And Word 6 uses multiple dialog boxes all the time.

Author: But workarounds are available—the unfolding dialog box, the tabbed dialog box, and others. Cascading menus seem to be a favorite of the Excel 5 development team. Or you can let things change dynamically. Witness the Word 6 Go To dialog box. Note also that the Excel Go To dialog box could have easily incorporated the same economy but didn't. Instead, it opens another dialog box with 13 option buttons. Go figure.

Developer: But what about wizards? They force people through several dialog boxes.

Author: Rules are made to be broken. The characteristic that distinguishes a wizard from a dialog drill-down is its purpose: Wizards are structured guides to a multistep process. Plus they let you fast-forward to the end. This is in marked contrast to Printer Setup, which requires that you slog through four dialog boxes to get to the Advanced Options dialog box for PostScript printers. Maybe Microsoft should redesign Printer Setup as a wizard.

Principle #4. Show, Don't Tell

Remember that nobody reads the directions. This is not to say that people don't *follow* directions—they just don't read them unless all else fails. So what does this mean to IS professionals? Take a guess:

a. The documentation doesn't matter.

b. You need to provide personalized instruction for all business applications.

c. The interface itself needs to indicate what to do next.

If you picked C, you're right. A good user interface leads users through the process to accomplish the task at hand. Organization is key. Follow the principles below to help ensure that users can follow your unwritten instructions.

■ Organize controls logically.

■ Organize menus according to Microsoft Office standards.

■ Organize main screens with standard Windows graphics.

Organize controls logically

The first control that users see in the upper left corner of a window (whether that window serves as the main screen, a dialog box, or a form) should be the first thing that they need to do or the thing that they will do most often. The second control should be the logical next step, and so on. Make sure that the tab order reinforces the visual order. Use frames, not lines, to group related elements together. (See the section titled "Principle #6. Hold Up Your End of the Conversation" later in this chapter.)

Organize menus according to Office standards

A quick look at Office confirms Microsoft's commitment to standardizing a look and feel across applications (see Figure 4-15). The standard menu bar is identical in Excel, Word, and PowerPoint except for a single title (the third from the right) that is particular to each application. In Excel, this application-specific menu title is Data; in Word, it's Table; and in PowerPoint, it's Draw.

| File | Edit | View | Insert | Format | Tools | App-Specific | Window | Help |

Figure 4-15. *The standard Office menu bar contains only one menu that differs for each application. Office users will find it easier to use your business application if you stick to this standard.*

The importance of menus—which are often the first place users look for clues about what an application can do—is borne out by an observation made by a participant in the *Microsoft Word Challenge* video:

> I think the learning curve on Microsoft Word was immediate. I figured it out in ten minutes, and I spent less than five minutes going through the menus.

Accordingly, Microsoft assigned standard menu positions to 46 commands (see Figure 4-16). For example, the Undo and Repeat commands are always the first and second items on the Edit menu, the Zoom command is in the last group of items on the View menu, the Spelling command is the first command on the Tools menu, and so on.

Menu	Commands	Menu	Commands
File	New	View	Full Screen
	Open		Toolbars
	Close		Ruler
	Save		Zoom
	Save As		
	Find File	Insert	Picture
	Summary Info		Object
	Page Setup		
	Print Preview	Format	Style
	Print		
	Most-recently-used list	Tools	Spelling
	Exit		Macro
			Customize
Edit	Undo		Options
	Repeat		
	Cut	Window	New Window
	Copy		Arrange/Arrange All
	Paste		Open-window list
	Paste Special		
	Clear	Help	Contents
	Find		Search For Help On
	Replace		Index
	Go To		Quick Preview
	Links		Examples And Demos
	Object		Tip Of The Day
			Technical Support
			About...

Figure 4-16. *Standard commands in standard positions on standard menus.*

Use the following guidelines to organize the menus in your own applications so that users familiar with Office will find your application easy to use.

- Eliminate unnecessary menus—for example, if your application doesn't use commands on the Format menu, delete it—but maintain the standard menu order.

- Use the Window menu only with MDI (Multiple Document Interface) applications—in other words, with applications that support the use of multiple documents or forms.

- Position standard Office commands used in the application (such as Print, Undo, or Toolbars) in their standard menu positions—which is where Office users will look for them first.

FYI

Toolbar Icons vs. Application Icons

Do you know the *stylistic* difference between icons used to launch applications and those that sit on toolbars? The latter must be easy to identify and learn. (For example, a scissors means "cut.") The former must be easy to recognize (for example, Excel's 3-D "XL"). Each application's icon should be original, while toolbar-type icons should be as standard as possible across your entire suite of business applications.

Organize main screens with standard Windows graphics

Space is always a problem—there's either too little or too much. When there's too much space, developers frequently resort to the "big button look" to use it up and to give the application a distinctive look (see Figure 4-17 on the next page). This look consists of a main screen with six or so buttons big enough to absorb a 640 by 480 display. (Graphics are optional.) Its chief advantages:

- Easy implementation. (An all-purpose main screen eliminates the need to choose a form to load at startup.)

- Familiarity. (It's a common solution for developers of business applications.)

As an alternative to the big button look, you can use a custom toolbar (an appropriate variation of the standard menu bar), and load the form used most often as the main, or first, form. Let users set the main form through the Options command on the Tools menu (where user preferences should be stored).

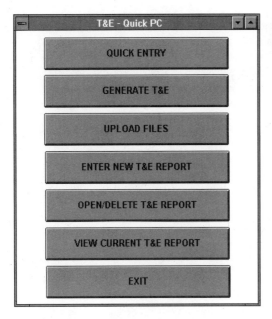

Figure 4-17. *The "big button look" (left), also called the "switchboard," is a popular way of taking up space, making the application easy to recognize and skirting the problem of which form to show at startup. The toolbar (right) is an easy-to-implement alternative.*

NOTE Several of my colleagues have argued that database applications benefit most from the big button look because a main screen separate from any particular form simplifies implementation of security. The sample TimeNtry application in Chapter 10 uses a main screen with buttons, although a toolbar and a user-specified startup form would provide a user interface more consistent with Office standards.

Use of a toolbar and a user-specified startup form offers several advantages:

■ It fosters a more user-friendly interface because users can choose the main form that best suits their work schedule and style. A different form is still only one mouse click away, so nothing is lost in terms of speed.

■ It makes the application look more like a commercial Windows-based product.

■ The smaller buttons allow VGA users to see the application's commands without maximizing the application window.

Buttons should be on toolbars. This is true even in spreadsheet-based applications, in which you'll often find a series of command buttons along the top or bottom of the sheet. *Use a toolbar.* If you want to make the application's commands easier to recognize, use a floating toolbar at startup that users can anchor later.

FYI

Ready-Made Icons

Too often, the judgment as to what's a good GUI graphic is dismissed as "a matter of taste" and is left to the developer, to the application's users, or to the boss. To be sure, taste is an element of graphics, but the more important element is experience and awareness of standard practices in a particular medium. One of the worst software designers I've ever met was skilled in designing graphics of other sorts; what works for architecture and interior design does not necessarily work for user interfaces. If no one on staff has experience with good GUIs, look at the commercial applications used in your office, evaluate their GUIs in light of your needs, and borrow ideas as appropriate.

The Office products, Visual Basic, and Windows itself provide a large number of graphics that you can borrow for toolbars and button bars. Although you need an application that saves to .ICO format to create icons for Program Manager (the maximum size is 32 by 32 pixels), toolbar and button bar icons are nothing more than appropriately sized graphics. They use any graphics format supported by the Clipboard. The maximum size for toolbar icons is 16 by 16 pixels; button bar icons should never be larger than icons in Program Manager.

The following applications and libraries provide ready-made icons:

- PROGMAN.EXE.

- MORICONS.DLL. (Many of these icons are for MS-DOS–based applications, but they're a good starting point for custom buttons.)

- All Windows-based executables—including Access, Excel, Word, PowerPoint, and File Manager (WINFILE.EXE)—come with at least one icon and sometimes several.

- Visual Basic provides more than 450 icons (in .ICO format).

- Excel and Word provide two dozen or so toolbar-style icons.

NOTE When you create custom toolbars, don't redefine existing toolbar icons.

The following three tools can help you use these icons: IconWorks, a sample application that comes with Visual Basic and handles the .ICO format; the Button Editors that come with Excel and Word; and Paintbrush, which comes with Windows.

If you use Paintbrush (which handles the .BMP format but not the .ICO format), you have to take a screen snap of the icon. Although many screen snap programs let you capture a particular area of the screen (I use SnapPRO! by Window Painters), Windows has a built-in version that captures the entire screen and copies it to the Clipboard. Simply press the Print Scrn key. You can then paste the screen capture into Paintbrush and edit it there. (To change the size of the Paintbrush image to 16 by 16 pixels or 32 by 32 pixels, use the Image Attributes command on the Options menu.)

Principle #5. Do, Don't Ask (Unless It's Important)

Business-application developers are often too cautious. They make sure that when users click the OK button, a dialog box appears asking whether they're sure they want to carry out the action.

Assume that people use the same logic in business applications that they do elsewhere in Windows, and ask for confirmation only when an action has irreversible consequences (for example, deleting records).

Principle #6. Hold Up Your End of the Conversation

The fact that nobody reads the directions doesn't mean that you shouldn't *have* directions. Sometimes you need to put things into words. The challenge is to do so in a useful way.

Labels, status bars, and ToolTips

Text that accompanies labels, status bars, and ToolTips should be short enough for users to absorb at a glance, almost subconsciously. For example, use a single word for field labels in dialog boxes and forms (see Figure 4-18). Use two or three words at most for ToolTips. Use a short phrase starting with a verb for messages in the status bar.

NOTE Every command should display an instruction in the status bar—for example, *Type the customer's last name* or *Show customer data sorted by date.* And please don't say "please."

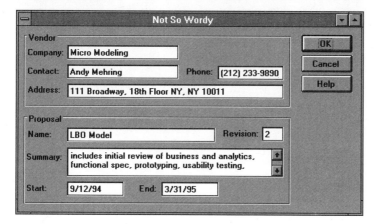

Figure 4-18. *The top form has twice as many words as the bottom form. Is it twice as clear? Frames make it easy to group controls according to topic or task, and they can help reduce the word count dramatically.*

Message boxes

Keep explanatory messages brief: One short sentence with the appropriate icon (see Figure 4-19 on the following page) and a Help button are all anyone has time for. (And remember: Many people will simply click OK and try again.)

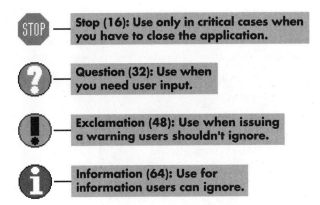

Figure 4-19. *The standard message box icons and their values. The value and meaning are the same in all Office applications, Visual Basic, and Visual C++.*

Help

By the time users open Help, they're ready to do anything—even read—to solve the problem at hand. Still, they're not about to read more than they have to, so here's a technique to make things easier on them: Create two versions of Help—a short version (called, perhaps, *Must Know*) and a complete version (called *Technical Reference*). The idea is to provide documentation that gives busy people the gist of what they need with a few short sentences and a picture, plus a "bible" that lets motivated users and support staff learn everything there is to know about an application.

Principle #7. Let the Driver Drive

IS professionals and developers tend to divide the world into people who are good with PCs and people who aren't. We tend to build for proficient users and grumble about all the others. To develop more usable business applications, Alan Cooper, the creator of Visual Basic, recommends classifying users by how frequently—not how proficiently—they use PCs. A good GUI accommodates all comers: infrequent or first-time users, expert users, mouse users, and keyboard users. To put Cooper's theory into practice, follow these guidelines as you develop your interface:

- Put all commands on menus. (Infrequent and first-time users rely heavily on menus.)

- Create toolbars for the commands that people will use all the time.

- Provide shortcut keys for the commands on toolbars.

- List shortcut keys on menus. (Excel doesn't support this.)

- Add access keys for keyboard users. (Access keys are the underlined letters on menus and in dialog box labels. Press Alt plus the underlined letter to access the command or control.) Add them to menus so keyboard users don't have to use a mouse. Add them to labels in dialogs and forms so keyboard users can move to controls out of tab order.

- When appropriate, use pop-up menus (accessible via the right mouse button) as a shortcut for mouse users. (This option isn't available when you develop applications with Access, Excel, or Word.)

- Use ToolTips to accelerate learning for toolbar users. (This capability is built into Microsoft products starting with Office version 4, Visual Basic version 4, and Visual C++ version 1.5.)

- Be forgiving. Provide a graceful way for users to continue when they make mistakes (which is inevitable). For example, display instructions rather than error messages. (Don't display a message box that says "Wrong date format!" Instead, tell users what the correct format is.)

- Let the preferences set in Control Panel—including color—govern your application. Period.

  Developers frequently complain that users create color schemes that spoil *their* color schemes and make the text boxes turn yellow, baby blue, or some other "objectionable" color. Because of this, they hard-code the colors in their applications. As a stark reminder of Microsoft's commitment to letting users choose their own color schemes, a colleague once demonstrated the freedom users have to change the default colors in Word. He set the button face to green, the application workspace to yellow, and the window background to light gray. If a leading software vendor can allow people to do this to a flagship application, so can you.

GUI Development Methodology

As I mentioned in Chapter 3, which outlines an application development methodology that works well with Office products and with Visual Basic, GUI development is separate from application development. GUI development focuses on how users work with an application rather than on how the application works. The following five steps are the keys to developing an easy-to-use interface:

1. Identify users and their goals.
2. Identify tasks.
3. Build GUI prototypes.
4. Test for usability.
5. Try again.

Step #1. Identify Users and Their Goals

The first thing to do is identify who will use the application and why. The "who" is usually pretty straightforward—for example, the accounting department or the customer service department. The next question: *Why* will people use this application? The obvious answer: They want to do a particular task more efficiently. But is this the real reason?

Alan Cooper encourages developers to "think big" so they can understand the "real goals" of the people who use business applications—to impress the boss, to win a contract, to earn frequent-flyer miles, and so on.

Developers shouldn't fool themselves into thinking that the application itself is of any interest to users, beyond how it can help them make headway toward their real goals. Applications that are so easy to use that they actually boost productivity help *everybody*.

FYI

The Hierarchy of Users

How do managers who spearhead an application's development—but who aren't end users—fit into the GUI development process? They don't. To produce better applications, the GUI development process must focus on the true end users. If an application boosts productivity, managers know that IS has done a good job.

Step #2. Identify Tasks

Both application development and GUI development are rooted in business (or task) analysis. However, the GUI development process doesn't focus on business tasks in order to analyze requirements but rather to investigate how users think about and perform these tasks.

Interview the people who will use the application. If an application has more than one user population, interview each population separately. (For example, travel and entertainment [T&E] systems have two populations: general users and the accounting department.) The following interview techniques can help you obtain the necessary information:

- Ask people to describe what they do.

- Watch them do it. Note the process and the sequence. For example, if they're currently using a computerized system, are they using the numeric keypad? Users rarely mention such details.

- Switch places with them, and do it yourself. You're bound to learn the unspoken assumptions that the users neglect to mention.

Answers to the following key questions will help you develop a good interface:

- What tasks do the users typically perform? List these tasks, put them in order, and write out the possible scenarios. (The application itself might need to perform any number of tasks, but these aren't relevant here.)

- How often do the users perform these tasks? Because exceptional cases are more memorable than everyday cases, people tend to dwell on the exceptions. Be sure to understand the frequency with which each task and scenario occurs. The goal is to develop an interface that makes it easy to handle everyday tasks and makes it possible to handle the exceptions.

- How do the users perform these tasks now? When and where do they perform these tasks? What physical *things* do they work with— for example, currencies, letters from customers, and so on? This line of questioning is especially valuable in trying to establish the language and icons for the application. If people work with "case files" now, they should work with them in the new application.

Map the results of the interviews onto a user interface. For example, let's say you've identified two tasks. If users typically perform task 2 after task 1, a good GUI will provide a one-step way to access task 2 from task 1. If task 2 always occurs after task 1, a good GUI will combine them into a single task.

Here's another example: Users might do data entry all day every day, do data lookup now and then, and print 100 reports as a single batch once a week. In this case, a good GUI would make data entry the main screen, Data Lookup a menu command, and Print Reports a menu command that defaults to Print All Reports.

Step #3. Build GUI Prototypes

So far, you've identified users, tasks, and how users perform and think about these tasks, but you still haven't done anything on the PC. And that's as it should be. Before you start coding a prototype, draw some pictures (see Figure 4-20 on the following page). With pencil in hand, explain to users how you understand the tasks, how you might organize the screens, and how tasks will be accessible via the menu, mouse, and keyboard. Get feedback. Rip up the drawings. Try again.

The bottom line: Before you start coding, make sure that what you're thinking jibes with what users are thinking.

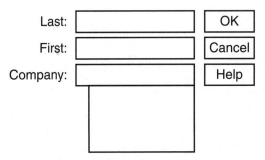

Figure 4-20. *Use drawings to test your understanding of the tasks people perform before you begin building a GUI prototype.*

Step #4. Test for Usability

When you do start building the GUI, test its usability. Testing needn't be a formal or complicated process. Studies show that testing an application with five to seven people reveals 80 percent of the problems.

Chris Peters, a vice president at Microsoft, once talked about conducting informal usability tests. As you're creating an application, he said, you should just call over the developers next door, have them try whatever you're working on, and then *believe what you see.* If the tester can't perform the task, you should probably change it. Peters admitted that he was once one of those people who got usability results back and *didn't* believe what he saw: "I always figured that they'd just found 10 stupid people."

Usability tests are particularly important because you often get unexpected results. Designers of airport signs decided to test people's recognition of some of the symbols (or icons, if you will) that they'd created (see Figure 4-21). A large number of people guessed that the plane pointing straight up meant "airport," the plane angled upward meant "departures," and the plane angled downward meant "crash landings." (The designers intended it to mean "arrivals.") Always test your work.

Figure 4-21. *Why you don't see signs with downward-pointing planes: Tests showed that a large number of people thought the symbol on the right meant "crash landings" instead of "arrivals."*

Step #5. Try Again

GUI development—like application development in general—is an iterative, evolutionary process. "Trying again" is what makes any process successful.

FYI

The Five-Minute GUI Makeover

At the end of a workshop that Steve Koeppel (leader of the GUI Standards Project) and I gave at Bankers Trust, we guided participants through the GUI development process for redesigning a business application that they all used—and hated: the T&E reimbursement system. Due to an accounting department requirement, the existing application made people enter all expenses for a given date consecutively. A good GUI would let people enter the dollar amount, the date, and the required business information for each receipt *in any order*. The application itself would order the information according to date, so the accounting department wouldn't know the difference.

Steve and I played the role of developers (asking questions), and two dozen participants played the role of users (answering questions). We wrote their responses on a whiteboard. Here's the gist of what happened:

Q *Who will use the T&E reimbursement system?*

A ■ Everybody who wants to get reimbursed
■ The people who work in accounting

Q *Why will people use the system?*

A ■ To get reimbursed
■ To get a check
■ They have to
■ They have to travel for their jobs

Q *What is the business task?*

A ■ To enter the information that accounting needs to write checks
■ To organize the information the way accounting needs it
■ To maintain records

Q *What information does the system need to maintain records?*

A ■ Date
■ Description
■ Amount
■ Currency

- Location
- With whom
- Expense type (air/rail, hotel/lodging, and so on)

Q *Describe the current process. What items do you have when you sit down to enter information into the system?*

A ■ Receipts
- Receipts in hotel envelopes
- Receipts organized by date

Q *Let's try drawing a picture of a good GUI for this application. What's the most important element to you, the user? What element belongs in the screen's upper left corner?*

A ■ Date
- Location

It took a few tries before someone hit on "amount" as the most important element. Even then, several voices protested on behalf of the people in accounting (who needed the information organized by date) until they saw that the application itself could organize the information.

This example proved something to all of us. First, it demonstrated how hard it is to redesign something—even something we don't like. Second, it showed *why* this is so hard—how tempted we are to idealize existing systems and belittle common sense. Third, it showed the depth of our bias in favor of business requirements over users, even when it's *not* a zero-sum game (as in this example).

One developer who participated in the workshop admitted afterward that he'd seen where our line of questioning was headed, but he believed he had the trump card—the accounting department's requirements. He was taken aback that his bias had impaired his professional judgment.

5

Data at Your Desktop

You could say that Alexander Graham Bell created the first network when he invented the telephone in 1876. In the 1950s, digital computers made it possible to computerize the telephone network, and shortly thereafter computers themselves started communicating over this network. We began to distinguish between local area networks (LANs), which are confined to a small physical region such as an office building, and wide area networks (WANs), which span geographical regions.

Although the earliest telecommunications were faster than mail, they were still quite slow. For example, it could take up to 10 hours to send Jane Austen's *Emma*—a 396-page (1.3-MB) document. Today, the same amount of information can speed across wide area networks from New York to Los Angeles in a matter of seconds.

It used to be that electronic communication was limited to conversations—"I want," "I need," "I know." *What* you knew—the underlying data—was stored on magnetic tapes and disks. You didn't *communicate* data—you had to ship it back and forth like cargo. One could argue that the PC network's most important contribution is that it has transformed data from bulky packages into a purer electronic form.

In this chapter, I first introduce the networks that make it possible to deliver data to corporate desktops. Next I explain how Open Database Connectivity (ODBC), Microsoft's standard interface for accessing data, helps companies use these networks to build the push-button business. I also discuss techniques for using ODBC to automate data access from end-user development tools.

The Back End (Server, Mainframe, or Mini—Does It Matter?)

Jean-Louis Gassée, former president of Apple Products, once observed:

> Someday the computer network will become like the phone system:
> We won't worry about its underpinnings, we'll use it, we'll enjoy it,
> and we'll pervert it (the mark of success), putting it to uses not
> foreseen by the inventors.

We're clearly moving in that direction. For example, I don't hear as many sto-
ries about executives' resistance to using the computer network as I used to.
(My favorite story is about the senior manager with the big corner office and
the couch who insisted that the technician installing his networked PC put it
on an end table—not on his desk—because he had "work to do.")

Today electronic mail is standard for many companies, and executives who
once shunned PCs are now using e-mail. The head of administrative computing at a major New York college mentioned recently that "executives who can't
open their e-mail" are the help desk's most frequent callers. He cites this as
proof that the PC network has become *the* way to do business. In many companies, shared network drives, the networked printer, and online services
such as CompuServe are facts of life, like the phone and the photocopier.

Of course, the physical setups for PC networks are as varied as the communications that pass through them, but most companies use one—or a combination—of the following three models. These models differ primarily in how
they manage communications and affect business-application development.

- Networks with central file servers

- Client-server computing

- Peer-to-peer computing

Networks with Central File Servers

File servers are computers with specialized software for sharing data. Networks
built around *central* file servers require that PCs on the LAN communicate by
sending files to the server. The server then:

- Routes files to PCs according to address (e-mail)

- Stores files that others can use (shared network drives)

- Stores files that only the owner—with a password—can use (private
  network drives)

NOTE   Although there is a class of computer called a "file server," a server is just as likely to be a minicomputer, a mainframe, or a plain old PC.

Traditional file server applications (which support multiple users) are generally structured in one of two ways: either they run entirely from the file server or, in the case of some database applications, they run entirely from the PC, which accesses data from the server. Client-server architecture modifies this model to improve performance, security, and reliability.

Client-Server Computing

Client-server computing is the latest network computing model. In the simplest sense, any PC that gets data from the network server (which provides data) is a client (which receives data). Technically, however, client-server architecture takes things one step further. It actually splits client-server applications into a *front end* (the client), which runs on the PC, and a *back end* (the server), which runs on a network server.

The goal of client-server architecture is to structure appropriately the processing performed by each end of an application. An application's front end typically consists of a user interface that lets users enter, edit, view, sort, and publish data. The client PC itself does all of this work and "places orders" with the server: "Please enter this data into the database," or "I need data on the Ford Motor Company."

An application's back end gets the orders and fills them: "Data duly entered," or "Here's all the data I have on Ford." The server does whatever processing is necessary to store the data, find it, and maintain its integrity.

Peer-to-Peer Computing

Not long ago, the *New York Times* ran an article that mentioned a technologically advanced (though fictitious) Wall Street firm that essentially built a supercomputer by soaking up the spare processing power from the clerical staff's PCs when the staff went to lunch. That's what peer-to-peer computing under Microsoft Windows will be able to do for you...someday soon.

For now, peer-to-peer computing is a humbler feature that lets networked PCs use printers, fax boards, hard drives, CDs, and so on that belong to another PC. System 7 for the Macintosh, Microsoft Windows for Workgroups, and Microsoft Windows NT all support peer-to-peer computing. Peer-to-peer networks turn every PC into a potential server as well as a client. PCs that share their resources with others act as de facto servers, and PCs that borrow resources act as clients.

The more powerful the PCs, the better peers they'll be. However, one of the charms of peer-to-peer networks is that companies of all sizes can take advantage of them. For example, small companies that can't afford a dedicated file server can use peer-to-peer networks to share data. Larger companies that have networks can add peer-to-peer functionality so users can retrieve data directly from others' hard drives.

FYI

Faster Than FedEx—From NY to LA in 6.77 Seconds

Investment banking is built on financial analyses, client presentations, and legal documents—all of which must be stored in such a way that they're easy to find. In the early days of PC computing (before networks), document management was an exercise in tracking down floppy disks. Miriam Anderson, network administrator for the investment banking group at Donaldson, Lufkin & Jenrette (DLJ), recalled those times:

> People didn't even know how to handle floppy disks. They would mark them with ballpoint pens, paper-clip them together, then lose them. We were constantly retyping presentations.
>
> Eventually, we hired someone to be responsible for document management. The hardest part of the job was to get people to hand over their floppies. The manager put every document into its own binder with a disk, and she invented a document-naming convention—client name, date, and banker—so that we could find it. We had hundreds of these binders, and every once in a while someone would misplace one and there would be a crisis.

In 1983–84, DLJ's investment banking group installed its first network: a file server and a shared printer for a bull pen of 10 analysts. Ten years ago, *that* was state-of-the-art. Since then, the group has grown from 40 people to 500 people and has built a network infrastructure that spans six cities. Now, using the client-server model, DLJ has a document management system that tracks more than 40,000 Microsoft Excel and Microsoft Word documents.

The department's half-dozen IS professionals manage the network from its hub on the 47th floor of a New York City skyscraper. They deliver three broad categories of services:

■ A local area network, which provides document management, desktop faxing, and access to a growing cache of business applications

■ Desktop Quotron services (for real-time market data)

■ A wide area network using the frame relay cloud (see Figure 5-1), including:

   ▫ Nationwide instant-delivery e-mail

   ▫ WAN information transfer at 193 KB per second (see Figure 5-2)

   ▫ Nationwide dial-up financial services (including CompuServe, FactSet, and Securities Data) through a pool of modems in the 47th-floor hub

   ▫ Remote nationwide dial-up so users can connect via laptops and home computers

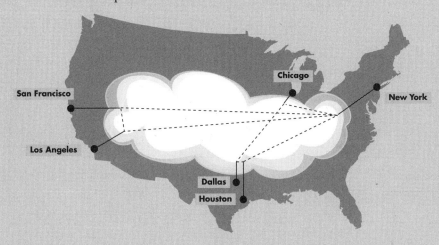

Figure 5-1. *DLJ's WAN uses a frame relay cloud that provides high-speed data transfer at a fraction of the price of long distance phone service. The solid rules in the diagram indicate T1 (dedicated, high-volume) lines, and the dotted rules represent the frame relay connections between offices. (These are nondirect; data takes the fastest route available.)*

Equipment	KB per Second	Time
WAN	193	6.77 seconds
LAN	1544	0.85 seconds
Modem (14,400 bps)	1.80	12.09 minutes
Modem (2400 bps)	0.30	72.56 minutes

Figure 5-2. *This table shows the relative transmission rates of four kinds of communications equipment. The rightmost column shows the time it takes to transmit Jane Austen's* Emma *(396 pages = 187,000 words = 1306 KB of data).*

DLJ's WAN takes a giant step toward the push-button business. The investment banking group can now move information of all sorts—including client presentations and legal documents—from desktop to desktop and coast to coast with one keystroke. One interesting side benefit of the WAN is that the group (which runs 24-hour word processing shifts in New York and Los Angeles) can now manage the word processing *workload* as well as the documents themselves to take advantage of time differences and downtime.

Open Database Connectivity

In about 500 BC, Heraclitus pointed out that "all things are one....The road up and the road down are one and the same." If he were philosophizing today, he might say that the back end and the front end form a single system to store and retrieve data and to analyze and present information.

Indeed, this is the primary purpose of many business processes: to turn raw data into usable information. As companies reengineer their businesses, many are developing front-end applications in Excel and Word that make it easier for users to transform data into the information they need. However, there's a stumbling block along this route: the difficulty of getting data from the back-end database into the front-end application. Enter ODBC.

ODBC at Your Fingertips

To access data stored in any database management system, you need a standard way to connect to all databases and a standard language for entering and retrieving data. Open Database Connectivity (ODBC) provides the first capability, and Structured Query Language (SQL—pronounced "sequel") provides the second (see Figure 5-3). ODBC, which uses SQL statements to communicate with database management systems, is designed to handle common database functions, including:

- Creating, editing, and deleting tables

- Creating and deleting views and indexes

- Selecting, updating, inserting, and deleting fields

- Granting and revoking access privileges

In addition to accommodating these lowest-common-denominator functions (which ODBC handles through its built-in driver manager, available through Control Panel), many database management systems let users access data using a variety of other features and functions. To take advantage of these, client applications use the database's ODBC driver (provided by the database manufacturer). Developers who need greater control over the database system than ODBC provides can access a database's application programming interface (API) directly.

> **NOTE** Most major database management systems—including Microsoft Access, Microsoft FoxPro, Oracle, SQL Server, Paradox, dBASE, SyBase, and DB2—provide ODBC drivers.

Client application
The front end generally lets users enter, edit, and retrieve data. It uses ODBC to connect to a data source (any database that supports ODBC), sends and receives data, and then disconnects.

Driver manager
All ODBC applications communicate with the driver manager and not directly with the driver. Communications are in SQL.

Driver
A driver is a DLL that processes ODBC function calls to a data source. It connects to the database, translates SQL statements, retrieves data, and returns it to the client application (via the driver manager). It handles any network protocols for communicating with the data source.

Server application
A back end is generally the database or database management system (DBMS) that lets users store, manage, and retrieve data.

Figure 5-3. *ODBC architecture.*

FYI

Making ODBC Work for You

ODBC makes it easy to retrieve data that is stored centrally and to use it at the desktop. You can add ODBC capabilities to your PC environment in three ways:

- By installing Access, Excel, or Word (which include ODBC drivers for FoxPro, Paradox, dBASE, and SQL Server)

- By installing a separate product called Microsoft ODBC Desktop Database Drivers (which includes drivers for Excel and text files as well as those drivers that come with Office products, and help files)

- By using the Microsoft ODBC SDK 2.0 (which is necessary if you plan to use the ODBC API)

After you install ODBC (Figure 5-4 lists the standard files), an icon labeled "ODBC" appears in Control Panel. This is the driver manager, which you use to:

- Set up databases as *data sources* for your applications. (A data source is a name that ties a particular database or directory to its ODBC driver.)

- Add ODBC drivers.

- Check versions of the installed ODBC drivers.

- Delete ODBC drivers and data sources. (Deleting a data source does not delete the underlying database.)

- Turn ODBC call tracing on or off to help track down errors.

Filename	Description
ODBC.DLL	Driver manager
ODBCADM.EXE	Interface for the driver manager
ODBCINST.DLL	File for the driver manager
ODBCINST.HLP	Help for the driver manager
ODBC.INI	INI file maintained by the driver manager
SIMBA.DLL	Query processing engine
MSJETDSP.DLL	Jet dispatcher (accepts requests from SIMBA.DLL and routes them to the appropriate driver)
SIMADMIN.DLL	ODBC Simba administrator
XBS110.DLL/XBS200.DLL	ODBC driver for dBASE and FoxPro
DRVDBASE.HLP	Help for the ODBC dBASE driver
DRVFOX.HLP	Help for the ODBC FoxPro driver
PDX110.DLL	ODBC driver for Paradox
DRVPARDX.HLP	Help for the ODBC Paradox driver
RED110.DLL	ODBC driver for Access version 1.1
DRVACCSS.HLP	Help for the ODBC Access driver
ODBCJT16.DLL*	ODBC driver for Access version 2
ODBCTL16.DLL*	ODBC helper function

Figure 5-4. *ODBC files installed with the complete installation of Access, Excel, or Word. Starred files (*) are installed only with Access version 2.*

You must set up data sources to use ODBC (see Figure 5-5). To do this, use the ODBC driver manager in Control Panel to: 1) select the database driver to use (for example, Access version 2.0 for MS Office); 2) type a unique descriptive name for the data source (for example, "Purchasing" or "Payroll"); and 3) select the full path to the database or directory (for example, C:\ACCESS2\ CS-SMPL.MDB).

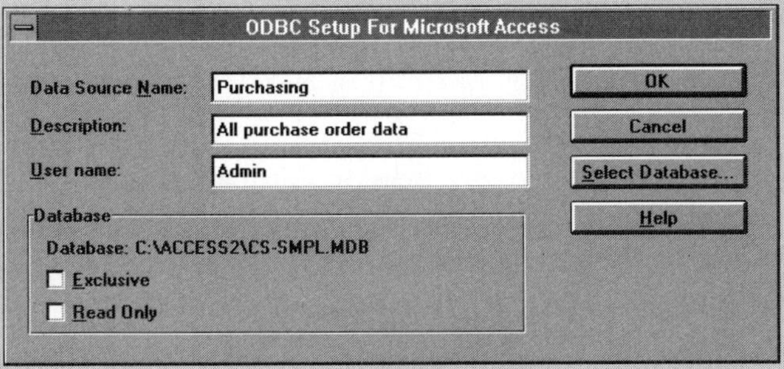

Figure 5-5. *Use the ODBC driver manager to set up data sources. Front-end applications use these data sources to connect to database management systems.*

Data Source: Database or Directory?

ODBC is structured to handle databases, such as Access, that contain several tables. In such cases, the data source points to the actual database file (for example, an .MDB file). When you query the data source, the driver manager prompts you to select the tables to use.

However, some databases don't *contain* tables per se; rather, what we call the "database" is actually a group of related files that serve as data tables. In these cases, the data source points to the directory where these database tables are stored. When you query the data source, the driver manager opens the directory and prompts you to select the specific files you want to use. This allows you to use a group of dBASE files, Excel files, or even text files as a single database.

Integrating Data at the Desktop

Although ODBC was conceived as a standard that simplifies the use of data from multiple database management systems, you don't have to be faced with the "Tower of Babel of databases" (as a colleague of mine put it) to find ODBC useful. ODBC makes it easier to use centrally stored corporate data at the desktop.

■ ODBC brings developers one step closer to "assembling" business applications rather than coding them from scratch. Developers need only change the connection string in a front-end application to hook it up to another ODBC database. (See the sidebar titled "Using Connection Strings" later in this chapter.) One advantage of this is the ability to develop and test front-end applications locally using, for example, an Access database. Simply change the connection string to connect to the network database and "go live" with the application.

- ODBC lets users access data stored in nontraditional databases (such as text files and Excel worksheets) in a structured way, just as they would a "real" database. (See the section titled "Integrating Desktop Data into the Enterprise" later in this chapter.)

- ODBC makes it easier to build front-end applications using end-user development tools. For example, a financial services company is building a front end in Excel to track and analyze investment data stored in SQL Server. (See the section titled "Building Database Front Ends with End-User Development Tools" later in this chapter.)

FYI

ODBC Database? Have We Got a Query Tool for You....

Microsoft Query enables you to perform sophisticated queries to bring data stored in any ODBC database—such as Access, Oracle, and Paradox—into Excel and Word. From there, you can analyze the data, report it, publish it, present it, or fax it.

To retrieve data with MS Query (which uses ODBC), users don't have to know where a database is (local or remote) or even *what* it is (Access, an Excel spreadsheet, Oracle, and so on). They need only know the name of the data source. (Figure 5-6 shows a typical MS Query session.)

MS Query is primarily an end-user tool (as opposed to a developer tool). However, developers can update queries easily through code using Excel query definitions and Word fields (see Appendix A).

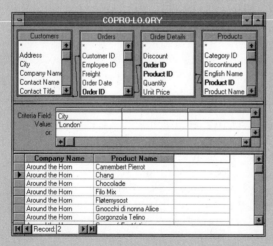

Figure 5-6. *Diagram of the MS Query window.*

Using MS Query from Excel or Word

1. In Excel, choose the Add-Ins command from the Tools menu to install the MS Query add-in. If MS Query isn't listed in the Add-Ins dialog box, use the Browse button to find the file. (All add-ins use the .XLA extension.) If it *is* listed, select its check box.

    ■ When the MS Query add-in is installed correctly, the Get External Data command appears on the Data menu. Choose this command to run MS Query.

    ■ In Word, choose the Database command from the Insert menu, and then click the Get Data button. If MS Query is installed correctly, a button with its name appears in the Open Data Source dialog box. Choose this command to run MS Query.

2. MS Query displays the data sources that you set up using the ODBC driver manager. You have the following options:

    ■ Select a data source, and then click Use to use it for the query.

    ■ Click the Other button and then the New button to add a data source. (This opens the ODBC driver manager.)

    ■ If no data source is listed, click the Other button.

3. After selecting a data source, MS Query prompts you to choose the tables or files from which to get data. After choosing these tables, select the fields of data to retrieve (see Figure 5-6).

    MS Query enables you to perform the following tasks:

    ■ Specify criteria for selecting records. (Use the commands on the Criteria menu.)

    ■ Sort the records. (Use the Sort command on the Records menu.)

    ■ Calculate fields. (Type the SQL expression for the calculation in an empty field. See the sidebar titled "Introducing SQL" later in this chapter.)

    ■ Save the query. (You can, however, update queries without saving them.)

    ■ Retrieve unique records. (Use the Query Properties command on the View menu.)

    ■ Execute a SQL statement or procedure to perform operations that you can't do in the query window, such as modifying existing tables or creating an index.

    ■ Join tables. (Use the Joins command on the Table menu.)

4. To retrieve the data into Excel or Word, choose the Return Data command from the File menu or click the Return Data button. To ensure that you can update the data, select the Keep Query Definition option for Excel and the Insert Data as Field command for Word.

5. To update the query in Excel, use the Refresh Data command on the Data menu. To update the query in Word, use the F9 key.

Integrating Desktop Data into the Enterprise

It's been said that 70 percent of the world's data is stored in spreadsheets and word processing files. Whenever I test this figure on business managers and IS professionals, they say that they wouldn't be surprised if it were even higher. You can see why an important benefit of ODBC is the ability to use spreadsheet data in a more structured way—for example, to perform queries on the data from Access, Word, or Visual Basic. ODBC helps integrate desktop data enterprise-wide in three ways:

- By making it easier to perform queries across multiple sheets from applications other than Excel

- By making it easier to build front-end applications that let people other than the spreadsheet's owner use the data

- By making it easier to automate the integration of these sheets into centralized databases

The key to making enterprise-wide data a reality is automation. Automation and standardization of such things as field names, data types, and formatting go hand in hand, and although standardization has at least as many detractors as it has fans, users can't share data easily without it. "CASE STUDY: From Desktop Data to a Central Database" on page 94 illustrates some benefits of standardization.

When companies start to integrate desktop data such as spreadsheets into enterprise-wide data—or even into department-wide data—the biggest hurdle they face isn't the technology but users' dislike of standardization. One problem with standardization is that it interferes with users' "mental maps" of their data—their picture of how certain elements fit together and why they're important. Standardization is sure to eliminate someone's "favorite" field of data.

Another problem with standardization is that users feel that it's *their* data. Tom Facciolo, who has run into this in his role as administrative vice president of the CUNY Research Foundation, compares spreadsheet data to a beloved pet: "People interact with this data 30 hours or so a week. They enter it. They maintain it. They let others borrow it. It's *theirs*."

When you remember that business data stored in spreadsheets is often treated as "personal" data, it's not so surprising that more people aren't eager to receive the benefits of standardization (ease of use, broader use, and better integrity). They look at it as "trading in Fido."

Using ODBC to integrate desktop data

Although the Excel ODBC driver (XLSISAM.DLL) isn't currently included with Access, Excel, or Word, you can obtain it through a separate product called Microsoft ODBC Desktop Database Drivers. Using an ODBC driver for Excel enables you to build front-end applications from Word and Visual Basic that query workbooks and retrieve specified data.

Although Access enables you to import Excel workbooks, in some cases it's better to use ODBC even from Access, because by doing so you guarantee use of the most recent version of the workbook, and you eliminate the step of importing it.

I provide a sample Visual Basic version 3 application (ODBC-XL.EXE) on the *Office Solutions* disk included with this book, which lets you investigate the structure of any Excel "database" consisting of several Excel version 4 worksheets (see Figure 5-7). It uses ODBC and Visual Basic's data access objects to return information about the structure of the database—i.e., the tables (sheets) available and the fields (columns) for each table. (You can modify the code to return such information about other database management systems as well.)

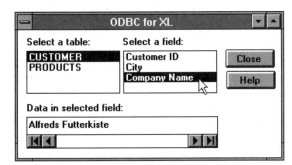

Figure 5-7. *This sample Visual Basic version 3 application from the* Office Solutions *disk lets you drill down into an Excel "database" consisting of several Excel version 4 worksheets. To use this sample application, you must have the ODBC driver for Excel (XLSISAM.DLL); CMDIALOG.VBX and VBRUN300.DLL must be loaded in your Windows system directory; and the Excel sheets you want to view (such as Customer.XLS and Products.XLS) must be loaded in a single directory.*

NOTE As of this writing, the ODBC driver for Excel (version 1.01.2115, dated 9/15/93) supports Excel version 3 and Excel version 4 files. By the time you read this, Microsoft might have a version that supports Excel version 5. Note that Excel versions 3 and 4 require you to define a name for the database range as "database." Define the name, save the file as Excel 4, and you're ready to go.

CASE STUDY: From Desktop Data to a Central Database

Most people who store data in spreadsheets do so for one of two reasons:

- They know how to use spreadsheets (but not databases).
- They use spreadsheets to do their jobs.

People who work in business units that track transactions and financial data frequently fall into these categories. Unfortunately, while a spreadsheet is often the best tool for analyzing data, it's not the best place to store data for querying and reporting. And the more data that is stored in spreadsheets, the harder it is to manage.

When Doubling Your Business Is Bad News

A department at a large bank responsible for tracking financial instruments recently discovered the pitfalls associated with storing corporate data in spreadsheets. The department produces daily reports for senior management on the current market value of each instrument in their portfolio. For a long time, they reported on about 200 deals (worth a half-billion dollars) from eight regions around the world.

To do this, the staff used a semiautomated reporting system in Excel that required significant manual labor. For example:

- They had to reformat each sheet because the eight regions supplied data in different formats.
- They had to paginate each report by hand. (Reports were typically 40 pages long.)
- They had to manually create summaries for deals over $5 million.

One month, the volume of transactions doubled. To produce these daily reports, the department hired eight temporary staff from Ernst & Young and borrowed three people from other departments. Lenore Michaels, a director at Micro Modeling Associates who reengineered the process and designed the new system, described the atmosphere of crisis: "Everyone was working 16 hours a day. They were all ordering in lunch and dinner, and they still couldn't do it."

Interestingly enough, the reason wasn't solely the amount of manual processing. Rather, the process itself couldn't handle the extra people any more than it could handle the extra transactions. Michaels explained:

> One problem was that the "system" didn't function multiuser, but they did. They had all these files open read-only. They had to run around and ask, "Who has this file open?" No one knew which one was really the one in use because everybody had their own copy.

> No one had any control over the data. They checked and rechecked and hoped the people who had a good eye would catch the problems.

This lack of control had one particularly disturbing side effect. Although the report's purpose was to compare yesterday's current market value (CMV) with today's, there was no automated way to track the date on which deals started or ended. When the volume doubled, they literally lost track of deals.

For example, let's say that today's $1 billion CMV includes a three-month, $.1 billion ($100 million) deal with Company A that gets paid off tomorrow. This means that tomorrow's report has to include Company A in "yesterday's" $1 billion total, even though it won't figure in tomorrow's CMV. But this isn't what happened. Because there was no mechanism for tracking dates, people couldn't make the adjustment. The result was that future reports reduced "yesterday's" $1 billion CMV to $.9 billion.

Consolidating Excel Worksheets in Access

The most interesting thing about the solution that Michaels designed is that it required remarkably little change from the department. They still collect, calculate, and analyze data in Excel workbooks. The main difference is that each of the eight regions supplying data uses worksheets that are formatted according to a clearly defined standard.

In addition, they use a fully automated Access application to consolidate the workbooks and generate the reports. The application tracks when deals start and end. It generates error logs flagging current deals that don't have data and "done deals" that do. It automatically summarizes deals over $5 million. And it ensures that no two deals have the same deal number.

Now the department handles more than twice the original volume of transactions (upwards of $1 billion) with the original three staff members, minus overtime.

Building Database Front Ends with End-User Development Tools

Because so many people use Word and Excel to turn raw data into usable business information, these tools are good front ends for job-specific data access. For example, companies build database front ends in Word to simplify data access for reports and publications. Companies build database front ends in Excel for analysis and decision support.

There are three general approaches to ODBC automation through Word and Excel :

- One approach uses templates to store and update specific queries. For example, you can build publication templates in Word that include prefab queries to a database (such as sales data organized by product, region, and salesperson). Users can then update information from the database with a single command. (See the section titled "Retrieving Data Using ODBC and Word Fields" on the facing page.)

- The second approach automates queries using an ODBC connection string (which provides the database path and other required information, such as a password) and a set of specialized functions. For example, you can build an Excel application that manages workbooks containing accounting data and that has the ability to capture certain data automatically and enter it in a central database. One client I work with is currently building such a system, in part as a way of turning desktop data into enterprise-wide data. (See the section titled "Retrieving Data Using ODBC Functions" later in this chapter.)

- The third approach uses the ODBC API directly. You can use this API with any Windows programming language, including Access Basic, C/C++, VBA for Excel, WordBasic, and Visual Basic. Besides being the most direct way to access data, it's also the most consistent across programming languages. The set of specialized ODBC functions mentioned in the previous bullet point are *wrappers* for the ODBC API functions. (In other words, they are commands that simplify use of the API.) The *Microsoft ODBC 2.0 Programmer's Reference and SDK Guide* provides complete reference materials for the ODBC API.

What Are Fields?

Fields are instructions that tell Word how to handle data. Word uses fields for page numbering, tables of contents, embedded materials, linked materials, and queries. Use the Field command on the Insert menu to get a complete list of fields. You can view fields within a Word document in two different ways:

- As results (formatted text or graphics).

- As the field codes or instructions themselves. These instructions are enclosed by field characters ({}). (They look like brackets but aren't.)

There are five field-related operations that you should know:

- Switch between field codes and field results using the View tab for the Options command on the Tools menu (or position the insertion point in the field and press Shift+F9).

- Update field codes—in other words, get the most recent version of whatever they locate or generate—by positioning the insertion point in the field and pressing F9.

- Unlink field codes—in other words, turn them permanently into results without the underlying instructions—by positioning the insertion point in the field and pressing Ctrl+Shift+F9.

- Create field characters by pressing Ctrl+F9.

- Delete field codes by selecting them and then pressing the Del key. (You can't just backspace over them.)

Retrieving Data Using ODBC and Word Fields

According to the dictionary, a "template" is a pattern that artisans use to ensure that items are made consistently—knobs, for example, or a popular design for cups. Templates enable users to reuse the same design or to retrieve the most recent data for the same query. Although Access, Excel, and Word all use templates in some form, Word relies on them most heavily. In fact, to create applications in Word, you have to create templates.

Developers can prepare templates that contain queries, formatting, calculations, and so on that users can update easily. For example, an easy way to automate data access in Word is to create a template that includes a field code generated using MS Query. To do this, follow these steps:

1. Create a new Word document.

2. Create a query as described in the sidebar titled "ODBC Database? Have We Got a Query Tool for You...." earlier in this chapter. When you insert the data into Word, make sure you choose the Insert Data As Field command.

3. Save the Word document as a template. (Select Document Template as the file type.) That way, users can start new documents based on this template without spoiling the original. To get the latest data available for the query, place the insertion point in the field and press F9.

Field codes not only make it easy to update the query, but they let you edit it directly, bypassing MS Query altogether.

FYI

Introducing SQL

SQL is a standard language used to store, maintain, and retrieve data from database management systems. When developing front-end applications that handle data stored in ODBC-compliant databases, use code to build the SQL statements required to enter, retrieve, and delete data. The section titled "Managing Data from Word Using ODBC and SQL" in Chapter 10 provides the syntax for four main SQL statements: SELECT, UPDATE, DELETE, and INSERT. However, since the sample code in this chapter uses the SQL SELECT statement, I provide the basic syntax here:

```
SELECT [Predicate] NameOfFields FROM NameOfTable WHERE→
  ListOfCriteria [ORDER BY] NameOfField
```

The predicate (such as ALL or DISTINCT, which returns unique records) restricts the records returned. For example, the following SQL statement (used in the next section) returns unique records from the Product Name field in the Products table and sorts them by product name. Since SQL doesn't support multiword field names directly, enclose such names within single quotes (` `). (This is ASCII character 96.)

```
"SELECT DISTINCT Products.`Product Name` FROM→
  Products Products ORDER BY Products.`Product Name`"
```

Editing queries using Word fields

After you retrieve data into Word using MS Query, turn on the field codes (choose the Options command on the Tools menu, and then select the Field Codes check box on the View tab) and examine the instructions, which will resemble the following:

```
{ DATABASE \c "DSN=Product Listing;DBQ=C:\\ACCESS2\\PRODUCTS.MDB;→
  DefaultDir=C:\\ACCESS2;Description=Current Product Listing;FIL=MS→
  Access;JetIniPath=msacc20.ini;SystemDB=C:\\ACCESS2\\system.mda;→
  UID=Admin;" \s "SELECT DISTINCT Products.`Product Name` FROM→
  Products Products ORDER BY Products.`Product Name`" \h }
```

> **NOTE** For ease of reading, the → character represents a line break that does not appear in the actual code.

Field codes—like any set of programming commands—have a specific structure and syntax. They always start with a keyword (in this case, "Database"), followed by a series of *switches* that specify where things are, what they are, or how to format them.

The following explains the bold items in the field code shown above:

- The \c switch in the Database field specifies the connection string.

- DSN is the data source name listed in the ODBC driver manager.

- The \s switch specifies the SQL instructions that query the database. (The SQL statements themselves are in capital letters.)

- The \h switch inserts an empty paragraph at the end of the list.

> **NOTE** Because the \ character precedes switches, use \\ to identify pathnames in fields.

To change either the data source or the query, type new instructions. For example, the following SQL statement selects records from the Customers table (rather than Products, as in the example above) and from the Company Name field (rather than Product Name). It then sorts them by company name:

```
\s "SELECT DISTINCT Customers.`Company Name` FROM Customers→
  Customers ORDER BY Customers.`Company Name`"
```

FYI

Using Connection Strings

No matter what front-end development tool you use, connection strings are the key to accessing an ODBC database. When you set up a data source in the ODBC driver manager, you're essentially setting up its connection string—in other words, you're telling Windows the data source's name, path, password, and so on. To connect to a data source by means of code, you must provide the same information. Figure 5-8 describes the keywords commonly used in connection strings.

Keyword	Description
DSN*	Name of the data source, as specified in the ODBC driver manager
UID	User login ID
PWD	Password
DBQ*	Path to the database or directory (DBQ stands for "database query")
FIL*	File type (Access version 1.1 = RedISAM; Access version 2.0 = MS Access; Excel = Excel; Paradox = Paradox; and so on)

Figure 5-8. *Keywords used in ODBC connection strings. The starred (*) items are necessary to connect to all ODBC databases. Other items are required to connect to Access databases. Some ODBC drivers might require additional information.*

The following connection string opens an Access version 2 data source named Accounting, located in the path C:\ACCESS. The filename for the database is ACCT.MDB.

```
"DSN=Accounting;UID=Admin;DBQ=C:\ACCESS\ACCT.MDB;FIL=MS Access"
```

NOTE Some data sources prompt you for a user ID and a password. For example, an Access version 2 database requires a user ID. The default is "Admin," and the default password is an empty string. (Don't enter anything.) Also, in some cases you can connect using only the data source name.

To open an Excel data source named Products in the directory C:\ODBC, use this connection string:

```
"DSN=Products;DBQ=C:\ODBC;FIL=EXCEL"
```

Direct connect using Word fields

Once you understand the syntax used in fields, you can create and edit fields using WordBasic. This provides automated control over queries to any ODBC database, completely bypassing MS Query. For example, the following code, which is in Solution.DOT on the *Office Solutions* disk included with this book, uses a bookmarked field to edit queries under WordBasic macro control. (*Bookmarks* let you easily return to a particular location in a template, paragraph, table, or field code.) To use this code, set up a data source named Solution Database that points to the Access file Solution.MDB (also on the *Office Solutions* disk), edit the field code to reflect your data source, and then run the ODBCFields macro.

```
Sub MAIN
  On Error Goto ErrorTrap

'Message regarding required data source.
  Msg$ = "To use this macro, you must set up an ODBC data source "
  Msg$ = Msg$ + "pointing to Solution.MDB, which is on the "
  Msg$ = Msg$ + "Office Solutions disk. The data source name "
  Msg$ = Msg$ + "should be Solution Database. Have you done this?"
  Response = MsgBox(Msg$, "Office Solutions", 20)
  If Response = 0 Then Goto BYE

'Retrieves data from Solution.MDB in the Access directory.
'Turn on field codes if they're not on. Set flag.
  If ViewFieldCodes() = 1 Then
    Flag = 1
  Else
    ViewFieldCodes 1
  End If

'Display input box so user can quickly select the field
'data to retrieve.
  WhichField$ = InputBox$("Type a field: Customer ID, Company→
    Name, or City.", "Office Solutions")

'Go to bookmark for SQL statement in query.
  EditGoTo "Changeling"

'Replace existing SQL query with the new field
'specified by user.
  Insert WhichField$

'Select new field.
'If you don't reset bookmark you'll be able to run macro only once.
'Find preceding instance of the ` character.
```

(continued)

101

```
  ExtendSelection
  EditFind .Find = "`", .Direction = 1, .MatchCase = 0, .WholeWord→
    = 0, .PatternMatch = 0, .SoundsLike = 0, .Format = 0, .Wrap = 0
  Cancel
  CharRight 1, 1

'Reset bookmark.
  EditBookmark .Name = "Changeling", .Add

'Update fields to display results of latest query.
  EditSelectAll
  UpdateFields

CleanUp:
'Position cursor to see query.
  EditGoTo "SeeQuery"

'Turn off field codes if they weren't on at start.
  If Flag <> 1 Then ViewFieldCodes 0

'Exit sub.
  Goto BYE

ErrorTrap:
  If Err <> 0 And Err <> 102 Then MsgBox "An error occurred. Error→
    code is" + Str$(Err), "Office Solutions", 64
  Goto CleanUp

BYE:
End Sub
```

Although the ODBCFields macro requires users to type the field to return an input box, you can create an interface through which users can construct sophisticated queries. For example, they can select the fields for which they want data and the sort order.

Retrieving Data Using ODBC Functions

There's a clear, direct relationship between how Word accesses MS Query and how you automate queries, but there's no relationship between MS Query and automation in Excel. Excel stores the information necessary to refresh MS Queries as hidden names, which you can't view through the Name command on the Insert menu. However, you can view these hidden names through the VBA for Excel code shown on the facing page. This code writes *all* defined names to an Excel sheet. To use it, run the ShowNames macro in Solution.XLS on the *Office Solutions* disk included with this book.

```
Sub ShowNames()
'Names are always returned in two columns--the name and its
'definition.
'objDefinedName is a variable representing a name object.
'Names is a collection of name objects.
'objDefinedName.Name is the name property of each name object.
'objDefinedName.RefersTo is the RefersTo property of each name
'object.
  On Error GoTo ShowNamesError
  Dim objDefinedName As Object
  Dim intCount As Integer

'Select specific sheet.
  Sheets("wrkShowNames").Select

'Select cell A1.
  Range("A1").Activate

'Select any existing data and delete it.
  Selection.CurrentRegion.Select
  Selection.Delete
  Range("A1").Select

'Start counter.
  intCount = 1
  For Each objDefinedName In Names
    Cells(intCount, 1) = objDefinedName.Name

'This line ensures that the text looks like text to Excel.
    Cells(intCount, 2) = "'" & objDefinedName.RefersTo
    intCount = intCount + 1
  Next

'Best-fit columns.
  ActiveSheet.Range("A1").CurrentRegion.EntireColumn.AutoFit

ShowNamesExit:
'Go home.
  Range("A1").Select
  Exit Sub

ShowNamesError:
  If Err <> 0 Then MsgBox "An unidentified error occurred.", 64, ⮐
    "ShowNames"
  Resume ShowNamesExit
End Sub
```

You can use VBA for Excel to replicate the functionality of Word's field codes by modifying MS Queries and then writing them back to hidden names, but it's not worth the trouble. Unlike Word's field codes, which bypass MS Query, Excel works *through* MS Query. (The Refresh Data command actually opens MS Query.) Therefore, you should use Excel's ODBC functions to build front-end applications for data stored in ODBC-compliant database management systems.

Using ODBC functions from Excel

The easiest way to query and retrieve data in ODBC-compliant database management systems from Excel is to use a special set of ODBC functions (see Figure 5-9).

Function	Description
SQLOpen	Connects to a data source using a connection string. If successful, it returns a unique connection ID number.
SQLClose	Disconnects from a data source using the connection ID as an argument.
SQLExecQuery	Executes a query on a data source using the connection ID as an argument. Use SQLRetrieve or SQLRetrieveToFile to get the results of the query.
SQLRequest	Connects to an external data source using a connection string, runs a query (as a SQL statement) from a worksheet, and then returns the result as an array.
SQLRetrieve	Retrieves the results from a previously executed query. Before using this function, establish a connection with SQLOpen, and then execute a query with SQLExecQuery. SQLRetrieve uses the connection ID as an argument.
SQLRetrieveToFile	Retrieves the results from a previously executed query and places them in a file. Before using this function, establish a connection with SQLOpen, and then execute a query with SQLExecQuery. SQLRetrieveToFile uses the connection ID as an argument.
SQLGetSchema	Returns information about the structure of the data source on a particular connection ID. It requires that you specify at least one of 14 available actions, including a list of available data sources and a list of tables for a given database.
SQLBind	Specifies where results are placed when they are retrieved using the SQLRetrieve function. It uses the connection ID as an argument.
SQLError	Returns detailed error information when called after one of the other ODBC functions fails.

Figure 5-9. *ODBC functions for Excel and Word.*

Before you can use these commands, you must make them available through the ODBC add-in, which comes with Excel. To do this, follow these steps:

1. In an Excel module, choose the References command from the Tools menu.

2. If XLODBC isn't listed, use the Browse button to find the file (XLODBC.XLA). If it *is* listed, select its check box. Now you can use the Object Browser to view Excel's ODBC functions (which all start with "SQL").

NOTE Because Excel version 5 and Word version 6 both use ODBC functions packaged as add-ins, it's likely that future versions will provide other means of using ODBC. Also, see the sidebar titled "OLE vs. ODBC" in Chapter 11 for a comparison of ODBC and OLE.

The code below, which is in Solution.XLS on the *Office Solutions* disk, shows how to use Excel's ODBC functions to retrieve data from Solution.MDB (also on the *Office Solutions* disk) and write it to an Excel sheet. To use this code, set up a data source named Solution Database that points to the Access file Solution.MDB, and then run the CallingODBC macro.

```
Sub CallingODBC()
'ConnectID is the unique connection ID returned by SQLOpen.
'ConnectStr is the connection string.
'QRY1-3 shows different query options valid for Solution.MDB.
'blnConnectFailed indicates whether connection failed.
  On Error GoTo CallingODBCError
  Dim ConnectID As Integer
  Dim ConnectStr As String
  Const QRY1 = "SELECT Customers.`Company Name` FROM Customers→
    Customers "
  Const QRY2 = "SELECT Orders.`Product Name` FROM Orders Orders"
  Const QRY3 = "SELECT Orders.`Product Name`, Customers.`Company→
    Name` FROM Customers Customers, Orders Orders WHERE→
    Orders.`Customer ID`= Customers.`Customer ID` ORDER BY→
    Orders.`Product Name`"
  Dim blnConnectTried As Boolean

'Sets connection string.
  ConnectStr = "DSN=Solution Database"

'Select specific sheet to write to.
  Sheets("wrkCallingODBC").Select

'Select any existing data and delete it.
  Selection.CurrentRegion.Select
```

(continued)

```
      Selection.Delete
      Range("A1").Select

'Connect to data source. blnConnectTried is initially False.
'The documentation says that you should be able to display the
'SQL Data Sources dialog box if the connection fails, but this
'works unreliably. If the connection fails, code traps error 13.
'If the Boolean flag is False, it displays the dialog by passing
'SQLOpen an empty string and sets the flag to True. If users click
'Cancel, code traps error 13, and because the flag is True, exits.
Connecting:
      ConnectID = SQLOpen(ConnectStr)

'Query from customer table. You can change this query.
      SQLExecQuery ConnectID, QRY3

'Retrieve query into sheet.
      SQLRetrieve ConnectID, Sheets("wrkCallingODBC").Cells(1, 1)

CallingODBCExit:
      On Error Resume Next

'Close data source.
      SQLClose ConnectID

'Best-fit selected range.
      ActiveSheet.Range("A1").CurrentRegion.EntireColumn.AutoFit

'Go home.
      Range("A1").Select
      Exit Sub

CallingODBCError:
'If users click Cancel in SQL Data Sources dialog box...
      If Err = 13 Then
        If Not blnConnectTried Then
          blnConnectTried = True
          ConnectStr = ""
          Resume Connecting
        End If

'Otherwise, notify user of error and exit.
      ElseIf Err <> 0 Then
        If Err <> 0 Then MsgBox "An unidentified error occurred. Error→
          code is" & Err, 48, "Calling ODBC"
      End If
      Resume CallingODBCExit
End Sub
```

Using ODBC functions from Word

Although you can use the ODBC functions listed in Figure 5-9 from Word as well as from Excel, they're more awkward to use in Word because they're implemented through a WLL (a DLL written specifically for Word). (See the section titled "The DLL Solution" in Chapter 6 for more information on WLLs.) This implementation presents two small hurdles:

- To use the ODBC functions, you must install WBODBC.WLL, provided on the *Office Solutions* disk included with this book.

- Because these functions are implemented through a WLL, you must declare them—just as you declare Windows API functions.

The following code uses the ODBC functions to replicate Excel's CallingODBC macro shown on the facing page. To use this code (which is in Solution.DOT on the *Office Solutions* disk), set up a data source named Solution Database pointing to the Access file Solution.MDB; copy the WBODBC.WLL to your Word template directory; add it using the Templates command on the File menu; and then run the ODBCFunctions macro. (See the section titled "SAMPLE APPLICATION: Business Information Manager [BIM]" in Chapter 10 for more information on using Word to access data in ODBC-compliant database management systems.)

```
Declare Function SQLOpen Lib "WBODBC"(ConnectionString$,→
    output_string$, driver_prompt As Integer) As Integer
Declare Function SQLClose Lib "WBODBC"(ConnectID As Integer) As→
    Integer
Declare Function SQLExecQuery Lib "WBODBC"(ConnectID As Integer,→
    query_text$) As Integer
Declare Function SQLRetrieveRows Lib "WBODBC"(ConnectID As Integer)→
    As Integer
Declare Function SQLRetrieveColumns Lib "WBODBC"(ConnectID As→
    Integer) As Integer
Declare Function SQLRetrieveItem$ Lib "WBODBC"(ConnectID As→
    Integer, COLUMN As Integer, ROW As Integer) As String

Sub MAIN
    On Error Goto ErrorTrap

'Define queries.
    Query1$ = "SELECT Customers.`Company Name` FROM Customers→
        Customers"
    Query2$ = "SELECT Orders.`Product Name` FROM Orders Orders"
    Query3$ = "SELECT Orders.`Product Name`, Customers.`Company→
```

(continued)

```
      Name` FROM Customers Customers, Orders Orders WHERE⟶
      Orders.`Customer ID`= Customers.`Customer ID` ORDER BY⟶
      Orders.`Product Name`"

'Connect to data source.
   ConnectID = SQLOpen("DSN=Solution Database", ret$, 4)

'Although (according to the documentation) you should be able to
'display the SQL Data Sources dialog box if the connection fails,
'this works unreliably. So if SQLOpen fails, display the SQL Data
'Sources dialog box by calling SQLOpen with the first argument being
'an empty string.
ShowDataList:
   If ConnectID = 0 Then ConnectID = SQLOpen("", ret$, 2)

'If user clicks Cancel in the Data Source Selection dialog box, clean
'up and exit function.
   If ConnectID = 0 Then Goto CleanUp

'Execute Query1$, Query2$, or Query3$.
   x = SQLExecQuery(ConnectID, Query3$)

'Get the number of rows and columns.
   COLUMN = SQLRetrieveColumns(ConnectID)
   ROW = SQLRetrieveRows(ConnectID)

'Create new document for query results.
   FileNew

'Insert table using the number of rows and columns from query.
   TableInsertTable .ConvertFrom = 0, .NumColumns = COLUMN,⟶
      .NumRows = ROW

'Populate table with query results.
   For R = 1 To ROW
     For C = 1 To COLUMN
      ITEM$ = SQLRetrieveItem$(ConnectID, C, R)
      Insert ITEM$
      If C <> COLUMN Or R <> ROW Then NextCell
     Next
   Next

CleanUp:
   On Error Resume Next

'Close data source.
   x = SQLClose(ConnectID)
   Goto BYE
```

```
ErrorTrap:
'If the user selects an incorrect data source...
  If Err = 512 Then
    MsgBox "The data source you selected is incorrect.", "Office→
      Solutions", 16
    FileClose 2
    ConnectID = 0
    Goto ShowDataList
  ElseIf Err <> 0 And Err <> 102 Then
    MsgBox "An unidentified error occurred. Error code is" +→
      Str$(Err), "Office Solutions", 48
    Goto CleanUp
  End If

BYE:
End Sub
```

6

The Windows API: Not Just for C Programmers

The code-reusability bandwagon is a big one, and people have been getting on it for a long time—for the past half century, in fact. What's especially interesting about it is that outside the application development community, no one actually discusses reusability. It's taken for granted. Use and reuse are pretty much the same thing.

Within the development community, however, reusability has been a hot topic since the mid-1940s, when assembly-language programmers started using macros to bundle frequently used commands into a single, reusable instruction. In 1951, researchers at Cambridge University developed another means of reusing code: libraries that store general subroutines and functions. Today, both macros and libraries are essential to programming for Microsoft Windows.

This chapter describes a library of reusable code available to every Windows user: the Windows Application Programming Interface (API). It also introduces the Windows Open System Architecture (WOSA), explains how to use the Windows API with the Microsoft BASICs, and explains how to use custom dynamic link libraries (DLLs) to provide capabilities that otherwise aren't available to the BASICs.

Reusing Code

Despite the attention given to code reuse, the challenge isn't to reuse code (which nearly every developer does) but to *formalize* reuse of code—in other words, to provide a method by which a group of developers can share code. Like most developers, I reuse dozens of general routines: I know what they do, I know where to find them, and—most important—I know that they work. If someone has trouble coding a function and I have a solution, I give that person my code. This is how every developer I know works. We reuse our own code constantly. We reuse someone else's code only when we need a little help.

Let's be honest: It's rarely easy to use someone else's code. Even assuming that it's well documented (which is a big assumption), you still have to figure out exactly what the code does, test it, and then tweak it into exactly what you need. All things considered—unless you're faced with a substantial coding job—it's usually faster to write code than to borrow it.

An application-development unit at a company I have worked with considered establishing a companywide code library. Several big issues surfaced immediately: Who would guarantee the code's quality? What would the documentation requirements be, and who would enforce them? Would the author have to support the code? Who would maintain the library and let developers know what was available? Add to these the usual political problems of sharing among departments, and you can begin to understand the scope of the problem. In the end, they made two decisions:

- To keep code reuse largely informal
- To provide developers with application shells (templates) for the two development tools they used most often—Excel and Visual Basic

Open Architecture and Code Reuse

Although Microsoft developed software for all the early PC companies—Apple, Commodore, and Radio Shack (now Tandy)—its big break came when IBM started a top secret effort, code-named "Project Chess," to launch its own line of PCs. Bill Gates, cofounder of Microsoft, convinced IBM that he could write a new operating system to take full advantage of the new PC's capabilities. Gates also convinced IBM to make the machine specs public. This *open architecture* approach—a radical departure from the computer industry's traditional mode of doing business—was one of the keys to the PC's success and to Microsoft's later success with Windows.

Before this point, hardware and software had been highly proprietary, highly integrated, and highly unstandardized. Companies bought into the DEC way of solving business problems, or the IBM way, or the WANG way, and so on. They got all of the software and the hardware—from the mainframe or minicomputer right down to the printer—from the same vendor.

The open architecture approach completely revamped the old model. Today businesses essentially build their own systems, choosing from a wide variety of computer vendors, printer manufacturers, monitor manufacturers, and software developers to put together highly customized solutions that fit their business.

F Y I

The Application Shell

Application shells—also known as *templates*—and developer tools provide a relatively simple, practical means of promoting both code reuse and a standard look and feel. For example, an application shell might include a standard menu bar, a standard toolbar, and a standard About box. Developer tools and utilities might include wizards, subroutines, or functions that simplify common tasks that developers perform. For example, the sample application Menu-BldR.MDA (on the *Office Solutions* disk included with this book) simplifies the use of menu commands in Access Basic code. (See the sections titled "SAMPLE APPLICATION: AppMakeR.XLT" and "SAMPLE APPLICATION: DevelopR.XLS" in Chapter 9 for an Excel application shell and a set of developer utilities.)

The open architecture model provides three major advantages over the proprietary model:

- Open architectures are published. This facilitates *standardization* by making it easy for unrelated computer companies to build hardware and software to the same spec.

- Standardization in turn makes software *portable* so that it runs on a wider variety of hardware—not only on PCs but, with minor modifications, on Macintosh computers and workstations as well. For example, roughly 80 percent of the code in Microsoft Excel version 5 and Microsoft Word version 6 is the same for both the Windows and the Macintosh editions. Platform-independent software makes users' skills platform-independent as well.

- Standardization also facilitates *interoperability* so components built by different companies fit together. This lets businesses share information across computer platforms and, in the best client-server tradition, locate their processing needs on the machine that makes the most sense. Compaq PCs, a DEC mainframe, IBM AS/400 servers, and a variety of software can all contribute to the same solution.

WOSA Means Standardization...and Freedom

Microsoft developed Windows on the Windows Open Services Architecture (WOSA) model. In WOSA, a published API sits on the "black box" of proprietary software. The API lets anyone access and use the black box without knowing the details of what goes on inside. For example, the Windows API contains the information necessary to call the functions that make up Windows, including their names, what they do, the arguments or parameters they take, and what they return.

By providing published specs to hardware and software manufacturers, WOSA promotes the standardization necessary to integrate at the desktop a wide variety of evolving hardware and software. It's easy to see how this works if you think of an API as a "connector," not unlike a phone jack. You can use any Windows-based application with any back end (from hardware back ends such as printers and monitors to software back ends such as databases), as long as they both plug into the API.

WOSA offers two advantages to developers:

- There's no need to worry about the specific "ends" that people might dream up. You simply attach your end to the standard interface. If your end fits and their end fits, everything works.

- Windows is infinitely extensible. Applications can add their own APIs that you can then use to build custom applications. For example, FactSet, a financial data vendor, developed an API that allows its customers to build front ends to retrieve FactSet data. (For more information, see "CASE STUDY: More than a PIF—Reengineering an Application for Windows" later in this chapter.)

There are three broad categories of services currently available through WOSA: 1) common application services, which let applications connect to anything from Windows itself to telephones; 2) communication services, which provide standard access to network communications; and 3) a number of vertical market services, which let applications access capabilities particular to specialized markets (see Figure 6-1).

FYI

Extending Windows

You could say that a Windows API consists of two things: a *dynamic link library* (DLL) and the DLL's documentation. DLLs add functionality that Windows-based applications can use at runtime. Developers don't have to write their own code for these functions—they can simply call a function in the DLL.

One benefit of a DLL-based architecture such as the Windows architecture is that you can update DLLs independent of the applications that use them. The next time an application calls an updated DLL, it gets the new functionality instead of the old. You can also add custom DLLs. (See the section titled "When the Windows API Alone Isn't Enough" later in this chapter.) In fact, when Microsoft adds a new API (such as MAPI or ODBC), it's actually adding a set of DLLs.

Service Category	Description
Common application services	The Windows API lets applications use any of the 1000 functions in Windows. (See the next section, "API Calls to Die For.")
	The Open Database Connectivity (ODBC) API lets Windows-based applications access any ODBC database. (See Chapter 5.)
	The Messaging API (MAPI) lets mail-enabled applications access any MAPI mail system.
	The Telephony API (TAPI) lets applications use any PC-telephone connection to access corporate telephone networks.
	The License Service API (LSAPI) makes it easier for corporations to manage software licenses centrally.
	The OLE API enables developers to create OLE-compatible applications.
Communication services	The Sockets API lets applications access network services across a variety of protocols, such as TCP/IP, IPX/SPX, and AppleTalk.
	The SNA API provides open access to IBM's SNA API to standardize the method for connecting to a host.
	The RPC API lets you access remote procedure calls that are compatible with the Open Software Foundation's DCE RPC. This makes it easier to build distributed client-server applications across a variety of networks.
Vertical market services	WOSA Extensions for Financial Services let applications access services commonly used in the banking industry.
	WOSA Extensions for Real-Time Market Data let applications receive live data (such as stock prices) from a variety of sources.
	WOSA Extensions for Control, Engineering, and Manufacturing let applications access these types of data sources.

Figure 6-1. *WOSA services.*

API Calls to Die For

Too many people learn about the Windows API the way they learned about sex—either from their friends or by piecing together veiled references in books and magazines. A few months back, I joined second-year programmers at a large company for a discussion about what they wish they had known about Windows programming when they started their jobs. The Windows API was the first thing on their list. One developer mentioned that he'd spent a lot of time trying to figure out how to determine the display driver used on a given machine. He had written a lot of useless code by the time someone gave him the GetPrivateProfileString API function. It worked great, but he thought it was a special case. No one told him that there were more than 1000 such functions that he could use—for free.

The "free" part becomes important when you realize that a number of custom controls for Access Basic and Visual Basic are nothing more than C/C++ "wrappers" (or interfaces) that make it easier to use the Windows API functions. Of course, sometimes you need a wrapper because the Microsoft BASICs can't directly use all of the functions available through the API. Two limitations curb the use of API functions from the Microsoft BASICs:

■ When an application relies on Windows to do something for it, Windows sometimes calls a function in the application (known as a *callback function*) to get whatever information it needs to proceed. *None of the Microsoft BASICs supports callback functions.*

■ Some API functions (such as PeekMessage) use special data structures. Because WordBasic doesn't let you define your own data types, you can't use functions of this kind in WordBasic. (In some cases, you can work around this problem by using other API functions to allocate memory for these data structures.)

What You Need to Know to Learn More

As powerful as the BASICs are, they can't do everything. But with the API you can make them do a lot more than they otherwise could. To use an API function with the BASICs, you must declare it using the Declare statement. This statement—which tells your code where to find the API function and how to use it—requires the following information:

■ The function's name

■ The function's library location (based on its purpose): *Kernel* (low-level operating system functions, such as memory management), *User* (window management functions), or *GDI* (graphical interface management functions)

■ The arguments or information the function requires

■ The function's return type

A typical Declare statement for Access Basic, VBA for Excel, and Visual Basic looks like this:

```
Declare Function GetDriveType Lib "Kernel" (ByVal nDrive As⤳
   Integer) As Integer
```

In this example, the API function is GetDriveType, the DLL is Kernel, and the one argument the function needs is an integer representing the drive that you want to check (A = 0, B = 1, and so on, up to Z = 25). The words *As Integer* at the very end of the function indicate that the function returns an integer.

As with any function, assign it to a variable of the correct type (as given by the function's return type) to store the return value. After you declare the function, the following code calls it and returns information about the type of drive 3 (which is the D drive):

```
Dim DriveType As Integer
DriveType = GetDriveType(3)
```

WordBasic and the ByVal keyword

Essentially, the ByVal keyword (used in the Declare statement above) provides the API function with the *value* of information rather than its address, or location in memory.

Unlike the other BASICs, WordBasic never uses the ByVal keyword. Otherwise, WordBasic Declare statements look pretty much like the others, as does the code used to call the API function:

```
Declare Function GetDriveType Lib "Kernel" (nDrive As Integer) As⤳
   Integer
```

NOTE Throughout this chapter, the code samples use the standard Declare statements—including the ByVal keyword—for Access Basic, VBA for Excel, and Visual Basic. To use these samples in WordBasic, delete every occurrence of ByVal.

FYI

Using Handles and Pointers

Because the objects used in Windows programming can be quite large, Windows uses numeric identifiers to make them easier to manipulate. Two types of numeric identifiers are available: *handles* and *pointers*.

■ A handle is a reference number that Windows uses to identify an object, such as a window or a task. Nearly every object in Windows has a handle, and a large percentage of API functions either require a handle as an argument or return a handle. Some do both.

■ A pointer is a memory address. Although pointers are widely used in programming, none of the BASICs uses them. If you look at the API documentation, you'll see that many API functions take pointers as arguments. When calling these functions from one of the BASICs, use a variable of the type indicated by the pointer. For example, if one of the arguments to an API function is a pointer to a string—in other words, a memory address that stores a string—use a string variable.

Getting strings from API functions

When an API function retrieves a string, it requires two arguments: a *string buffer* (which is a variable for storing the string retrieved) and an integer specifying the length of the string buffer. You must ensure that the buffer is big enough to accept the whole string. One way to do this is to use the String$ function to create a "spaceholder" of the maximum length that you think you'll need. If the string exceeds the estimated length, you'll get only the part of the string that fits.

NOTE WordBasic doesn't require that you create a spaceholder for strings. However, I use this method in WordBasic for compatibility with the other BASICs. Also, because API functions return strings that end with a null character (ANSI code 0), always add an extra character of space to the buffer.

The following example uses the GetSystemDirectory function to get the pathname for the WINDOWS\SYSTEM directory. The Declare statement for the GetSystemDirectory function is as follows:

```
Declare Function GetSystemDirectory Lib "Kernel" (ByVal lpBuffer As→
    String, ByVal nSize As Integer) As Integer
```

Here's a sample subroutine that uses this function:

```
Sub cmdSysDirectory_Click ()
'Display the system directory pathname in a message box.
'Variable for this pathname.
  Dim StringHolder As String

'Variable for the length of this pathname.
  Dim iLength As Integer

'Provide StringHolder enough space to hold the pathname.
  StringHolder = String$(256, 0)

'Copy the pathname into StringHolder.
  iLength = GetSystemDirectory(StringHolder, Len(StringHolder))

'Trim StringHolder to the pathname's actual size.
  StringHolder = Left$(StringHolder, iLength)

  MsgBox "The system directory is " & StringHolder
End Sub
```

In addition to the GetSystemDirectory function, the following API functions (which are described in this chapter) retrieve strings and require similar handling: GetWindowsDirectory, GetClassName, GetProfileString, GetPrivateProfileString, and GetWindowText.

Passing strings to API functions

When you pass a string variable to an API function, it treats the variable as a pointer. In general, you don't need to think about this, but a few functions (such as FindWindow and the GetProfileString and WriteProfileString functions) do things differently when you give them the equivalent of a null pointer instead of a string. The way to pass a null pointer in Access Basic, VBA for Excel, and Visual Basic is to use ByVal 0& (which is zero represented as a long integer). When you do this, be sure to change the Declare statement to account for the fact that you're not passing a string. This is one of the few cases in which you list the argument's type as As Any, which allows for either a string or a long. Because the Any type is the least efficient, use As String if your application always passes a string or As Long if you always pass ByVal 0&. In WordBasic, simply pass a zero.

Here's an example of how null pointers work. The WritePrivateProfileString function, which writes to initialization (INI) files other than WIN.INI, accepts four arguments: 1) the name of the section in the INI file, 2) the name of the entry for the INI file, 3) the entry itself, and 4) the name of the INI file. If you pass a null pointer instead of a string for the third argument (the entry), the function deletes the entire entry.

119

The following two subroutines write to an INI file named TEST.INI, which has a section called "Presidents" containing an entry titled "First President." The first subroutine, WriteINIEntry, takes a string argument strEntry and writes it in the First President line of the INI file. The second subroutine, DeleteINIEntry, removes the First President line entirely. (See the section titled "INI File Functions" later in this chapter for more information about INI files.)

```
Declare Function WritePrivateProfileString Lib "Kernel" (ByVal→
  lpSectionName As String, ByVal lpEntryName As Any, ByVal lpString→
  As Any, ByVal lpFileName As String) As Integer

Sub WriteINIEntry()
'This writes "George Washington" as the entry for "First
'President" in the [Presidents] section of the TEST.INI file.
  Dim iRet As Integer
  iRet = WritePrivateProfileString("Presidents", "First→
    President", "George Washington", "TEST.INI")
End Sub

Sub DeleteINIEntry()
'This deletes the entry for "First President" in the [Presidents]
'section of the TEST.INI file.
  Dim iRet As Integer
  iRet = WritePrivateProfileString("Presidents", "First→
    President", ByVal 0&, "TEST.INI")
End Sub
```

An API Primer

The following sections describe a few dozen of the 1000-plus function calls in Windows. Hundreds of other functions are available through the different APIs—for example, MAPI and ODBC. The listing is far from complete (my husband calls them "API-tizers"), but it includes some of the most commonly used functions from the Kernel and User DLLs, and the samples work with all the Microsoft BASICs. (I have omitted GDI functions, although they are invaluable for multimedia applications.)

I have organized the API functions into seven broad categories:

- Drive and directory functions
- INI file functions
- Task functions
- Window display functions
- Window information functions
- Window input functions
- Miscellaneous functions

NOTE Most of the code samples in this chapter are written in Access Basic, but you can copy them to VBA for Excel or Visual Basic—the syntax is identical. I wrote a few of the samples in WordBasic because the syntax is slightly different, and I wrote one sample, which manipulates Excel win-dows, in VBA for Excel. All of the sample code is in Solution.MDB, Solution.XLS, and Solution.DOT on the *Office Solutions* disk included with this book. The Declare.TXT file on the disk contains standard Declare statements for all API functions listed in this chapter. See Appendix A for additional sources of information on the Windows API.

FYI

Aliasing API Functions

In some cases, you might have to *alias* API functions so you can call them by a name other than the one defined in the Windows DLL. This technique is helpful in several circumstances:

- When you want to use an API function with a name that is identical to a function defined by a given version of the Microsoft BASICs. (For example, WordBasic has its own version of the GetPrivateProfileString function.)

- When you want to use an API function with a name that contains a character that is "illegal" for a BASIC function name. (For example, you have to alias API functions that start with an underscore, such as _lopen.)

- When you want to avoid "duplicate procedure" error messages in Access Basic when using libraries that call API functions.

To alias an API function, use the Alias keyword in the function's Declare statement. The syntax follows:

```
Declare Function NewName Lib "NameOfLib" Alias "NameOfFunction"→
  (ListOfArguments)
```

For example, this is the Declare statement for the GetDriveType function:

```
Declare Function GetDriveType Lib "Kernel" (nDrive As Integer) As→
  Integer
```

Use the following Declare statement to call this function by the alias "Hardware":

```
Declare Function Hardware Lib "Kernel" Alias "GetDriveType"→
  (nDrive As Integer) As Integer
```

Drive and Directory Functions

Drive and directory functions return information about a PC's drives and directories (see Figure 6-2). For example, the following WordBasic code identifies the D drive (a CD-ROM drive on my machine) as "Remote."

```
Declare Function GetDriveType Lib "Kernel"(nDrive As Integer) As→
   Integer

Sub MAIN
'Return values are: 2 = Removable; 3 = Fixed; 4 = Remote.
'The following line calls the API function. The argument
'is a number corresponding to the drive: 0 for A, 1 for B, etc.
  DriveType = GetDriveType(2)

  Select Case DriveType
    Case 2
      MsgBox "The specified drive is REMOVABLE."
    Case 3
      MsgBox "The specified drive is FIXED."
    Case 4
      MsgBox "The specified drive is REMOTE."
    Case Else
      MsgBox "Function failed."
  End Select
End Sub
```

FYI

Using Windows API Constants

A number of Windows API functions use predefined constants with descriptive names. The Windows Software Development Kit (SDK) provides the names of these constants, but not their values. For example, the GetDriveType function identifies drives according to one of three constants: DRIVE_REMOVABLE, DRIVE_FIXED, or DRIVE_REMOTE. However, the documentation doesn't tell you that DRIVE_REMOVABLE = 2, DRIVE_FIXED = 3, or DRIVE_REMOTE = 4, even though 2, 3, or 4 is what the function returns.

The documentation for the professional edition of Visual Basic includes the values for these constants. You can also find two text files from Microsoft (WIN30API.TXT and WIN31EXT.TXT) that contain values for these constants on the *Office Solutions* disk.

Function	Description
GetDriveType	Determines the drive type.
	`Declare Function GetDriveType Lib "Kernel"`↵ `(ByVal nDrive As Integer) As Integer`
	Arguments: 0 = A drive, 1 = B drive, and so on, through 25 = Z.
	Returns: One of the following: 2 if it's a removable drive, 3 if it's fixed, 4 if it's remote (or a CD), or 0 if the function fails.
GetSystemDirectory	Returns the Windows system directory.

	`Declare Function GetSystemDirectory Lib`↵
	    `"Kernel" (ByVal lpBuffer As String,`↵
	    `ByVal nSize As Integer) As Integer`

	Arguments: lpBuffer is a string buffer that holds the Windows system directory path. The integer nSize is the maximum number of characters to copy to lpBuffer. (See the section titled "Getting Strings from API Functions" earlier in this chapter.)
	Returns: The length of the string copied into lpBuffer, or 0 if the function fails.
GetWindowsDirectory	Returns the Windows directory.

	`Declare Function GetWindowsDirectory Lib`↵
	    `"Kernel" (ByVal lpBuffer As String,`↵
	    `ByVal nSize As Integer) As Integer`

	Arguments: Same as GetSystemDirectory.
	Returns: Same as GetSystemDirectory.

Figure 6-2. *Drive and directory functions.*

INI file functions

INI file functions let you read from and write to INI files (see Figure 6-3 on the next two pages). An INI file is a text file structured as follows:

```
[SECTION NAME]
EntryName=
```

INI files typically store information required by applications at startup, such as user preferences. However, you can use INI files to store any application-related information. For example, the sample Visual Basic application Tracker (described later in this chapter) uses an INI file to store the time spent in Word documents.

Three categories of API functions control INI files:

■ Functions that get text data from INI files (GetPrivateProfileString, GetProfileString)

- Functions that get numeric data from INI files (GetPrivateProfileInt, GetProfileInt)

- Functions that write text or numeric data to INI files *as strings* (WritePrivateProfileString, WriteProfileString)

These functions are quite similar. The following Declare statement for the GetPrivateProfileString function (which retrieves data from a given private INI file) is typical of Get functions. (The arguments are in bold.)

```
Declare Function GetPrivateProfileString Lib "Kernel" (ByVal→
    lpSectionName As String, ByVal lpEntryName As Any, ByVal→
    lpDefault As String, ByVal lpReturnedString As String, ByVal→
    nSize As Integer, ByVal lpFilename As String) As Integer
```

The following Declare statement for the WritePrivateProfileString function (which enters data in a given private INI file) is typical of Write functions. (The arguments are in bold.)

```
Declare Function WritePrivateProfileString Lib "Kernel" (ByVal→
    lpSectionName As String, ByVal lpEntryName As Any, ByVal lpString→
    As Any, ByVal lpFileName As String) As Integer
```

Function	Description
GetPrivateProfileInt	Retrieves an integer value from an INI file.
	```Declare Function GetPrivateProfileInt→ Lib "Kernel" (ByVal lpSectionName As→ String, ByVal lpEntryName As String,→ ByVal nDefault As Integer, ByVal→ lpFilename As String) As Integer```
	Arguments: See the next section, "INI Arguments."
	Returns: If the function is successful, it returns the integer corresponding to the given entry. If it can't find the entry, it returns nDefault. If the given entry isn't an integer, the function returns 0.
GetPrivateProfileString	Retrieves a string from an INI file.
	```Declare Function GetPrivateProfileString→ Lib "Kernel" (ByVal lpSectionName As→ String, lpEntryName As Any,→ ByVal lpDefault As String, ByVal→ lpReturnedString As String, ByVal→ nSize As Integer, ByVal lpFilename As→ String) As Integer```
	Arguments: Described in the next section, "INI Arguments," except for lpReturnedString, which is a string buffer that receives the requested entry, and nSize, which is the maximum number of characters to copy to lpReturnedString.

Function	Description
	Returns: The length of the string copied into lpReturnedString.
| GetProfileInt | Retrieves an integer value from WIN.INI.<br><br>```
Declare Function GetProfileInt Lib→
  "Kernel" (ByVal lpSectionName As→
  String, ByVal lpEntryName As String,→
  ByVal nDefault As Integer) As Integer
```<br><br>**Arguments:** See the next section, "INI Arguments."<br>**Returns:** Same as GetPrivateProfileInt. |
| GetProfileString | Retrieves a string from WIN.INI.<br><br>```
Declare Function GetProfileString Lib→
  "Kernel" (ByVal lpSectionName As →
  String, lpEntryName As Any, ByVal→
  lpDefault As String, ByVal→
  lpReturnedString As String, ByVal→
  nSize As Integer) As Integer
```<br><br>**Arguments:** Same as GetPrivateProfileString, except for lpFilename, which this function doesn't need.<br>**Returns:** Same as GetPrivateProfileString. |
| WritePrivateProfileString | Writes a string to an INI file. If the file doesn't exist, this function creates it.<br><br>```
Declare Function→
  WritePrivateProfileString Lib "Kernel"→
  (ByVal lpSectionName As String,→
  lpEntryName As Any, lpString As→
  Any, ByVal lpFileName As String) As→
  Integer
```<br><br>**Arguments:** See the next section, "INI Arguments."<br>**Returns:** Nonzero if the function is successful; 0 otherwise. |
| WriteProfileString | Writes a string to WIN.INI.<br><br>```
Declare Function WriteProfileString Lib→
  "Kernel" (ByVal lpSectionName As→
  String, lpEntryName As Any,→
  lpString As Any) As Integer
```<br><br>**Arguments:** See the next section, "INI Arguments."<br>**Returns:** Same as WritePrivateProfileString. |

Figure 6-3. *INI file functions.*

INI arguments

Given the SectionName/EntryName structure of INI files, it's not surprising that all INI-related functions require two arguments: the section name (lpSectionName) and the entry name (lpEntryName). In addition, the Get functions require a default argument (lpDefault), such as an empty string (" "), which the function uses if it can't find the specified entry.

You can retrieve *all* entries in a given section by passing ByVal 0& as the entry name (lpEntryName), as long as you make sure the buffer (lpReturnedString) is long enough to hold them. (See the section titled "Getting Strings from API Functions" earlier in this chapter for more information on using ByVal 0&.)

The Write functions require an argument specifying the string to enter in the INI file (lpString). In addition to entering data in files, the Write functions enable you to delete data. (See the section titled "Passing Strings to API Functions" earlier in this chapter.)

You control which data to delete in the following two ways:

■ Delete an entire entry by using ByVal 0& for the string to enter (lpString).

■ Delete an entire section by using ByVal 0& for the entry name (lpEntryName).

The Private INI functions require an argument specifying the name of the INI file (lpFileName).

The following Access Basic code uses the GetPrivateProfileString function to determine the display driver currently in use:

```
Declare Function GetProfileString Lib "Kernel" (ByVal lpAppName As→
    String, lpKeyName As Any, ByVal lpDefault As String, ByVal→
    lpReturnedString As String, ByVal nSize As Integer) As Integer


Function ShowDisplayDriver()
'This function reads the display driver listed in SYSTEM.INI
'and displays it in a message box.
    Dim iLength As Integer
    Dim sBuffer As String

'Initialize sBuffer with a string of 128 null characters
'to provide space to hold the display driver.
    sBuffer = String$(128, 0)

'Read the display driver name into sBuffer.
    iLength = GetPrivateProfileString("boot.description",→
      "display.drv", "", sBuffer, Len(sBuffer), "system.ini")
```

```
'If iLength is 0, the function didn't get a string.
  If iLength = 0 Then
    MsgBox "Couldn't find display driver."

'Otherwise, trim sBuffer to the actual length
'of the string retrieved, and display a message box.
  Else
    sBuffer = Left$(sBuffer, iLength)
    MsgBox "The display driver is " & sBuffer
  End If
End Function
```

FYI

Private vs. Public INIs

There are two types of INI files: private INIs and WIN.INI (which is public). Use "nonprivate" functions, such as GetProfileString and WriteProfileString, to manipulate the WIN.INI. Be careful when doing this. Although you can add sections and entries to WIN.INI, it's better to use private INI files. Use the "private" INI functions (the ones with the word "Private" in their name) to manipulate all other INI files (including SYSTEM.INI and EXCEL5.INI).

FYI

Argument Names for API Functions

The prefixes for API function arguments use C/C++ naming conventions, as described below:

lp = long pointer, generally to a string; in the Microsoft BASICs, use a string variable

n = numeric; use an integer variable

dw = unsigned long integer; in the Microsoft BASICs, this represents an integer from 0 through 2,147,483,647. You can represent integers through 4,294,967,295 using a conversion formula described by Daniel Appleman (see Appendix A).

w = unsigned integer; in the Microsoft BASICs, this represents an integer from 0 through 32,767. You can represent integers through 65,535 using a conversion formula described by Daniel Appleman (see Appendix A).

h = handle, which is an integer

Task Functions

In Windows parlance, the term *task* describes any application currently running under Windows. (To see the current Windows Task List, press Ctrl+Esc.) Task functions let you work with tasks—from functions that exit Windows or run an MS-DOS application to those that check whether a given task handle is still valid (see Figure 6-4).

The following Access Basic code uses the GetNumTasks function to determine the number of applications currently running under Windows and uses the GetFreeSystemResources function to determine the percentage of free resources. (See the section titled "Miscellaneous Functions" later in this chapter.) It then displays a message box with this information.

```
Declare Function GetNumTasks Lib "Kernel" () As Integer
Declare Function GetFreeSystemResources Lib "User" (ByVal→
   fuSysResource As Integer) As Integer

'To use API constants, you must declare them.
Const GFSR_SYSTEMRESOURCES = 0
Const GFSR_GDIRESOURCES = 1
Const GFSR_USERRESOURCES = 2

Function ShowSysInfo()
'Displays a message box listing the number of tasks and the
'percentage of free system resources.
   Dim iTasks As Integer
   Dim iFreeRes As Integer
   iTasks = GetNumTasks()
   iFreeRes = GetFreeSystemResources(GFSR_SYSTEMRESOURCES)
   MsgBox "The current number of tasks is " & iTasks & Chr$(13) &→
   "System Resources: " & iFreeRes & "% Free"
End Function
```

Function	Description
ExitWindows	Restarts or terminates Windows.

	`Declare Function ExitWindows Lib "User" (ByVal→`
	`   dwReturnCode As Long, ByVal wReserved As→`
	`   Integer) As Integer`

	Arguments: Set dwReturnCode to 66 to close and restart Windows, or set it to 67 to close Windows and reboot. Set wReserved to 0.
	Returns: No return if successful, or 0 if one or more applications won't close.

Function	Description
ExitWindowsExec	Terminates Windows and runs an MS-DOS application. ```Declare Function ExitWindowsExec Lib "User"→ (ByVal lpExe As String, ByVal lpParams As→ String) As Integer``` **Arguments:** lpExe is the pathname and filename of the MS-DOS executable you want to run after Windows has terminated, and lpParams is a string containing command-line parameters required by that executable. If you don't need parameters, set this argument to an empty string (" "). **Returns:** Same as ExitWindows.
GetCurrentTask	Returns the current task handle. ```Declare Function GetCurrentTask Lib "Kernel" ()→ As Integer``` **Arguments:** None. **Returns:** The handle of the current task, or 0 if the function fails.
GetNumTasks	Returns the current number of tasks. ```Declare Function GetNumTasks Lib "Kernel" () As→ Integer``` **Arguments:** None. **Returns:** The number of tasks currently running under Windows.
GetWindowTask	Returns the task associated with a window. ```Declare Function GetWindowTask Lib "User" (ByVal→ hWnd As Integer) As Integer``` **Arguments:** hWnd is the window handle. **Returns:** The handle of the task associated with the given window, or 0 if the function fails.
IsTask	Determines whether a task handle is valid. ```Declare Function IsTask Lib "Kernel" (ByVal→ hTask As Integer) As Integer``` **Arguments:** hTask is the task handle you're checking. **Returns:** Nonzero if hTask is a valid task handle; 0 otherwise.

Figure 6-4. *Task functions.*

Window Display Functions

Window display functions (see Figure 6-5 below) control windows and provide information about them (for example, whether they're maximized or minimized). The following WordBasic code uses the GetWindowText function, the SetWindowText function, and the GetActiveWindow function (see the section titled "Window Input Functions" later in this chapter) to change the text in the title bar temporarily. The only difference between the following Declare statements and those used in Access Basic, VBA for Excel, and Visual Basic is that WordBasic doesn't use the ByVal keyword.

```
Declare Function GetActiveWindow Lib "User"() As Integer
Declare Function GetWindowText Lib "User"(hWnd As Integer,
  lpString As String, nSize As Integer) As Integer
Declare Sub SetWindowText Lib "User"(hWnd As Integer, lpString As
  String)

Sub MAIN
'This macro temporarily changes the title of the program window;
'to change it back, maximize or restore the document window.
  hWnd = GetActiveWindow
  MsgBox "The active window handle is" + Str$(hWnd)
  Length = GetWindowText(hWnd, WindowText$, 255)
  MsgBox "The current window text is " + WindowText$ + "... but
    not anymore..."
  NewWindowText$ = "hi!"
  SetWindowText(hWnd, NewWindowText$)
End Sub
```

Function	Description
BringWindowToTop	Uncovers an overlapped window.
	`Declare Sub BringWindowToTop Lib "User"` `(ByVal hWnd As Integer)`
	Arguments: hWnd is the window handle.
	Returns: Nonzero if the function is successful; 0 otherwise.
CloseWindow	Minimizes a window.
	`Declare Sub CloseWindow Lib "User" (ByVal` `hWnd As Integer)`
	Arguments: hWnd is the window handle.
	Returns: This function doesn't return a value.

Function	Description

GetWindowText	Copies the window text to a buffer.
	
	``
	Declare Function GetWindowText Lib "User"→
	    (ByVal hWnd As Integer, ByVal lpString→
	    As String, ByVal nSize As Integer) As→
	    Integer
	``
	
	Arguments: hWnd is the window handle, lpString is a buffer to receive the window text, and nSize is the maximum number of characters to copy into lpString.
	
	Returns: The number of characters copied into lpString.

GetWindowTextLength	Returns the length of window text. ``` Declare Function GetWindowTextLength Lib→ "User" (ByVal hWnd As Integer) As Integer ``` **Arguments:** hWnd is the window handle. **Returns:** The length of text in the window title bar or the control window.
IsIconic	Determines whether a window is minimized. ``` Declare Function IsIconic Lib "User"→ (ByVal hWnd As Integer) As Integer ``` **Arguments:** hWnd is the handle of the window to be checked. **Returns:** Nonzero if the window is minimized; 0 otherwise.
IsWindowVisible	Determines the visibility state of a window. ``` Declare Function IsWindowVisible Lib→ "User" (ByVal hWnd As Integer) As Integer ``` **Arguments:** hWnd is the window handle. **Returns:** Nonzero if the window is visible; 0 otherwise.
IsZoomed	Determines whether a window is maximized. ``` Declare Function IsZoomed Lib "User"→ (ByVal hWnd As Integer) As Integer ``` **Arguments:** hWnd is the handle of the window to be checked. **Returns:** Nonzero if the window is maximized; 0 otherwise.

(continued)

Function	Description
OpenIcon	Activates a minimized window.
|          | ```
Declare Function OpenIcon Lib "User"→
   (ByVal hWnd As Integer) As Integer
``` |
	Arguments: hWnd is the handle of the minimized window.
	Returns: Nonzero if successful; 0 otherwise.
SetWindowText	Sets text in a caption title or a control window.
|          | ```
Declare Sub SetWindowText Lib "User"→
   (ByVal hWnd As Integer, ByVal lpString→
   As String)
``` |
| | **Arguments:** hWnd is the window handle, and lpString is the text to put in the title bar or the control window. |
| | **Returns:** This function doesn't return a value. |

Figure 6-5. *Window display functions.*

Window Information Functions

Window information functions (see Figure 6-6, beginning on page 134) provide a variety of information about the windows that are currently open. For example, you can use these functions to determine the relationships among windows. These relationships are described using a familial vocabulary. A "child" window belongs to another window, called the "parent" window. (For example, command buttons and list boxes are generally children of their parent dialog box.) "Siblings" are children of the same parent window.

The following VBA for Excel code uses the GetClassName function, the GetWindow function, and the GetActiveWindow function to determine class names for all active child windows of the Excel application window (the parent).

```
Declare Function GetActiveWindow Lib "USER" () As Integer
Declare Function GetClassName Lib "USER" (ByVal hWnd As Integer,→
   ByVal lpClassName As String, ByVal nMaxCount As Integer) As→
   Integer
Declare Function GetWindow Lib "USER" (ByVal hWnd As Integer,→
   ByVal wCmd As Integer) As Integer

Sub AllMyChildren()
'Handle to Excel; returned by GetActiveWindow.
   Dim hExcel As Integer

'Handle to Excel's child windows; returned by GetWindow.
   Dim hChild As Integer
```

```
'Counter.
  Dim iNumChildren As Integer
  Dim sBuffer As String
  Dim iLength As Integer
  Dim sClassList As String

'Gets the handle to Excel's application window.
  hExcel = GetActiveWindow()
  sBuffer = String$(128, 0)

'Gets class name and checks that it's XLMain. If not, exits.
  iLength = GetClassName(hExcel, sBuffer, Len(sBuffer))
  sBuffer = Left$(sBuffer, iLength)
  If sBuffer <> "XLMain" Then Exit Sub
  sClassList = "The children of Excel's main window have the➔
    following classes: " & Chr$(13)

'Loop through and get all child windows.
  Do

'First time through the loop, get the first child window.
    If iNumChildren = 0 Then
      hChild = GetWindow(hExcel, 5)

'After the first time through the loop, get the next child window,
'specified by the constant 2.
    Else
      hChild = GetWindow(hChild, 2)
    End If

'If there are no more child windows, stop looping.
    If hChild = 0 Then Exit Do

'Get the class name of the child window.
    sBuffer = String$(128, 0)
    iLength = GetClassName(hChild, sBuffer, 127)
    sBuffer = Left$(sBuffer, iLength)

'Build list of classes; Chr$(13) is the linefeed.
    sClassList = sClassList & sBuffer & Chr$(13)
    iNumChildren = iNumChildren + 1
  Loop
  If iNumChildren = 0 Then
    MsgBox "The Excel main window has no children."
  Else
    MsgBox sClassList
  End If
End Sub
```

Function	Description
FindWindow	Returns the handle of a window with a given class and/or the window name (from the title bar). This function doesn't search child windows.
| | ```
Declare Function FindWindow Lib "User" (ByVal→
    lpClassName As Any, ByVal lpWindowName As→
    Any) As Integer
``` |
	Arguments: lpClassName is the class name of the window you're looking for, and lpWindowName is its title bar text.
	Returns: The window handle, or 0 if the function fails.
GetClassName	Returns a window-class name.
| | ```
Declare Function GetClassName Lib "User"→
    (ByVal hWnd As Integer, ByVal lpClassName As→
    String, ByVal nMaxCount As Integer) As Integer
``` |
	Arguments: hWnd is the window handle, lpClassName is a string buffer that receives the class name, and nMaxCount is the maximum number of characters to copy to lpClassName.
	Returns: The length of the string copied to the buffer, or 0 if the function fails.
GetNextWindow	Returns the next or the previous window in the window manager list.
| | ```
Declare Function GetNextWindow Lib "User"→
    (ByVal hWnd As Integer, ByVal wFlag As→
    Integer) As Integer
``` |
	Arguments: hWnd is the window handle. Set wFlag to 2 to get the handle of the next window in the window manager list, or set it to 3 to get the handle of the previous window.
	Returns: The handle specified by the wFlag argument.
GetParent	Returns the parent window handle.
| | ```
Declare Function GetParent Lib "User" (ByVal→
    hWnd As Integer) As Integer
``` |
	Arguments: hWnd is the window handle.
	Returns: The handle of the parent window, or 0 if the given window doesn't have a parent.
GetTopWindow	Returns a handle for the top-level child of the window.
| | ```
Declare Function GetTopWindow Lib "User"→
    (ByVal hWnd As Integer) As Integer
``` |
```

Function	Description
	Arguments: hWnd is the window handle.
	Returns: The handle of the top-level child of the window, or 0 if there are no child windows.
GetWindow	Returns the handle of the window with the specified relationship to the given window.

```
Declare Function GetWindow Lib "User" (ByVal⇥
    hWnd As Integer, ByVal wCmd As Integer) As⇥
    Integer
```

Arguments: hWnd is the window handle. Set wCmd as follows:

0 for the handle of its first sibling
1 for the handle of its last sibling
2 for the handle of its next sibling
3 for the handle of its previous sibling
4 for the handle of its owner
5 for the handle of its first child

Returns: The window handle specified by the wCmd argument, or 0 if the function fails.

Function	Description
GetWindowLong	Returns a long integer value from extra window memory. You can use this to get window style information.

```
Declare Function GetWindowLong Lib "User"⇥
    (ByVal hWnd As Integer, ByVal nIndex As⇥
    Integer) As Long
```

Arguments: hWnd is the handle of the window. Set nIndex to −16 to get the window style, or set it to −20 to get the extended window style.

Returns: A long integer that depends on the nIndex argument.

Function	Description
GetWindowWord	Returns an integer value from extra window memory. You can use this to get an instance handle.

```
Declare Function GetWindowWord Lib "User"⇥
    (ByVal hWnd As Integer, ByVal nIndex As⇥
    Integer) As Integer
```

Arguments: hWnd is the handle of the window. Set nIndex to −6 to retrieve the instance handle of the application that owns the window. If it's a child window, set nIndex to −8 to get the handle of its parent window; set it to −12 to get its child window ID number.

Returns: An integer that depends on the nIndex argument.

(continued)

135

Function	Description
IsChild	Determines whether a window is a child of a given parent window.

	`Declare Function IsChild Lib "User" (ByVal→`
	`    hWndParent As Integer, ByVal hWnd As→`
	`    Integer) As Integer`

	Arguments: hWndParent is the window handle of the parent window; hWnd is the handle of the window in question.
	Returns: Nonzero if the window is a child of a given parent; 0 otherwise.
IsWindow	Determines whether a window handle is valid.
	`Declare Function IsWindow Lib "User" (ByVal→` `    hWnd As Integer) As Integer`
	Arguments: hWnd is the window handle to check.
	Returns: Nonzero if hWnd is a valid window handle; 0 otherwise.

Figure 6-6. *Window information functions.*

FYI

I SPY

SPY is a handy application that comes with the Windows SDK. It lets you spy on Windows to determine how windows relate to one another and what messages are generated when you move the mouse, click a button, press a key, and so on. When you use SPY, it becomes obvious that Windows (with a capital "W") is a collection of windows (with a lowercase "w"). There's the *application window* in which Access, Excel, or Word runs. Then there's the *detail window* (or *document window*), which contains the individual files you work with (see Figure 6-7). Every window belongs to a particular *class*.

- The Access application window belongs to the class OMain.
- The Excel application window belongs to the class XLMain.
- The Word application window belongs to the class OpusApp.
- The Visual Basic application window (which is invisible) belongs to the class ThunderMain (which I discovered using the SPY application and the GetClassName API function). Application windows for Visual Basic applications that you create yourself belong to the class ThunderForm.

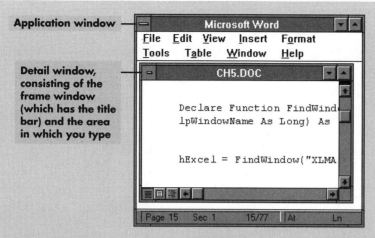

Application window

Detail window, consisting of the frame window (which has the title bar) and the area in which you type

Figure 6-7. *Word's application window and its detail (or document) window.*

Among Microsoft's Office development tools, Excel has the simplest structure: Each workbook, including the workbook's title bar and all of its worksheets, is a single window. (Status bars, scroll bars, toolbars, rulers, dialog boxes, and so on are *always* separate windows.) In Word, each document has (in addition to status bars and the rest) two windows: a *frame window*, which includes the title bar, and a child of the frame window, which is the area in which you type (see Figure 6-7).

Access has a far more complex structure. Each Access table consists of four to seven separate windows (see Figure 6-8 on the following page):

- The table itself is a window. It includes the title bar and contains the other windows. It is, in effect, the parent of the other windows. Its class is OTable.

- The table's grid is a window of the class OGrid. The grid is a child of the table.

- The active (or "editable") cell is a child window of the grid. Its class is OKttbx.

- The navigation buttons (of the class OSUI) are a child of the table.

- Each scroll bar is a separate window of the class Scrollbar (as are scroll bars in most Windows-based applications) and is a child of the table.

- The blank space where the scroll bars meet is a separate window of the class OBlank (true for every Windows-based application that uses Windows scroll bars) and is a child of the table.

When you use API functions to get information about a window, you have to be aware of the relationships among windows to identify the one you want. (See the sidebar titled "Determining Which Document Has the Focus" later in this chapter.)

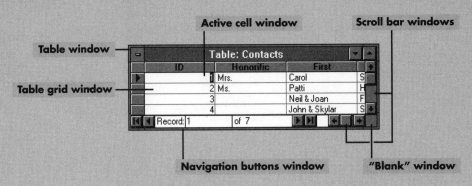

Figure 6-8. *The windows in an Access table.*

Window Input Functions

Window input functions (see Figure 6-9 on the next two pages) provide three broad categories of information:

■ Whether a window is *active* (whether it is the main window in the application that has the focus).

■ Whether a window is *enabled* (whether it can receive mouse or keyboard input). For example, dialog box command buttons might or might not be enabled.

■ Whether a window has the *focus* (whether it is actually receiving mouse or keyboard input). For example, an Access dialog box might have several controls, all of them enabled, but only one has the focus.

The following Access Basic code uses the FindWindow function to determine a handle for Excel's application window. If Excel is running, FindWindow returns a valid (nonzero) handle; the code then calls the SetActiveWindow function to make Excel the active application. If Excel isn't running, the code launches it with the Shell statement.

> **NOTE** If more than one copy of an application is running, the FindWindow function might not find the window you want.

```
Declare Function FindWindow Lib "User" (ByVal lpClassName As Any,→
  ByVal lpWindowName As Any) As Integer
Declare Function SetActiveWindow Lib "User" (ByVal hWnd As→
  Integer) As Integer

Function SwitchToExcel ()
'Excel must be in your path for this to work. This function checks
'to see whether Excel is open. If so, it makes Excel the
'active application. If not, it launches Excel.

'Handle to Excel.
  Dim hExcel As Integer

'Handle to previous active window, returned by SetActiveWindow.
  Dim hPrevActive As Integer

'Instance handle for Excel, returned by the Shell function.
  Dim hinstExcel As Integer

'Call the API function FindWindow to see whether Excel is open.
'XLMain is the class name for Excel's main window. Setting the
'window title argument to ByVal 0& causes the function to search
'by class name only.
  hExcel = FindWindow("XLMain", ByVal 0&)
  If hExcel <> 0 Then

'If Excel is open, call SetActiveWindow to switch to Excel.
    hPrevActive = SetActiveWindow(hExcel)
  Else

'If Excel isn't open, launch it using the Shell statement.
    hinstExcel = Shell("excel.exe", 1)
  End If
End Function
```

Function	Description
EnableWindow	Enables or disables input to a window.

	`Declare Function EnableWindow Lib "User"→`
	`  (ByVal hWnd As Integer, ByVal bEnable→`
	`  As Integer) As Integer`

	Arguments: hWnd is the window handle and bEnable is a Boolean variable. If bEnable = 1, the window is enabled, and if bEnable = 0, the window is disabled.
	Returns: Nonzero if the window was previously disabled; 0 otherwise.

(continued)

Function	Description
GetActiveWindow	Retrieves the handle of the active window.
	``` Declare Function GetActiveWindow Lib→ "User" () As Integer ```
	Arguments: None.
	Returns: The handle of the active window.
GetFocus	Returns the handle of the window with the focus.
	``` Declare Function GetFocus Lib "User" ()→ As Integer ```
	Arguments: None.
	Returns: The handle of the window with the focus.
IsWindowEnabled	Determines whether a window accepts user input.
	``` Declare Function IsWindowEnabled Lib→ "User" (ByVal hWnd As Integer) As Integer ```
	Arguments: hWnd is the window handle.
	Returns: Nonzero if the window is disabled; 0 otherwise.
SetActiveWindow	Makes a top-level window active.
	``` Declare Function SetActiveWindow Lib→ "User" (ByVal hWnd As Integer) As Integer ```
	Arguments: hWnd is the window handle.
	Returns: The handle of the previously active window.

Figure 6-9. *Window input functions.*

Miscellaneous Functions

The following three API functions (see also Figure 6-10 on page 142) contribute to an application's professional look and feel:

- GetFreeSystemResources checks the status of your system resources.

- WinHelp launches a custom Help file.

- GetTickCount tracks elapsed time.

The first Access Basic code example uses the WinHelp function to launch WINHELP.HLP. Although you have to use this function to launch custom Help from Access Basic and Visual Basic, both VBA for Excel and WordBasic include their own commands for launching Help files.

```
Declare Function WinHelp Lib "User" (ByVal hWnd As Integer, ByVal ➔
   lpHelpFile As String, ByVal wCommand As Integer, dwData As Long) ➔
   As Integer

Function OpenWindowsHelp ()
'Opens the Windows Help file if you have it installed
'in your Windows directory.
'Return value of WinHelp function.
   Dim iRet As Integer

'Open the Help file.
   iRet = WinHelp(Forms!APIDEMO.hWnd, "c:\windows\winhelp.hlp", ➔
      HELP_CONTENTS, 0)

'Notify user if action fails.
   If iRet = 0 Then MsgBox "Can't open the Windows Help file."
End Function
```

The following example (written in Access Basic) demonstrates how to use the GetTickCount function to stopwatch code.

```
Declare Function GetTickCount Lib "User" () As Long

Function CountTimer ()
'Computes the number of milliseconds it takes the system to count
'from 1 to 300 and to display the numbers in a text box.
   Dim i As Integer
   Dim lTickCount As Long

   Forms!APIDEMO.txtCount.Visible = True

'GetTickCount gets the milliseconds since Windows started.
   lTickCount = GetTickCount()

'Count from 1 to 300.
   For i = 1 To 300
      Forms!APIDEMO.txtCount = Str$(i)
      Forms!APIDEMO.Repaint
   Next i

'Call GetTickCount again, and then subtract to get the elapsed time.
   lTickCount = GetTickCount() - lTickCount
   MsgBox "Counting from 1 to 300 took " & lTickCount & " ➔
      milliseconds."
   Forms!APIDEMO.txtCount = ""
   Forms!APIDEMO.txtCount.Visible = False
End Function
```

Function	Description
GetFreeSystemResources	Returns the percentage of free system resource space.

	``
	Declare Function GetFreeSystemResources→
	    Lib "User" (ByVal fSysResource As→
	    Integer) As Integer
	``

	Arguments: Set fSysResource to 0 to retrieve system resource information, set it to 1 to retrieve graphics resource information, or set it to 2 to retrieve user resource information.
	Returns: The percentage of free space for resources of the type indicated by the fSysResource argument.
WinHelp	Opens a Windows Help file. You must use this function if you launch a custom help file from a menu command in both Access Basic and Visual Basic.

	``
	Declare Function WinHelp Lib "User"→
	    (ByVal hWnd As Integer, ByVal→
	    lpHelpFile As String, ByVal wCommand→
	    As Integer, dwData As Long) As Integer
	``

	Arguments: hWnd is the handle of the window from which help was requested. lpHelpFile is the filename (and pathname, if necessary) of the desired help file. Set wCommand to 3 and dwData to 0 to display the contents screen of the help file, or set wCommand to 2 and dwData to 0 to tell the help file it's no longer needed. If no other application is using the help file, it is closed.
	Returns: Nonzero if the function is successful; 0 otherwise.
GetTickCount	Returns the number of milliseconds since Windows started.
	``` Declare Function GetTickCount Lib→ "User" () As Long ```
	Arguments: None.
	Returns: The number of milliseconds since Windows started.

Figure 6-10. *Miscellaneous functions.*

SAMPLE APPLICATION: Tracker

Although you can improve most business applications using the Windows API—if only to create INI files to store user preferences and other application-related information—some applications rely on API functions for core processing. The sample Visual Basic application called Tracker (which is in the VB directory on the *Office Solutions* disk) is one example.

Even developers not familiar with Visual Basic who read through the application code shown in this section will see that BASIC isn't the only common macro language currently available: You can think of the Windows API as another one. Tracker's API code can be ported wholesale into Access Basic and VBA for Excel and, with minor modifications to the Declare statements, to WordBasic as well.

Of course, a main feature that *can't* be ported to the other BASICs is the ability to deliver Tracker's functionality with an 11-KB footprint (the size of Tracker's .EXE file). Even if you add the VBRUN300.DLL (which is 400 KB), remember that Excel's .EXE file (to give one example) is more than 4 MB. If you check system resource usage, you'll see that Tracker typically decreases free system resources by 4 percent, while launching Excel decreases them by 13 percent.

PRODUCT SHEET: Tracker

Purpose:	Tracker automatically logs the time spent in every Word document. This makes it easier for high-volume word processing centers to bill clients accurately and quickly.
Development tools used:	Visual Basic Professional Edition version 3; Windows API
How Tracker works:	Tracker stores the amount of time spent in every Word document in a private INI file (which is essentially a structured text file). The file's default name is TF (for "time file") plus the current date (formatted as *mmddyy*) and a text file extension (for example, TF061894.TXT). The time file's default location is the same directory as Tracker itself. You can change both the name and the location.

You can launch Tracker manually after Word is running or automatically whenever you open Word. To launch Tracker automatically, write a Word macro named "AutoExec" and save it in NORMAL.DOT. The code for the macro is a single line that points to Tracker's .EXE file. For example:

```
Shell "c:\offsoln\tracker\tracker.exe"
```

The diagram on the following page shows how Tracker works.

143

How Tracker Works

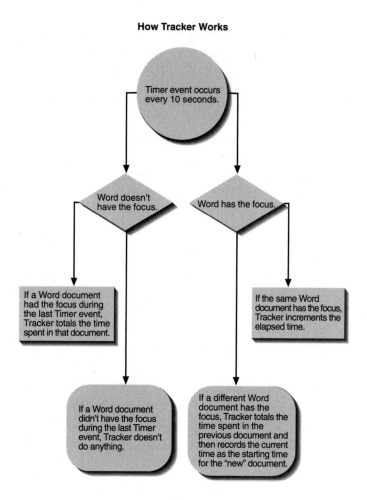

A number of companies that I work with run 24-hour word processing centers (which are quite common in big law firms and investment banks). For the most part, the work done in these centers is billed back to clients through a labor-intensive manual system: Word processors fill in time sheets listing the documents in which they worked and the time spent, and someone else enters these times into a database for billing purposes.

In addition to being redundant, this system is prone to inaccuracy because word processors frequently work in more than one document, shifting between them as questions get answered and more material (such as charts and exhibits) comes in. This makes it hard to record accurately the time spent working in any particular document.

About a year ago, a client asked me to create a system that tracks the time that word processors spend in each document. The goal was to completely automate the billing with a system that directly feeds an Access database.

Tracker is an early version of this system. It runs in the background and checks every 10 seconds to see whether a Word document has the focus. If a Word document has the focus, Tracker logs it in what I call the "time file." If something other than a Word document has the focus, Tracker stops timing and checks until a Word document gets the focus, at which point it starts timing again.

Two key programming techniques make Tracker tick:

- Finding the focus (in other words, determining which window is receiving mouse or keyboard input)

- Accessing private INI files (the time file is an INI file)

Both techniques rely on API functions. Here is Tracker's declarations section, in which I declare the eight API functions used: FindWindow, GetClassName, GetFocus, GetParent, GetWindowText, IsChild, GetPrivateProfileString, and WritePrivateProfileString.

```
'General declarations.
  Option Explicit
  Option Compare Text

'Windows API functions for getting window information.
  Declare Function FindWindow Lib "User" (ByVal lpClassName As Any,→
    ByVal lpWindowName As Any) As Integer
  Declare Function GetClassName Lib "User" (ByVal hWnd As→
    Integer, ByVal lpClassName As String, ByVal nMaxCount As→
    Integer) As Integer
  Declare Function GetFocus Lib "User" () As Integer
  Declare Function GetParent Lib "User" (ByVal hWnd As Integer) As→
    Integer
  Declare Function GetWindowText Lib "User" (ByVal hWnd As Integer,→
    ByVal lpString As String, ByVal aint As Integer) As Integer
  Declare Function IsChild Lib "User" (ByVal hWndParent As Integer,→
    ByVal hWnd As Integer) As Integer

'Windows API functions for writing and reading the INI file.
  Declare Function GetPrivateProfileString Lib "Kernel" (ByVal→
    lpSectionName As String, ByVal lpEntryName As String, ByVal→
    lpDefault As String, ByVal lpReturnedString As String, ByVal→
    nSize As Integer, ByVal lpFileName As String) As Integer
```

(continued)

```
Declare Function WritePrivateProfileString Lib "Kernel" (ByVal⤍
    lpSectionName As String, ByVal lpEntryName As String, ByVal⤍
    lpString As String, ByVal lpFileName As String) As Integer

'Declare variables and constants.
'Name of the last Word document used while the application was
'running.
    Dim sLastDoc As String
'Name of text file logging time information.
    Dim sTimeFileName As String

'Constants for GetPrivateProfileString function.
    Const BUFFER_LENGTH = 255
    Const TIME_STRING_LENGTH = 8

'Error code constant.
    Const ERR_ILLEGAL_CALL = 5
```

Who's Got the Focus?

Tracker logs and calculates time data for the Word document that has the focus—in other words, the document that the word processor is currently processing. The following points provide a general description of how the application tracks the focus. (See the sidebar on the facing page for a detailed look at the code that does this.)

- Tracker first seeks Word's application window by searching for its particular class, OpusApp.

  The following line of code retrieves the window handle for OpusApp:

  ```
  hWndApp = FindWindow("OpusApp", ByVal 0&)
  ```

- If Tracker can't find OpusApp, it knows that Word isn't open and it closes itself down.

- Although several Word documents can be open at any time, only one has the focus. Tracker uses a static string variable called sCurrentDoc to track it.

- Because static variables don't change between procedure calls, Tracker "remembers" the last document in which word processors worked. When they start work in a different document, Tracker totals the time spent in the previous document; either finds the section in the time file for the new document or creates one; and then starts timing.

■ Because Word documents are made up of several windows, the key to tracking them is determining which document is being edited. The class of the Word document currently being edited (the document that has the focus) is OpusWwd. An OpusWwd window is always the child of a frame window (which has the title bar and the class OpusMwd).

■ Word processors might not be working in Word at all. If they're not in Word, Tracker totals the time spent in sCurrentDoc and then stops timing.

FYI

Determining Which Document Has the Focus

Take the following steps (illustrated here with code samples from Tracker's tmrCheckFocus_Timer subroutine) to determine which document has the focus:

1. Get the class name of the window with the focus:

```
'Check whether the focus is in a Word child window.
'hWndApp is the handle for Word; hWndFocus is the handle of the
'window with the focus.
'If the focus is in a Word child window...
    If IsChild(hWndApp, hWndFocus) <> 0 Then

'...get the class name of that window.
        iRet = GetClassName(hWndFocus, sStringBuffer,➔
        BUFFER_LENGTH)
    sClassName = Left$(sStringBuffer, iRet)
```

2. If the class name is OpusWwd, get the handle of its parent window:

```
'If the focus is in an editable Word child window, get the name
'of the document.
    If sClassName = "OpusWwd" Then
        hAppDoc = GetParent(hWndFocus)
```

3. Get the window text from the frame window's title bar:

```
        iRet = GetWindowText(hAppDoc, sStringBuffer,➔
        BUFFER_LENGTH)
        sWinTitle = Left$(sStringBuffer, iRet)
```

4. The window text (which contains the document's name) can also include the full pathname. Eliminate any pathname information using Tracker's ExtractFileName procedure:

```
        sWinTitle = Extract(sWinTitle, 1)
```

The Timer Procedure

Tracker's main procedure, the Timer procedure, determines which document has the focus. The Timer control runs this procedure every 10 seconds.

```
Sub tmrCheckFocus_Timer ()
'Name of the Word document currently in use.
   Static sCurrentDoc As String

'Window handle for Word.
   Dim hWndApp As Integer

'Handle for the window with the focus.
   Dim hWndFocus As Integer

'Handle for the Word document in use.
   Dim hAppDoc As Integer

'Generic placeholder for values returned by Windows API functions.
   Dim iRet As Integer

'Buffer to hold strings retrieved by Windows API functions.
   Dim sStringBuffer As String * BUFFER_LENGTH

'Class name of the window with the focus.
   Dim sClassName As String

'Title of the Word document with the focus.
   Dim sWinTitle As String

'Compute/record elapsed time for the document currently
'in use by calling the ComputeElapsedTime subroutine.
   ComputeElapsedTime (sCurrentDoc)

'Use FindWindow to see whether Word is open.
'OpusApp is the class name for Word's main window; replace
'this with XLMain or OMain to track Excel or Access usage.
'If Word isn't open, terminate Tracker.
   hWndApp = FindWindow("OpusApp", ByVal 0&)
   If hWndApp = 0 Then
     tmrCheckFocus.Enabled = False
     Unload Me
     Exit Sub
   End If

'Get the handle of the window with the focus.
   hWndFocus = GetFocus()
```

```
'If GetFocus is successful
  If hWndFocus <> 0 Then

'Check whether the focus is in a Word child window.
'hWndApp is the handle for Word; hWndFocus is the handle of the
'window with the focus. If the focus is in a Word child window...
    If IsChild(hWndApp, hWndFocus) <> 0 Then

'...get the class name of that window.
      iRet = GetClassName(hWndFocus, sStringBuffer, BUFFER_LENGTH)
      sClassName = Left$(sStringBuffer, iRet)

'If the focus is in an editable Word child window, get the name
'of the document.
      If sClassName = "OpusWwd" Then
        hAppDoc = GetParent(hWndFocus)
        iRet = GetWindowText(hAppDoc, sStringBuffer, BUFFER_LENGTH)
        sWinTitle = Left$(sStringBuffer, iRet)
        sWinTitle = Extract(sWinTitle, 1)

'If the new document is different, stop timing the previous
'document and start timing the new one.
        If sWinTitle <> sCurrentDoc Then

'The StopTime function computes the elapsed time for the
'current work session and adds it to the total time for
'sCurrentDoc. It records this time in the time file and
'clears the start time and elapsed time for sCurrentDoc.
          StopTime sCurrentDoc

'Enters the current time as the StartTime for the new document.
          WriteToTimeFile sWinTitle, "StartTime", Time$

'Record the name of the new document in the global variable
'sLastDoc and in the local variable sCurrentDoc.
          sLastDoc = sWinTitle
          sCurrentDoc = sWinTitle
        End If
      End If

'If focus isn't in a Word child, no document is current.
'Stop timing sCurrentDoc and clear it.
    Else
      StopTime sCurrentDoc
      sCurrentDoc = ""
    End If
  End If
End Sub
```

FYI

Is Anybody There?

When I first started thinking about the Tracker application, I wanted to be able to determine whether word processors were hard at work or out to lunch—by checking for keyboard and mouse activity. Unfortunately, the API functions that do this require callbacks, which Visual Basic can't handle. This left three options:

- Write the application in C/C++.

- Write a custom DLL to determine whether there was keyboard and mouse activity. (Generally, DLLs are written in C/C++.)

- Use a screen saver; when the screen saver comes on, Word loses the focus.

The version of Tracker in this chapter uses the third option. If you're concerned about whether the Windows screen saver is indeed on, write a Visual Basic procedure to check and then to turn it on if necessary.

The INI Log

Every 10 seconds, Tracker checks which Windows-based application has the focus and, if it's Word, Tracker logs that document in a private INI file. Because INI files are structured by sections ([]) and entries (=), you can access data easily at any point in the file. Tracker's INI files (or time files) have the following structure:

```
[WORD DOCUMENT NAME]
StartTime=
ElapsedTime=
TotalTime=
```

Here's a sample time file produced by Tracker:

```
[CHAPTER.DOC]
StartTime=
ElapsedTime=
TotalTime=00:49:32

[MISC.DOC]
StartTime=
ElapsedTime=
TotalTime=00:03:21
```

```
[Document2]
StartTime=
ElapsedTime=
TotalTime=00:00:40
```

When Tracker determines that a Word document has the focus, it either recomputes the elapsed time for the most recently used document or sets the StartTime for the document in which word processors have just started (or restarted) work.

Recomputing elapsed time

When Tracker updates the time spent in the Word document currently in use, it uses the WriteToTimeFile procedure. After computing the elapsed time (current time less the StartTime recorded in the INI file), Tracker writes it to the INI file's ElapsedTime entry. The code for WriteToTimeFile follows:

```
Sub WriteToTimeFile (ByVal sDocName As String, ByVal sEntryName As ↴
   String, ByVal sEntryValue As String)
'Return value of WritePrivateProfileString.
   Dim iRet As Integer

'String for message box warning.
   Dim sMsg As String

'Flag to indicate whether this is the first write operation to INI.
   Static fNewTimeFile As Integer

'Constant for MsgBox function.
   Const MB_ICONEXCLAMATION = 48

'Constant for SetAttr function.
   Const ATTR_HIDDEN = 2

'Calls API function to write string.
   iRet = WritePrivateProfileString(sDocName, sEntryName, ↴
      sEntryValue, sTimeFileName)

'If there's a problem writing to INI file, alert user.
   If iRet = 0 Then
      sMsg = "Couldn't write value for " & sEntryName
      sMsg = sMsg & " in the file " & sTimeFileName & ". "
      sMsg = sMsg & "If the file is open, you should close it."
      MsgBox sMsg, MB_ICONEXCLAMATION, "Time File Unavailable"
```

(continued)

```
'If this is the first write operation (i.e., the creation
'of a new time file), set the hidden attribute.
  ElseIf fNewTimeFile = 0 Then
    SetAttr sTimeFileName, ATTR_HIDDEN
    fNewTimeFile = 1
  End If
End Sub
```

NOTE Not surprisingly, Tracker can't write to an open time file. To prevent time files from being opened, I set the hidden attribute, which is cleared in the Unload procedure when the application closes.

Handling the start time

When Tracker first logs a Word document as the one currently in use, it records the StartTime in the form *hh:mm:ss*. The code for this is located toward the end of the Timer procedure:

```
'Enters the current time as the StartTime for the new document.
  WriteToTimeFile sWinTitle, "StartTime", Time$
```

Tracker also stops timing any document it was tracking and calls the StopTime procedure. After computing ElapsedTime and adding it to TotalTime, the StopTime procedure sets the StartTime and ElapsedTime entries in the INI file to empty strings.

When the Windows API Alone Isn't Enough

Although the Windows API can extend the capabilities of the Microsoft BASICs considerably, it has limitations. As mentioned earlier, the BASICs can't take advantage of some API functions (for example, those requiring callbacks); and, indeed, you can't expect standard APIs to provide functions tailor-made to your business needs. You can circumvent these limitations by writing custom DLLs.

The DLL Solution

DLLs come in several flavors, including:

■ DLL (which any application can use)

■ XLL (which only Excel can use)

■ WLL (which only Word can use)

XLLs and WLLs are specialized DLLs that you can "add in" to Excel and Word. These add-in libraries have four advantages over general DLLs:

- They provide menus, menu items, toolbars, and so on, from which you can access the library's functions—which eliminates the need to write macros to call these functions.

- Not only can XLLs and WLLs add functions to Excel and Word, but they can also execute commands from VBA for Excel or WordBasic directly, eliminating the need for macros.

- Because XLLs and WLLs eliminate the need for macros (which run relatively slowly), they speed up your business applications.

- Because XLLs and WLLs stay in memory until you specifically unload them (or exit Excel or Word), you don't have to call them repeatedly to use them repeatedly. This also speeds up processing.

The difficulty with DLLs is that you have to use a low-level programming language such as C/C++ to create them. Nonetheless, if you need the speed and the extra capabilities that these tools provide, a DLL is the only solution. I have used custom DLLs in several circumstances:

- To test for mouse and keyboard activity

- To rotate graphics and text in Word

- To create a Word dialog box featuring a text box with a vertical scroll bar

The next section illustrates the last instance mentioned: use of a custom DLL to create a Word dialog box featuring a text box with a vertical scroll bar—a control that, for some reason, Word itself doesn't provide.

For C Programmers Only

Companies that build WordBasic applications to provide online entry for business forms or to enter descriptive text into a database generally need an interface that streamlines handling of multiple paragraphs of text. Unfortunately, this is one of WordBasic's chronic weak spots. The first two versions of WordBasic didn't support multiline text boxes. Although Word version 6 supports multiline text boxes, it doesn't add a vertical scroll bar to alert people to the fact that the text boxes *are* multiline text boxes.

I know of two successful solutions to this problem:

■ Use a Visual Basic dialog box with a multiline text box and a vertical scroll bar, and control that dialog box using Dynamic Data Exchange (DDE). (See Chapter 12 for information on using DDE from Word.)

■ Use a DLL or a WLL.

I have provided a sample DLL and a sample WLL (plus source code) on the *Office Solutions* disk. Both files have a single function (MLTBDlgBoxDLL and MLTBDlgBox, respectively) that creates a multiline text box with a vertical scroll bar for Word (see Figure 6-11). Although the DLL and the WLL do the same thing, they do it in different ways, providing an object lesson in the differences between general DLLs and application-specific DLLs (such as XLLs or WLLs).

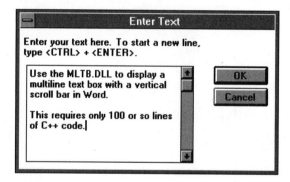

Figure 6-11. *To use this text box, call the MLTBDlgBoxDLL function in MLTB-D.DLL or add MLTB.WLL. Both are in the API directory on the* Office Solutions *disk, as is the C source code.*

Using MLTB-D.DLL
To use the DLL, follow these steps:

1. Copy the file MLTB-D.DLL into your WINDOWS\SYSTEM directory.

2. Write a WordBasic macro (such as the one shown on page 156) that calls the DLL function MLTBDlgBoxDLL and inserts the string from the text box into your document. The MLTBDlgBoxDLL function requires two arguments:

■ TextHolder—a string variable to hold the contents of the text box

■ HolderLength—the length of TextHolder

The function returns an integer for the actual length of the text that users type in the text box.

FYI

Got the Message?

When I first toyed with the idea of creating a multiline text box with a vertical scroll bar in Word, I expected that I could do it using the Windows API. My spirits rose when I discovered the DialogBox function, which displays a modal dialog box. My spirits fell when I discovered that it requires a callback function.

Then I found the CreateWindow function. This was very promising. It displays a text box that you can type in and scroll through, but *I couldn't get the text into Word.* Eventually, I had to admit that this makes sense. The function doesn't return users' responses (what they typed or what they clicked). It simply returns the handle of the window that it creates.

Still feeling optimistic, I created a dialog box using Word's dialog editor and then called the CreateWindow function to draw the multiline text box with a vertical scroll bar. The dialog box appeared, but as soon as I clicked the text box, I got a General Protection Fault. So I gave up.

I finally realized that the real problem wasn't scroll bars, but messages: Windows operates on messages. For example, in the space of four or five seconds, I generated 415 messages simply by waving my mouse around the screen and typing the word "testing." (I used SPY to capture these messages; see the sidebar titled "I SPY" earlier in this chapter.) Although the most obvious messages are those generated by keyboard and mouse input, there are thousands of others, covering every aspect of Windows functionality.

Because messages are central to Windows, every window needs a way to respond to them. This is why the API's DialogBox function requires a callback function—to handle messages. When you create a dialog box using Excel's dialog sheets, Word's dialog editor, or an Access Basic or a Visual Basic form, the message handling is done for you. You write the code to respond to various events, but the message handling happens automatically.

When you create a window using API functions, however, you must write code to handle the messages. This creates a catch-22 situation because even though you must write this code, you can't—at least not with the Microsoft BASICs. You have to move to a lower-level programming language such as C/C++. This means that if you want to display a multiline text box with a vertical scroll bar in Word, you have to write a DLL or a WLL (or settle for DDE).

The following macro is in Solution.DOT on the *Office Solutions* disk:

```
'MLTB-D.DLL must be in your WINDOWS\SYSTEM directory.
Declare Function MLTBDlgBoxDLL Lib "MLTB-D.DLL"(TextHolder As→
   String, HolderLength As Integer) As Integer

Sub MAIN
'Limits length of string returned by MLTB to 1000 characters.
   YourText$ = String$(1000, 0)
   iLen = MLTBDlgBoxDLL(YourText$, 1000)
   If iLen <> 0 Then
     YourText$ = Left$(YourText$, iLen)
     Insert YourText$
   End If
End Sub
```

Using MLTB.WLL

To use the WLL, follow these steps:

1. Copy MLTB.WLL into your Word template directory.

2. Choose Templates from the File menu, and then click the Add button. Select MLTB.WLL from the list.

3. Although you must use a WordBasic macro to run the DLL, the WLL runs itself—simply choose the Enter Text command from the Edit menu. (The WLL added this menu item.)

Although it's not necessary, you can call the WLL's MLTBDlgBox function from a WordBasic macro (such as the one shown below) the same way you call other DLL functions. This macro doesn't require arguments or a return value because the WLL itself inserts text from the text box automatically when users click the OK button.

The following macro (which duplicates the functionality of the previous macro) is in Solution.DOT on the *Office Solutions* disk:

```
Declare Sub MLTBDlgBox Lib "MLTB.WLL"()

Sub MAIN
  MLTBDlgBox
End Sub
```

CASE STUDY: More than a PIF—
Reengineering an Application for Windows

FactSet, a data vendor that provides real-time and historical financial data, had trouble with its user interface: Although FactSet is known for being able to do nearly anything with data, it wasn't able to do it in Windows dialog boxes. It's now finishing up a yearlong project that promises to change that...sort of.

FactSet has developed a Windows emulator and its own API to provide data at clients' desktops—directly from the remote FactSet VAX. The emulator provides the Windows look and feel, and the API enables clients to build, among other things, their own front ends to FactSet data.

The Nature of the Beast

FactSet started out nearly 20 years ago with a single hard-copy product called "the company fact set"—an overview of a company's financial position. Today, FactSet is an online service that lets clients (primarily investment analysts and portfolio managers) use more than 60 gigabytes of domestic and international financial data stored on a VAX mainframe. It also lets clients add private databases to the VAX so that they can integrate FactSet's standard data with their own, analyze it, and report on it as if it came from the same source.

Although FactSet has developed hundreds of products that let clients use data in various ways, most clients perform four tasks:

- They use FactSet data to generate custom reports in a spreadsheet.

- They generate standard FactSet reports (of which there are hundreds).

- They use FactSet to chart data.

- They screen the FactSet databases to come up with a list of securities that meet certain criteria.

Unfortunately, clients have had to access these products and services through a DEC terminal emulator and a modem—a relatively slow, nonintuitive, and expensive process. A year ago, FactSet started a project to fix this problem by developing a Windows interface and adding wide-area-network (WAN) access.

GUI on a VAX?

Although FactSet has wowed the market with its number-crunching capabilities, its products generally have a steep learning curve. Mike Oeth, who heads FactSet's new Windows Technology Group, described how steep.

> Right now, it's not unusual for us to spend three to six hours on the phone explaining how to do some of the sophisticated calculations and reporting that our clients need. People have to *learn* how to use FactSet, but they don't have time to learn it. FactSet isn't their whole job. Their job is to manage money or value companies, and FactSet is just one of the tools they use to do that.

Although FactSet's goal had been to provide clients with the point-and-click access that has become synonymous with "ease of use," it hasn't been easy: FactSet's applications include several million lines of code that run on a VAX, not on a PC. Upon analysis, FactSet felt it had two choices:

- Preserve the architecture of the distributed system in which the logic and functionality reside on the VAX.

- Build a true client-server system in which the logic resides on the PC and the VAX becomes a data server.

FactSet decided to do both—or, I should say, to *try* both—and let the best solution win.

Even Client-Servers Get the Blues

There's no doubt that you can build a better interface in Windows than you can on a VAX, and this fact was the strongest argument for trying the client-server solution. The problem that FactSet wrestled with was how to access 60 gigabytes of remote data seamlessly using a local PC interface. (FactSet's most viable competitors surrendered this point long ago and simply put everything at the client site; the farthest that data gets from the PC is a LAN server.)

Of course, you can't put 60 gigabytes of data at a client's site, so these competitors essentially bargained with the devil and traded data for a slick interface. They got color, fonts, bitmaps, drag and drop, and so on, at the cost of having a relatively small data set.

FactSet decided not to make that deal. Instead, it designed a system that included a Visual C++ front end that uses the "FactSet API" to retrieve data from the VAX. However, the deeper they got into this project, the more reasons they found to stay with the current architecture. The problems fell into three broad categories:

- Constraints imposed by the PC as a development tool

- A lower-than-expected level of performance from the PC product

- The unacceptable fact that they would be forced to abandon their "continuous upgrade" policy in favor of scheduled releases

FactSet has thrived on its continuous upgrade policy. Because its applications run on a VAX, FactSet can compile three new versions of an application in a single day, with minor tweaks that affect only one or two clients. Or a client might call and ask FactSet to add a particular calculation, such as a harmonic mean, to one of the standard reports. During the past six or seven years, FactSet has developed 1006 versions of one of its most popular applications.

This continuous upgrade policy is at the heart of a virtuous circle: FactSet has a set of applications that incorporates literally thousands of user requests and a product that no one can duplicate—and the clients know it. Clients know that an engineer sat down for however long it took—a day or two—to program a new feature that they asked for.

FactSet explored various technologies that might provide a similar capability on the PC, but came up empty-handed. As Bill Faulkner, director of product development, said, "We didn't want to tell our clients, 'We'll make a note of your request, and we'll try to get it into the next release.' That's not how we work here, and it's not the way we want to work. We succeed because we can wow people."

Back to the VAX

Now that everyone at FactSet understands the PC development environment better than before, they feel better about the decision to stay on the VAX. They overhauled their Windows-based terminal emulator to look and feel much more like a standard Windows-based application.

Here's how it works: Clients dial in to FactSet (or log on through the WAN). The application logic, which is on the VAX, sends a series of commands to the Windows emulator (FDSW.EXE) running on the user's PC. The Windows emulator uses these commands to build the appropriate dialog box. When users click a button in that dialog box or press a key, that event is passed along to the VAX and the application provides a real-time response.

For example, FactSet handles list boxes by imaging the list box with the first 20 or so elements to the Windows emulator on the PC. When users click the scroll bar, the system passes that event along to the VAX, and the VAX application images the next 20 elements. In spite of the fact that the system is handling massive amounts of data—such as 40,000-element lists—the distance is virtually transparent to users.

The main thing that FactSet loses with the new Windows emulator is the ability to take advantage of all the graphical controls available to PC applications: FactSet is limited to emulating only those controls that it programmed. Mike DiChristina, director of engineering, summed up the efforts.

The engineer who was in charge did a decent subset of Windows widgets, so we can use list boxes, radio buttons, edit boxes, and so on. But can we do tabbed dialog boxes? No. Color? No. Different fonts? No. Of course, we can program all these things eventually, but it's something that our competitors get free.

On the other hand, they can't do a 40,000-element list.

The FactSet API: Intermediary Between the VAX and Excel

The most important side benefit of FactSet's attempt to design a client-server system is an API: FDSAPI.DLL (written in C++). This API (which is platform-independent and runs on Windows, MS-DOS, SUN Workstations, and the Mac) communicates directly with an interpreter on the VAX (also written in C++). It has two important features:

■ It lets the VAX communicate with Windows-based applications (such as Excel).

■ It lets clients build their own PC-based front ends.

Company Look-Up, which lets Excel access FactSet data, is one of the first applications that FactSet released using the new Windows emulator, the API, and an XLL (FDS.XLL). Here's how it works. Let's say you're in Excel and you want to get a standard FactSet report on a company, such as Microsoft. You click a button (provided by the XLL) to open the Company Look-Up application; you select Microsoft's ticker; and then FactSet populates your sheet with the report.

Or let's say you want to get specific financial data and you know the code. Simply type that code into a cell, and then press Enter to retrieve the data. Because it all happens real-time, you don't realize that the API sends your request to the VAX, which then sends the data to the API, which then DDEs it into your sheet.

Even though FactSet decided not to go the client-server route, the API gives users the opportunity to head in that direction. FactSet's clients can use such tools as Visual C++, Visual Basic, PowerBuilder, and Excel to build their own front ends, their own automated reports, their own analyses, and so on. To a large extent, the API gives FactSet the best of both worlds—powerful VAX applications for data retrieval and number crunching, and custom PC-based applications for anyone who wants them.

Making Things Local on the WAN

With the wide area network, FactSet is no more remote than a network server. In the old days—because it took a minute or so to dial in—people didn't log onto FactSet to follow through on a broker's hot tip. But now, because of FactSet's wide area network, users can click the FactSet icon and instantly pull up a dossier on any given security. And because clients pay a fixed monthly fee for the WAN, they can stay on as long as they like. It's not surprising that people are now using FactSet as an interactive tool rather than as a remote "batch research" service.

It will take a while to convert all clients to the WAN, but FactSet already sees the difference it makes: One client has about 15 users whose collective average use was previously about 33 hours per month. Since they hooked up to the WAN, *each* of the 15 people uses FactSet about 33 hours per month.

Ease of use isn't all in the GUI.

TWO

The Integrated Office

An IS professional at Bankers Trust (BT) told me how his organization came to realize the importance of the integrated desktop. In 1989, they finished a state-of-the-art system for the BT trading floor called BIDDS, the Broadgate Information Distribution & Display System. It was the first of its kind—a major client-server application delivering external market data and trading-floor data real-time to traders. BT implemented it first in London and delivered it to desktops on VAX workstations. The application worked perfectly. The traders loved it. They could do everything they always wanted to do. And they all put PCs on their desks, right next to their VAXs.

In 1989, *this* was an integrated desktop.

The problem (other than the obvious problem that the actual desktops weren't built to accommodate both a VAX workstation and a PC) was that no matter how powerful their VAXs were, none of the traders had one at home. They had PCs at home. And what they wanted was to bring home their favorite Lotus 1-2-3 spreadsheets—sheets they didn't have on their VAXs.

As Stanley Rose, a vice president at Bankers Trust, put it, "That was when we decided that we had to start with a standard, integrated desktop. Since it's much easier to build an interface from a PC into anything than to build an emulated PC environment from other desktops, the PC became that standard."

Part 2 of this book illustrates how to use Microsoft Office to turn the standard PC desktop into a custom business tool. My purpose isn't to teach, step-by-step, how to write Access Basic, VBA for Excel, or WordBasic code, but rather to demonstrate how to use these languages to develop applications and utilities. To do this, I organize "how to" information around actual applications and utilities that I've been involved in building or that my colleagues have built. I use these sample applications and utilities to highlight the following:

- "Bulletproofing" and professionalizing applications
- Methods for organizing code into libraries

- Vehicles for delivering applications, including templates and add-ins

- Ways to structure applications

- Essential coding techniques

- Development features introduced with the latest release of Office, including Microsoft Word's document variables and dynamic dialog boxes; the ability to create add-ins for Microsoft Excel; and Microsoft Access wizards and builders

I comment the code heavily so that less experienced developers can learn from it. I have tried to follow the best programming practices throughout, but every day I discover better practices, and no doubt I could improve on some of the code—and I will. Or you will.

Here's a brief description of the chapters in Part 2:

Chapter 7 provides an overview of how to structure Office-based business applications so that they look and feel like commercial Windows-based products rather than a bunch of macros.

Chapters 8 through 10 take an up close look at a variety of business applications and utilities built with each of the Office development tools: Access, Excel, and Word. These chapters feature a grab bag of sample applications, utilities, and techniques for developing robust business applications.

Chapters 11 and 12 demonstrate how to use OLE and DDE to develop business applications that use multiple Office products.

7

Turning Office Products into Custom Business Applications

Many companies don't use off-the-shelf software straight off the shelf. As Miriam Anderson, who administers the LAN in Donaldson, Lufkin & Jenrette's investment banking group, put it, "We customize everything. We have to. We need more than vanilla word processors and spreadsheets—we need specialized tools that make it easier for people to get particular jobs done."

Traditionally, business tools and applications have been delivered in the form of stand-alone executables, as Visual Basic applications are. However, applications created with Microsoft Office development tools don't have executables. Instead, they're packaged in various "containers" associated with the shrink-wrapped product:

- Access databases
- Access add-ins
- Excel workbooks
- Excel templates
- Excel add-ins
- Word templates
- Some combination of the above, plus DLLs, XLLs, or WLLs

Applications built with end-user development tools differ in form from those built with more traditional tools, but the two have a common purpose: to simplify tasks through automation. This chapter covers the following issues that affect your success in achieving this goal.

- Developing for different PC configurations

- Launching Office-based applications

- Using templates

- Securing Office-based applications

- Following good housekeeping practices

- Installing Office-based applications

- Making Office-based applications easy to maintain

- Planning for upgrades

Developing for Different PC Configurations

The conventional wisdom about PC configuration is that developers should test applications on the full range of hardware available in a company, but I've never seen this done: Development deadlines are too tight and testing requires too much legwork. The "minimum-alist" approach, as I call it, is often more feasible (see Figure 7-1). By following this approach, you can develop applications that run on the minimum standard configurations mandated by many companies using Office—and thereby ensure that your applications work well without further customization.

Configuration	Guidelines
Colors	Use only the 16 colors available for standard VGA.
Disk space	Check disk space before installing the application on a local drive.
Fonts	Use MS Sans Serif in dialog boxes. (See the section titled "Handling Text in GUIs" in Chapter 4 for more information on standard font usage.)
	Use standard TrueType fonts, or use the Normal style in Excel and Word.
	For publishing applications that require special fonts, write routines that check for those fonts and display clear messages when they're not found.
Monitors	If any user of your applications uses a VGA monitor, design for VGA.
RAM	Memory problems can usually be solved by closing applications, but this isn't necessarily an option when you create business applications that use OLE automation or DDE. In such cases, you should test applications extensively on the minimum configuration, whether it's 4 MB, 8 MB, or 16 MB.

Figure 7-1. *Developing for the minimum standard configuration.*

FYI

What Do You *Mean,* You Don't Use an 8514/a (Small Fonts) Display?

The lower the resolution, the less information that fits on screen. For example, a spreadsheet that displays 40 rows and 8 columns in Super VGA (SVGA) mode (800 by 600 pixels, or 1024 by 768 pixels) might display only 30 rows and 6 columns in VGA mode (640 by 480 pixels). A common mistake is to build applications (and dialog boxes) in SVGA and then "discover" that they don't fit in VGA.

Even if your company has standardized on SVGA, some people (like me) often use VGA because they find the larger display easier to read. If you design for VGA, your applications will always fit on higher resolution displays. On the other hand, don't hard-code maximization into your designed-for-VGA applications. (See the section titled "Following Good Housekeeping Practices" later in this chapter.) Not only is this generally considered poor programming practice (although it's sometimes hard to avoid), but maximized applications that look fine in VGA often look lopsided in SVGA mode (or higher). This is because the size difference between the two resolutions results in blank space along the right side of maximized windows at higher resolutions.

In cases in which higher resolutions display more data, let windows grow as large as users want. If screen dimensions are important to the application, use the Windows API function GetSystemMetrics with the SM_CXSCREEN and SM_CYSCREEN constants (which equal 0 and 1, respectively) to obtain the screen size, and then size windows accordingly. The following code returns the current display resolution:

```
Declare Function GetSystemMetrics Lib "User" (ByVal nIndex As↴
   Integer) As Integer

Sub ScreenSize()
'Constant for horizontal display = 0.
'Constant for vertical display = 1.

  Dim x As Integer
  Dim y As Integer

  x = GetSystemMetrics(0)
  y = GetSystemMetrics(1)
  MsgBox "The resolution is" & Str$(x) & " x" & Str$(y) & "."
End Sub
```

Certain resolutions, such as 8514/a (small fonts) and 1280 by 1024 displays, change not only the amount of information that fits on screen but also the proportions of the screen. Because of this, bitmaps that look fine in VGA or SVGA (which have the same proportions) look distorted on an 8514/a (small fonts) display or on a 1280 by 1024 display. To avoid this problem in applications that include graphics, use Microsoft's Multiple-Resolution Bitmap Compiler (MRBC.EXE), which comes with Visual C++, the professional edition of Visual Basic, and WHAT6 (see Appendix A).

Launching Office-Based Applications

Arguably, the easiest way to launch business applications is in the usual Microsoft Windows manner: by double-clicking an icon in Program Manager. But with template-based applications built with end-user development tools such as Microsoft Excel and Microsoft Word, it sometimes makes more sense to launch them using the New command or the Open command on the File menu. Some companies add business applications and custom utilities to startup directories so that they launch automatically when users run Excel or Word. (See Chapters 8 and 9 for more information on creating Word-based and Excel-based applications, respectively.)

Attaching Program Manager Icons to Office-Based Applications

You can launch .MDB (Access) files, .XL* (Excel) files, and .DOC (Word) files directly from icons in Program Manager. To do this, follow these steps:

1. Locate the file in File Manager.

2. Use Ctrl+Esc to open the Task List, and then tile the open Windows applications.

3. Arrange File Manager and Program Manager so that you can click the file you want to turn into an icon and drag it into a Program Manager group, and then do so. The file uses the icon associated with its host application (for example, Microsoft Access).

4. To change the icon, click it once, and then choose Properties from the File menu. Use the Change Icon button to browse through your files until you find the icon you want. (See the sidebar titled "Ready-Made Icons" in Chapter 4 for information on icons that ship with Windows.)

To set up an icon for an Access-based or Excel-based business application, this is all you need to know. But if you're launching an application from a Word template, there's a wrinkle. Unlike Excel, Word opens the actual template, not a new document based on the template. To circumvent this problem, open a *dummy* template when users double-click the application icon in Program Manager. The purpose of the dummy is to run an AutoOpen macro that creates a new document based on the actual Word template for the business application.

Using Templates

Templates are essentially models—for example, sheets on which you model other sheets and documents on which you model other documents. Templates make it easy to create documents, charts, and even Excel dialog boxes—with standard formatting and functions.

To create an Excel template or a Word template, you must do the following:

1. Save the file as a template. (Use the Save File As Type option in the Save As dialog box.)

2. Use a specific filename extension (.XLT for Excel or .DOT for Word).

3. Store the template in a specific directory (for example, XLSTART for Excel or TEMPLATE for Word).

> **NOTE** You can access templates in directories other than the Word template directory by typing the full pathname.

Both Excel and Word templates can include standard text, formatting, and macros—all the things that let you perform a specific task more easily.

Excel Templates

Excel uses two categories of templates: those designed for specific tasks; and *autotemplates*, which have specific filenames and are stored in the XLSTART directory (or in an alternate startup directory). Use Excel's autotemplates to customize new workbooks, inserted sheets, and inserted dialog boxes. For example, companies sometimes add the file's name to the header or footer in the workbook autotemplate so that they can track files more easily.

Excel recognizes the following autotemplate names:

- BOOK.XLT (for workbooks)
- CHART.XLT (for charts)
- DIALOG.XLT (for dialog boxes)
- MACRO.XLT (for Excel version 4 macro sheets)
- SHEET.XLT (for worksheets)

When you store templates for Excel applications or an autotemplate for a workbook in the XLSTART directory (or in an alternate startup directory), Excel lists these templates in the New dialog box (see Figure 7-2). When you store other autotemplates in a startup directory, Excel uses them automatically whenever you insert a chart sheet or a dialog sheet into your workbook.

Figure 7-2. *Excel's New dialog box lists the workbook autotemplate plus application-specific templates stored in the XLSTART directory (or in an alternate startup directory). If you don't have templates stored in a startup directory, Excel doesn't display a dialog box when you choose New from the File menu.*

Word Templates: The Only Way to Develop Word Applications

To develop business applications in Word, you must use templates. Although you can store macros in Excel workbooks (and can therefore create applications in workbooks), you can store Word macros only in templates. Documents based on a given template automatically use that template's styles, macros, and AutoText entries. Even "document-based" business applications (in which users modify existing documents rather than create new ones) require that documents be attached to templates that provide, in essence, the application's engine.

A Word template can include any of the following elements:

- AutoText entries
- Bookmarks
- Macros
- Menus
- Menu items
- Shortcut keys
- Styles

- Text and other Word elements (including sections, headers and footers, and frames)

- Toolbars

Macros stored in Word's global templates are available to all Word documents. Word automatically uses NORMAL.DOT as a global template, but you can mark other templates as global by storing them in the Word startup directory or by loading them through the Templates command on the File menu. (See the section titled "How Word-IBK Works" in Chapter 8 for more information on how Word's global templates can fit into an application development strategy.)

Access Templates

In Access, templates have a reduced role. While Excel and Word use templates to store the code and dialog boxes that form an application and to create new files that use a template's specific formatting and functions, Access templates contain only formatting for forms and reports.

Securing Office-Based Applications

Generally, you can implement two levels of security in business applications: *access control* and *integrity control*.

- Access control limits user access to data (for example, giving everyone in an accounting department access to nonsensitive personnel records while granting payroll-record access to only select managers).

- Integrity control prevents accidental damage to the application (preventing users from changing or deleting key elements) and to the code (making it tamperproof).

FYI

How Secure Is Secure?

When companies downsize from mainframe applications to those built with Office products, they tend to be concerned about security issues, particularly the following:

- How secure are PCs and LANs compared to mainframes?

- How bulletproof are Office-based applications compared to those compiled in Fortran and C/C++?

The best answer I've ever heard to the first question was when someone followed up the usual "not as secure" with the observation that people have actually *walked off with servers* (remember, I live in New York City)—which is not something you worry about with mainframes (even in New York). The honest answer to the second question is "It depends." If you compare Access-based applications to compiled applications, the answer is "very bulletproof"; in the case of Excel-based applications, it's "quite bulletproof"; and in the case of Word-based applications, it's "not so bulletproof." (See the section titled "Insecurity" later in this chapter.) Note that virtually all passwords can be hacked if people are determined to hack them.

Security

Security in Access (which I describe in the section titled "Securing Your Data" in Chapter 10) is far more powerful—and proportionately more complex—than security in either Excel or Word. Although Excel provides greater integrity control than Word does, implementation of security in Excel and Word is quite similar. When securing applications built with end-user development tools, think through these issues:

- Excel and Word have two different levels of password protection, which are set through the Options button in the Save As dialog box and through the Protection command on the Tools menu, respectively. (The exact command in Word is Protect Document.) Use the command in the Options dialog box to prevent unauthorized people from opening files (implement access control). Use the command on the Tools menu to protect elements in documents and templates (implement integrity control).

NOTE I rarely see access control implemented in business applications through the Options dialog box. Often it's done through network security, or it's simply omitted as unnecessary.

- All Office products let you open files as read-only. The Options dialog box in both Excel and Word also lets you mark files as Read-Only Recommended, which prompts users to open them as read-only.

- When you use the Protection commands on the Tools menu in Excel or Word, use password protection. If you don't, you haven't protected anything. (See "CASE STUDY: Lock 'Em Out" later in this chapter.)

■ If you hide windows in Excel, make sure that users can't inadvertently unhide them. Although you can do this by removing the Hide and Unhide commands from the Window menu, this also prevents people from using these commands productively. One solution is to hide worksheets by setting the Visible property to xlVeryHidden, which hides the object in such a way that it can only be made visible if you reset this property to True. Another solution is to distribute Excel-based business applications as add-ins. (See Chapter 9 for more information on Excel add-ins.)

Figure 7-3 summarizes the security-management techniques available for the Office development tools.

Protection Scheme	Access	Excel	Word
Set up password protection.	Assign permissions to database objects for particular groups of users. (One password gets users into all objects for which they have permissions.) You can assign permissions for the following database objects, but you can't revoke *run* permissions on modules. ■ forms ■ tables ■ macros ■ modules ■ queries ■ reports	Excel lets you protect the following: ■ workbooks ■ individual sheets (including worksheets, charts, dialog boxes, modules, and Excel version 4 macro sheets) ■ individual cells ■ individual graphic objects For worksheets, charts, and Excel version 4 macro sheets, you can protect: ■ contents ■ objects ■ scenarios	Word lets you selectively protect the following: ■ entire documents ■ annotations ■ forms ■ master documents ■ revisions ■ sections ■ subdocuments ■ templates To protect sections, use the Forms option of the Protect Document command on the Tools menu.
Use the protection property settings for objects and controls.	Access lets you "enable" and/or "lock" controls. (An enabled control can have the focus, and a locked control doesn't accept input.)	Excel allows you to specify whether an object is movable and sizable and to "lock" it. (This takes effect only when you protect the worksheet or workbook.) You can also disable controls in Excel dialog boxes using code.	You can't "lock" controls in Word dialog boxes, but you can disable them using code. Use the Protect Document command to prevent forms from being changed, *except* by entering data into controls.

(continued)

175

Protection Scheme	Access	Excel	Word
Hide elements so that users can't access them.	Hide database objects, including forms and tables.	Hide worksheets, workbooks, names, and formulas for cells.	Hide characters, including whole paragraphs of text. Unfortunately, users can inadvertently delete this text unless you put it in a protected section.
Delete standard commands, menus, menu items, shortcut keys, and so on.	Use the Menu Builder to customize menus. Attach menus to forms and reports by specifying the name of the menu bar macro in the MenuBar property.	Use the Menu Editor command on the Tools menu (available only when you're in a module).	Use the Customize command on the Tools menu to customize menus.
Scramble (or "encrypt") elements so they can't be read by text editors or utility programs.	Use the File Encrypt/Decrypt Database command (available only when you don't have a database open) to "encrypt" Access databases. To benefit from encryption, you must first implement Access security.	Use the Make Add-In command on the Tools menu (available only when you're in a module) to "encrypt" VBA code.	Use the Word-Basic command MacroCopy, and specify the ExecuteOnly option to "encrypt" WordBasic macros.

Figure 7-3. *For Access, Excel, and Word: Use the File Properties command in File Manager to mark files as read-only and/or as hidden; use code to open files as read-only in particular circumstances; use network permissions to secure files on network drives.*

Insecurity

Word is the least secure of the Office development tools. While Access and, to a lesser extent, Excel enable you to prevent users from deleting necessary elements, Word does not. For example, the only way to prevent users from deleting necessary bookmarks, fields, or text (including hidden text) is to store these elements in a protected section, which isn't always feasible.

Although Excel lets you protect data and functions stored in individual cells, it has a few vulnerable spots too. The following are two precautions that you can take to minimize the possibility that users will overwrite the named ranges assigned in Excel-based applications:

- Make named ranges local to worksheets. (See the sidebar titled "Using Defined Names" in Chapter 9 for more information.)

- Hide the named ranges.

Hidden names don't appear in the Define Name, Paste Name, or Go To dialog boxes. But even though you can unhide (or hide) such names only through code, users can *overwrite* them simply by using that name for another range. If you define the name locally, however, this is unlikely to happen. The following code creates a hidden name ("Invisible") for a range on Sheet1:

```
Sub HideName()
  ActiveWorkbook.Names.Add Name:="Invisible",→
    RefersToR1C1:="=Sheet1!R1C1:R3C4", Visible:=False
End Sub
```

CASE STUDY: Lock 'Em Out

Access, Excel, and Word let you customize their environments so completely that you can render the native application unrecognizable (see Figure 7-4). You can eliminate native functionality by deleting menus, menu items, toolbars, shortcut keys, scroll bars, and so on; launch your application from an icon; or run it from a series of dialog boxes. In short, you can build an application that has relatively little to do with the Office development tool you used to program it.

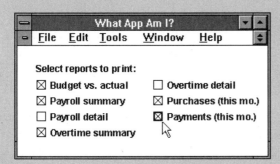

Figure 7-4. *This interface was created with an Office development tool. Which one?*

Of course, although you can do all these things, presumably you're using an end-user development tool for its native functionality—or at least for a specific piece of that functionality. In some cases, however, that piece is quite small.

For example, about two years ago I was part of a team that built an Excel-based application that essentially locked users out of Excel and locked them into this particular application. The application worked as follows (see Figure 7-5):

- Every midnight (from Monday through Friday) the application formatted a text file generated by the mainframe into a read-only Excel spreadsheet. This spreadsheet served as a flat-file database that populated a series of Excel sheets known as "data boxes." The point of the data boxes was to make available to everyone in the firm key financial data, ratios, and projections on publicly traded companies.

- Analysts could add their own projections to the data box.

- Brokers had read-only access to these data boxes, which let them view in a consistent format the most recent financial data on companies and analysts' latest opinions and projections.

Essentially, this firm delivered company data in a personal spreadsheet form but ensured that it was usable only as company data. Excel was the perfect platform because everyone had it already and analysts knew how to use it.

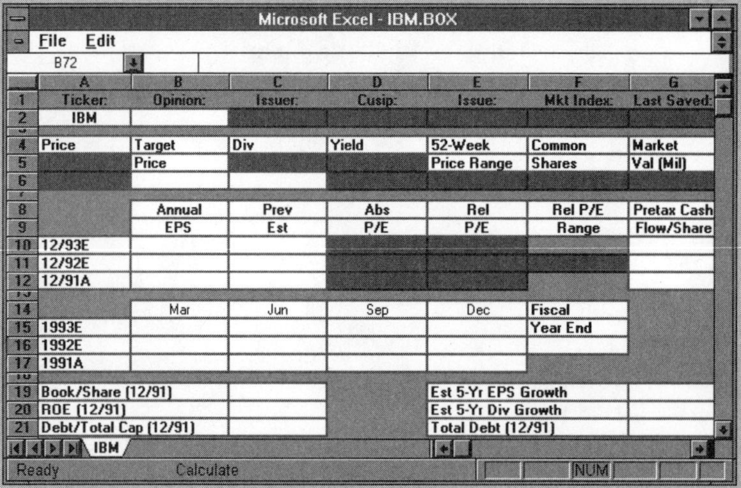

Figure 7-5. *This data box, built for a financial firm, has a dozen commands, three of which are native to Excel: Copy, Paste, and Exit. The others are specific to the data box system, including New Data Box, Open Data Box, and Restore Cell (which overwrites data that analysts have entered manually with values from the database). Analysts can enter data into the blank white cells. Shaded cells perform calculations based on data read from the database.*

Following Good Housekeeping Practices

It takes more code to create solid business applications than to create a group of macros and modules. Here's a checklist of things your applications should do:

- Turn off screen redraw

- Trap errors

- Close files that applications open

- Return to the starting point

- Restore users' original settings

- Return to the original drive and directory

Turn Off Screen Redraw

To achieve a more professional look for your applications, turn off screen redraw. (*Screen redraw* updates the screen so that users see files opening and data appearing as code executes.) Not only does this improve the look and feel of applications (it doesn't seem like a video on fast-forward), it improves performance dramatically. (See the sidebar titled "Tips for Boosting Performance" on the next page.) To test this yourself, use the TestRedrawDrag module in Solution.XLS on the *Office Solutions* disk included with this book. On my PC (a Dell Dimension XPS 466V with 16 MB of RAM), this test runs in 1044 milliseconds with screen redraw *on* and in 275 milliseconds when it's *off*.

Below is the VBA for Excel subroutine from the TestRedrawDrag module. It uses the Windows API function GetTickCount to stopwatch the code.

```
Declare Function GetTickCount Lib "USER" () As Long

Sub InsertLotsOSheets()
  Dim i As Integer
  Dim lTickCount As Long

'Turns off screen redraw; comment out this line to see how long
'the code takes to run when screen redraw is ON.
  Application.ScreenUpdating = False

'Computes the number of milliseconds it takes the code to run.
'Calls GetTickCount to get the milliseconds since Windows started.
  lTickCount = GetTickCount()

'Insert new sheets.
```

(continued)

```
   For x = 1 To 7
      Sheets.Add

'Select the top three cells.
      Range("A1:C1").Select

'Format them.
      With Range("A1:C1")
        .font.Bold = True
        .font.Underline = xlSingle
        .HorizontalAlignment = xlCenter
      End With

'Insert column headings.
      Range("A1").Formula = "Company"
      Range("B1").Formula = "Contact"
      Range("C1").Formula = "Phone"
   Next

'Go home.
   Range("A1").Select

'Call GetTickCount again, and subtract to get the elapsed time.
   lTickCount = GetTickCount() - lTickCount
   MsgBox "Procedure took" & Str$(lTickCount) & " milliseconds."

'Turns on screen redraw.
   Application.ScreenUpdating = True
End Sub
```

FYI

Tips for Boosting Performance

A system can never run fast enough. You should stopwatch your code using the Windows API function GetTickCount to test how long it takes to run on your company's PCs. Here are some tips for making code run faster:

■ Shorten your code. (I remember reworking a procedure that ran on a 386 PC several times, until I finally whittled it down by almost a third. At that point, performance was OK even on the 386, and I'd written some very good code.)

■ Use in-line code in place of subroutine calls. (Even though subroutines produce shorter code, they tend to run more slowly. Test this the next time you're trying to boost performance.)

- Use integer variables and integer math. (WordBasic doesn't support this technique.)

- Use variant variables only if absolutely necessary. (WordBasic doesn't support variants.)

- Use progress indicators. (This doesn't boost actual performance, but it boosts "perceived" performance, which is nearly as important.)

Trap Errors

Handle errors gracefully. Alert users to which error occurred and what they should do next. Solid business applications require solid error-trapping routines, and there are several good strategies for putting these together.

Here's the strategy used throughout this book. Start procedures with the code On Error GoTo *NameOfErrorTrap*. End procedures with the error trap, which uses If…Then or Select Case to handle errors. At the end of the error trap, use Resume *NameOfCleanUpRoutine* to clean up and exit the procedure. This strategy works for all the Microsoft BASICs, although WordBasic requires minor modifications because it doesn't have an Exit Sub or an Exit Function statement. (See the section titled "Return to the Original Drive and Directory" later in this chapter for an example of an error trap in WordBasic.)

The following Access Basic code (which is in Solution.MDB on the *Office Solutions* disk included with this book) demonstrates how such an error trap works. (The section titled "Maintenance Tools" later in this chapter illustrates an error trap in the context of a small application.)

```
Function ErrorSample() As Integer
  On Error GoTo ErrorSampleError
  Dim strMsg As String

'Turn off screen redraw.
  Application.Echo False
  DoCmd OpenTable "tblxxx"
  DoCmd OpenForm "frmxxx"

ErrorSampleExit:
'Put cleanup routines, such as turning on screen redraw, here.
  Application.Echo True
  Exit Function

ErrorSampleError:
  Select Case Err
```

(continued)

```
'Table exists but form doesn't.
   Case 2102
      strMsg = "The form you specified doesn't exist."
      MsgBox strMsg, 64, "Sample Code"
   Case Else
      strMsg = "An error occurred in ErrorSample. Check whether "
      strMsg = strMsg & "the command did what you expected, and "
      strMsg = strMsg & "if not, try again. If the error still "
      strMsg = strMsg & "occurs, call the Help Desk at x5678, "
      strMsg = strMsg & "and mention Error #: " & Err & "."
      MsgBox strMsg, 64, "Sample Code"
   End Select

'Go to cleanup routine before exiting function.
   Resume ErrorSampleExit
End Function
```

> **NOTE** If you rework this routine into a centralized form, store the Err value
> in a variable to prevent it from being reset to 0.

FYI

On Errors

The Microsoft BASICs support several statements and functions that provide
information regarding errors, including the following:

- Err: Returns the number of the error that occurs.

- Error[(*ErrorNumber*)]: Returns the built-in message string for an error
  that occurs. This function (which is not supported by WordBasic)
  returns "User-defined error" for errors that aren't defined by the Office
  application.

- Error *ErrorCode*: Simulates an error and lets you test an error trap.

Close Files That Applications Open

Business applications built with end-user development tools sometimes open
extra files—for example, workbooks or Word documents. Unless users need
to manipulate these files directly, it's generally best to keep them invisible. Use
the following rules of thumb.

- In Excel, hide workbooks that applications require but that users don't use directly.

- Close files that applications open as soon as they're no longer needed.

- Automatically save files that should be saved.

- Automatically close files without saving them if your code makes changes that shouldn't be saved. If you need to leave files open but unchanged when the procedure ends, close them automatically without saving, and then reopen them.

> **NOTE** These files will be *truly* invisible if you turn off screen redraw when manipulating them through code.

Return to the Starting Point

In Access, as in Visual Basic, you can manipulate Jet engine objects without physically going to them. On the other hand, when you manipulate Access objects (such as tables, forms, and reports)—and often when you're working in Excel and Word—the focus moves as code runs. For example, when you create a sheet in code or execute the Find command, the focus moves to that sheet or to the found item. In general, you should return users to the location from which they ran the procedure, or, if the purpose of the code is to create something (such as a table of contents or a report), you should leave them at the start of the element created.

In Word, use bookmarks to return to the user's original location. Although you can use named ranges to do this in Excel (Excel's named ranges are analogous to Word's bookmarks), it's faster to set the original selection as a Range object and then return to it at the end of the macro. Whenever a procedure creates temporary bookmarks or named ranges, delete them at the procedure's end.

> **NOTE** In Access, use the Bookmark property for Recordset objects to return to specific records, *not* to return to the user's on-screen starting point.

Sample code for VBA for Excel and WordBasic is shown on the next page. All code is in Solution.XLS or Solution.DOT on the *Office Solutions* disk included with this book.

VBA for Excel

The macro on the next page sets the active cell(s) as a range object, applies a number format to contiguous cells, and then returns to the original selection. By creating a range object instead of defining a temporary named range, you don't have to delete the range at the procedure's end.

```
Option Explicit

Sub BackToTheBeginning()

  Dim CurrentSelection As Object

'When macro is invoked, set active cell as a range object.
  Set CurrentSelection = ActiveCell

'Select contiguous cells.
  Selection.CurrentRegion.Select

'Apply the following number format.
  Selection.NumberFormat = "#,##0_);[Red](#,##0)"

'Return to the originally active cell(s).
  CurrentSelection.Select
End Sub
```

WordBasic

The following macro deletes all empty paragraphs in a document. It's handy for cleaning up documents brought into Word from other file formats. In Word, the only way to return to the user's original location is by creating a temporary bookmark that you delete at the macro's end.

```
Sub MAIN
'Mark cursor location when macro is invoked.
  EditBookmark "HereIAm"
  StartOfDocument
  n = AtEndOfDocument()
  While n = 0
    EditGoTo .Destination = "\Para"
    EmptyPara$ = Selection$()
    p = Asc(EmptyPara$)
    If p = 13 Then
      EditClear
    Else
      CharRight
    End If
    n = AtEndOfDocument()
  Wend

'Return to original cursor position.
  EditGoTo "HereIAm"

'Delete bookmark.
  EditBookmark .Name = "HereIAm", .Delete
End Sub
```

Restore Users' Original Settings

Many applications built with Office development tools (especially Excel and Word) change settings used by the Office application—for example, whether Excel's gridlines are displayed or whether the toolbars are displayed. When business applications do this, they should restore the original settings when users close the application, including:

- Settings available through the Options command on the Tools menu in Excel and Word and on the View menu in Access

- Toolbars

- Zoom percentage

- The state of the application window and the document window

The key to restoring these settings is a two-step process that captures them when the business application loads and then returns them to their original state when the application ends. (In some cases, you'll change settings at the start of a *procedure* and restore them when you exit that procedure.) For example, the section titled "AppMakeR's Auto_Open and Auto_Close Procedures" in Chapter 9 provides sample routines for Excel. Auto_Open captures the toolbars in use and the state of the formula and status bars when you open a workbook or a template; stores this information in variables; and then changes these elements as the application requires. Auto_Close restores the original elements when you close the application.

NOTE If you store a sizable amount of information relating to Excel's or Word's last-saved user configuration, consider using INI files rather than variables. Also, hold down the Shift key to *prevent* auto macros from running when you open an Access database, an Excel workbook, or a Word document.

In some cases, it makes sense to read settings stored in INI files rather than to capture information at startup. For example, this technique provides a single-step method for restoring the window state last saved by users.

The VBA for Excel code on the next page uses an Auto_Open procedure to set the workbook window to a specified state (in this case, maximized). When you close the application, the Auto_Close procedure reads the [Microsoft Excel] section of the EXCEL5.INI file for the Maximized entry's value (described in Figure 7-6 on page 187), which is the user's last-saved window state. The Auto_Close procedure uses a Select Case routine to reset the windows accordingly. (The code is in Solutions.XLS on the *Office Solutions* disk.)

```
Declare Function GetPrivateProfileString Lib "KERNEL" (ByVal→
  lpSectionName As String, ByVal lpEntryName As String, ByVal→
  lpDefault As String, ByVal lpReturnedString As String, ByVal→
  nSize As Integer, ByVal lpFileName As String) As Integer

Sub Auto_OpenII()
'Maximize the workbook (or document) window.
  Set CurrentWindow = Application.ActiveWindow
'Note that xlMaximized is an intrinsic constant.
  Application.ActiveWindow.WindowState = xlMaximized
End Sub


Sub Auto_CloseII()
  Dim ReturnVal As Integer
  Dim MaximizedSetting As String
  Set CurrentWindow = Application.ActiveWindow

'Set the size of MaximizedSetting.
  MaximizedSetting = String$(3, 0)

'Call the Windows API INI function.
  ReturnVal = GetPrivateProfileString("Microsoft Excel",→
    "Maximized", "", MaximizedSetting, 2, "EXCEL5.INI")
  MaximizedSetting = Left$(MaximizedSetting, ReturnVal)

'Message box providing information from the INI file.
  MsgBox "Back to the original window state, Case" &→
    MaximizedSetting

'Reset to the user's last saved window state.
  Select Case Val(MaximizedSetting)
    Case 0
      Application.WindowState = xlNormal
      CurrentWindow.WindowState = xlNormal
    Case 1
      Application.WindowState = xlMaximized
      CurrentWindow.WindowState = xlNormal
    Case 2
      Application.WindowState = xlNormal
      CurrentWindow.WindowState = xlMaximized
    Case 3
      Application.WindowState = xlMaximized
      CurrentWindow.WindowState = xlMaximized
    Case Else
      MsgBox "Maximized setting not properly restored."
  End Select
  Application.Quit
End Sub
```

Value	Access	Excel
−1	n/a	n/a
0	Access is not maximized.	Both Excel and the open workbook are set by the Pos entry in the INI file.
1	Access is maximized.	Excel is maximized, but the open workbook is not.
2	n/a	Excel's size is set by the Pos entry in the [Microsoft Excel] section of the EXCEL5.INI file, and the workbook is maximized within that window.
3	n/a	Both Excel and the open workbook are maximized.

Figure 7-6. *Values for the window state stored in INI files.*

FYI

INI Files

Access, Excel, and Word each have private INI files that store a variety of information—from the Most Recently Used file list to the application's last window state (maximized, restored, or minimized). Sometimes you must read these files (using the Windows API function GetPrivateProfileString) to get information relevant to your business application—for example, the default path for an end-user development tool, the add-ins loaded at startup, or the Word template path. (See the section titled "SAMPLE APPLICATION: InstallR" later in this chapter.) You can also edit these INI files directly (using the Windows API function WritePrivateProfileString) to establish the settings you need. However, if you need to store application-related information such as user preferences, it's generally safest to create a dedicated INI file for your business application.

The INI files for Office development tools are stored in the Windows directory under the following names:

- MSACC20.INI
- EXCEL5.INI
- WINWORD6.INI

See the section titled "INI File Functions" in Chapter 6 for more information on INI files.

Restoring the window state using Access Basic and WordBasic

To restore the original window state in Access Basic, use a routine nearly identical to the VBA for Excel routine shown in the previous section, but substitute the Maximize and Restore actions for VBA's WindowState properties. Because Word doesn't store the window state in its INI file, restoring it requires a two-step process:

1. Capture this state when you launch the application (use the AppMaximize and DocMaximize functions), and store it as a document variable.

2. Restore the original state when users exit the application. (Use an AutoExit routine.)

> **NOTE** You can also use a two-step process to restore the original window state in VBA for Excel: Use WindowState properties to capture the state of Excel's windows on startup, and then store the settings for use on exit.

Return to the Original Drive and Directory

Business applications often access different drives and directories. When they do, make sure that they reset the current drive and directory. The next time users open or save a file, they should be in the same drive and directory as the last time they opened or saved that file.

Each of the two code samples below (written in Access Basic and in WordBasic) performs the following tasks:

■ It determines whether the specified directory exists.

■ It stores the current drive and directory in a variable, changes to the user-specified path, and then restores the original path.

All code is in Solution.MDB or Solution.DOT on the *Office Solutions* disk included with this book. The code for VBA for Excel and Visual Basic is identical to that for Access Basic.

Access Basic

```
Function ChangeDir ()
   Dim strOldDirectory As String
   Dim strNewDirectory As String
   On Error GoTo ChangeDirError
```

```
'Record the current directory.
  strOldDirectory = CurDir$
  MsgBox "The current directory is " & strOldDirectory

'Let the user enter a new directory and switch to it.
  strNewDirectory = InputBox$("Type a new directory:", "Change➔
    Directory")
  If strNewDirectory = "" Then
    Exit Function
  Else
    ChDir strNewDirectory
  End If

'Display the value of the CurDir$ function to verify that the
'directory has been changed to the directory that the
'user entered.
  MsgBox "Now the current directory is " & CurDir$

ChangeDirExit:
'Change the directory back to its original setting.
  ChDir strOldDirectory

'Display the value of the CurDir$ function to verify that the
'directory has been restored to its original setting.
  MsgBox "The directory has been restored to " & CurDir$
  Exit Function

ChangeDirError:
'Handle error when path not found.
  If Err = 76 Then
    MsgBox "The directory you entered doesn't exist."

'Handle miscellaneous errors.
  ElseIf Err <> 0 Then
    MsgBox "Unexpected Error " & Err & ": " & Error$
  End If
  Resume ChangeDirExit
End Function
```

WordBasic

```
Sub MAIN
  On Error Goto ChangeDirError

'Record the current directory.
```

(continued)

```
    OldDirectory$ = Files$(".")
    MsgBox "The current directory is " + OldDirectory$

'Let the user enter a new directory and switch to it.
    NewDirectory$ = InputBox$("Type a new directory:", "Change↴
      Directory")
    If NewDirectory$ = "" Then
      Goto BYE
    Else
      ChDir NewDirectory$
    End If

'Display the value of the Files$(".") function to verify that
'the directory has been changed to the directory that the
'user entered.
    MsgBox "Now the current directory is " + Files$(".")

ChangeDirExit:
'Change the directory back to its original setting.
    ChDir OldDirectory$

'Display the value of Files$(".") to verify that the
'directory has indeed been restored to its original setting.
    MsgBox "The current directory has been restored to " + Files$(".")

'WordBasic doesn't have an Exit statement, so use Goto.
    Goto BYE

ChangeDirError:
'Handle error when path not found.
    If Err = 76 Then
      MsgBox "The directory you entered doesn't exist."

'Handle error when users click Cancel.
    ElseIf Err = 102 Then
    Goto BYE

'Handle miscellaneous errors.
    ElseIf Err <> 0 Then
      MsgBox "Unexpected Error " + Str$(Err) + ": " + Error$
    End If
    Goto ChangeDirExit

BYE:
End Sub
```

SAMPLE APPLICATION: InstallR

No matter how you distribute business applications—on floppy disks or over a network—installation is easier if you provide an installation program. This is especially true when business applications consist of several files to be installed in specific directories, the names of which might vary from PC to PC.

For example, Word templates are typically installed in the template directory (which might be C:\WINWORD\TEMPLATE, D:\WORD6\TEMPLATE, and so on); Excel templates are typically installed in the XLSTART directory (which could be in any path); and INI files are stored in the Windows program directory (which might also be in any path). Without an installation program, installation can be time-consuming and complicated.

This section presents a sample installation program called InstallR (written in Visual Basic), which simplifies the process of installing business applications built with Office products.

PRODUCT SHEET: InstallR

Purpose:	InstallR is an installation program that consists of two executable files: InstallR.EXE and INSTALL.EXE. These two programs simplify the installation process.
	Developers use InstallR.EXE to prepare business applications for distribution and installation. Users use INSTALL.EXE to install these applications on their PCs.
Development tools used:	Visual Basic Professional Edition, version 3; Windows API
How InstallR and INSTALL work:	InstallR.EXE makes it easier for developers to create installation routines for business applications built with Office development tools. One way it does this is by locating five standard directories (whose paths vary from PC to PC) at install time—the Word Template directory, the Word startup directory, the Excel startup directory, the Windows directory, and the Windows system directory. This feature enables developers to create dynamic installation routines that install files based on the configuration of the target PC.
	INSTALL.EXE not only enables users to install business applications, but it provides a list of the files installed and their locations for easy reference.
	The diagram on the following page illustrates the division of labor between InstallR.EXE and INSTALL.EXE:

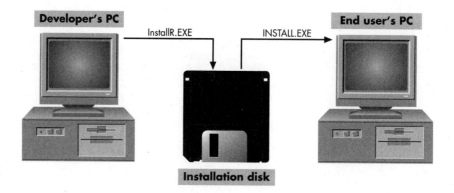

InstallR consists of a pair of applications—InstallR.EXE and INSTALL.EXE—that provide an easy-to-use interface for both developers and end users. (Both the applications and the Visual Basic source files are on the *Office Solutions* disk included with this book.) To create an installation disk, developers run InstallR.EXE. They select the files for the application and the directories in which to install these files. The installation disk (which can be a floppy disk or a directory on the network) contains three elements:

- Application files

- INSTALL.INI (a list of application files and their destination directories)

- INSTALL.EXE

To install the application, users run INSTALL.EXE.

InstallR.EXE is essentially an interface that handles basic file management—which is what installation boils down to. It consists of four dialog boxes:

- The Select Files dialog box (SELFILES.FRM) uses drag and drop to let you select the application files to be installed.

- The Select Directories dialog box (DEST.FRM) lets you enter the directory in which to install each file in the application. You can either type the pathname or use the Select Final Destination dialog box (SELDEST.FRM).

- The Select Final Destination dialog box (SELDEST.FRM) lets you select a specific drive and directory. This dialog box lists five standard directories (such as the Windows program directory and the Excel startup directory) in which to install files.

■ The Select INSTALL Directory dialog box (INSTDIR.FRM) lets you select the path *from* which to install the application files—generally a floppy disk or a network drive. Click OK to 1) create this path, 2) copy the application files and INSTALL.EXE to it, and 3) write the application filenames and destination directories to INSTALL.INI.

> **NOTE** InstallR doesn't include a routine to install an icon or set up a Program Manager group, but you can certainly add these capabilities. You might also want to add a file compression routine.

The Select Files Dialog Box

The Select Files dialog box (see Figure 7-7) implements drag and drop using the following four event procedures and the PtInControl function:

■ filSource_MouseDown (filSource is the Filename list box)

■ filSource_MouseMove

■ lstSelectedFiles_MouseUp (lstSelectedFiles is the Files to Install list box)

■ lstSelectedFiles_DragDrop

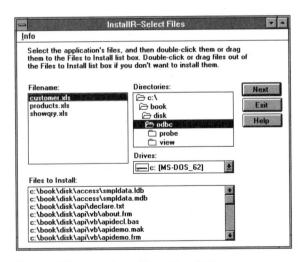

Figure 7-7. *InstallR's Select Files dialog box.*

MouseDown

The subroutine on the next page records the position of the pointer when users press the mouse button. The PtInControl function (shown later) uses this information to verify that the pointer was in the Filename list box.

```
Sub filSource_MouseDown (Button As Integer, Shift As Integer, X As→
   Single, Y As Single)

'Record mouse position at start of drag and drop from filSource list
'box to lstSelectedFiles.
   xDragStart = X + filSource.Left
   yDragStart = Y + filSource.Top
End Sub
```

MouseMove

The following subroutine allows users to *drag* files by invoking the drag
method of the Filename list box.

```
Sub filSource_MouseMove (Button As Integer, Shift As Integer, X As→
   Single, Y As Single)

'When left mouse button is down, initiate drag-and-drop operation
'from filSource to lstSelectedFiles.
   If Button = 1 Then filSource.Drag
End Sub
```

MouseUp

The following subroutine allows users to *drop* files by invoking the drag
method with argument 2, which generates a DragDrop event. (The event
procedure is shown in the next section.)

```
Sub lstSelectedFiles_MouseUp (Button As Integer, Shift As Integer,→
   X As Single, Y As Single)

'Finish the drag-and-drop operation from filSource_MouseMove event;
'generate a DragDrop event for lstSelectedFiles.
   If Button = 1 Then filSource.Drag 2
End Sub
```

DragDrop

The following subroutine is the DragDrop event procedure. It calls the
PtInControl function to verify that users were in the Filename list box when
they pressed the mouse button. If so, it completes the drag-and-drop operation by adding the file to the Files to Install list box.

```
Sub lstSelectedFiles_DragDrop (Source As Control, X As Single, Y As→
   Single)
```

```
'Call PtInControl to determine whether initial mouse position was in
'filSource. If so, complete drag and drop by adding the selected file
'from filSource to lstSelectedFiles.
   If PtInControl(filSource, xDragStart, yDragStart) Then
      lstSelectedFiles.AddItem filSource.Path & "\" &→
         filSource.List(filSource.ListIndex)
   End If
End Sub
```

Is the mouse pointer in the list box?

The following function, PtInControl, verifies that the mouse pointer was in the Filename list box when users pressed the mouse button to initiate the drag-and-drop operation.

```
Function PtInControl (ctrl As Control, X As Single, Y As Single)→
   As Integer

'Returns True if the point (x,y) is in ctrl, False otherwise.
   Dim xMin As Single
   Dim xMax As Single
   Dim yMin As Single
   Dim yMax As Single

   xMin = ctrl.Left
   xMax = ctrl.Left + ctrl.Width
   yMin = ctrl.Top
   yMax = ctrl.Top + ctrl.Height

   If (X >= xMin) And (X <= xMax) And (Y >= yMin) And→
     (Y <= yMax) Then
     PtInControl = True
   Else
     PtInControl = False
   End If
End Function
```

The Select Directories Dialog Box

The files selected in the Select Files dialog box populate the Select Directories dialog box (see Figure 7-8 on the next page). Specify the path in which to install each application file by typing the pathname in the text box or by clicking the command button to the right of the text box.

195

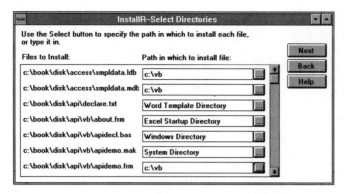

Figure 7-8. *InstallR's Select Directories dialog box.*

The Select Final Destination Dialog Box

If you click the command button to the right of the text box, InstallR.EXE displays the Select Final Destination dialog box (see Figure 7-9). Select either a specific path or one of five standard directories:

- Word template directory

- Word startup directory

- Excel startup directory (XLSTART)

- Windows program directory

- Windows system directory

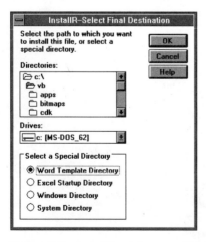

Figure 7-9. *InstallR's Select Final Destination dialog box.*

By selecting a standard directory, you prevent hard-coding of an installation routine that might not work on all PCs. Later, the installation program (INSTALL.EXE) checks the PC on which it's installing an application to determine the path for the standard directory, and then it installs the application file accordingly.

The Select INSTALL Directory Dialog Box

The last step in creating an installation routine is to specify the path *from* which to install the application files. The Select INSTALL Directory dialog box (see Figure 7-10 on page 200) allows you to choose this path either by selecting the appropriate directory or by typing the pathname in the Path text box. When you click the OK button, InstallR.EXE calls the MakeInstallDirectory procedure (shown below), which performs two tasks:

- It creates INSTALL.INI, which contains a list of the application files and the directories in which to install them.

- It copies the application files and INSTALL.EXE to the installation directory. (Make sure that INSTALL.EXE is in the same directory as InstallR.EXE.)

```
Sub MakeInstallDirectory ()
'Path to the installation directory.
  Dim sInstallDir As String

'Drive for the installation directory.
  Dim sDrive As String

'Full path and name for INSTALL.INI.
  Dim sINIFile As String

'Source filename to be written to INSTALL.INI as an entry name.
  Dim sSourceFile As String

'Destination directory to be written to INSTALL.INI as an entry.
  Dim sDestination As String

'Loop counter.
  Dim i As Integer

'Return value of WritePrivateProfileString.
  Dim iRet As Integer

'Error constant.
  Const ERR_FILE_NOT_FOUND = 53
```

(continued)

```
'Width of horizontal fill gauge on progress indicator.
  Const GAUGE_WIDTH = 3195

'Read the path to the installation directory from txtInstallDir.
  sInstallDir = txtInstallDir

'Get the drive part of the path.
  sDrive = Left$(sInstallDir, 2)

'Check the drive by calling IsDrive.
  Select Case IsDrive(sDrive)

'Notify the user if the drive is unavailable or unintelligible.
    Case ISD_NO
      MsgBox "Drive " & sDrive & " is unavailable.  Select a→
        different drive for the installation directory."
      Exit Sub
    Case ISD_ERROR
      MsgBox "Couldn't understand drive specification in the→
        path " & sInstallDir & ". Make sure you specify a full path→
        for the installation directory."
      Exit Sub

'Otherwise, if the drive is available...
    Case ISD_YES

'...call the IsDir function to check the installation directory.
      Select Case IsDir(sInstallDir)

'If the directory isn't there, create it.
        Case ISD_NO
          MkDir sInstallDir

'If there's a problem with the directory string, notify the user.
        Case ISD_ERROR
          MsgBox "Path garbled " & sInstallDir
          Exit Sub

      End Select          'IsDir(sInstallDir)
  End Select              'IsDrive(sDrive)

'Change mouse pointer to hourglass.
  Screen.MousePointer = 11

'Display progress indicator. The shape control shpSoFar is used
'as a gauge--by adjusting its width, the program notifies the
'user of the progress of the installation.
  frmProgress.shpSoFar.Width = GAUGE_WIDTH \ (2 * iNumSourceFiles)
```

```
    frmProgress.lblDirectory = sInstallDir
    frmProgress.Show

    If Right$(sInstallDir, 1) <> "\" Then sInstallDir =⟶
      sInstallDir & "\"
    sINIFile = sInstallDir & "install.ini"
    For i = 0 To iNumSourceFiles - 1

'Get the source filename and destination path from frmDestination,
'and write them to INSTALL.INI.
      sSourceFile = frmDestination.lblSource(i).Caption
      sDestination = frmDestination.txtDestination(i).Text
      iRet = WritePrivateProfileString("Locations", sSourceFile,⟶
        sDestination, sINIFile)
      If iRet = 0 Then MsgBox "Couldn't write to INI file."

'Write names of current install file on progress indicator.
      frmProgress.lblFile = sSourceFile
      frmProgress.Refresh

'Copy the source files for the application to the installation
'directory.
      FileCopy frmSelectFiles.lstSelectedFiles.List(i),⟶
        sInstallDir & sSourceFile
      frmProgress.shpSoFar.Width = ((i + 1) * GAUGE_WIDTH) \⟶
        iNumSourceFiles
    Next i

'If INSTALL.EXE is in the same directory as InstallR, copy it
'to the installation directory. Otherwise, notify users that they
'will have to put it there themselves.
    On Error Resume Next
    FileCopy app.Path & "\" & "INSTALL.EXE", sInstallDir &⟶
      "INSTALL.EXE"
    If Err = ERR_FILE_NOT_FOUND Then MsgBox "Couldn't find⟶
      INSTALL.EXE. You must copy it to " & sInstallDir & " manually."

'Unload the progress indicator and restore the mouse pointer.
    Unload frmProgress
    Screen.MousePointer = 0

    MsgBox "The source files have been copied to " &⟶
      Left$(sInstallDir, Len(sInstallDir) - 1)
    Unload frmSelectFiles
    End
End Sub
```

Figure 7-10. *InstallR's Select INSTALL Directory dialog box.*

About INSTALL.INI

INSTALL.INI is a private INI file with a single section, [Locations]. The entry names are the application files to be installed, and the entries are the paths in which to install them, as in the following example:

```
[Locations]
yourapp.exe = c:\yourapp
yourapp.dot = Word Template Directory
yourapp.dll = System Directory
```

INSTALL.INI lists the files installed and their locations, so users can print this file for reference regarding the application files copied to their PC. Or they can copy it from the installation disk, rename it, and store it for future use.

INSTALL.EXE

To install a business application, users simply run INSTALL.EXE (see Figure 7-11), which performs four tasks:

■ It uses the Windows API function GetPrivateProfileString to read from INSTALL.INI the application files to install and their destinations.

■ It verifies that all application files are on the installation disk.

- It verifies the destination directories and determines whether application files already exist in those paths. If so, it notifies the end user.

- It copies files from the installation disk to the destination directories.

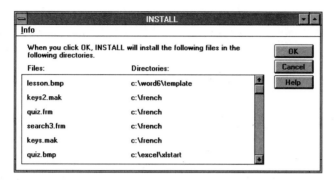

Figure 7-11. *InstallR's INSTALL dialog box. Users click OK to install the application files listed.*

Installing files in standard directories

When developers use InstallR.EXE's Select Final Destination dialog box to specify one of five standard directories (rather than a specific path), the program stores these directories in INSTALL.INI as simple descriptions: Word Templates, Word Startup, Excel Startup, Windows, and System. The GetSpecialDirectories procedure (shown below) then locates these directories on the user's PC:

```
Sub GetSpecialDirectories ()
'Return value of the Windows API functions used in this procedure;
'the length of the text retrieved.
   Dim iLength As Integer

'String buffer to hold retrieved text.
   Dim sBuffer As String

'Length of buffer.
   Const BUFFER_LENGTH = 128

'Length of Excel pathname.
   Dim iXLPathLen As Integer

'Get Word template path; initialize sBuffer with null characters.
   sBuffer = String$(BUFFER_LENGTH, 0)
```

(continued)

```
'Read the Word template path from WINWORD6.INI.
  iLength = GetPrivateProfileString("Microsoft Word", "USER-DOT-↴
    PATH", "", sBuffer, BUFFER_LENGTH - 1, "winword6.ini")

'If no text was retrieved, notify the user.
  If iLength = 0 Then
    MsgBox "Couldn't read Word template path from INI file."
  End If

'Record the path in the global variable sWordTemplate.
  sWordTemplate = RemoveBackslash(Left$(sBuffer, iLength))

'Get Word startup path; initialize sBuffer with null characters.
  sBuffer = String$(BUFFER_LENGTH, 0)

'Read the Word startup path from WINWORD6.INI.
  iLength = GetPrivateProfileString("Microsoft Word", "STARTUP-↴
    PATH", "", sBuffer, BUFFER_LENGTH - 1, "winword6.ini")

'If no text was retrieved, notify the user.
  If iLength = 0 Then
    MsgBox "Couldn't read Word startup path from INI file."
  End If

'Record the path in the global variable sWordStartup.
  sWordStartup = RemoveBackslash(Left$(sBuffer, iLength))

'Get Excel startup path.
'The path for EXCEL.EXE is recorded in the [Extensions] section
'of WIN.INI. The startup directory--always called XLSTART--is
'in the same directory as EXCEL.EXE.
  sBuffer = String$(BUFFER_LENGTH, 0)
  iLength = GetProfileString("Extensions", "xls", "", sBuffer,↴
    BUFFER_LENGTH - 1)
  If iLength = 0 Then
    MsgBox "Couldn't read Excel startup path from INI file."
    sXLStartup = ""
  Else
    sBuffer = Left$(sBuffer, iLength)

'Extract the path string from the full path to EXCEL.EXE and
'append the name of the startup directory.
    iXLPathLen = InStr(1, sBuffer, "EXCEL.EXE", 1)
    sXLStartup = Left$(sBuffer, iXLPathLen - 1) & "XLSTART"
  End If

'Get Windows directory path.
```

```
  sBuffer = String$(BUFFER_LENGTH, 0)
  iLength = GetWindowsDirectory(sBuffer, BUFFER_LENGTH - 1)
  If iLength = 0 Then
    MsgBox "Couldn't get Windows directory."
  End If
  sWindows = RemoveBackslash(Left$(sBuffer, iLength))

'Get System directory path.
  sBuffer = String$(BUFFER_LENGTH, 0)
  iLength = GetSystemDirectory(sBuffer, BUFFER_LENGTH - 1)
  If iLength = 0 Then
    MsgBox "Couldn't get System directory."
  End If
  sSystem = RemoveBackslash(Left$(sBuffer, iLength))
End Sub
```

Making Office-Based Applications Easy to Maintain

The best business applications make it easy for users to change the things that change most often. In particular, applications should do the following:

- Present options likely to change in list boxes (using the extended multiselect property) rather than in check boxes.

- Provide tools whose purpose is to enable users to maintain applications.

List Boxes, Not Check Boxes

The classic Print Reports routine—the one I see in most business applications that provide this capability—is hard to maintain. It's a dialog box with check boxes listing the available reports, and users click these boxes to indicate which reports to print. The problem is that adding a report—and *everyone* wants to add a report—requires that a developer create a new dialog box and write additional code. In other words, it pushes users back into the mainframe-esque situation of queuing up at a programmer's door when they need to make changes.

So you should change the approach. Use a list box with the extended multi-select property rather than check boxes, and have this list box read the available reports dynamically. (Depending on the Office development tool you're using, you might read from a text file, a table, or an Excel worksheet.) This is great for those who use the application, because they can control it (to a certain extent), and it's great for developers, because they can reuse this code for other applications. Plus, you can extend this idea to a host of things other than Print Reports.

Maintenance Tools in Excel and Word

Maintenance tools enable users to maintain business applications. Although the Maintenance utility explained in the following section is written in Access Basic, you can duplicate it quite easily in VBA for Excel because Excel can also use tables to store list box items. The main difference between Access and Excel in this regard is that Access lets you create continuous forms and Excel doesn't, which means that users have to edit the tables using edit boxes.

Unfortunately, this utility is trickier to implement in Word because Word's list boxes don't read directly from tables. But you can write a procedure that does this. (See the section titled "QuickSwitch" in Chapter 8 for an example that uses a Word table to populate a list box; see the section titled "Managing Members" in the same chapter for an example that uses an INI file.)

Maintenance Tools

One key to developing applications that users can maintain is to use list boxes that read dynamically from files that users can edit, but business applications require a secure procedure for making such edits. Maintenance utilities enable users to edit information for the application without breaking the application.

For example, I was part of a team that developed a departmental accounting and financial reporting system in Access, which was designed to give users significant control over maintenance. The program presents most options as drop-down lists, the elements of which are maintained in Access tables. People in the Administration group (with the broadest security access) use the Maintenance utility to change the options presented in the application's drop-down lists (see Figure 7-12). When users select the category of information for which they want to change options, the application displays a dialog box listing the relevant options. Users can add to this list, delete from it, or edit it. They never enter the actual tables that store the information.

The Access Maintenance utility (the code is in Solution.MDB on the *Office Solutions* disk included with this book) has three essential elements:

- The OnClick event procedure, which is called when users click the OK button (in the form module for L_frmMaintenanceTable).

- The MaintenanceTable function, which is called by the OnClick event procedure. This function opens and closes the forms used to maintain the tables.

- Property settings that use the data in the tables to populate controls (see Figure 7-13).

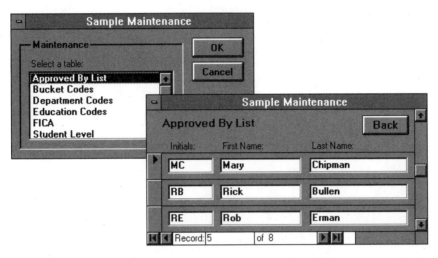

Figure 7-12. *The Maintenance utility dialog box on the left lets users with administrative access modify the tables that populate the application's list boxes. Selecting the Approved By List option displays the dialog box on the right, which lets users edit the list of people who can approve purchase orders. This list populates the Approved By drop-down list that appears on the Purchase Order form.*

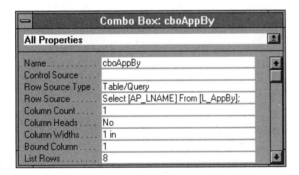

Figure 7-13. *Property settings for the Approved By drop-down list on the Purchase Order form (L_frmPO). The Row Source property is set to populate this control with data from the AP_LNAME field in the Access table L_AppBy.*

The OnClick event procedure

The code on the next page returns the index of the item selected in the Maintenance utility list box and calls the MaintenanceTable function.

```
Sub btnOKMainMenu_Click ()
'List box selection.
  Dim SelectedItem As Integer

'List box object.
  Dim MaintenanceControl As Control
  Set MaintenanceControl = lstMaintenance

'Return value for MaintenanceTable.
  Dim ReturnVal As Integer

'Move focus to specified control.
  MaintenanceControl.SetFocus

'Get index for selected item.
  SelectedItem = MaintenanceControl.ListIndex

'Clear list box.
  Me!lstMaintenance.value = ""

'Call MaintenanceTable function.
  ReturnVal = MaintenanceTable(SelectedItem)

'Redisplay form if an error occurs in MaintenanceTable.
  If ReturnVal = 0 Then Me.visible = True
End Sub
```

The MaintenanceTable function

The code below opens the maintenance table that users selected from the Maintenance utility list box:

```
Function MaintenanceTable (listindex As Integer) As Integer
  On Error GoTo MaintenanceTableError

'Name of form.
  Dim strFrm As String

'Calls form based on listindex.
  Select Case listindex
    Case 0
      strFrm = "l_frmAppBy"
    Case 1
      strFrm = "l_frmBucket"
    Case 2
      strFrm = "l_frmDept"
  End Select

'Hide main menu.
```

```
  forms!L_frmMaintenanceTable.visible = False

'Open form.
  DoCmd OpenForm strFrm
  DoCmd Restore
  MaintenanceTable = -1

MaintenanceTableExit:
  Exit Function

MaintenanceTableError:
  If Err = 2494 Then
    MsgBox "You can't edit this table. Function under→
      construction.", 64, "Maintenance Utility"
  Else
    MsgBox "An unidentified error occurred. Check to see→
      whether the command did what you expected, and if not, try→
      again.", 64, "Maintenance Utility"
  End If
  MaintenanceTable = 0
  Resume MaintenanceTableExit
End Function
```

FYI

Programming "Best Practices" Using Word and Excel

An IS professional at one company I work with observed, "If we don't customize applications, people have too many choices."

He meant that people have too many choices in situations that don't require any. For example, in Word there are at least three ways to keep a page number from appearing on the first page of a new section: 1) Format the page number as white; 2) format it as hidden text; or 3) select the Different First Page option on the Layout tab of the Page Setup dialog box.

Similarly, there are at least three ways to hide zero values in Excel worksheets (this is especially useful when linking Excel worksheets, because blank cells automatically fill with zeros): 1) Format the font for these cells as white; 2) create a custom number format that formats zero values automatically as white (for example, #,##0.00_);[Red](#,##0.00);[White]General); 3) turn off the Zero Values option in the Options dialog box.

Some of these methods are better than others. The best way to suppress page numbers in Word is to use the Different First Page option because this gives you instant uniformity among all sections in a document. The best way to hide *all* zero values in Excel is to turn off the Zero Values option, and the best way to hide them selectively is to use a number format. I refer to such methods as *best practices*. They require the fewest steps both to do and to *un*do because they rely on the way Word and Excel were designed to work.

Automating "Best Practices" to Make Materials Easier to Maintain

For many corporate materials (such as legal documents, policy manuals, and financial reports), maintenance is a far larger part of the life cycle than is creation. Often, users update these materials dozens—if not hundreds—of times. If the materials aren't created using best practices, they can be difficult to update. This is especially true when several people (each with a preferred practice) work on the same materials.

The best way to improve how materials are maintained, despite continuous updates and many pairs of hands, is to build utilities that automate common tasks, especially formatting tasks. Automation provides consistency, not only in how the resulting material is formatted but also in the technique used to format it. Automating best practices makes materials easier to maintain as well as to create.

It also provides a focus for training. When people learn applications such as Word and Excel in the context of their jobs—using business applications and utilities to create and update actual materials—three things happen consistently:

■ They learn to use Word and Excel *faster* because they learn them on a need-to-know basis.

■ They learn how to use the best practices for Word and Excel, which makes them more productive users of these tools.

■ They create materials that are easier to maintain and update.

Planning for Upgrades

The flip side of making business applications easier for users to maintain is making them easier for developers to maintain. In many cases, what's good for users is good for developers too. For example, using list boxes rather than check boxes makes it easier for both users and developers to update the options that applications provide. (See the section titled "Making Office-Based Applications Easy to Maintain" earlier in this chapter.)

Developers should plan for upgrades and build the first version with the inevitable next version in mind. They should provide a mechanism for upgrading applications that doesn't wipe out the user's existing application-related data or preferences. In practice, this means storing data and preferences in files that are separate from the application itself—in separate workbooks, text files, document files, INI files, and so on.

I once had to use an Excel application that didn't do this. It stored code and application-related data that users entered (which often consisted of several dozen entries) in the same workbook. Every time the developer upgraded the system (seemingly every other month), I had to reenter all my data. Imagine the complaints that this developer heard.

8

Developing Business Applications with Word

What's in a word? Thomas Peters and Robert Waterman, in their book *In Search of Excellence*, tell how little Lanier, Inc., beat its giant competitors (including IBM, Xerox, and Wang) in sales of stand-alone word processors *by not calling them word processors*. They quote an individual in the industry who observes that there isn't a bigger put-off than the term "word processor."

Not only is the term off-putting, but it's often misused. When businesspeople use word processing software to prepare faxes, letters, contracts, proposals, reports, and sales materials, they're frequently doing much more than word processing. They're thinking things up and getting them down on paper. They're editing and repackaging data to present it as useful information.

And despite the highly repetitive nature of most word processing tasks and the size of the user population, IS professionals have spent little energy in the realm of word processing, choosing instead to focus on the automation of traditional data processing tasks. Historically, automation for document processing has been confined to the word processor itself.

This is starting to change for a variety of reasons, from budget-induced cutbacks in support staff to the fact that end-user development tools make it increasingly practical to build customized document processing applications. Over the past few years, I've used Microsoft Word to build the following broad categories of business applications.

- **Publishing applications.** Not only can Word handle most desktop publishing functions required by businesses, but it enables companies to automate these functions. As a result, more are building Word-based applications for publishing. PaineWebber moved its equity research publishing system (which produces 2400 reports each year) to Word from a UNIX-based product. (See "CASE STUDY: Faster, Faster…" later in this chapter.)

- **Mail merge applications.** Although companies that deal directly with customers frequently store related data on a mainframe or on servers, Word-based mail merge systems enable those responsible for specific categories of contact to send mailings from their desktops. For example, a banking department I work with uses such a system to send account information to customers.

- **Applications that turn business correspondence into corporate data.** Companies are beginning to experiment with using fax and letter templates as front ends for collecting and using essential data on business contacts. (See the section titled "SAMPLE APPLICATION: Business Information Manager [BIM]" in Chapter 10.)

- **Word processing department templates.** For example, when Donaldson, Lufkin & Jenrette's investment banking group developed highly automated templates for word processing in the investment banking department, they created a new, more sophisticated look for their materials *and* cut processing time.

- **Business forms.** As companies move from handwritten forms to online entry, they find that the simplest solution is often to automate this process in an application that employees already use for word processing—Word.

This chapter presents three sample business applications and explains some of the programming techniques and practices that can help you develop business applications in Word. These sample applications can be found on the *Office Solutions* disk included with this book. They are as follows:

- WW-IBK.DOT and Global.DOT, two Word templates that demonstrate how to turn the shrink-wrapped version of Word into a custom product that aids in streamlining business operations.

- WrdGroup.DOT, a publishing application that facilitates workgroup activities. (I don't mean Microsoft Windows for Workgroups, I mean a group of people working on a single publication.)

- WriteR.DOT, a version of the template and utilities that I used to write this book.

SAMPLE APPLICATION: The Investment Banking Edition of Word (Word-IBK)

A central feature of Microsoft's end-user development tools is the ability to "roll your own commands" if you don't like the way these products work. In other words, you can customize the commands *built into* Word and Microsoft Excel to perform business-specific tasks. I regularly work with companies that customize Word's built-in commands (such as New, Open, Find File, and Summary Info) to better integrate Word with systems that handle essential operations—for example, document management systems, billing systems, or publishing systems.

The sample application Word-IBK (IBK stands for "investment banking") demonstrates key techniques for turning the shrink-wrapped version of Word into a highly customized product streamlined for a particular business. It uses two templates:

- Global.DOT (stored in Word's startup directory)

- WW-IBK.DOT (stored in Word's template directory)

PRODUCT SHEET: Word-IBK

Purpose:	Word-IBK takes the first step toward transforming Word from a generic word processor confined to stand-alone PCs into a business-document processor tightly integrated with a company's overall computing needs. The original version of this system (developed for a leading investment bank) customizes NORMAL.DOT to integrate Word with a document management system.
Development tool used:	Word
How WW-IBK.DOT and Global.DOT work together:	WW-IBK.DOT and Global.DOT (which, for demonstration purposes, replaces NORMAL.DOT) together provide a structure for extensively customizing Word's environment. These templates use three techniques to accomplish this:

■ They replace standard Word commands with custom procedures. For example, Global.DOT customizes the New command on the File menu, and WW-IBK.DOT customizes the Style command on the Format menu.

■ They provide custom tools that make it easier to produce documents and publications with a specific format. These tools are stored in document-specific templates—in this case, WW-IBK.DOT.

■ They *protect* document-specific templates (WW-IBK.DOT) to preserve the application's integrity.

The diagram on the following page illustrates Word-IBK's overall structure.

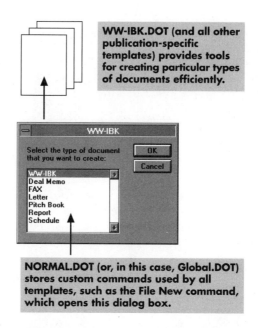

WW-IBK.DOT (and all other publication-specific templates) provides tools for creating particular types of documents efficiently.

NORMAL.DOT (or, in this case, Global.DOT) stores custom commands used by all templates, such as the File New command, which opens this dialog box.

FYI

Creating Custom Dialog Boxes

Although you can put controls in Word documents (using the Forms toolbar), the most flexible and professional-looking way to get information from users is through custom dialog boxes. Follow these steps to create a custom dialog box in Word:

1. Launch Word's Dialog Editor (see Figure 8-1), an application that enables you to "draw" controls in dialog boxes. (The file for the Dialog Editor, MACRODE.EXE, is installed automatically in Word's program directory.)

2. The Dialog Editor opens a blank Word dialog box. This application works rather like a drawing program:

   - To add a control, choose it from the Item menu.

   - To reposition a control, drag it to a new location.

   - To resize a control (or the dialog box itself), drag the edges.

   - To change the name of a control (or the dialog box), double-click it. You can also reposition and resize a control precisely by double-clicking it and then editing the resulting dialog box.

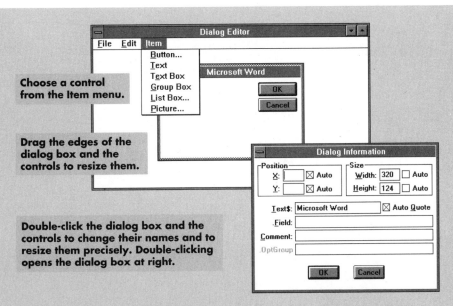

Choose a control from the Item menu.

Drag the edges of the dialog box and the controls to resize them.

Double-click the dialog box and the controls to change their names and to resize them precisely. Double-clicking opens the dialog box at right.

Figure 8-1. *Use Word's Dialog Editor (MACRODE.EXE) to create custom dialog boxes.*

3. After you "draw" a dialog box, use the Select Dialog command on the Edit menu, and then copy the dialog box to the Clipboard.

4. Paste the dialog box into your macro. The Clipboard translates the Dialog Editor's graphic image into WordBasic code (called a *dialog box definition*), which describes the position and name of each control. In the example below, the names of the controls (three text boxes) are in bold. Note that the order in which the controls are listed defines the tab order.

```
Begin Dialog UserDialog 592, 120, "New"
   Text 25, 40, 123, 13, "Company Name:"
   TextBox 153, 36, 320, 18, .Company
   TextBox 153, 62, 320, 18, .Presentation
   TextBox 153, 88, 320, 18, .Head
   Text 6, 66, 143, 13, "Presentation Date:"
   Text 42, 90, 107, 13, "First Heading:"
   Text 152, 13, 233, 13, "Type the following information."
   OKButton 491, 10, 88, 21
   CancelButton 491, 34, 88, 21
End Dialog
```

5. To display the dialog box under macro control, add the following two lines of code:

```
Dim dlg As UserDialog
x = Dialog(dlg)
```

The first line of code stores dialog box settings in the dialog record, dlg, which is of the type UserDialog. (See the sidebar titled "About Dialog Records" later in this chapter for more information.) All custom dialog boxes are of the type UserDialog.

The second line sets a variable to store the value that the dialog box returns. This value depends on the button the user clicks. If the user clicks OK, x = −1; if the user clicks Cancel, x = 0; and if the user clicks another command button, x = 1, 2, 3, and so on, depending on the number of command buttons in the dialog box. For example, if a dialog box has four command buttons—OK, Cancel, Help, and Next—OK and Cancel equal −1 and 0, respectively; Help equals 1; and Next equals 2.

6. Write code that performs a series of actions depending on the user's selections. For example, the following code displays a message box when the user clicks OK.

```
If x = -1 Then MsgBox "OK!"
```

(For an example of a dialog box in context, see the section titled "The New Command on Global.DOT's File Menu" later in this chapter.)

How Word-IBK Works

The original version of Word-IBK (developed for a leading investment bank) includes a custom NORMAL.DOT and more than a dozen *document-specific* templates, including a marketing presentation in landscape orientation, a report in portrait orientation, schedule makers and project management documents, memos, faxes, letters, and several legal documents. NORMAL.DOT customizes basic Word commands (such as New, Open, and File Find), which affects Word's functionality throughout the entire investment bank. Each of the document-specific templates provides custom functionality for the types of documents and publications the division produces.

The miniature version of Word-IBK presented here replicates this structure. Global.DOT is used in lieu of NORMAL.DOT to replace Word's standard New command with a custom New command. WW-IBK.DOT is a sample template with several tools that make it easier to produce reports.

NOTE   Companies that store all templates on a network and want to customize Word for everyone on the network generally do so by customizing
NORMAL.DOT. Use another global template (stored in Word's startup
directory) to customize individual installations of Word.

FYI

Listing Word's Built-In Commands

To list Word's built-in commands, open the Macro dialog box from the Tools
menu, and then select Word Commands from the Macros Available In drop-
down list (see Figure 8-2). This list includes all 840 WordBasic commands.
Since commands listed on menus start with the menu name, they're easy to
locate. To replace commands with a custom version, create a macro that uses
the same name. For example, to customize the FileFind command, create a
macro named FileFind.

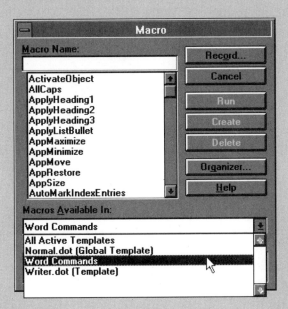

Figure 8-2. *To see Word's built-in commands, select Word Commands from the
Macros Available In drop-down list.*

Using Word-IBK

To use Word-IBK, store Global.DOT in Word's startup directory and store WW-IBK.DOT in Word's template directory.

1. After launching Word, choose the New command (customized by Global.DOT) from the File menu. (The custom New command is designed to list the templates available by easily recognized descriptive names. In this case, the list is hard-coded for demonstration purposes, and the only template available is WW-IBK.)

2. Create a new report based on WW-IBK by selecting it from the list box.

   The following specific features of Word-IBK are described in later sections of this chapter:

   ■ The custom New command on Global.DOT's File menu (see "Global.DOT: Customizing Word's Built-In Commands")

   ■ WW-IBK.DOT's menu (see "WW-IBK.DOT: Building a Better Template")

   ■ Protection (see "Getting In When You're Locked Out")

   ■ Templates structured to provide solid business applications (see "Structuring Word-Based Business Applications")

Global.DOT: Customizing Word's Built-In Commands

Global.DOT has a single purpose: It changes the New command on Word's File menu so the command opens a custom dialog box that lists templates by descriptive names (see Figure 8-3).

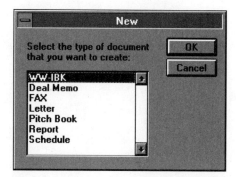

Figure 8-3. *When you choose the New command from Global.DOT's File menu, Word opens this dialog box.*

To replace a built-in Word command with a custom command, create a macro that uses the same name. Word then runs the custom command rather than the built-in command. Word runs only the first macro of a given name that it finds, and it searches in this order: current template, NORMAL.DOT, other global templates, and then Word's built-in commands (see Figure 8-4).

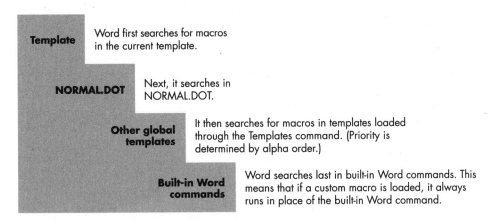

Template — Word first searches for macros in the current template.

NORMAL.DOT — Next, it searches in NORMAL.DOT.

Other global templates — It then searches for macros in templates loaded through the Templates command. (Priority is determined by alpha order.)

Built-in Word commands — Word searches last in built-in Word commands. This means that if a custom macro is loaded, it always runs in place of the built-in Word command.

Figure 8-4. *The Word template hierarchy.*

The New command on Global.DOT's File menu

This section explains how to customize the New command on the File menu (as I did for Global.DOT).

1. In the Macro dialog box, type the macro name *FileNew*, and then click the Create button. Word opens the following macro:

```
Sub MAIN
Dim dlg As FileNew
GetCurValues dlg
Dialog dlg
FileNew dlg
End Sub
```

Here's how this four-line macro works. (See the sidebar titled "About Dialog Records" later in this chapter for more information.)

■ The first line, Dim dlg As FileNew, creates a dialog record (dlg) for the built-in dialog box "FileNew." (A dialog record is a special variable that stores dialog box settings.)

■ The second line, GetCurValues dlg, retrieves the current dialog box settings.

- The third line, Dialog dlg, displays the dialog box (in this case, the New dialog box).

- The fourth line, FileNew dlg, executes the File New command with the user-specified settings. (In this case, it creates a new document based on the selected template.)

2. Add WordBasic code to select settings for the FileNew dialog box. For example, in the following macro the line of code shown in bold causes the New dialog box to default to the template WW-IBK rather than to Normal.

```
Sub MAIN
'In case user clicks Cancel.
On Error Resume Next
Dim dlg As FileNew
GetCurValues dlg
dlg.Template = "WW-IBK"
Dialog dlg
FileNew dlg
End Sub
```

3. To replace Word's New dialog box with a custom version, delete the standard code and write your own. The FileNew macro in Global.DOT, shown below, replaces Word's built-in File New command. (See the sidebar titled "Creating Custom Dialog Boxes" earlier in this chapter for more information.)

NOTE   For ease of reading, the ⟶ character represents a line break that does not appear in the actual code.

```
Sub MAIN
   On Error Goto FileNewProblem
   ScreenUpdating 0

'Create array for list box.
'I've hard-coded this list for demo purposes.
'Only the first item, WW-IBK, will work because
'it's the only template included.
   Dim NewArray$(7)
      NewArray$(0) = "WW-IBK"
      NewArray$(1) = "Deal Memo"
      NewArray$(2) = "FAX"
      NewArray$(3) = "Letter"
      NewArray$(4) = "Pitch Book"
      NewArray$(5) = "Report"
      NewArray$(6) = "Schedule"
```

```
'Create custom dialog box.
  Begin Dialog UserDialog 358, 162, "New"
    ListBox 15, 49, 213, 102, NewArray$(), .New
    OKButton 260, 11, 88, 21
    CancelButton 260, 35, 88, 21
    Text 16, 15, 215, 13, "Select the type of document", .Text1
    Text 16, 27, 183, 13, "that you want to create:", .Text2
  End Dialog

  Dim dlg As UserDialog
  x = Dialog dlg

'User clicks OK.
  If x = -1 Then
    Select Case dlg.New
      Case 0
        FileNew .Template = "WW-IBK.DOT"
      Case Else
        MsgBox "This template isn't hooked up.", "Word-IBK", 64
    End Select
  End If

CleanUp:
  ScreenUpdating 1
  Goto BYE

FileNewProblem:
  If Err > 0 Then
    Msg$ = "An error occurred in Word-IBK. Create another➞
      document"
    Msg$ = Msg$ + " to ensure correct formatting. Error code ="
    Msg$ = Msg$ + Str$(Err) + "."
    MsgBox Msg$, "Word-IBK", 48
    Goto CleanUp
  End If
BYE:
End Sub
```

FYI

About Dialog Records

WordBasic uses variables called *dialog records* to store settings for both built-in and custom dialog boxes. Developers use dialog records for three tasks:

■ To retrieve or change dialog box settings (such as the After setting in the Paragraph dialog box) without opening the dialog box.

■ To display built-in Word dialog boxes and to select settings for these dialog boxes. For example, you might want the New dialog box to default to the template WW-IBK rather than to the Normal template. (See the section titled "The New Command on Global.DOT's File Menu" earlier in this chapter for more information.)

■ To display a custom Word dialog box. Once you define a dialog record, you can manipulate each dialog box setting individually. For example, the FormatParagraph dialog record includes these settings: .LeftIndent, .RightIndent, .Before, .After, .LineSpacingRule, .LineSpacing, .Alignment, .WidowControl, .KeepWithNext, .KeepTogether, .PageBreak, .NoLineNum, .DontHyphen, .Tab, and .FirstIndent.

To *retrieve* a dialog record, follow the first two steps below. To *change* a dialog record, follow all four steps.

1. **Define the dialog record.** The WordBasic syntax for defining a dialog record is similar to the syntax for defining variables in Microsoft's other BASICs:

```
Dim DialogRecord As DialogBoxName
```

For example, the following code creates the variable FPara to store data for the FormatParagraph dialog box:

```
Dim FPara As FormatParagraph
```

2. **Retrieve the current dialog box settings.** The current settings vary, depending on one of two things: the last thing the user did (for example, the current FileOpen settings depend on the last directory from which the user opened a file) *or* the current cursor position (for example, the settings in FormatParagraph change depending on the paragraph selected). The following code builds on the previous code and retrieves *all* settings in the FormatParagraph dialog box for the currently selected paragraph:

```
GetCurValues FPara
```

At this point, you can use any setting from the FormatParagraph dialog box. For example, to display the amount of space that follows the currently selected paragraph, use the MsgBox statement:

```
MsgBox FPara.After
```

3. **To change settings, assign a new value.** For example, the following line of code eliminates space after the currently selected paragraph:

```
FPara.After = "0"
```

4. "Write" changes to the dialog box so that they take effect. For example, this line of code writes the setting in the previous line to the FormatParagraph dialog box:

```
FormatParagraph FPara
```

Of course, to change the space after a paragraph without opening the Paragraph dialog box, you can use a single line of code:

```
FormatParagraph .After = "0"
```

However, to retrieve a setting's current value or to open a dialog box, you must use a dialog record.

Using Word's Built-In Dialog Boxes

Whether or not you change settings in Word's built-in dialog boxes, five lines of code are necessary to open these dialog boxes and handle them correctly under macro control. Three lines (the first two and the last) are identical to the code for handling individual dialog records. The third line displays the dialog box. The following code opens the FormatParagraph dialog box:

```
SubMAIN
Dim FPara As FormatParagraph
GetCurValues FPara
Dialog FPara
FormatParagraph FPara
EndSub
```

The problem with this code is that if the user clicks the Cancel button, WordBasic generates error message #102: "Command failed." To prevent this, use On Error Resume Next or work into your error trap a line of code that suppresses this message. In the following error trap, And Err <> 102 suppresses the "Command failed" message. (See the section titled "Getting In When You're Locked Out" later in this chapter to see this error trap in context.)

```
If Err > 0 And Err <> 102 Then MsgBox "An error occurred in WW-IBK.↵
   Check to see whether it did what you expected, and if not, try↵
   choosing the command again.", "WW-IBK", 48
```

WW-IBK.DOT: Building a Better Template

WW-IBK.DOT includes a handful of features and custom commands. Some commands provide specific functionality that makes it easier to create this particular type of report, and others demonstrate good template-building practices generally. For example, it's a good practice to store custom commands added to templates in a single place. (I use the Utilities menu for this purpose.) It's also a good practice to use macros to apply styles.

I once developed a Word system for a company that told me it "had templates already." These templates consisted of a header and a footer and a few dozen styles with names such as Th, b1, Sh, and Head. Since people didn't know *when* to use these styles, they didn't use them at all. Instead, they formatted everything manually.

WW-IBK.DOT's Utilities menu (see Figure 8-5) lists the *items* that people want to format (such as main heads, subheads, and exhibit titles) rather than the corresponding style names (Headings 1, 2, and 4). Besides being easier to use, this method of formatting offers another advantage: It keeps custom styles to a minimum. If a particular element requires complex formatting and the use of several styles (a table, for example), you can apply these styles automatically as part of a macro.

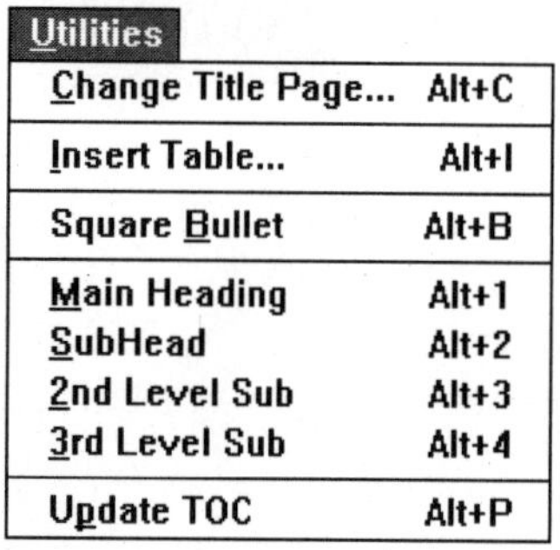

Utilities	
Change Title Page...	Alt+C
Insert Table...	Alt+I
Square Bullet	Alt+B
Main Heading	Alt+1
SubHead	Alt+2
2nd Level Sub	Alt+3
3rd Level Sub	Alt+4
Update TOC	Alt+P

Figure 8-5. *The custom menu for WW-IBK.DOT. Note that it includes both macros that perform multistep tasks and those that apply styles.*

Getting In When You're Locked Out

WW-IBK.DOT uses *protection* to lock users out of a single section—the title page, which contains bookmarks that affect the header. By protecting section one, I prevent users from accidentally deleting these bookmarks. Unfortunately, protection requires added work for the developer.

When you look at the code for WW-IBK.DOT, you'll notice two lines that pepper every macro: WordLibrary.Unprotect and WordLibrary.Protection. These commands refer to the Unprotect and Protection routines in the macro library named WordLibrary. (See the sidebar titled "Macro Libraries" later in this chapter for more information.) Every time a macro that uses a protected Word feature runs, you have to *unprotect* the document when the macro starts and *reprotect* it when the macro ends.

FYI

Protecting Macros

Use WordBasic's MacroCopy statement to make macros *execute-only*—in other words, to prevent users from reading or editing them. This is a good way to distribute applications. To use this statement, both the template *from* which you copy and the one *to* which you copy must be open. Use the following syntax:

```
MacroCopy Template1:Macro1$, Template2:Macro2$, 1
```

For example, the following code copies the macro LIB in the template WW-IBK.DOT to the macro LibEXE in the same template. LibEXE is execute-only:

```
Sub MAIN
   MacroCopy "c:\template\ww-ibk:LIB", "c:\template\ww-ibk:LibEXE", 1
End Sub
```

If you don't specify a template name, MacroCopy uses the NORMAL.DOT template. For example, the following code copies the macro LIB in the template WW-IBK.DOT to LibEXE in NORMAL.DOT:

```
Sub MAIN
   MacroCopy "c:\template\ww-ibk:LIB", "LibEXE", 1
End Sub
```

If you omit the third argument for the MacroCopy statement, it copies macros without making them execute-only.

Although a few gurus claim to have hacked execute-only WordBasic code, no one has published the secret. Until someone does, consider this process irreversible and be careful not to overwrite original code with an execute-only version.

Protection in Word version 6

The Protect Document command in Word version 6 comes with some baggage: As soon as you lock users out of a particular section, they're prevented from using nearly one-third of Word's menu commands *no matter what section they are in* (see Figure 8-6 on the following page).

Invoking code to unprotect and reprotect the document as macros run is inconvenient, but it's easy to do. Re-enabling commands that Protect Document disables isn't much harder, but it's more time-consuming. For each command that you want people to be able to use in the nonprotected areas of a document, substitute a custom command for Word's built-in command, as described in the section titled "The New Command on Global.DOT's File Menu" earlier in this chapter.

File	Edit	View	Insert	Format	Tools
Templates	Select All	Outline	Page Numbers	Drop Cap	Hyphenation
Page Setup	AutoText	Master Document	Annotation	Heading Numbering	Word Count
	Bookmark	Header And Footer	Form Field	AutoFormat	AutoCorrect
	Links	Footnotes	Footnote	Style Gallery	Mail Merge
		Annotations	Caption	Style	Envelopes And Labels
			Cross-reference	Frame	Revisions
			Index And Tables	Picture	Macro
			File	Drawing Object	Customize
			Frame		
			Picture		

Figure 8-6. *If you protect one section of your document, you lose access to these commands throughout your document.*

For example, in WW-IBK.DOT, I customized the Style command on the Format menu. I renamed it "Styles" for demonstration purposes, and I assigned it the keyboard shortcut Alt+S. The code, which follows, doesn't change the Style dialog box at all; it simply turns the standard Style dialog box into a template-specific command that the developer controls.

```
Sub MAIN
   On Error Goto StylesProblem

'Calls the Unprotect sub in the WordLibrary macro.
   WordLibrary.Unprotect

'Makes styles available despite protection.
   Dim FStyle As FormatStyle
   GetCurValues FStyle
   FormatStyle FStyle
   Dialog FStyle

CleanUp:
   On Error Resume Next
   WordLibrary.Protection
   Goto BYE
```

```
StylesProblem:
  If Err > 0 And Err <> 102 Then
    Msg$ = "An error occurred in the Styles command. "
    Msg$ = Msg$ + " Error code =" + Str$(Err) + "."
    MsgBox Msg$, "WW-IBK", 48
    Goto CleanUp
  End If

BYE:
End Sub
```

In addition to re-enabling commands that protection disables, you have to contend with disabled toolbar buttons. (These aren't "grayed out" like disabled menu commands are—instead, they beep when you click them.) One way to handle this is to customize toolbars to include only those commands that work.

FYI

Macro Libraries

There are two kinds of Word libraries: the *WLL*, which requires some C/C++ programming (see Chapter 6 for more information); and the humbler *macro library*. Storing frequently used subroutines and functions in macro libraries makes them easier to reuse: Simply copy the macro library into the template in which you're working. (Use the Organizer command in the Macro dialog box to do this.)

For example, the three sample applications in this chapter use the macro library called WordLibrary, which includes four routines that I use often:

- The WindowsDirectory$ function, which returns the path for the Windows directory. If you use Windows API calls regularly, consider writing library functions for them. That way, you declare these functions once—in the library—and can use them ever after.

- The WhichView function, which returns a value that indicates which view is in effect when the macro starts—Normal, Page Layout, and so on—so macros that change this view can restore it to the original when they finish.

- The subroutines UnProtect and Protection, which unprotect and reprotect documents. As you can tell from reading the code for these subroutines, the password for WW-IBK.DOT is "xxx." To secure this template, make macros that use passwords execute-only. (See the previous sidebar, "Protecting Macros," for instructions.)

WordLibrary's code follows:

```
Declare Function GetWindowsDirectory Lib "Kernel"(lpBuffer As→
  String, nSize As Integer) As Integer

Function WindowsDirectory$
'Make StringHolder long enough to hold the system directory
'path.
  StringHolder$ = String$(256, 0)

'Call the API function, which reads the directory path into
'StringHolder.
  iLength = GetWindowsDirectory(StringHolder$,→
  Len(StringHolder$))

'Trim StringHolder$ down to its actual size.
  StringHolder$ = Left$(StringHolder$, iLength)
  WindowsDirectory$ = StringHolder$
End Function


Function WhichView
  If ViewNormal() = -1 Then
    View = 0
  ElseIf ViewOutline() = -1 Then
    View = 1
  ElseIf ViewPage() = -1 Then
    View = 2
  ElseIf ViewMasterDocument() = -1 Then
    View = 3
  End If
  WhichView = View
End Function


Sub Protection
'Protect document.
  ToolsProtectDocument .DocumentPassword = "xxx", .Type = 2
  ToolsProtectSection .Protect = 1, .Section = 1
End Sub


Sub Unprotect
'Unprotect document.
  ToolsUnprotectDocument .DocumentPassword = "xxx"
End Sub
```

Structuring Word-Based Business Applications

Three techniques help you structure Word-based business applications as logical extensions of Word:

- Use auto macros (see Figure 8-7). These macros run automatically whenever a particular event occurs. For example, the AutoNew macro runs whenever you create a new document based on the template. Auto macros provide one of WordBasic's rare nods to event-driven programming.

- Use custom menus to house custom commands.

- Use custom dialog boxes. Users shouldn't have to scroll through documents to create or edit standard elements, such as title page and cover information, disclaimers, the table of contents, headers and footers, and "end material" such as the index. For example, every standard element in the original version of Word-IBK uses a dialog box when user input is required, or it is handled automatically through code when user input isn't necessary.

Macro	Event Trigger
AutoExec	Runs when users launch Word. (You have to store this macro in NORMAL.DOT or in another global template stored in Word's startup directory.)
AutoNew	Runs when users create a new document based on the template that contains the AutoNew macro.
AutoOpen	Runs when users open an existing document.
AutoClose	Runs when users close a document.
AutoExit	Runs when users quit Word.

Figure 8-7. *Auto macros.*

WW-IBK.DOT demonstrates the use of auto macros and dialog boxes to handle its title page (see Figure 8-8 on the following page):

- AutoNew handles first-time input of the report's title (usually a company's name) and the presentation date.

- ChangeTitlePage handles editing of this information.

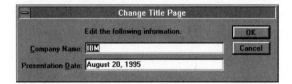

Figure 8-8. *WW-IBK.DOT's AutoNew macro opens the dialog box on top, which includes code to ensure that users fill in the required fields. The ChangeTitlePage macro opens the dialog box on the bottom, which uses bookmarks to retrieve the current company name and presentation date from the document.*

WW-IBK.DOT's AutoNew macro

WW-IBK.DOT's AutoNew macro (shown below) includes a routine to ensure that users type information for required fields before continuing. If a text box is blank when users click OK, the macro displays a message box explaining that they must type information into every text box and that they can edit it later with the Change Title Page command. When users click the message's OK button, the system displays the original dialog box, *preserving the information they already entered.* The code uses four features:

- The ReDim statement, which lets you redefine a dialog box variable on the fly

- Variables that store user-entered information

- A label (called Starter in this example) to which the macro returns to redisplay the dialog box

- Code that resets the dialog box controls equal to the variables that store user-entered information

```
Sub MAIN
  On Error Goto AutoNewProblem
  ViewToolbars .Toolbar = "WW-IBK Utilities", .Show

'Display hourglass pointer.
  WaitCursor 1
  Print "Creating document..."

'Turn off screen redraw.
  ScreenUpdating 0
  WordLibrary.Unprotect
```

```
'Custom dialog box.
  Begin Dialog UserDialog 592, 120, "WW-IBK"
    Text 25, 40, 123, 13, "&Company Name:"
    TextBox 153, 36, 320, 18, .Company
    TextBox 153, 62, 320, 18, .Presentation
    TextBox 153, 88, 320, 18, .Head
    Text 6, 66, 143, 13, "Presentation &Date:"
    Text 42, 90, 107, 13, "&First Heading:"
    Text 152, 13, 233, 13, "Type the following information."
    OKButton 491, 10, 88, 21
    CancelButton 491, 34, 88, 21
  End Dialog

'Hook up input form.
  Redim dlg As UserDialog

Starter:
  dlg.Company = Company$
  dlg.Presentation = Presentation$
  dlg.Head = Head$
  x = Dialog(dlg)

'User clicks OK.
  If x = -1 Then
    Company$ = dlg.Company
    Presentation$ = dlg.Presentation
    Head$ = dlg.Head

'Make sure that all fields are filled.
    If Company$ = "" Or Presentation$ = "" Or Head$ = "" Then
      MsgBox "Type information for each item in this dialog box.➞
        These items appear on the report's title page. You can➞
        edit them later using the Change Title Page command.",➞
        "WW-IBK", 48
      Goto Starter
    End If

'Insert information from dialog box and reset bookmarks.
    EditGoTo "Company"
    Insert Company$
    EditGoTo "\Para"
    ShrinkSelection
    EditBookmark .Name = "Company"        'Reset Bookmark
    EditGoTo "PresentDate"
    Insert Presentation$
    EditGoTo "\Para"
    ShrinkSelection
    EditBookmark .Name = "PresentDate"    'Reset Bookmark
    EditGoTo "Head"
    Insert Head$                          (continued)
```

(continued)

```
'Update TOC.
    EditGoTo "TOC"
    UpdateFields

'Position cursor for typing.
    EditGoTo "StartHere"

'User clicks Cancel.
  ElseIf x = 0 Then
    AreYouSure = MsgBox("Are you sure you want to exit this➝
      template? Click on YES to exit.", "WW-IBK", 36)
    If AreYouSure = 0 Then
      Goto Starter
    Else

'Set flag that closes document at macro's end.
'This avoids error message generated by the Protection
'command when no document is open.
      Flag = 1
    End If
  End If

CleanUp:
  If Flag = 1 Then FileClose 2
  If Flag <> 1 Then WordLibrary.Protection

'Turn on screen redraw.
  ScreenUpdating 1
  WaitCursor 0
  Goto BYE

AutoNewProblem:
  If Err > 0 And Err <> 102 Then
    Msg$ = "An error occurred in WW-IBK. Create another document"
    Msg$ = Msg$ + " to ensure correct formatting. Error code ="
    Msg$ = Msg$ + Str$(Err) + "."
    MsgBox Msg$, "WW-IBK", 48
  End If
  Goto CleanUp

BYE:
End Sub
```

WW-IBK.DOT's ChangeTitlePage macro

WW-IBK.DOT's ChangeTitlePage macro (shown on the facing page) uses the GetBookmark$ function to display the current company name and presentation date when it opens the dialog box.

NOTE Although you can use a dialog function to display information in dialog controls (see the sidebar titled "Creating Dynamic Dialog Boxes" later in this chapter), I always try to follow Occam's razor: *Entities should not be multiplied needlessly.* In other words, the simpler the better. One subroutine is clearly simpler than a subroutine plus a function, unless you need that function to do something you can't do otherwise—such as make a dialog box respond dynamically to user selections.

```
Sub MAIN
  On Error Goto TitlePageProblem

'Make sure necessary bookmarks exist.
  If ExistingBookmark("Company") = 0 Or→
    ExistingBookmark("PresentDate") = 0 Then
    MsgBox "The title page of this document is corrupt. The title→
      should be bookmarked as Company and the date as PresentDate.→
      You need to correct this manually. If the title isn't→
      bookmarked as Company, the name won't appear correctly in→
      the header.", "WW-IBK", 16
    Goto CleanUp
  End If
  ScreenUpdating 0
  WordLibrary.Unprotect

'Custom dialog box.
  Begin Dialog UserDialog 592, 94, "Change Title Page"
    Text 25, 40, 123, 13, "&Company Name:"
    TextBox 153, 36, 320, 18, .Company
    TextBox 153, 62, 320, 18, .Presentation
    Text 6, 66, 143, 13, "Presentation &Date:"
    Text 152, 13, 225, 13, "Edit the following information."
    OKButton 491, 10, 88, 21
    CancelButton 491, 34, 88, 21
  End Dialog

'Hook up input form.
  Dim dlg As UserDialog
  dlg.Company = GetBookmark$("Company")
  dlg.Presentation = GetBookmark$("PresentDate")
  x = Dialog(dlg)

'User clicks OK.
  If x = -1 Then
    Company$ = dlg.Company
    Presentation$ = dlg.Presentation

'Insert information from the dialog box and reset bookmarks.
    EditGoTo "Company"
    Insert Company$
```

(continued)

```
        EditGoTo "\Para"
        ShrinkSelection
        EditBookmark .Name = "Company"          'Reset Bookmark
        EditGoTo "PresentDate"
        Insert Presentation$
        EditGoTo "\Para"
        ShrinkSelection
        EditBookmark .Name = "PresentDate"      'Reset Bookmark
        CharRight

'Update the REF field in the header.
        ViewHeader
        UpdateFields
        CloseViewHeaderFooter
      End If

CleanUp:
    WordLibrary.Protection

'Turn on screen redraw.
    ScreenUpdating 1
    Goto BYE

TitlePageProblem:
    If Err > 0 Then
        Msg$ = "An error occurred in Change Title Page. "
        Msg$ = Msg$ + "Error code =" + Str$(Err) + "."
        MsgBox Msg$, "WW-IBK", 48
        Goto CleanUp
    End If

BYE:
End Sub
```

CASE STUDY: Faster, Faster...

A few years ago, PaineWebber's equity research department (which publishes more than 2400 reports each year—or a total of about 30,000 pages) decided to replace its WANGs with PCs and to invest in a new publishing system. The existing system, a proprietary UNIX-based publishing platform, had three problems:

- It was expensive to run.

- Few people knew how to operate it.

- It was slow.

One reason it was so slow was that it wasn't compatible with anything. For example, it wasn't compatible with any word processing software (WANG, Word, or WordPerfect) or any of the department's printers. As a result, the department had to *reprocess* all text through a series of translation tables to get it into the UNIX system, and after formatting the text into pages, it had to run those pages through another series of translation tables to print them.

Candy Schwartz, vice president in charge of publishing at PaineWebber, summed up the problem this way: "We had 56 analysts, and three operators published all their reports. It got to the point where we either had to beef up the publishing staff or think of another way to do it." They decided to find another way to do it.

The Need for a Desktop Publisher

First, the department investigated proprietary typesetting systems. But because the prices were astronomical and turnaround time would remain relatively slow, they decided that a PC-based desktop publishing system might make more sense. But when they compared the leading desktop publishing systems—Ventura, PageMaker, and FrameMaker—they found that these packages weren't much easier to use than the proprietary systems. The hardware for the desktop systems was cheaper, but the department would still have to funnel publications through a small group of highly trained people.

Meanwhile, the department had chosen Excel and Word as their main applications, and a closer look at Word revealed that it might be able to double as a desktop publisher. It did nearly everything they wanted, with two exceptions: It had weak typesetting capabilities (especially *kerning*—the ability to adjust spacing between letters), and it didn't support printer pagination. But it did almost everything else the department needed, and it offered these advantages:

- It eliminated the need for specially trained staff.

- It eliminated the need to translate text from one system to another.

- It eliminated significant manual labor because the department could use WordBasic to automate tasks.

In the end, Word's timesaving potential won out. As Candy Schwartz said, "Of course you want the product to look as good as possible, but it's also important to get it out there before everyone else. Our competitors are analyzing and making recommendations on the same companies we follow, so we want people to read our analysis first."

Ring Out the Old...

With the old UNIX-based typesetting system, publishing was often a seven-step process:

1. Analysts dictated reports, typed them into WANG, or wrote them out longhand.

2. Clerical staff typed the reports into WANG if they weren't already typed in; printed them out; attached tables and charts; and then walked them over to the publishing group.

3. The publishing group edited the reports and then sent them through the approval process.

4. Supervisory staff read and approved the reports.

5. Clerical staff made corrections.

6. The publishing group translated the reports into the UNIX-based publishing system, input any further corrections, and formatted the pages.

7. Analysts reviewed the reports in their finished form and then approved them.

Of course, in some cases, analysts *didn't* sign off on the reports. Instead, they put in motion a whole new round of editing and formatting. At its fastest, the process took nearly a week.

...And Ring In the New

When PaineWebber switched to Word, it got more than a new publishing system—it got a whole new process. The department built automated templates that enabled analysts and clerical staff to format reports as they typed. The publishing group still edits (using annotations and revision marks) and checks formatting—and the approval process is unchanged—but turnaround time is down to 24 hours for most reports.

Although there was some initial concern that analysts and clerical staff were doing more work up front, it soon became obvious that they were doing less work on the whole. For example, use of Word's annotations and revisions eliminated the need to input corrections. Plus, analysts now have more control over their reports.

Candy Schwartz noted that although analysts aren't necessarily writing more than they used to, "they're certainly able to take better advantage of what they have written and to repackage it for different audiences. If they've done a quick memo for our sales force, it's now easier for them to include information from that memo in a larger report for clients. They get a lot more mileage out of research than they used to."

SAMPLE APPLICATION: WrdGroup.DOT

WrdGroup.DOT is a version of a publishing template used by a financial publishing group. It stores in an INI file standard information (such as name, title, phone, and assistant) for each member who authors publications. This makes it easier for the clerical staff to handle publications for everyone in the group.

WrdGroup.DOT has three main macros, which I examine in the following sections:

- AutoNew calls the MembersOnly macro, which enables users to select a member. It then opens a main dialog box that displays information particular to the selected member and in which users type other information for the publication.

- MembersOnly populates a list box with names of the members stored in the WW-GRP.INI file. If users add or edit members, it calls the OpenDefaultsFile macro.

- OpenDefaultsFile manages the process of adding member information to the INI file and editing it.

PRODUCT SHEET: WrdGroup

Purpose:	WrdGroup makes it easier for people who regularly work together on projects to collaborate more closely. The original version of this application stores standard publishing information (such as name, phone number, and so on) for workgroup members who author financial reports. This makes it easy for clerical staff to pull up an author's standard information and start new reports.
Development tool used:	Word
How WrdGroup works:	When you create a new publication based on WrdGroup.DOT (to do this, choose New from the File menu), WrdGroup opens a dialog box that lists workgroup members. You can add new members or edit information for existing members. When you select the member who is authoring the publication, WrdGroup populates the main dialog box with that author's standard information. When you click OK in this dialog box, the application enters the standard information into the publication's footer.
	The diagram on the next page shows WrdGroup's three main features: the *member dialog box*, the *main dialog box* (which includes standard author information and other document information), and the *document template*.

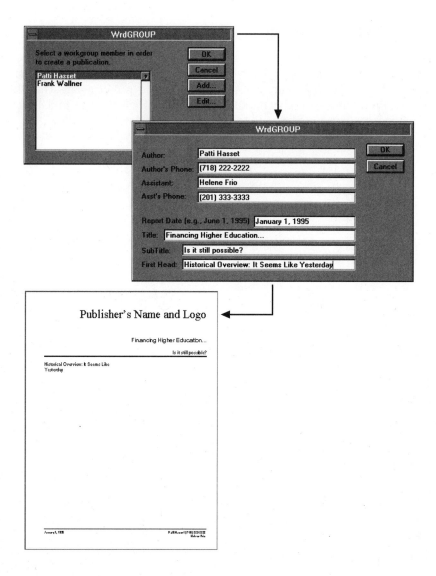

AutoNew

WrdGroup.DOT's AutoNew macro, shown below, manages the document creation process. To do this, it performs three specific tasks:

- It uses Page Layout view because it has a two-column format. AutoNew therefore calls the WhichView function in the WordLibrary macro to determine the last view that users set. It stores this information in a

document variable (using the SetDocumentVar statement). The
AutoClose macro uses the GetDocumentVar statement to reset the view.

> **NOTE** WordBasic's *document variables* are similar to global variables in that
> they enable you to share information among macros. However, they
> do this by storing the information in the document itself (rather than in
> memory), which means that when you reopen the document, you can
> still use its document variables.

- It calls the MembersOnly macro to open a dialog box from which users
  select the publication's author.

- It opens the main dialog box where users type information and then
  inserts this information into the publication.

```
Sub MAIN
   On Error Goto AutoNewProblem
   WaitCursor 1
   ScreenUpdating 0

'Get current view and restore in file close.
   WhichView = WordLibrary.WhichView
   If WhichView <> 2 Then
     Select Case WhichView

'Normal.
       Case 0
         SetDocumentVar "WhichView", "0"

'Outline.
       Case 1
         SetDocumentVar "WhichView", "1"

'Master doc.
       Case 3
         SetDocumentVar "WhichView", "3"
     End Select
   End If

'This calls the macro that opens a list box with member names.
   MembersOnly

'MembersOnly macro sets this variable if user clicks Cancel.
   c$ = GetDocumentVar$("cancel")
   If c$ = "0" Then Goto CleanUp
```

(continued)

```
DefineDialog:
  Begin Dialog UserDialog 632, 222, "WrdGROUP"
    Text 16, 25, 56, 13, "&Author:"
    TextBox 144, 20, 361, 18, .Author
    Text 16, 47, 121, 13, "Author's &Phone:"
    TextBox 144, 42, 361, 18, .AuthorPhone
    Text 16, 67, 75, 13, "A&ssistant:"
    TextBox 144, 65, 361, 18, .Assistant
    Text 16, 89, 104, 13, "Ass&t's Phone:"
    TextBox 144, 87, 361, 18, .AssistantPhone
    Text 16, 126, 248, 13, "&Report Date (e.g., June 1, 1995)"
    TextBox 274, 124, 232, 18, .ReportDate
    Text 16, 149, 40, 13, "T&itle:"
    TextBox 67, 146, 438, 18, .Title
    Text 16, 172, 69, 13, "&SubTitle:"
    TextBox 110, 168, 395, 18, .SubTitle
    Text 16, 193, 84, 13, "&First Head:"
    TextBox 110, 190, 395, 18, .Head
    OKButton 530, 12, 88, 21
    CancelButton 530, 37, 88, 21
  End Dialog

'Hook up input form.
  Redim dlg As UserDialog

'Get number for selected member from doc variable "Member" stored
'by MembersOnly macro, and read the defaults for that member
'from WW-GRP.INI into the dialog box.
  MemberNum$ = GetDocumentVar$("Member")
  If MemberNum$ <> "" Then
    MemberSection$ = "Member" + MemberNum$
    dlg.Author = GetPrivateProfileString$⮑
      (MemberSection$, "Author", "ww-grp.ini")
    dlg.AuthorPhone = GetPrivateProfileString$⮑
      (MemberSection$, "AuthorPhone", "ww-grp.ini")
    dlg.Assistant = GetPrivateProfileString$⮑
      (MemberSection$, "Assistant", "ww-grp.ini")
    dlg.AssistantPhone = GetPrivateProfileString$⮑
      (MemberSection$, "AssistantPhone", "ww-grp.ini")
  End If

'Get information from dialog box.
  x = Dialog(Dlg)

'If user clicks OK.
  If x = -1 Then
    ViewPage
```

```
'First pg footer.
   ViewFooter
   Insert dlg.ReportDate + Chr$(9) + dlg.Author + "   "↵
     + dlg.AuthorPhone
   Insert Chr$(11)
   Insert Chr$(9) + dlg.Assistant

'Enter other info.
   EditGoTo .Destination = "Title"
   Insert dlg.Title
   EditGoTo .Destination = "Sub"
   Insert dlg.SubTitle
   EditGoTo .Destination = "Head"
   Insert dlg.Head
   EditGoTo .Destination = "StartHere"

'If user clicks Cancel.
  Else
    FileClose 2
    Goto CleanUp
  End If

CleanUp:
  WaitCursor 0
  ScreenUpdating 1

'If user clicked Cancel button in member list dialog box,
'close the file.
  If c$ = "0" Then FileClose 2
  Goto BYE

AutoNewProblem:
  If Err > 0 And Err <> 102 Then
    Msg$ = "An error occurred in WrdGROUP. Create another document"
    Msg$ = Msg$ + " to ensure correct formatting. Error code ="
    Msg$ = Msg$ + Str$(Err) + "."
    MsgBox Msg$, "WrdGROUP", 48
  End If
  Goto CleanUp

BYE:
End Sub
```

Managing Members

WrdGroup.DOT's MembersOnly macro, shown in the next section ("Members-Only"), manages the list of members. It reads member information stored in WW-GRP.INI and displays names in a list box. If users add or edit member information, MembersOnly calls the OpenDefaultsFile macro, which modifies the INI file.

When I first started to design this system, I considered three ways to store member information:

- In a single text file
- In separate text files
- In an INI file

Although each method has its pros and cons, the single text file method is clearly the worst choice. Each line in the file would have to contain the information for a given member separated by commas, as shown below:

```
Author, AuthorPhone, Assistant, AssistantPhone
```

You would then have to navigate the text file with WordBasic's file I/O functions (Open, Close, Read, Write, and Seek), which requires writing a fair amount of code. In addition, there would be no way to delete members (other than opening the text file and deleting them manually).

WrdGroup.DOT uses an INI file, but I'm not convinced that separate text files are a worse choice. (The original version of the system uses separate text files.) Although it's certainly *cleaner* to have a single INI file than to have a slew of tiny text files, the code for managing the text files is simpler (for example, to delete a member, use the Kill statement). To delete a member using the INI file, use the Windows API ProfileString functions (the other INI file routines use Word's version of these functions) and write a procedure to renumber the members.

Here is the structure of the WW-GRP.INI file:

```
[NumberOfMembers]
number=

[Member1]
Author=
AuthorPhone=
Assistant=
AssistantPhone=
```

FYI

Creating Dynamic Dialog Boxes

Dynamic dialog boxes change on screen in response to users' actions. Here are a few examples of dynamic dialog boxes in Word:

- In the Open dialog box, the files that are displayed change depending on the directory you select.

- In the Style dialog box, the Delete button is either enabled or disabled depending on the style you select. (You can't delete Word's built-in styles, such as Normal, Headings 1 through 9, and Annotation Text.)

- In the Insert Picture dialog box, the Preview window shows the image in the currently selected graphics file.

Dynamic dialog boxes require slightly different code than do other dialog boxes. To make a dialog box dynamic, follow these steps:

1. Add a dialog function.

2. List that function in the dialog definition.

The dialog box calls the dialog function whenever users select a control. The MembersOnly and QuickSwitch macros, which are shown later in this chapter, provide sample code for dynamic dialog boxes.

Listing a Dialog Function

The following code shows the syntax for listing a dialog function in the dialog definition. (The function's name is in bold.)

```
Begin Dialog UserDialog 472, 188, "TitleBarText", .NameOfFunction
    Series of statements
End Dialog
```

Dialog Function Syntax

The following code shows the syntax for dialog functions:

```
Function NameOfFunction(ControlID$, Action, SupplementalValue)
    Series of statements
End Function
```

ControlID$ is the name of the control that users select—for example, the ControlID$ for a control named .ControlName is "ControlName."

Action is the value of one of six actions that occur in dialog boxes. (Figure 8-9 summarizes the dialog function Action values. See the WordBasic Help topic "Dialog Function Syntax" for complete information.)

Action Value	Meaning
1	Corresponds to dialog box initialization, which occurs *after* the Dialog function is called and *before* the dialog box appears on screen.
2	Corresponds to clicking a control—including command buttons, option buttons, and list boxes, but not including text boxes and combo boxes.
3	Corresponds to typing in a text box or a combo box. The value is passed to the dialog function when the text box or combo box loses the focus.
4	Corresponds to a change in focus. In this case, the ControlID$ identifies the control that gets the focus, and the SupplementalValue identifies the control that lost the focus (you can't call a message box in response to this action).
5	Corresponds to an idle state.
6	Corresponds to the user moving the dialog box.

Figure 8-9. *Dialog function Action values.*

SupplementalValue receives additional information about a change in a dialog box control, depending on the Action. (See the WordBasic Help topic "Dialog Function Syntax" for more information.)

Using Special Statements and Functions

Use the following statements and functions to create dynamic dialog boxes. (See WordBasic Help for complete information.)

- DlgControlID(*"ControlName"*)—Returns the numeric identifier for the control represented by *ControlName*.

- DlgEnable, DlgEnable( )—The statement enables or disables controls (1 = Enabled; 0 = Disabled; Omitted toggles). The function determines the state of controls (1 = Enabled; 0 = Disabled).

- DlgFilePreview, DlgFilePreview$( )—The statement previews the specified file. The function returns the pathname and the filename currently previewed.

- DlgFocus, DlgFocus$( )—The statement sets the focus to the specified control. The function returns the string identifier for the control that currently has the focus.

- DlgListBoxArray, DlgListBoxArray$( )—The statement fills a list box with the contents of an array variable. The function returns an array variable with the contents of a list box or the number of items in the list box.

- DlgSetPicture—Sets the graphic displayed by a picture control.

- DlgText, DlgText$( )—The statement sets the label for a control. The function returns a label.

- DlgUpdateFilePreview—Updates a file preview created by FilePreview$.

- DlgValue, DlgValue( )—The statement selects or clears a control. The function returns a value indicating whether a control is selected.

- DlgVisible, DlgVisible( )—The statement hides or unhides a control (1 = Visible; 0 = Hidden; Omitted toggles). The function returns a value indicating whether a control is visible (1 = Visible; 0 = Hidden).

MembersOnly

The MembersOnly macro, shown below, takes advantage of three features that are new to WordBasic version 6:

- It uses Word's GetPrivateProfileString$ function to read the members into the list box.

- It uses a dialog function (SelectName) to disable the Edit button if there are no members (for example, the first time you run the application).

- It uses the SetDocumentVar statement to store each member's name for use in both the OpenDefaultsFile macro and the AutoNew macro.

```
Dim Shared iNumNames

Sub MAIN
'Read member names from WW-GRP.INI into the list box array.

ShowDialog:
  iNumNames = Val(GetPrivateProfileString$→
    ("NumberOfMembers", "number", "ww-grp.ini"))

'Handles case where there are names in the INI file.
  If iNumNames <> 0 Then
    Redim MemberName$(iNumNames - 1)
    For i = 0 To iNumNames - 1
      MemberName$(i) = GetPrivateProfileString$("Member" +→
        LTrim$(Str$(i + 1)), "Author", "ww-grp.ini")
    Next
  Else
```

(continued)

```
'Handles case where there aren't names in the INI file.
   Redim MemberName$(0)
  End If

'Create list box of members.
  Begin Dialog UserDialog 472, 188, "Members List", .SelectName
    Text 20, 14, 273, 13, "Select a workgroup member in order"
    Text 20, 27, 177, 13, "to create a publication."
    ListBox 20, 46, 269, 127, MemberName$(), .MemberList
    OKButton 371, 10, 88, 21
    CancelButton 371, 34, 88, 21
    PushButton 371, 58, 88, 21, "&Add...", .Add
    PushButton 371, 82, 88, 21, "&Edit...", .Edit
  End Dialog

'Display dialog box.
  Dim dlg As UserDialog
  iRet = Dialog(dlg)

  Select Case iRet

'Respond to user input.
'The document variable Cancel indicates whether or not
'the Cancel button was clicked.
'The document variable Member indicates the number of the
'selected member as recorded in WW-GRP.INI.

'Cancel button.
    Case 0
      SetDocumentVar "Cancel", "0"

'OK button.
    Case -1
      SetDocumentVar "Cancel", "1"
      SetDocumentVar "Member", LTrim$(Str$(dlg.MemberList + 1))

'Add button.
    Case 1
      SetDocumentVar "Cancel", "1"
      SetDocumentVar "Member", ""
      OpenDefaultsFile           'RUN MACRO
      Goto ShowDialog

'Edit button.
    Case 2
      SetDocumentVar "Cancel", "1"
      SetDocumentVar "Member", LTrim$(Str$(dlg.MemberList + 1))
```

```
        OpenDefaultsFile              'RUN MACRO
        Goto ShowDialog
    End Select

Bye:
End Sub


'This function enables the Edit button. When you first
'use this sample application, no members are listed
'and the Edit button is disabled.
Function SelectName(ControlID$, Action, SupplementalValue)
    If iNumNames = 0 Then DlgEnable "Edit", 0
End Function
```

DefaultsFile

The OpenDefaultsFile macro, shown on the next page, manages the task of adding members to and editing in the WW-GRP.INI file. As you can see in the section titled "Managing Members" earlier in this chapter, which shows WW-GRP.INI's structure, this macro tracks members by the sequential number assigned when the member is added. It uses the document variable (Member-Num$) stored by the MembersOnly macro (described above) to determine which member users selected from the Members List dialog box.

■ If MemberNum$ is an empty string, OpenDefaultsFile opens an Add & Edit dialog box (see Figure 8-10) so a user can type information for a new member. When the user clicks OK, it adds this member to the INI file.

■ If MemberNum$ isn't empty, OpenDefaultsFile opens an Add & Edit dialog box that displays information for the selected member. When the user clicks OK, it reads the information from the dialog box into the INI file.

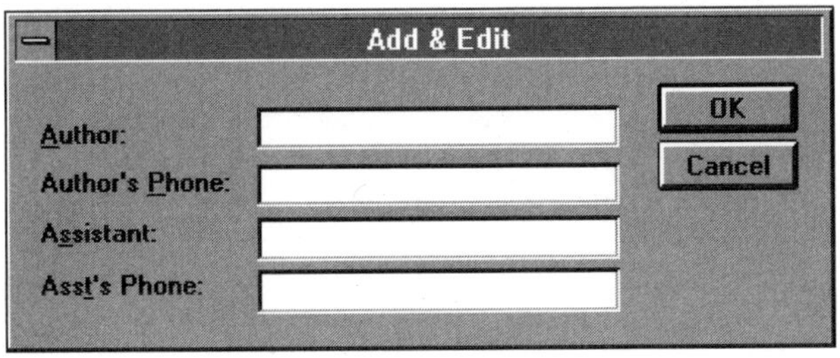

Figure 8-10. *WrdGroup.DOT's Add & Edit dialog box.*

```
Sub MAIN
'Create and display Add & Edit dialog box.
  Begin Dialog UserDialog 506, 118, "Add & Edit"
    Text 16, 24, 56, 13, "&Author:"
    Text 16, 45, 121, 13, "Author's &Phone:"
    Text 16, 66, 75, 13, "A&ssistant:"
    Text 16, 88, 104, 13, "Ass&t's Phone:"
    TextBox 152, 20, 226, 18, .DefaultAuthor
    TextBox 152, 43, 226, 18, .DefaultAuthorPhone
    TextBox 152, 66, 226, 18, .DefaultAsst
    TextBox 152, 88, 226, 18, .DefaultAsstPhone
    OKButton 401, 10, 88, 21
    CancelButton 401, 34, 88, 21
  End Dialog
  Redim dlg As UserDialog

'Display defaults. Get document variable Member (set in
'MembersOnly) to determine which member you're working with.
  MemberNum$ = GetDocumentVar$("Member")

'If MemberNum$ is an empty string...
  If MemberNum$ = "" Then

'...Set iNew to 1 to indicate that a new member is being added.
    iNew = 1

'Otherwise, set iNew to 0.
  Else
    iNew = 0
  End If

'If not a new member, get information from WW-GRP.INI and
'display it in the dialog box.
  If iNew = 0 Then
    MemberSection$ = "Member" + MemberNum$
    dlg.DefaultAuthor = GetPrivateProfileString$(MemberSection$,➥
      "Author", "ww-grp.ini")
    dlg.DefaultAuthorPhone = GetPrivateProfileString$➥
      (MemberSection$, "AuthorPhone", "ww-grp.ini")
    dlg.DefaultAsst = GetPrivateProfileString$(MemberSection$,➥
      "Assistant", "ww-grp.ini")
    dlg.DefaultAsstPhone = GetPrivateProfileString$➥
      (MemberSection$, "AssistantPhone", "ww-grp.ini")
  End If

'Set or reset member information.
  x = Dialog(dlg)
```

```
'User clicks OK.
  If x = -1 Then

'If a new member, increment the NumberOfMembers entry in the INI file
'and create a new section name.
    If iNew = 1 Then
      iNumNames = Val(GetPrivateProfileString$→
        ("NumberOfMembers", "number", "ww-grp.ini")) + 1
      MemberNum$ = LTrim$(Str$(iNumNames))
      SetPrivateProfileString "NumberOfMembers", "number",→
        MemberNum$, "ww-grp.ini"
      MemberSection$ = "Member" + MemberNum$
    End If

'Read new information from the dialog box into the INI file.
    SetPrivateProfileString MemberSection$, "Author",→
      dlg.DefaultAuthor, "ww-grp.ini"
    SetPrivateProfileString MemberSection$, "AuthorPhone",→
      dlg.DefaultAuthorPhone, "ww-grp.ini"
    SetPrivateProfileString MemberSection$, "Assistant",→
      dlg.DefaultAsst, "ww-grp.ini"
    SetPrivateProfileString MemberSection$, "AssistantPhone",→
      dlg.DefaultAsstPhone, "ww-grp.ini"

'Set the document variable Member to the new member number.
    SetDocumentVar "Member", MemberNum$

  End If
End Sub
```

SAMPLE APPLICATION: WriteR

WriteR is what I dubbed the template that I used to write this book. It consists of a dozen or so styles (many of which were specified by the publisher, Microsoft Press) and several utilities that make the mechanics of writing a little easier. I provide code for three utilities in this section:

■ The SEQuencer utility makes it easy to sequence multiple items with different formats using SEQ fields.

■ The REFeree utility makes it easy to reference bookmarked items using REF fields.

■ The QuickSwitch utility makes it easy to switch to frequently used directories to open and save files.

PRODUCT SHEET: WriteR

Purpose:	WriteR includes utilities that are useful for most publishing and document processing tasks.
Development tool used:	Word
How WriteR works:	WriteR lets you access its commands through the Utilities menu, the custom toolbar, or shortcut keys. The Utilities menu (which lists the shortcut keys) and the custom toolbar are shown below.

Utilities	
FieldsOn	Alt+Z
FieldsOff	Alt+X
Sequencer	Alt+S
QuickSwitch	Alt+Q
Referee	Alt+R
Square**B**ulletNStyle	Alt+B
Heading1	Alt+1
Heading2	Alt+2
Heading3	Alt+3
Heading4	Alt+4
Heading5	Alt+5
CodeLibrary	Alt+C

SEQuencer

Word's fields are powerful developer tools, especially when controlled through code. SEQuencer (see Figure 8-11) provides an interface for using Word's SEQ (sequence) fields, which are designed to automatically number items in your document. For example, you can automate the numbering of tables, figures, appendixes, and items in a list (see Figure 8-12).

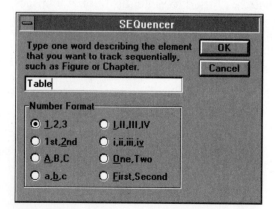

Figure 8-11. *The dialog box for WriteR.DOT's SEQuencer utility.*

NOTE To insert a SEQ field manually, choose the Field command from the Insert menu, and then select the Numbering option. Also, you can display and hide field codes by using WriteR.DOT's Fields On and Fields Off utilities.

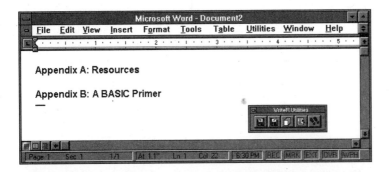

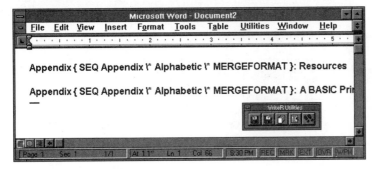

Figure 8-12. *The window on the top shows the results of the field codes in the window on the bottom.*

The syntax for the SEQ field is:

```
{SEQ Identifier \* Options \* MERGEFORMAT}
```

Because SEQ fields count the number of times *Identifier* appears in a document, you can track multiple *Identifier*s simultaneously. Figure 8-13 on the following page lists the possible switches for the argument *Options* and the sequence formats that they produce. The MergeFormat switch preserves the field's text formatting during an update.

Switch	Result
Arabic	1, 2, 3
Ordinal	1st, 2nd, 3rd
Alphabetic	A, B, C
alphabetic	a, b, c
Roman	I, II, III
roman	i, ii, iii
CardText	one, two, three
OrdText	first, second, third
Hex	9, 1A, 1B
DollarText	one and 00/100, two and 00/100

Figure 8-13. *Switches for the SEQ fields.*

The examples in Figure 8-14 number both tables and figures automatically. Note the result in each case.

Table/Figure	Field Code	Result
Table	{SEQ Table * alphabetic * MERGEFORMAT}	Table a
Figure	{SEQ Figure * Arabic * MERGEFORMAT}	Figure 1
Table	{SEQ Table * alphabetic * MERGEFORMAT}	Table b
Table	{SEQ Table * alphabetic * MERGEFORMAT}	Table c
Figure	{SEQ Figure * Arabic * MERGEFORMAT}	Figure 2

Figure 8-14. *Automatic numbering with SEQ.*

The code for SEQuencer, shown below, is simple. It opens a dialog box in which users "build" a SEQ field. The code's "core" is a Select Case statement that enters a switch for the field based on the option button users selected.

```
Sub MAIN
    On Error Goto SequencerProblem
    WaitCursor 1
    ScreenUpdating 0

'Mark where cursor is when macro is invoked.
    EditBookmark "BackToHere"

'Custom dialog box.
DisplayDialog:
    Begin Dialog UserDialog 418, 196, "SEQuencer"
        Text 11, 10, 289, 13, "Type one word describing the element"
        Text 12, 23, 268, 13, "that you want to track sequentially,"
```

```
    Text 10, 35, 201, 13, "such as Figure or Chapter."
    TextBox 10, 53, 276, 18, .Sequencer
    GroupBox 10, 81, 276, 102, "Number Format"
    OptionGroup  .NumberFormat
    OptionButton 20, 100, 100, 16, "&1,2,3"
    OptionButton 20, 120, 87, 16, "1st,&2nd"
    OptionButton 20, 140, 68, 16, "&A,B,C"
    OptionButton 20, 160, 68, 16, "a,&b,c"
    OptionButton 140, 100, 100, 16, "&I,II,III,IV"
    OptionButton 140, 120, 100, 16, "i,ii,iii,i&v"
    OptionButton 140, 140, 112, 16, "&One,Two"
    OptionButton 140, 160, 124, 16, "&First,Second"
    OKButton 313, 8, 88, 21
    CancelButton 313, 32, 88, 21
  End Dialog
  Dim Dlg As UserDialog
  x = Dialog(Dlg)

'User clicks OK.
  If x = -1 Then

'Check if sequence is empty.
    If dlg.Sequencer = "" Then
      MsgBox "You have to enter the element that you want to➔
        sequence!", "SEQuencer", 64
      Goto DisplayDialog
    End If
    Sequence$ = dlg.Sequencer

'Get user's "switch" selection, which determines formatting.
    Select Case dlg.NumberFormat
      Case 0
        Format$ = "Arabic"
      Case 1
        Format$ = "Ordinal"
      Case 2
        Format$ = "Alphabetic"
      Case 3
        Format$ = "alphabetic"
      Case 4
        Format$ = "Roman"
      Case 5
        Format$ = "roman"
      Case 6
        Format$ = "CardText"
      Case 7
        Format$ = "OrdText"
    End Select
```

(continued)

```
'Build SEQ field code using the InsertField command. You
'can also use the InsertFieldChars command (see REFeree macro).
    InsertField .Field = "SEQ " + Sequence$ + " \* " + Format$→
       + " \* MERGEFORMAT"

'Select document.
    EditSelectAll

'Update ALL fields in document.
    UpdateFields

'Return to the starting point.
    EditGoTo .Destination = "BackToHere"
    EndOfLine

'Cancel.
  Else
     Goto CleanUp
  End If

CleanUp:
   EditBookmark "BackToHere", .Delete
   ScreenUpdating 1
   WaitCursor 0
   Goto BYE

SequencerProblem:
   If Err > 0 Then MsgBox "An error occurred in SEQuencer. Check to→
      see whether it did what you expected, and if not, try the→
      command again.", "SEQuencer", 48
   Goto CleanUp

BYE:
End Sub
```

REFeree

The REFeree utility, like SEQuencer, uses Word's fields (in this case, the REF
fields) as the basis for automation. REFeree simplifies the use of Word's REF (reference) fields, which are designed to automatically display text for bookmarked
items in your document (see Figure 8-15). The utility does this by opening a list
box where you select the bookmark whose text you want to reference. For
example, you can use REF fields to automatically track references to bookmarked chapter titles or figure numbers (see Figure 8-16).

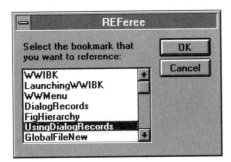

Figure 8-15. *The dialog box for WriteR.DOT's REFeree utility.*

NOTE To insert a REF field manually, choose the Field command from the Insert menu and then select the Links and References option.

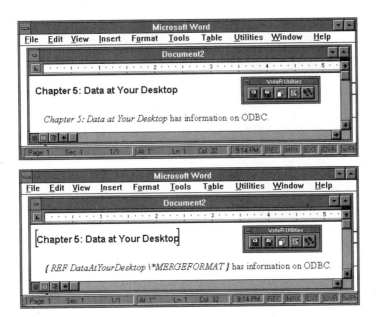

Figure 8-16. *The window on the top shows the results of the field codes in the window on the bottom.*

The syntax for the REF field is:

```
{REF BookMarkName \* MERGEFORMAT}
```

The code for REFeree, shown on the next page, is simple. It creates an array of bookmarks and then displays them in a custom dialog box. It uses the bookmark users select from this dialog box to build a REF field.

```
Sub MAIN
  On Error Goto RefereeProblem
  ScreenUpdating 0

'Bookmark original cursor position.
  EditBookmark .Name = "BackToHere"

'Turn on field codes if they're not on and create
'flag. Note that this is necessary because I build field
'codes manually using the InsertFieldChars command.
  If ViewFieldCodes() = 0 Then ViewFieldCodes 1 And Flag = 1

'Read bookmarks into list box.
  NoOfMarks = CountBookmarks()
  Dim ListArray$(NoOfMarks)

'No bookmarks.
  If NoOfMarks = 0 Then
    MsgBox "No bookmarks in this document!", "REFeree", 48
    Goto CleanUp
  End If

'Bookmarks.
  For i = 0 To NoOfMarks - 1
    ListArray$(i) = BookmarkName$(i + 1)
  Next

'Custom dialog box.
  Begin Dialog UserDialog 348, 144, "REFeree"
    ListBox 10, 44, 223, 90, ListArray$(), .MarksList
    OKButton 248, 10, 88, 21
    CancelButton 248, 34, 88, 21
    Text 12, 12, 192, 13, "Select the bookmark that"
    Text 12, 24, 172, 13, "you want to reference:"
  End Dialog
  Dim Dlg As UserDialog

'Return value for dialog.
  x = Dialog(Dlg)

'User clicks OK.
  If x = -1 Then

'Build REF field. Note that I do this slightly differently than
'in the code for SEQuencer. Here, I insert actual field characters,
'and then enter the text.
    InsertFieldChars
    Insert "REF " + ListArray$(dlg.MarksList) + " \* MERGEFORMAT"
```

```
'Select document and update ALL fields.
    EditSelectAll
    UpdateFields

'Return cursor to original position and delete
'temporary bookmark.
    EditGoTo .Destination = "BackToHere"
    EditBookmark .Name = "BackToHere", .Delete
  End If

CleanUp:
'Restore field codes display.
  If Flag = 1 Then ViewFieldCodes 0
  ScreenUpdating 1
  Goto BYE

RefereeProblem:
  If Err > 0 Then MsgBox "An error occurred in REFeree. Check to→
    see whether it did what you expected, and if not, try the→
    command again.", "REFeree", 48
  Goto CleanUp

BYE:
End Sub
```

QuickSwitch

The QuickSwitch utility (see Figure 8-17) stores paths that you use frequently
to eliminate the time-consuming process of switching directories manually.

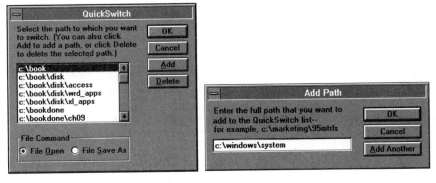

Figure 8-17. *The main dialog box and the Add Path dialog box for WriteR.DOT's
QuickSwitch utility.*

It stores these paths in a table in a Word document (Q_Switch.OPT) because this is an easy way to add, sort, and delete the path that users select (see Figure 8-18). I use the .OPT extension for the file because it provides a certain measure of security—users are less likely to delete .OPT files stored in the Windows directory than to delete .DOC files.

```
C:\book
C:\modeling
C:\bookdone\glossary
C:\bookdone\ch09
C:\word6\docs\tenth
C:\book\disk
C:\bookedit
C:\word6
C:\bookdone
C:\word6\template
```

Figure 8-18. *A sample table showing the format of Q_Switch.OPT.*

The QuickSwitch macro, shown below, is fairly complex. It consists of three subroutines (MAIN, FindTable, and FindRow) and a dialog function (EditItem), plus it uses the WindowsDirectory$ function in WordLibrary.

- The MAIN routine manages the utility's two dialog boxes (the main dialog box and the Add Path dialog box). It also handles such issues as whether Q_Switch.OPT exists, the number of rows in its table, and whether a document window is open. (If a document window is open, the utility stores the window's name and reactivates it if necessary—for example, if an error occurs.)

- The FindTable routine locates the table in Q_Switch.OPT, and the FindRow routine locates the path that users selected.

- The dialog function updates the screen dynamically as users delete paths from the list.

```
Dim Shared A, i, QWindow$, MainWindow$

Sub MAIN
  On Error Goto SwitchProblem
  ScreenUpdating 0

'Explicitly set Flag, which is used to indicate the windows
'that are open when users run this macro.
  Flag = 0

'Determine whether there's a document window open
'or whether only Document1 is open. If only Document1 is
'open, it will close when this macro runs, generating an error.
```

```
'You can't do this in a one-line If statement because if
'Window() = 0, WindowName$() generates an error.
  If Window() = 0 Then
    Flag = 1
  ElseIf WindowName$() = "Document1" And CountWindows() = 1 Then
    Flag = 1
  End If

'Get windows path; change to it; check whether INI file exists.
'Uses the WindowsDirectory$ function in WordLibrary macro.
  WindowsDirectory$ = WordLibrary.WindowsDirectory$
  ChDir WindowsDirectory$

'Check whether Q_Switch.OPT exists.
  FileFind .SearchName = " ", .SearchPath = WindowsDirectory$,→
    .Name = "Q_Switch.OPT", .SubDir = 0, .Title = "",→
    .Author = "", .Keywords = "", .Subject = "", .Options = 0,→
    .MatchCase = 0, .Text = "", .PatternMatch = 0,→
    .DateSavedFrom = "", .DateSavedTo = "", .SavedBy = "",→
    .DateCreatedFrom = "", .DateCreatedTo = "", .View = 0,→
    .SortBy = 0, .ListBy = 0, .SelectedFile = 0

'Count found files.
  A = CountFoundFiles()

'Handles case where no document windows are open.
  If Flag <> 1 Then MainWindow$ = WindowName$()

'Create Q_Switch.OPT if it doesn't exist.
  If A = 0 Then
    FileNew .Template = "Normal"

'Create table in Q_Switch.OPT if it doesn't exist.
    TableInsertTable .ConvertFrom = "", .NumColumns = "1",→
      .NumRows = "1", .InitialColWidth = "Auto", .Format = "0",→
      .Apply = "167"
    FileSaveAs .Name = "q_switch.opt"

'Rows in table; no paths entered yet.
    A = SelInfo(15)
    Dim PathArray$(A - 1)
    For i = 0 To A - 1
      PathArray$(i) = ""
    Next

'Read Q_Switch.OPT if it does exist; make sure you're in table.
  Else
    FileOpen .Name = "Q_Switch.OPT"
```

(continued)

```
'This label is for redisplaying the main dialog box.
Body:
    FindTable                'CALL SUB

'SelInfo(15) returns number of rows in table.
    A = SelInfo(15)

'Create array for list box.
    Redim PathArray$(A - 1)
    For i = 0 To A - 1
      EndOfLine
      StartOfLine 1
      A$ = Selection$()
      PathArray$(i) = A$
      LineDown
    Next

'If the table contains only 1 empty row...
    If A = 1 And Asc(A$) = 13 Then FirstTime = 1
  End If

'Set variable for Q_Switch.OPT window.
  QWindow$ = WindowName$()

'Return to original window.
'Handles case where no document windows are open or
'only Document1 is open.
  If Flag <> 1 Then Activate MainWindow$

'Custom MAIN dialog box.
  Begin Dialog UserDialog 380, 216, "QuickSwitch", .EditItem
    ListBox 12, 61, 244, 95, PathArray$(), .Path
    Text 13, 6, 224, 13, "Select the path to which you "
    Text 13, 18, 244, 13, "want to switch. Or, click on Add"
    Text 13, 30, 216, 13, "to add a path; and Delete to"
    Text 13, 42, 191, 13, "delete the selected path."
    OKButton 279, 11, 88, 21
    CancelButton 279, 35, 88, 21
    PushButton 279, 59, 88, 21, "&Add", .AddDialog
    PushButton 279, 83, 88, 21, "&Delete", .Delete
    GroupBox 12, 163, 244, 42, "File Command"
    OptionGroup  .FileCommand
    OptionButton 16, 180, 101, 16, "File &Open", .Open
    OptionButton 128, 180, 124, 16, "File &Save As", .Save
  End Dialog
  Redim Dlg As UserDialog

'Return value for dialog.
  x = Dialog(Dlg)
```

```
'User clicks OK.
  If x = -1 Then
    ChDir PathArray$(dlg.Path)

'Handles option button selection.
    If dlg.FileCommand = 0 Then

'Handles File Open.
        Dim FOpen As FileOpen
        GetCurValues FOpen
        x = Dialog(FOpen)
        If x = -1 Then FileOpen FOpen

'Handles File Save.
    Else
        Dim FSave As FileSaveAs
        GetCurValues FSave
        x = Dialog(FSave)
        If x = -1 Then FileSaveAs FSave
    End If

'User clicks add.
  ElseIf x = 1 Then

'Custom ADD dialog box.
'This label is for redisplaying the Add dialog box.
Add:
    Begin Dialog UserDialog 452, 94, "Add Path"
        Text 11, 9, 265, 13, "Enter the full path that you want to"
        Text 10, 22, 216, 13, "add to the QuickSwitch list--"
        Text 11, 35, 256, 13, "for example, c:\marketing\95mtrls"
        TextBox 10, 54, 285, 18, .AddText
        OKButton 320, 12, 121, 21
        CancelButton 320, 36, 121, 21
        PushButton 320, 60, 121, 21, "&Add Another", .AddAnother
    End Dialog
    Dim Dlg As UserDialog

'Handles the Add Path dialog.
    y = Dialog(Dlg)

'User clicks Add or Add Another.
    If y = -1 Or y = 1 Then

'Not valid path FORMAT. I don't check whether path exists...
        If InStr(dlg.AddText, ":") = 0 Or→
            InStr(dlg.AddText, "\") = 0 Then
            If Flag <> 1 Then Activate MainWindow$
```

(continued)

```
            Msg$ = "The format for the path is incorrect. A correct "
            Msg$ = Msg$ + "format is C:\WORD6."
            MsgBox  Msg$, "QuickSwitch", 64
            Goto ADD
          End If

'Activate Q_Switch.OPT.
          Activate QWindow$

          FindTable              'CALL SUB

'Test to find out whether there's more than one empty row.
          HowManyRows = SelInfo(15)
          EndOfLine
          StartOfLine 1

'Handle one empty row.
          If HowManyRows = 1 And Asc(Selection$()) = 13 Then
            CharLeft
            x = 1
          Else
            TableInsertRow
            CharLeft
          End If
          Insert dlg.AddText
          TableSelectTable
          TableSort .DontSortHdr = 0, .FieldNum = "Column 1",→
            .Type = 0, .Order = 0, .FieldNum2 = "", .Type2 = 0,→
            .Order2 = 0, .FieldNum3 = "", .Type3 = 0,→
            .Order3 = 0, .Separator = 0, .SortColumn = 0,→
            .CaseSensitive = 0
          If y = 1 Then Goto ADD

'User clicks Cancel in Add Path dialog box.
        Else
          Activate QWindow$
          Goto Body
        End If

'Delete is handled using the EditItem function.
      End If


CleanUp:
'Close and save Q_Switch.OPT.
      Activate QWindow$
      FileClose 1

'Turn on screen redraw.
      ScreenUpdating 1
      Goto BYE
```

```
SwitchProblem:
   If Err > 0 And Err <> 102 And Err <> 76 Then
      Msg$ = "An error occurred in QuickSwitch. Error code = "
      Msg$ = Msg$ + Str$(Err)
      MsgBox Msg$, "QuickSwitch", 64
   ElseIf Err = 76 Then
      Msg$ = "The selected path doesn't exist. Delete it "
      Msg$ = Msg$ + "from the list."
      MsgBox Msg$, "QuickSwitch", 64
      Activate QWindow$
      Goto Body
   ElseIf Err = 130 Then
      Resume Next
   End If
   Goto CleanUp

BYE:
End Sub


'Dynamically shows items deleted from list box...
Function EditItem(ID$, Action, SuppValue)
   If ID$ = "Delete" Then

'Delete path unless it's the last row.
'Index selected + 1 to equal row number.
      i = DlgValue("Path") + 1

'Activate Q_Switch.OPT.
      Activate QWindow$
      FindTable              'CALL SUB

'SelInfo(15) returns number of rows in the table.
      HowManyRows = SelInfo(15)
      FindRow               'CALL SUB

'Delete specified row of the table...
      If A = i And HowManyRows <> 1 Then
         TableDeleteRow

'...but always preserve a single row.
      ElseIf HowManyRows = 1 Then
         EndOfLine
         StartOfLine 1
         EditClear
      End If
```

(continued)

```
'Refill dialog with new array (less deleted path).
    FindTable              'CALL SUB

'Rows in table.
    A = SelInfo(15)

'Create array for list box.
    Dim PathArray2$(A - 1)
    For i2 = 0 To A - 1
      EndOfLine
      StartOfLine 1
      A$ = Selection$()
      PathArray2$(i2) = A$
      LineDown
    Next
    DlgListBoxArray "Path", PathArray2$()
    KeepDisplayed = 1
    DlgFocus "Path"
  End If
  EditItem = KeepDisplayed
End Function


Sub FindTable
'Find table in QWindow$ (Q_Switch.OPT).
  StartOfDocument

'SelInfo(12) returns -1 if selection is in a table.
  While SelInfo(12) <> -1
    LineDown
  Wend
End Sub


Sub FindRow
'Activate Q_Switch.OPT.
  Activate QWindow$

'Find row of selected path.
'SelInfo(13) returns the row # containing selection.
  A = SelInfo(13)
  StartOfDocument
  While A <> i
    LineDown
    A = SelInfo(13)
  Wend
End Sub
```

9

Developing Business Applications with Excel

I've heard people say—and I can't say they're wrong—that Microsoft Excel is the most versatile application on the market today. (One of my colleagues describes it as "the coolest application ever written.") Over the past few years, I've seen people use Excel to build a remarkable variety of powerful business applications:

- **Database front ends.** Since you can access virtually any data from Excel using ODBC, DDE, custom DLLs, and third-party tools, more companies are using Excel to deliver corporate data to the desktop. That way, people get the data where they can use it immediately— in a spreadsheet. One company I work with recently built an Excel application that lets senior management use 200 fields of personnel- related data stored in a DB2 database.

- **Financial models and analysis tools.** Many financial institutions rely on automated financial models built in Excel to analyze and report investments and to evaluate companies.

- **Publishing and presentation applications.** Excel is a powerful tool for publishing statistical data. Many companies that do this type of publishing use Excel to deliver camera-ready copy. The mutual funds research department at Merrill Lynch uses an Excel-based publishing application that has reduced the production schedule for quarterly reports from more than two weeks to less than a day. (See "CASE STUDY: Merrill Lynch's Mutual Funds Analysis System" later in this chapter.)

- **Executive information systems (EIS).** Senior management at a Fortune 100 consumer products company uses an Excel-based applica- tion to calculate the impact of various financial decisions, acquisitions, and investments on their earnings per share and on their long-term financial plan. This system combines a friendly, point-and-click front end with sophisticated financial calculations. The system also uses Excel's consolidation mechanism to enable senior management to view the company's finances at any level—by operating company, by a group of operating companies, or by the company as a whole.

■ **Reporting systems.** Since Excel can access virtually any data, companies use it as the reporting engine for delivering corporate data to desktops. Philip Morris recently built a human resources application in Excel for the Macintosh that provides senior management with a current snapshot of the top management layer of the entire company, including subsidiaries. The application queries a DB2 database and populates an Excel spreadsheet with the organization's name, the management positions, and the names of the people in those positions.

This chapter presents four sample applications and, in doing so, describes some of the programming techniques and practices that can help you develop professional business applications in Excel. The last section provides tips on how to develop applications that run on both the Microsoft Windows and the Macintosh versions of Excel.

The sample applications, listed below, can also be found on the *Office Solutions* disk included with this book:

■ AppMakeR.XLT, an Excel template that jump-starts the process of developing Excel-based business applications

■ DevelopR.XLS, a workbook with utilities for developers

■ WinAPI.XLA/.XLS, a common code library that uses custom Excel functions to simplify access to Windows API functions

■ Retrieve.XLS, an Excel application that demonstrates how to use custom Excel functions to retrieve external data into Excel sheets

SAMPLE APPLICATION: AppMakeR.XLT

AppMakeR.XLT is a template that jump-starts the process of developing Excel-based business applications by providing an application shell and a development framework. AppMakeR's main features are described in the following sections of this chapter:

■ Structural, programming, and naming conventions (see "Developing Applications with AppMakeR.XLT")

■ Sample Auto macros (see "AppMakeR's Auto_Open and Auto_Close Procedures")

- Centralized structure for using systemwide information and error traps (see "Managing Standard Procedures Centrally")

- Custom application menu, sample logon procedure, and custom Close routine (see "Other Tools in AppMakeR")

FYI

Template-Based Development

No matter which Office development tool you use, template-based development offers several advantages:

- It gives developers a framework in which to build business applications.

- It fosters code consistency among applications by establishing naming conventions and event-driven coding techniques.

- It's one of the easiest ways to promote code reuse.

Note that neither Visual Basic nor Microsoft Access uses templates per se to create this type of "shell" application. To create such a shell in Visual Basic, customize the AUTOLOAD.MAK file. To create a shell in Access, create a wizard.

PRODUCT SHEET: The AppMakeR Template

Purpose:	The AppMakeR template provides a structure for building Excel-based business applications, which includes: ■ Clearly defined naming and programming conventions ■ Sample Auto_Open and Auto_Close procedures ■ Sample code for common routines, such as a central error trap ■ An About box
Development tools used:	Excel; Windows API
How AppMakeR works:	Put AppMakeR.XLT in your XLSTART directory or in an alternate startup directory (which you set through the Options command on the Tools menu), and then load Excel. When you choose the New command from the File menu, the template appears in the New dialog box.

(continued)

PRODUCT SHEET: The AppMakeR Template

When you create a new business application based on the AppMakeR template, it opens a dialog box in which you enter basic information about the application. The application's name is used automatically in message boxes and custom dialog boxes, and the other information is used in the template's About box.

The following diagram illustrates AppMakeR.XLT's main features:

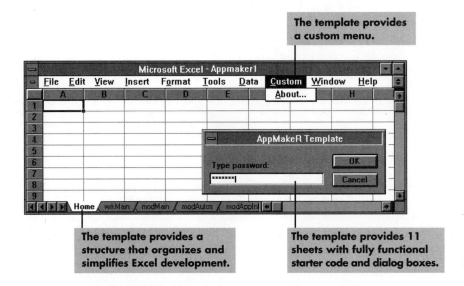

The template provides a custom menu.

The template provides a structure that organizes and simplifies Excel development.

The template provides 11 sheets with fully functional starter code and dialog boxes.

FYI

VBA vs. Excel

What I refer to throughout this book as "VBA for Excel" is in fact two language "libraries":

■ VBA (Visual Basic for Applications), a programming language that provides statements and functions you can use from applications such as Excel

■ The Excel Object Library, which contains programmable objects specific to Excel

Excel's Object Browser—which lists procedures, objects, methods, and properties currently loaded in Excel—lets you distinguish between VBA statements and functions and Excel's programmable objects. To use the Object Browser, open a module, and then choose Object Browser from the View menu:

- The dialog box's drop-down list shows the libraries and workbooks that are currently loaded. The VBA and Excel libraries are always loaded, as is the current workbook.

- The list box on the left shows the objects and modules in the selected library or workbook.

- The list box on the right shows the methods, properties, and procedures for the selected object or module.

Figure 9-1 lists the objects in the Excel Object Library and the methods and properties for the Button object (which is selected). Select VBA to display VBA statements and functions, or select an open workbook to display its procedures.

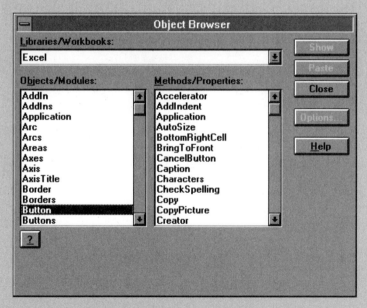

Figure 9-1. *The Object Browser lets you distinguish between VBA statements and functions and the objects available through the Excel Object Library. The Excel Object Library provides most of VBA for Excel's capabilities.*

Developing Applications with AppMakeR.XLT

The AppMakeR template uses the following set of structural, programming, and naming conventions to make business applications easier to maintain:

- It has a worksheet (called "home") in which the application leaves the user at startup. This home screen is designed as the location for your application's main worksheet functionality.

- It uses the worksheet wrkMain to store systemwide information, including the application's name and any application-specific lists that you maintain to populate dialog boxes.

- It has a module (modAutos) for the Auto macros used.

- It pairs dialog sheets with code. For example, modAppInfo contains the code for dlgAppInfo. (See the sidebar titled "Creating Custom Dialog Boxes" later in this chapter.)

- It uses an event-driven paradigm for writing dialog box code. This means that dialog box controls have their own procedures. In many cases, you can use a single procedure (such as cmdOK_Click, which is triggered when users click the OK button) to process the information in a dialog box.

- It uses modMain for miscellaneous (i.e., relatively short and general) procedures that don't have custom dialog boxes (for example, a custom File Close procedure). You'll generally want to create separate modules to house long or complex procedures that have their own functions and subroutines.

- It uses a standard, three-character prefix for naming variables, interface objects, and sheets. For example, a Boolean variable might be named blnResponse, and a command button cmdOK. Figures 9-2 through 9-4 list AppMakeR's naming conventions.

Data Type	Prefix	Storage Size	Info
Boolean	bln	2 bytes	True (−1) False (0)
Currency	cur	8 bytes	−922,337,203,685,477.5808 through 922,337,203,685,477.5807
Date	dat	8 bytes	1/1/100 through 12/31/9999
Double	dbl	8 bytes	−1.7976E308 through −4.9406E−324 4.9406E−324 through 1.7976E308

Data Type	Prefix	Storage Size	Info
Integer	int	2 bytes	−32,769 through 32,768
Long	lng	4 bytes	−2,147,483,648 through 2,147,483,647
Object	obj	4 bytes	Any object reference
Single	sng	4 bytes	−3.4028E38 through −1.4012E−45 1.4012E−45 through 3.4028E38
String	str	1 byte/character	1 to 65,535 bytes/characters
User-defined type	udt	Depends on elements	
Variant	vnt	16 bytes for numbers; 22 bytes + 1 byte/char for strings	All values/any text

Figure 9-2. *VBA for Excel's data types and the prefixes that AppMakeR uses to name them.*

Control	Prefix
Command button	cmd
Checkbox	chk
Combo box	cbo
Drawing object	drw
Drop-down list	drp
Edit box	edt
Frame	fra
Group box	grp
Horizontal scroll bar	hsb
Label	lbl
Line	lin
List box	lst
Option button	opt
Picture	pic
Spinner	spn
Text box	txt
Vertical scroll bar	vsb

Figure 9-3. *The prefixes that AppMakeR uses to name objects.*

Sheet Type	Prefix	Example
Dialog sheet	dlg	dlgAbout
Macro sheet	mac	macXL4Stuff
Module	mod	modAutos
Worksheet (system)	wrk	wrkMain

Figure 9-4. *The prefixes that AppMakeR uses to name sheets.*

FYI

Creating Custom Dialog Boxes

Although you can put controls in worksheets, usually the most flexible and professional-looking way to get information from users is through custom dialog boxes. Here's how to create custom dialog boxes in Excel (see Figure 9-5 on the facing page):

1. Insert a dialog sheet. (One way to do this is to choose Macro from the Insert menu and then select Dialog.) Excel opens a dialog sheet with a dialog box and the Forms toolbar. You can have only one dialog box per dialog sheet.

2. To add a control to the dialog box, select a type of control from the Forms toolbar and then draw that control in the dialog box. To resize a control, select it and drag its selection handles.

3. To rename a control, select it, type a new name in the name box, and then press Enter. (See Figure 9-3 for naming conventions for interface objects.)

4. To set properties and protection for controls, use the Object command on the Format menu.

5. To create event procedures for controls with Visual Basic–style names, click the Edit Code button on the Forms toolbar or use the Assign Macro command on the Tools menu. (Because controls don't have an intrinsic connection to code, you must use the Assign Macro command to manage this connection.)

6. To display a dialog box, use the Show method. For example, this code shows the dialog box on the dialog sheet named dlgSample:

```
DialogSheets("dlgSample").Show
```

7. One way to *initialize* a dialog box is to use an event procedure assigned to the dialog frame. Initialization procedures (which are used for such things as clearing edit boxes, enabling or disabling buttons, or changing title bar captions) run *after* you call the Show method and *before* Excel displays the dialog box. For example, this subroutine changes the title bar of the dialog box on dlgSample to "Sample":

```
Sub Dialog_Show()
  DialogSheets("dlgSample").DialogFrame.Caption = "Sample"
End Sub
```

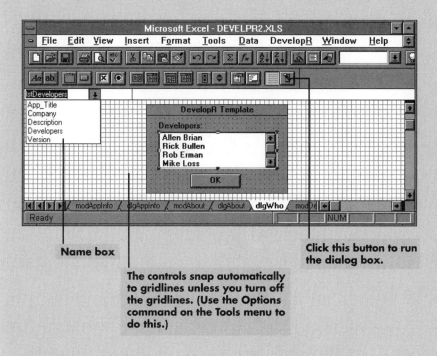

Name box

Click this button to run the dialog box.

The controls snap automatically to gridlines unless you turn off the gridlines. (Use the Options command on the Tools menu to do this.)

Figure 9-5. *Use Excel's dialog sheets to create custom dialog boxes.*

AppMakeR's Auto_Open and Auto_Close Procedures

Excel has two automatic procedures: Auto_Open and Auto_Close. Write an Auto_Open procedure to run specific code whenever users open a workbook, and write an Auto_Close procedure to run whenever users close the workbook. Although Excel version 5 retains the Auto_Activate and Auto_Deactivate macros for compatibility with the Excel version 4 macro language, use the

OnSheetActivate and OnSheetDeactivate properties when you program in VBA for Excel. For example, the following code runs the CheckOnActivate procedure whenever users activate Sheet1:

```
Sub Sheet1Activate()
  Worksheets("Sheet1").OnSheetActivate = ActiveWorkbook.Name↴
    & "!Module1.CheckOnActivate"
End Sub
```

NOTE For ease of reading, the ↴ character represents a line break that does not appear in the actual code.

To write an Auto_Open or Auto_Close procedure, assign a procedure with that reserved name. The Auto_Open procedure in AppMakeR.XLT performs four tasks:

■ Since many business applications hide or display toolbars, it stores the toolbars currently in use in the objTBs toolbar object.

■ Since many business applications change the state of the formula and status bars, it stores the original state in the variables blnShowFormula and blnShowStatus, respectively.

■ When you create a *new* business application, it displays a dialog box for entering the basic information about that application.

■ It leaves the user in the home cell of the home screen.

The next section lists the code for Auto_Open.

Auto_Open and the application information dialog box

Although the Auto_Open procedure (shown on the facing page) runs whenever you open the workbook, it prompts you to enter basic application information only when you create a *new* workbook. It determines whether a workbook is new by checking whether the filename has an extension—in other words, whether it has an Excel-given temporary name such as "AppMakeR1" or a user-given name such as "AcctsPay.XLS."

If the filename doesn't have a dot (.), Auto_Open calls the AppInfo procedure, which displays a dialog box for entering the basic information for the application, and passes it a value of True, which marks the file as a new workbook. In this case, the template clears the dialog box (except for the version number, which is set automatically to *1*) and displays it. (See the section titled "Managing Standard Procedures Centrally" later in this chapter for more information on the AppInfo procedure.)

```
Option Explicit
Dim objTBs() As Toolbar, varTB As Variant
Dim blnShowFormula As Boolean
Dim blnShowStatus As Boolean
Dim intTBCounr As Integer

Sub Auto_Open()
  On Error Resume Next

'Count visible toolbars. Save visible toolbars.
  intTBCount = 0
  For Each varTB In Toolbars
    If varTB.Visible Then
      intTBCount = intTBCount + 1
      ReDim Preserve objTBs(1 To intTBCount)
      Set objTBs(intTBCount) = varTB
    End If
  Next

'Capture the status of the formula and status bars.
  With Application
    blnShowFormula = .DisplayFormulaBar
    blnShowStatus = .DisplayStatusBar
  End With

'Display AppInfo dialog box and initialize
'to True if application is new.
  If InStr(ActiveWorkbook.Name, ".") = 0 Then
    AppInfo True
    ThisWorkbook.Worksheets("Home").Activate
  End If
End Sub
```

Auto_Close

AppMakeR's Auto_Close procedure, shown below, performs two tasks:

■ It restores the toolbars stored in the objTBs toolbar object.

■ It restores the state of the formula and status bars stored in the variables blnShowFormula and blnShowStatus.

```
Sub Auto_Close()
  On Error Resume Next
  Dim i As Integer
```

(continued)

275

```
'Restore toolbars captured at Auto_Open.
  For i = 1 To intTBCount
    objTBs(i).Visible = True
  Next

'Restore formula and status bar captured at Auto_Open.
  With Application
    .DisplayFormulaBar = blnShowFormula
    .DisplayStatusBar = blnShowStatus
  End With
End Sub
```

Managing Standard Procedures Centrally

The AppMakeR template handles two categories of standard procedures centrally (although you can give special treatment to specific cases):

■ It provides central storage of systemwide data, including application-specific lists that you maintain; the application name, which appears in title bars for message boxes and dialog boxes; and application information that appears in the About box.

■ It uses a central error trap.

Storing systemwide data

It's often useful to store systemwide data in a single worksheet. Such data falls into two categories: It's either used by more than one procedure or it's used to populate dialog boxes. The AppMakeR template uses the worksheet wrkMain (see Figure 9-6) to store this type of data, including what I call "application information"—the application's name, version number, description, and so on.

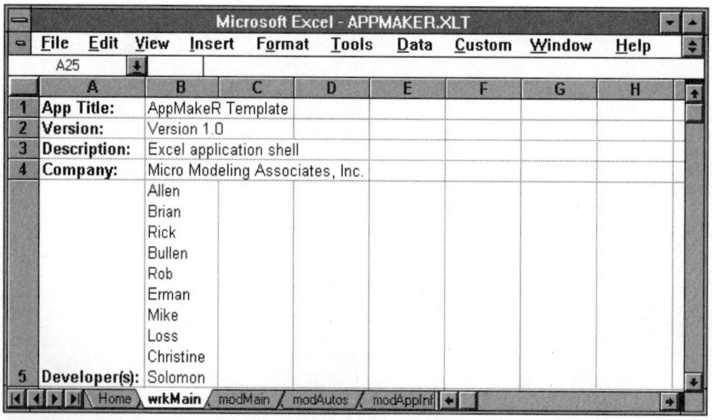

	A	B	C	D	E	F	G	H
1	App Title:	AppMakeR Template						
2	Version:	Version 1.0						
3	Description:	Excel application shell						
4	Company:	Micro Modeling Associates, Inc.						
		Allen						
		Brian						
		Rick						
		Bullen						
		Rob						
		Erman						
		Mike						
		Loss						
		Christine						
5	Developer(s):	Solomon						

Tabs: Home | **wrkMain** | modMain | modAutos | modAppInf

Figure 9-6. *AppMakeR.XLT's wrkMain stores systemwide data.*

When you start a new business application based on AppMakeR, the template opens the application information dialog box (see Figure 9-7). The template is designed to use this information (which you can change by running the CallAppInfo procedure) in two ways:

■ It uses the application's name for all title bars, including those in message boxes and custom dialog boxes. The following code does this:

```
'Declare strAppTitle as a global variable. This is done
'in modMain in the AppMakeR template.
  Global strAppTitle As String

'Set the value of strAppTitle for each dialog box. Message box
'title bars need only the application name. Dialog box title bars
'(such as the About box) often require an additional word.
  strAppTitle = "About " & Worksheets("wrkMain")↲
    .Range("App_Title").Value

'Use strAppTitle in the About dialog box title bar.
  ThisWorkbook.DialogSheets("dlgAbout").DialogFrame↲
    .Caption = strAppTitle
```

■ It uses all application information in the About box. (See the section titled "About the About Box" later in this chapter for more information.)

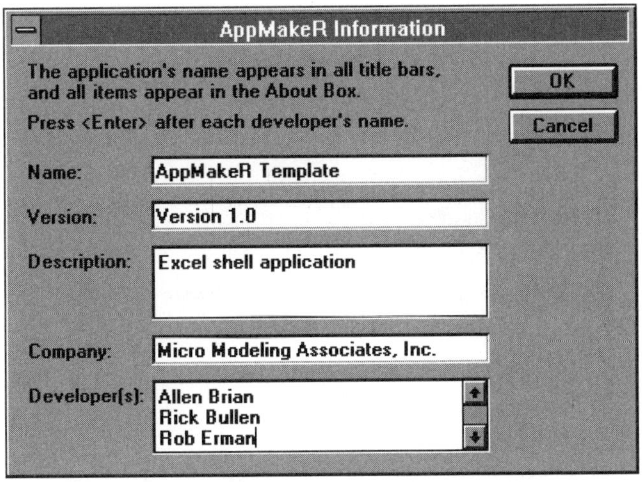

Figure 9-7. *The application information dialog box prompts you to enter the basic information for your application. This information appears in title bars and in the About box.*

AppMakeR.XLT calls the application information dialog box in two ways:

- From the Auto_Open macro, when you start a new workbook based on the AppMakeR template. (See the section titled "Auto_Open and the Application Information Dialog Box" earlier in this chapter.)

- From the password-protected CallAppInfo procedure, which lets developers change this information at any point. (See the next section, "Changing Application Information on the Fly.")

Changing application information on the fly To change the application information for an existing application, run the CallAppInfo procedure. This procedure is password protected to prevent end users from changing the application information. When developers enter the correct password ("xxx"), the procedure passes a value of False to AppInfo, which indicates that the file isn't a new one. (The first time Auto_Open calls AppInfo, it passes a value of True.) The application information dialog box displays the application information stored in wrkMain.

All the code for the application information dialog box is in the modAppInfo module (shown below). This module uses an event-driven structure for dialog box code, which means that dialog box events are broken into separate procedures. In this case, there are two main event procedures:

- Dialog_Show initializes the dialog box before it's displayed. It either clears the edit boxes (in the case of a new workbook) or retrieves data from wrkMain (using the GetAppInfo subroutine) and displays it in the edit boxes.

- cmdOK_Click uses the EnterAppInfo subroutine to store application information in wrkMain.

NOTE   See the sidebar titled "The Object-Dot Drill-Down" later in this chapter for information on how to use the Set statement to create an object variable (such as the objAIDialog variable that I use in modAppInfo).

```
Option Explicit
Dim objAIDialog As DialogSheet
Dim blnFlag As Boolean

'Call this procedure from a macro. It calls the password function.
'Password protection prevents users from running this macro
'and changing the application information.
Sub CallAppInfo()
  On Error Resume Next
```

```
      Dim strPassword As String
      Dim blnResponse As Boolean

 'Display message in the status bar.
      Application.StatusBar = "Type your password..."

 'Initialize blnFlag.
      blnFlag = False

 'Title bar.
      strAppTitle = Worksheets("wrkMain").Range("App_Title").Value & "→
        Information"

 'Call password function.
      blnResponse = GetSystemPassword(strAppTitle, "Type password:",→
        strPassword)

 'Process password.
      If blnResponse Then
        If strPassword = "xxx" Then
          AppInfo False
        Else
          MsgBox "Incorrect password. Access denied.", 16,→
            strAppTitle
        End If
      Else
        MsgBox "Logon canceled.", 16, strAppTitle
      End If

      Application.StatusBar = False
 End Sub


 'This procedure is called from Auto_Open and also from CallAppInfo
 'after users supply the correct password.
 Sub AppInfo(Init As Boolean)
   On Error GoTo AppInfoError
   Dim lngError As Long
   Application.ScreenUpdating - False

 'Display message in the status bar.
   Application.StatusBar = "Type the basic information for your→
     application..."
```

(continued)

```
'Title bar...necessary if called from Auto_Open.
  strAppTitle = Worksheets("wrkMain").Range("App_Title").Value & "⌐
    Information"

'Create dialog sheet object.
  Set objAIDialog = ThisWorkbook.DialogSheets("dlgAppInfo")
  If Init Then blnFlag = True

'Show dialog box.
  objAIDialog.Show

'Handle errors generated in other procedure.
  If Err <> 0 Then GoTo AppInfoError

AppInfoExit:
  Application.StatusBar = False
  Application.ScreenUpdating = True
  Exit Sub

AppInfoError:
'Code 20 is an error generated by Resume when handling an
'error from a procedure other than AppInfo.
  If Err <> 0 And Err <> 20 Then
    lngError = Err
    GlobalErrorMsg "modAppInfo", lngError
  End If
  Resume AppInfoExit
End Sub



'Initialize dialog box.
Sub Dialog_Show()
  On Error GoTo BYE

'Set caption.
  objAIDialog.DialogFrame.Caption = strAppTitle

'Clear all text boxes except Version.
  If blnFlag Then
    With objAIDialog
      .EditBoxes("edtAppTitle").text = ""
      .EditBoxes("edtDescription").text = ""
      .EditBoxes("edtCompany").text = ""
      .EditBoxes("edtDevelopers").text = ""
    End With

'Fill dialog box with current application information.
  Else
```

```
    With objAIDialog
      GetAppInfo "App_Title", "edtAppTitle"
      GetAppInfo "Version", "edtVersion"
      GetAppInfo "Description", "edtDescription"
      GetAppInfo "Company", "edtCompany"
      GetAppInfo "Developers", "edtDevelopers"
    End With
  End If

BYE:
End Sub


Sub cmdOK_Click()
  On Error GoTo BYE
  EnterAppInfo "App_Title", "edtAppTitle"
  EnterAppInfo "Version", "edtVersion"
  EnterAppInfo "Description", "edtDescription"
  EnterAppInfo "Company", "edtCompany"
  EnterAppInfo "Developers", "edtDevelopers"

BYE:
End Sub


'Gets information currently in wrkMain.
Sub GetAppInfo(RangeName As String, ControlName As String)
  On Error GoTo BYE
  objAIDialog.EditBoxes(ControlName).Caption =→
    Worksheets("wrkMain").Range(RangeName).Value

BYE:
End Sub


'Stores information in wrkMain.
Sub EnterAppInfo(RangeName As String, ControlName As String)
  On Error GoTo BYE
  Worksheets("wrkMain").Range(RangeName).Value =→
    objAIDialog.EditBoxes(ControlName).text

BYE:
End Sub
```

FYI

The Object-Dot Drill-Down

Excel's 128 objects are organized hierarchically so that lower-level objects (such as ranges) are contained in higher-level objects (such as worksheets). The highest-level object—the application object—contains all the other objects (see Figure 9-8). When you write VBA for Excel code, you often have to drill down using the dot (.) operator to get to the object that you want.

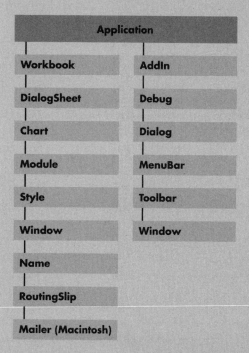

Figure 9-8. *The top layers of Excel's hierarchical object model.*

For example, the following code returns (in a message box) the contents of cell C6, located in the workbook "Sales.XLS" in the worksheet "May Sales." The first four items (shown in bold) drill down through Excel's object hierarchy. The last item, .Value, is the property that identifies the contents of the lowest-level object referenced—in this case, Range("C6").

```
MsgBox Application.Workbooks("Sales.XLS").Worksheets→
  ("May Sales").Range("C6").Value
```

You often can abbreviate code by taking into account the context in which it runs. For example, when running VBA for Excel code from Excel itself (rather than from Access or from Visual Basic), you can usually omit the reference to the application. The following code is functionally equivalent to the previous code. You can run it from anywhere in Excel, including from another workbook.

```
MsgBox Workbooks("Sales.XLS").Worksheets("May Sales")→
  .Range("C6").Value
```

The next line of code, though shorter, runs correctly only from within the workbook "Sales.XLS." If you run it from another workbook, it returns an error message—unless that workbook also has a worksheet named "May Sales."

```
MsgBox Worksheets("May Sales").Range("C6").Value
```

The next example provides the most succinct code, but it's also the most error-prone. You can run it from any worksheet, but a worksheet has to be active—otherwise it returns an error message. In addition, it returns the same answer as the previous code only if May Sales is the active worksheet.

```
MsgBox Range("C6").Value
```

ThisWorkbook

If you look through the code in this chapter, you'll see that a number of object references start with ThisWorkbook. The ThisWorkbook property makes it easy to reference objects in the same workbook as the VBA for Excel code currently running. It's a better way of identifying a workbook than, for example, Workbooks("Sales.XLS") because you can change the workbook's name and *not* change the code. Similarly, you can reuse the code more easily when you copy it to other workbooks.

The ThisWorkbook property also identifies the running workbook more reliably than does ActiveWorkbook because the active workbook might not be the one in which the VBA code is stored. On the other hand, if you want your code to run on whatever workbook is active, use ActiveWorkbook.

Two Techniques for Abbreviating VBA Code

VBA for Excel includes two syntactical techniques for minimizing the number of dots (.) in your code, which makes it run faster: the With statement and object variables.

> **The With statement:** The With statement is new in VBA for Excel. It lets you execute a series of statements on a single object (or on a user-defined type) without specifying that object each time. For example, the code on the following page formats the range C8 through G12 as 14-point bold and fills it with the formula = C$1 + C$2. (*$* indicates an absolute reference).

```
With ThisWorkbook.Worksheets("home").Range("C8:G12")
    .Font.Size = 14
    .Font.Bold = True
    .Value = "= C$1 + C$2"
    .FillRight
End With
```

Object variables: Creating an object variable is the most efficient way to reference objects that you use repeatedly. (Virtually all sample code in this book uses object variables.) There are two steps to creating an object variable: declaring it and setting it. The following code is functionally identical to the previous example—the only difference is that it uses the object variable objRngVar:

```
Dim objRngVar As Object
Set objRngVar = ThisWorkbook.Worksheets("home").Range("C8:G12")
With objRngVar
    .Font.Size = 14
    .Font.Bold = True
    .Value = "= C$1 + C$2"
    .FillRight
End With
```

Get, Set, or Do

VBA for Excel code that references objects always does one of three things:

- It gets (or returns) a property. For example, the following code gets the contents of cell C8:

```
MsgBox ThisWorkbook.Worksheets("May Sales").Range("C8").Value
```

- It sets a property. For example, the following code sets the contents of cell C8 equal to the sum of cells C1 and C2:

```
ThisWorkbook.Worksheets("May Sales").Range("C8").Formula = ⤸
    "= C1 + C2"
```

- It invokes a method to do something. For example, the following code uses the FillRight method to copy the contents and format of cell C8 into C8 through G8:

```
ThisWorkbook.Worksheets("home").Range("C8:G8").FillRight
```

About the About Box

The About command on AppMakeR's custom menu opens an About box popu-lated from the application information stored in wrkMain (see Figure 9-9), plus three items of system information:

■ The total amount of memory and the amount currently free

■ The percentage of system resources that are still free

■ Whether the system has a math coprocessor

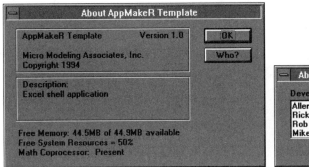

Figure 9-9. *AppMakeR.XLT's About Box (left) and the Developers list (right), which opens when you click the Who? button. Both dialog boxes read the application information stored in wrkMain.*

The code for these routines is in the Dialog_Show procedure of modAbout, shown below. VBA for Excel has properties that provide information about math coprocessors and the amount of memory available, but you have to use the Windows API function GetFreeSystemResources to get information on resources. (See Chapter 6 for more information on the Windows API.)

```
Declare Function GetFreeSystemResources Lib "USER"↵
  (ByVal fuSysResource As Integer) As Integer
Global Const GFSR_SYSTEMRESOURCES = 0

Option Explicit
Dim objAboutDialog As DialogSheet

'About box.
Sub DisplayAboutBox()
  On Error GoTo DisplayAboutBoxError
  Dim lngError As Long
  Application.ScreenUpdating = False
```

(continued)

```
'Display message in the status bar.
  Application.StatusBar = "System information..."

'Create dialog sheet object.
  Set objAboutDialog = ThisWorkbook.DialogSheets("dlgAbout")

'Show dialog box.
  objAboutDialog.Show

'Handle errors generated in other procedure.
  If Err <> 0 GoTo DisplayAboutBoxError

DisplayAboutBoxExit:
  Application.StatusBar = False
  Application.ScreenUpdating = True
  Exit Sub

DisplayAboutBoxError:
    If Err <> 0 And Err <> 20 Then
      lngError = Err
      GlobalErrorMsg "modAppInfo", lngError
    End If
  Resume DisplayAboutBoxExit
End Sub


'Initialize dialog box.
Sub Dialog_Show()
  On Error GoTo BYE
  Dim intRetVal As Integer, strAvail As String
  Dim strText As String, strFree As String

  With objAboutDialog

'Dialog box title bar.
    strAppTitle = Worksheets("wrkMain").Range("App_Title")↴
      .Value
    .DialogFrame.Caption = strAppTitle

'Application title; call sub.
    SetLabel "lblTitle", "App_Title"

'Version; call sub.
    SetLabel "lblVersion", "Version"

'Company; call sub.
    SetLabel "lblCompany", "Company"
```

```
'Description; call sub.
    SetLabel "lblDescription", "Description"

'Free resources.
    intRetVal = GetFreeSystemResources(0)
    objAboutDialog.Labels("lblFreeResources").text =⤸
      "Free System Resources =" & Str$(intRetVal) & "%"

'Math coprocessor.
    strText = "Not present"
    If Application.MathCoprocessorAvailable Then⤸
      strText = "Present"
    .Labels("lblMthProc").text = "Math Coprocessor:  "⤸
      & strText

'Free memory.
    strFree = Format(Application.MemoryFree / 1000000,⤸
      "#.#")
    strAvail = Format(Application.MemoryTotal / 1000000,⤸
      "#.#")
    .Labels("lblMemory").text = "Free Memory: " & strFree⤸
      & "MB of " & strAvail & "MB available"
  End With

BYE:
End Sub


'Sets labels in About dialog box.
Sub SetLabel(LabelName As String, RangeName As String)
  On Error GoTo BYE
  objAboutDialog.Labels(LabelName).text =⤸
    ThisWorkbook.Worksheets("wrkMain").Range(RangeName)

BYE:
End Sub


'Shows dialog box listing developers.
Sub cmdWho_Click()
  On Error GoTo BYE
  Dim Names As String
  Dim iPos As Integer
  Dim objList As ListBox
```

(continued)

```
'Create dialog sheet object.
  Set objList = ThisWorkbook.DialogSheets("dlgWho")→
    .ListBoxes("lstDevelopers")

  With ThisWorkbook.DialogSheets("dlgWho")
    strAppTitle = Worksheets("wrkMain").Range("App_Title")→
      .Value

'Dialog box title bar.
    .DialogFrame.Caption = strAppTitle

'List box.
    objList.RemoveAllItems

'Populate list box.
    Names = ThisWorkbook.Worksheets("wrkMain")→
      .Range("Developers").Value

'Parse range so that each developer is one item.
'Chr$(10) is the linefeed character.
    Do
      iPos = InStr(Names, Chr$(10))
      If iPos = 0 Then
        objList.AddItem Names
        Exit Do
      End If
      objList.AddItem Left$(Names, iPos - 1)
      Names = Right$(Names, Len(Names) - iPos)
    Loop

'Show dialog box.
    .Show
  End With

BYE:
End Sub
```

Using the central error trap

In addition to storing application information, the modAppInfo module (shown on page 278) demonstrates how to use AppMakeR's error trap. The main procedure (AppInfo) contains the trap. Although this particular trap is quite simple, you can easily expand it into a Select Case statement covering as many errors as you've identified. The global error message is designed to handle the most general case.

The following code in AppInfo calls the GlobalErrorMsg function and passes it two arguments: the name of the routine in which the error occurred and the error number. Both arguments appear in the message itself (see Figure 9-10).

```
'Code 20 is an error generated by Resume when handling
'error from a procedure other than AppInfo.
  If Err <> 0 And Err <> 20 Then
    lngError = Err
    GlobalErrorMsg "modAppInfo", lngError
  End If
```

Figure 9-10. *A sample error message produced by AppMakeR's central error trap.*

This is the GlobalErrorMsg function (located in modMain):

```
Sub GlobalErrorMsg(ProcedureName As String, ErrorNumber As Long)
  Dim ErrorMsg As String

'Title bar.
  strAppTitle = ThisWorkbook.Worksheets("wrkMain").→
    Range("App_Title").Value

'Global error message.
  ErrorMsg = "An error has occurred in " & ProcedureName & "."
  ErrorMsg = ErrorMsg & " Error code is " & ErrorNumber & "."
  MsgBox ErrorMsg, 48, strAppTitle
End Sub
```

FYI

Using Shortcut Keys in Excel

Developers must be very careful when adding shortcut keys in Excel.

■ Since custom shortcut keys don't appear on Excel's menus or in the Macro Run dialog box, you must communicate them to users in other ways. For example, you can list them as part of the message displayed in the status bar; list them in a separate, informational dialog box; or include them prominently in online help.

- In Excel, custom shortcut keys are limited to Ctrl+letter combinations. They're further limited because Excel itself uses many such combinations for its own shortcuts. When assigning shortcut keys, make sure you don't overwrite those provided by Excel.

- Consider providing an interface through which users can customize shortcut keys. That way, users can easily change shortcut keys that conflict with keys they use for other purposes.

Other Tools in AppMakeR

The AppMakeR template provides three other tools for developers:

- A custom application menu. To further customize this menu, use the Menu Editor command on the Tools menu (available only from modules). Remember to assign access keys.

- A custom Close routine (the CustomClose subroutine in modMain), which displays a message box that verifies whether users want to exit the current application.

- A standard function (GetSystemPassword) for procedures that require users to log on. (See the next section for more information.)

AppMakeR's logon routine

In addition to Excel's built-in security features (such as the Protection command on the Tools menu), you can write custom logon procedures to prevent unauthorized access to business application functions. For example, the CallAppInfo subroutine in the modAppInfo module (shown on page 278) uses the GetSystemPassword procedure to prevent end users from changing the application information. The more generic GetSystemPassword function (shown below) returns True if users enter the correct password and False otherwise. It takes three arguments:

- strTitleText (title bar text)
- strLabelText (instructions)
- strPassword (password)

```
Option Explicit

Dim objDialog As Object
Dim objBoxAway As EditBox
```

```
Dim objBoxAst As EditBox
Dim strPassword As String


Function GetSystemPassword(strTitleText, strLabelText, strPassword)⤳
  As Boolean
'Create dialog sheet object.
  Set objDialog = ThisWorkbook.DialogSheets("dlgGetPassword")

'Create edit box object that does not appear in the dialog box. This
'way, the password won't appear in the dialog box as users type.
  Set objBoxAway = objDialog.EditBoxes("edtBoxAwayFromSheet")

'Create edit box object that appears in the dialog box and fills with
'asterisks as users type.
  Set objBoxAst = objDialog.EditBoxes("edtAsteriskBox")

'Calls GHSPDisplayAsterisks sub.
  objBoxAway.OnAction = "GSPDisplayAsterisks"

'Initialize dialog box.
  objDialog.DialogFrame.Caption = strTitleText
  objDialog.Labels("lblLabel").text = strLabelText
  objBoxAway.text = ""
  objBoxAst.text = "|"
  objBoxAst.Enabled = False

'Show dialog box.
  GetSystemPassword = objDialog.Show
  strPassword = objBoxAway.text

'Clear asterisks. This isn't necessary, but it is
'good practice.
  objBoxAst.text = ""

'Clear edit box containing password.
'This is crucial for maintaining security.
  objBoxAway.text = ""
End Function

'Displays text as asterisk.
Sub GSPDisplayAsterisks()
  objBoxAst.text = String(Len(objBoxAway.text), "*") + "|"
End Sub
```

The GetSystemPassword function operates in conjunction with a dialog sheet and stores the password in an *undisplayed* edit box as the displayed edit box fills with asterisks (see Figure 9-11).

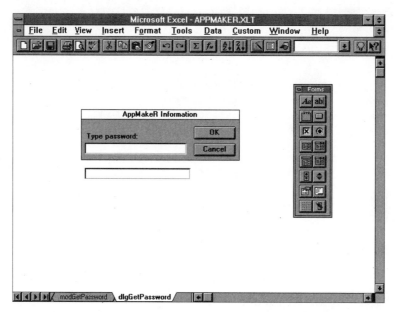

Figure 9-11. *AppMakeR's dlgGetPassword dialog sheet. Users enter the password in an edit box that is not displayed in the dialog box. A second edit box that is displayed in the dialog box fills with asterisks.*

FYI

Displaying a Built-In Dialog Box

Each of Excel's built-in dialog boxes (there are approximately 200) has a unique name. These names, each of which starts with xlDialog, are listed as constants in the Excel library of the Object Browser. Many built-in dialog boxes take arguments that correspond to their controls, and you can use these arguments to set dialog box options.

Here's a simple example of using a built-in dialog box. I added Excel's Define Name dialog box to DevelopR.XLS's Insert menu so that it's available to modules as well as to worksheets (which isn't normally the case). To do this, I created the following procedure in modMain and then assigned it to the menu using the Menu Editor command on the Tools menu. The key to using built-in dialog boxes is to invoke both the Dialogs method and the Show method as well as the dialog box's unique name (shown in bold).

```
Sub xlDefineNameDlg()
  Application.Dialogs(xlDialogDefineName).Show
End Sub
```

The only way I know to get a list of the arguments available to set dialog box options and their order is through the Reference Information section of Excel's Help file. Drill down into the Help file topic "Microsoft Excel Macro Functions Contents" and then "Macro Functions Listed by Category" and then "Command-Equivalent." Once you're in the section headed "Command-Equivalent," search for the dialog box you want to use.

For example, the Help topic for the Open command lists the following arguments in the following order:

```
OPEN(file_text, update_links, read_only, format, prot_pwd,⇥
  write_res_pwd, ignore_rorec, file_origin, custom_delimit,⇥
  add_logical, editable, file_access, notify_logical, converter)
```

This line of code displays the Open dialog box and uses the file_text argument to display only template (.XLT) files:

```
Application.Dialogs(xlDialogOpen).Show ".xlt"
```

This next line of code sets file_text = .xlt and read_only = True. The second comma serves as a placeholder for the second argument, update_links, which I omitted.

```
Application.Dialogs(xlDialogOpen).Show ".xlt",, True
```

Note that arguments for Excel dialog boxes historically have been *positional* arguments, which you must list in the specific order indicated by the Help topic. Although VBA for Excel supports this syntax, it also supports *named arguments*, which let you specify arguments without reference to their position. The following line of code is functionally equivalent to the previous line (the named arguments are in bold):

```
Application.Dialogs(xlDialogOpen).Show arg1:=".xlt", arg3:=True
```

Unfortunately, the new syntax still requires use of the "Command-Equivalent" Help topic mentioned earlier to determine that the file_text argument is named "arg1," that the read_only argument is "arg3," and so on. One step forward, one step back.

SAMPLE APPLICATION: DevelopR.XLS

DevelopR.XLS is a workbook with three utilities that enhance Excel's develop-ment environment. The original version of this workbook—which developers at Micro Modeling Associates have used and expanded for the past five years—has over two dozen such utilities. This section describes two in detail:

- Define Name, which simplifies the process of defining names that are local to sheets

- Book Browser, which displays all sheets in a workbook by type so you can go to a particular sheet easily

NOTE   Although DevelopR.XLS opens in a hidden window, you might prefer to convert this workbook to an add-in. (See the section titled "SAMPLE APPLICATION: The WinAPI Add-In" later in this chapter for informa-tion on how to do this.) The advantage of using this workbook from a hidden window is that it doubles as an informal code library.

PRODUCT SHEET: DevelopR Utilities

Purpose:	DevelopR.XLS provides a set of utilities that automates common programming tasks, including: ■ A utility for browsing through sheets in a workbook by category—modules, dialog sheets, and so on. (The shortcut is Ctrl+R.) ■ A utility for defining names that are local to sheets. (The shortcut is Ctrl+D.) ■ A utility for batch-handling hiding and unhiding sheets. (The shortcut is Ctrl+E.)
Development tool used:	Excel
How DevelopR works:	Put DevelopR.XLS (which opens in a hidden window) in your XLSTART directory or in an alternate startup directory (which you set through the Options com-mand on the Tools menu), and then load Excel. The DevelopR menu now appears on Excel's menu bar. To view DevelopR.XLS, use the Unhide command on the Window menu. The following illustration shows the DevelopR menu on Excel's menu bar:

FYI

Why Not Merge AppMakeR and DevelopR?

DevelopR's utilities aren't included in the AppMakeR template for two reasons:

- If you store these tools in AppMakeR, anyone who uses business applications based on AppMakeR has access to them and can damage the application inadvertently. Although you can try to prevent this with a policy requiring that developers delete these tools before delivering applications, it's safer to store them in a workbook available only to developers. You could password-protect these utilities, but it would make them cumbersome for developers to use.

- These utilities are meant to assist developers whenever they use Excel, not just when they're using AppMakeR. Again, storing them in a separate workbook accomplishes this.

DevelopR's Define Name Utility

Excel lets you define names *globally* or *locally*. (See the sidebar titled "Using Defined Names" on the following page for general information on defined names.) Global names are always listed in the Define Name dialog box (see Figure 9-12), and local names are listed only when the worksheet for which they're defined is active.

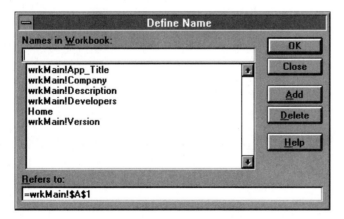

Figure 9-12. *The defined names starting with "wrkMain" are local to that sheet. The range named "Home" is global.*

FYI

Using Defined Names

You can name worksheet cells and then reference these names in formulas and in code. Defined names (available through the Name command on the Insert menu) are easier to read than cell references. For example, compare the following formulas (taken from column D in Figure 9-13 below), which average monthly sales over the days worked:

```
=MonthlySales/WorkDays
```

```
=B3/C3
```

To use named cells in formulas, first name those cells, and then type the name instead of the cell reference into the formula. Or use the Apply command on the Insert Name menu to convert cell references to names.

To use named ranges in code, replace the cell reference with its name. For example, the following lines of code are identical. They all select the range A2:A6, which is named "Months."

```
Range("Months").Select
```

```
Range("A2:A6").Select
```

```
Range(Cells(2, 1), Cells(6, 1)).Select
```

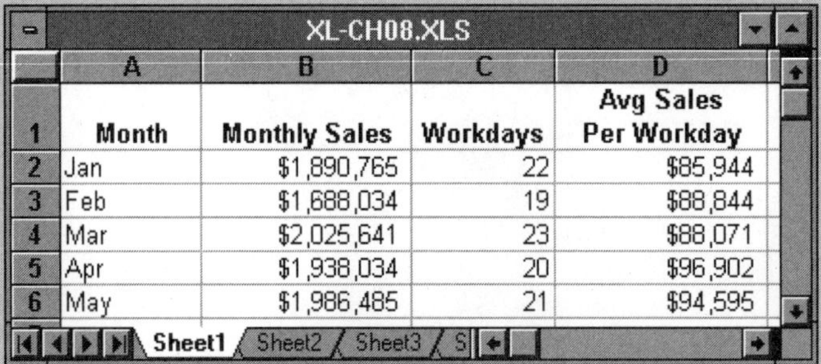

	A	B	C	D
1	Month	Monthly Sales	Workdays	Avg Sales Per Workday
2	Jan	$1,890,765	22	$85,944
3	Feb	$1,688,034	19	$88,844
4	Mar	$2,025,641	23	$88,071
5	Apr	$1,938,034	20	$96,902
6	May	$1,986,485	21	$94,595

XL-CH08.XLS — Sheet1 / Sheet2 / Sheet3 / S

Figure 9-13. *Using named cells in formulas and code makes it easier to manipulate worksheets.*

When you use the Name command on the Insert menu to define names, Excel automatically defines them globally. However, when building Excel-based applications, you should use local names (which reference the worksheet for which they're defined) for two reasons:

- Local names enable developers to use the same name on all similarly structured sheets.

- Local names prevent users from overwriting defined names used in code.

Although you can define names locally using the Name command on the Insert menu, it requires extra typing. For example, to define a range named "Dates" locally on a sheet named "May Sales," type the following in Excel's Define Name dialog box:

```
'May Sales'!Dates
```

DevelopR.XLS's Define Name utility (see Figure 9-14) simplifies the process of defining names locally. Because the edit property of the "Refers to" edit box is set to Reference, you can select the worksheet and cells to name, just as you can in Excel's Define Name dialog box. To define names locally, select the Local Name button and then type the defined name. The utility references the worksheet name automatically.

In addition to simplifying use of local names, DevelopR's Define Name utility (unlike Excel's Define Name dialog box) runs from modules. Although you can easily add a list box to this utility to display all names defined in the workbook, I added Excel's Define Name dialog box to the Insert menu in modules. The subroutine, xlDefineNameDlg, is in modMain. (See the sidebar titled "Displaying a Built-In Dialog Box" earlier in this chapter for more information.)

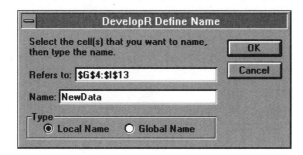

Figure 9-14. *DevelopR.XLS's Define Name utility makes it easier to define names locally.*

The code for DevelopR's Define Name utility follows:

```
Option Explicit
Dim objDNDialog As DialogSheet, objWhatAmI As Object
Dim strAppTitle As String, strRange As String
Dim strMyName As String
```

(continued)

```
'Main procedure.
Sub DefineName()
   On Error GoTo DefineNameError
   Dim blnDlgResult As Boolean
   Dim strSheetName As String, lngError As Long

'Don't use screen updating with dialog boxes
'that use Reference controls because users won't
'be able to see what they're selecting.

'Display message in the status bar.
   Application.StatusBar = "Select the worksheet range " &→
     "whose name you want to define..."

'Create dialog sheet object.
   Set objDNDialog = ThisWorkbook.DialogSheets("dlgDefineName")

'Is the active sheet a worksheet?
   Set objWhatAmI = ActiveWorkbook.Worksheets
   strMyName = ActiveWorkbook.ActiveSheet.Name
   For Each objWhatAmI In Worksheets
     strSheetName = objWhatAmI.Name

'If the active sheet is a worksheet...
     If strMyName = strSheetName Then
       strRange = Selection.Address

'If the active sheet is not a worksheet...
     Else
       strRange = ""
     End If
     Exit For
   Next

'Show dialog box.
   objDNDialog.Show

'Handle errors generated in other procedures.
   If Err <> 0 Then GoTo DefineNameError

DefineNameExit:
   Application.StatusBar = False
   Exit Sub

DefineNameError:
   If Err <> 0 And Err <> 20 Then
     lngError = Err
```

Register Today!

Return this
Developing Applications with Microsoft® Office
registration card for:

✔ a Microsoft Press® catalog

✔ exclusive offers on specially
priced books

U.S. and Canada addresses only. Fill in information below and mail postage-free. Please mail only the bottom half of this page.

Developing Applications with Microsoft Office—Owner Registration Card
1-55615-665-0A

_____

NAME

_____

INSTITUTION OR COMPANY NAME

_____

ADDRESS

_____

CITY   STATE   ZIP

MicrosoftPress.

Quality Computer Books

**For a free catalog of
Microsoft Press® products, call
1-800-MSPRESS**

BUSINESS REPLY MAIL
FIRST-CLASS MAIL   PERMIT NO. 53   BOTHELL, WA

POSTAGE WILL BE PAID BY ADDRESSEE

MICROSOFT PRESS REGISTRATION
DEVELOPING APPLICATIONS WITH
MICROSOFT OFFICE
PO BOX 3019
BOTHELL WA   98041-9946

NO POSTAGE
NECESSARY
IF MAILED
IN THE
UNITED STATES

```
      GlobalErrorMsg "Define Name", lngError
   End If
   Resume DefineNameExit
End Sub


'Initialize dialog box.
Sub Dialog_Show()

  With objDNDialog

'Dialog box title bar.
     strAppTitle = ThisWorkbook.Worksheets("wrkMain").Range→
       ("App_Title").Value & "Define Name"
     .DialogFrame.Caption = strAppTitle

'Edit boxes.
     .EditBoxes("edtRangeText").text = ""
     .EditBoxes("edtRangeName").text = ""
     .EditBoxes("edtRangeText").text = strRange

  End With
End Sub


Sub cmdOK_Click()
   On Error GoTo BYE
   Dim strRangeName As String
   Dim intFlag As Integer, intPos As Integer

'Display message in the status bar.
   Application.StatusBar = "Select the cell(s) that you want to→
     name..."

  With objDNDialog
     strRange = .EditBoxes("edtRangeText").text

'Get local or global name.
     intFlag = .OptionButtons("optGlobal").Value

'If global...
     If intFlag = 1 Then
       strRangeName = .EditBoxes("edtRangeName").text

'If local...
     Else
```

(continued)

```
'Parse range to extract sheet name.
    intPos = InStr(strRange, "!")
    strMyName = Left$(strRange, intPos)
    strRangeName = strMyName &↴
       .EditBoxes("edtRangeName").text
  End If
End With

'Define name.
  ActiveWorkbook.Names.Add strRangeName, "=" & strRange

BYE:
End Sub
```

DevelopR's Book Browser Utility

The Book Browser utility lets you browse through the sheets in a workbook by type. For example, you can browse through modules only or through worksheets. To go to a sheet, double-click it, or select it and click OK.

Book Browser's triggers

In VBA for Excel, the term *trigger* is used to describe controls that change dialog boxes dynamically depending on the option users select. For example, when you open the Book Browser utility, the dialog box (see Figure 9-15) lists all sheets in the workbook. However, clicking the option buttons—All Sheets, DialogSheets, Modules, and WorkSheets—updates the list box dynamically to show only sheets of the specified type. It does this by running a procedure, which depends on the option selected. The four option button procedures are optAll_Click, optDialog_Click, optModule_Click, and optSheet_Click.

1. Each procedure calls the DisplaySheets subroutine, with the appropriate sheet type as an argument. For example, if you select the DialogSheets option, the opt_Dialog_Click procedure calls DisplaySheets with Active-Workbook.DialogSheets (which specifies only the dialog sheets in the workbook).

2. The DisplaySheets subroutine then cycles through the sheets specified by its argument and adds each to the list box.

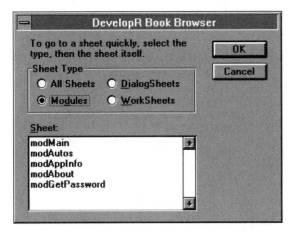

Figure 9-15. *DevelopR.XLS's Book Browser utility lets you browse through the sheets in a workbook by type.*

The code for DevelopR's Book Browser utility is shown below. Because it uses the ActiveWorkbook property rather than the ThisWorkbook property to reference code that reads the sheets, this utility works with any open workbook. (See the sidebar titled "The Object-Dot Drill-Down" earlier in this chapter for more information on the ThisWorkbook property.)

```
Option Explicit
Dim objBBDialog As DialogSheet
Dim objBBList As ListBox
Dim objCollection As Object
Dim objSheet As Object

Sub BrowseBook()
  On Error GoTo BrowseBookError
  Dim intSelect As Integer, intError As Integer
  Application.ScreenUpdating = False

'Display message in the status bar.
  Application.StatusBar = "Select type of sheet, and then " &→
    "click one to go to it..."

'Create dialog sheet object.
  Set objBBDialog = ThisWorkbook.DialogSheets("dlgBrowseBook")

'Create list box object.
  Set objBBList = objBBDialog.ListBoxes("lstSheets")
```

(continued)

```
'Show dialog box. Clear list box last displayed.
Show:
  objBBList.RemoveAllItems
  objBBDialog.Show

'Handle errors generated in other procedures.
  If Err <> 0 Then GoTo BrowseBookError

BrowseBookExit:
  Application.DisplayStatusBar = False
  Application.ScreenUpdating = True
  Exit Sub

BrowseBookError:
  If Err = 1006 Then
    MsgBox "Select a sheet!", 48, "DevelopR"
    GoTo Show
  ElseIf Err <> 0 And Err <> 20 Then
    lngError = Err
    GlobalErrorMsg "Browse Book", lngError
  End If
  Resume BrowseBookExit
End Sub


'Initialize dialog box.
Sub Dialog_Show()
  On Error GoTo BYE
  With objBBDialog

'Dialog box title bar.
    strAppTitle =
      ThisWorkbook.Worksheets("wrkMain").Range➞
      ("App_Title").Value &
      "BookBrowser"
    .DialogFrame.Caption = strAppTitle

'Call sub to populate list box.
    DisplaySheets ActiveWorkbook.Sheets

'Set option buttons.
    .OptionButtons ("optAll")
  End With

BYE:
End Sub
```

```
Sub optAll_Click()
'Call sub to populate list box.
  DisplaySheets ActiveWorkbook.Sheets
End Sub


Sub optDialog_Click()
'Call sub to populate list box.
  DisplaySheets ActiveWorkbook.DialogSheets
End Sub


Sub optModule_Click()
'Call sub to populate list box.
  DisplaySheets ActiveWorkbook.Modules
End Sub


Sub optSheet_Click()
'Call sub to populate list box.
  DisplaySheets ActiveWorkbook.Worksheets
End Sub


'Lists sheets of a particular type.
Sub DisplaySheets(SheetsOfTypeX As Object)
  On Error GoTo BYE
  Dim objSheet As Object

'Clear list box.
  objBBList.RemoveAllItems

'Add items for the type of sheet selected.
  For Each objSheet In SheetsOfTypeX
    objBBList.AddItem objSheet.Name
  Next

BYE:
End Sub


Sub cmdOK_Click()
  On Error GoTo BYE
  Dim intSelect As Integer
```

(continued)

```
'Get selected sheet.
  intSelect = objBBList.ListIndex

'Go to selected sheet.
  ActiveWorkbook.Sheets(objBBList.List(intSelect)).Activate

BYE:
End Sub
```

F Y I

Built for Speed

Excel is a good tool for building number-crunching applications (and, using OLE automation, the number-crunching modules of larger applications)—as long as you do the number crunching in worksheets and not in VBA for Excel code. When you rely on low-level worksheet functions that are built into Excel, you're using optimized, compiled code, and this makes number-crunching applications quite fast.

However, a certain percentage of Excel's functionality is written in macros and delivered as add-ins, including the Report Manager, the View Manager, and the financial and engineering functions included in the Analysis ToolPak. Although it's easy to spot most add-ins because you manage them through the Add-Ins command on the Tools menu, a few add-ins (such as Scenarios and Goal Seek) are loaded automatically. Using these tools can slow down custom applications, so time your code before committing to them. (See Chapter 7 for more information on timing code.)

People familiar with the Excel version 4 macro language often comment that VBA seems slower. In fact, one developer who reviewed this chapter scribbled in the margin, "There may be certain cases where the required performance is impossible...." The reason is that VBA for Excel functions are OLE automation objects, located in DLLs. VBA for Excel can be slower because it's passing through this extra layer.

SAMPLE APPLICATION: The WinAPI Add-In

An *add-in* is VBA for Excel code that other people can use but that they can't read or modify. (In fact, no one can read or modify add-ins because they're in a compiled form, so be sure to keep a copy of the original .XLS file.) Add-ins, which use the .XLA extension, can range from a series of stand-alone procedures or user-defined functions (such as WinAPI.XLA) to complete applications.

Because add-ins are execute-only, they're ideal for distributing Excel code. Their only drawback is that they can take a while to open. For example, on my PC (a Dell Dimension XPS 466V with 16 MB of RAM), the GetWinDir function from WinAPI.XLA takes 55 milliseconds to run the first time through. Once loaded, it requires only a fraction of a millisecond.

WinAPI.XLA shows how to deliver a code library as an add-in. It includes custom functions that serve as wrappers for three Windows API functions: GetWindowsDirectory, WritePrivateProfileString, and GetPrivateProfileString. Add-ins are particularly well suited to deliver code libraries for two reasons:

- They make it relatively easy for a central authority to maintain and distribute well-tested, tamperproof code to Excel developers.

- They imitate built-in features of Excel. For example, Excel lists an add-in's functions in the Function Wizard dialog box, which is available through the Insert menu. (See the sidebar titled "Building Add-Ins into Excel" later in this chapter.)

PRODUCT SHEET: The WinAPI Add-In

Purpose:	The WinAPI add-in provides a structure for maintaining and delivering a code library to Excel developers. This version of the library includes three custom Excel functions that serve as wrappers for common Windows API functions:
	■ GetWindowsDirectory. (The library function is GetWinDir.)
	■ WritePrivateProfileString. (The library function is PutStringToINI.)
	■ GetPrivateProfileString. (The library function is GetStringFromINI.)
	Wrapping API functions in VBA for Excel code makes it easier for developers to use these functions. For example, it eliminates two difficulties that developers face when using the API: declare statements and the need to allocate buffer size for functions such as GetPrivateProfileString.
Development tools used:	Excel; Windows API
How the WinAPI Add-In works:	The WinAPI add-in is a model for providing developers with a library of tested, tamperproof procedures. The diagram on the following page illustrates the principle.

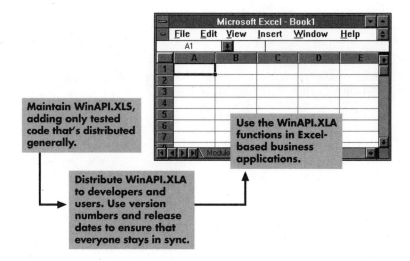

Maintain WinAPI.XLS, adding only tested code that's distributed generally.

Distribute WinAPI.XLA to developers and users. Use version numbers and release dates to ensure that everyone stays in sync.

Use the WinAPI.XLA functions in Excel-based business applications.

The code from WinAPI.XLS is shown below.

```
Option Explicit

'Declare statements for Windows API Functions.
Private Declare Function GetWindowsDirectory Lib "KERNEL"→
   (ByVal lpBuffer As String,→
   ByVal nSize As Integer) As Integer
Private Declare Function GetPrivateProfileString Lib "KERNEL"→
   (ByVal lpApplicationName As String,→
   ByVal lpKeyName As String,→
   ByVal lpDefault As String,→
   ByVal lpReturnedString As String,→
   ByVal nSize As Integer,→
   ByVal lpFileName As String) As Integer
Private Declare Function WritePrivateProfileString Lib "KERNEL"→
   (ByVal lpApplicationName As String,→
   ByVal lpKeyName As String,→
   ByVal lpString As String,→
   ByVal lplFileName As String) As Integer


'Function:   GetWinDir.
'Title:      Get name of Windows directory.
'Syntax:     OK = GetWinDir(strWinDir).
'Function:   1. Returns the name of the directory in strWinDir.
'            2. Returns OK = True/False to signal OK/Not OK.
'            3. If OK = False, strWinDir = "".
Function GetWinDir(strWinDir) As Boolean
   Dim strBuffer As String
   Dim intLen As Integer
```

```
'Allocate a string buffer.
  strBuffer = Space$(200)
  intLen = GetWindowsDirectory(strBuffer, Len(strBuffer))
  strWinDir = Left$(strBuffer, intLen)
  GetWinDir = (intLen <> 0)
End Function


'Functon:    PutStringToINI.
'Title:      Store a string and its value in an INI file.
'Syntax:     OK = PutStringToINI(Section,Item,Value,File).
'Function:   1. Invokes WritePrivateProfileString.
'            2. Returns OK = True/False to signal OK/Not OK.
'Notes:      1. Defaults to the Windows directory if no path is
'               specified.
Function PutStringToINI(strSection As String, strItem As String,→
  strSendString As String, strFile As String) As Boolean
  Dim blnRV
  blnRV = WritePrivateProfileString(strSection, strItem,→
    strSendString, strFile)
  PutStringToINI = (blnRV <> 0)
End Function


'Function:   GetStringFromINI.
'Title:      Using Section, Item, File...get value from INI file.
'Syntax:     OK = GetStringFromINI(Section,Item,Default, _
'            RetString,File).
'Function:   1. Allocates a buffer for the return string.
'            2. Gets the string from the INI.
'            3. Returns OK = True/False to signal OK/Not OK.
'            4. If OK = False, GetString = "".
'Notes:      1. Defaults to the Windows directory if no path is
'               specified.
'            2. Returns False only if params are bad AND the
'               default string is null; if there is a default string,
'               OK = True.
Function GetStringFromINI(strSection As String, strItem As→
  String, strDefault As String, strGetString As String,→
  strFile As String) As Boolean
  Dim intLen As Integer

'Allocate a string buffer.
  strGetString = Space$(200)
```

(continued)

```
intLen = GetPrivateProfileString(strSection, strItem,
  strDefault, strGetString, Len(strGetString), strFile)
strGetString = Left$(strGetString, intLen)
GetStringFromINI = (intLen <> 0)
End Function
```

FYI

Are Add-Ins Really Tamperproof?

Maybe not. Although Microsoft says that add-ins are secure, I hear that someone who frequents the Excel forum on CompuServe claims to have gotten
module code out of an add-in (although that person apparently didn't leave
instructions for the rest of us). In any case, it's certainly easy enough to peek
into add-ins. For example, you can use the following code to view the sheets
in the Microsoft Query add-in:

```
Sub PeekingAtXLAs()
  Dim i As Integer
  For i = 1 To Workbooks("xlquery.xla").Sheets.Count
    MsgBox Workbooks("xlquery.xla").Sheets(i).Name
  Next
End Sub
```

How to Use WinAPI.XLA

Excel includes two separate commands for using add-ins: the Add-Ins command and the References command. (Both are on the Tools menu.) The Add-
Ins command is primarily for end users; the References command (which is
available only when you're in a module) lets developers use an add-in's procedures and functions in their own code. For example, to use WinAPI.XLA, choose
References and then use the Browse button to locate this add-in. Once it's
listed and checked in the References dialog box, you can access its functions.

Using the GetWinDir function

The WinAPI add-in's GetWinDir function uses the GetWindowsDirectory API
call to get the Windows directory. The GetWinDir function returns True if it's
successful and False if it's not. (See the notes for the function in the code listing
for WinAPI.XLS, shown earlier.) To use this function, pass in a variable to hold
the string for the Windows directory, as shown in the following example:

```
Sub ChangeToWinDir()
  Dim strWinDir As String
  Dim OK As Integer
```

```
'Call custom function.
  OK = GetWinDir(strWinDir)
  If OK Then
    ChDir strWinDir
  Else
    MsgBox "Couldn't get Windows directory!"
  End If
End Sub
```

FYI

Building Add-Ins into Excel

Here are some tips on building add-ins that look and feel like seamless extensions of Excel:

■ In the .XLS that is destined to become an .XLA, type the add-in's title in the Summary Info dialog box (available through the File menu). This title appears in the Add-Ins dialog box (available through the Tools menu) when you load the add-in.

■ Type descriptive information in the Comments section of the Summary Info dialog box. This appears at the bottom of the Add-Ins dialog box.

■ Use the Options button in the Object Browser (available through the View menu when you're in a module) to type brief instructions. These appear in the Function Wizard.

■ When you use an add-in's procedures and functions in your code, make sure the add-in is always available to your users. One way to do this is to store it in the users' XLSTART directory (or in the alternate startup directory). That way, the add-in loads automatically whenever users run Excel.

Using the PutStringToINI function

The WinAPI add-in's PutStringToINI function uses the WritePrivateProfileString API call to create and/or write to a private INI file. The PutStringToINI function returns True if it's successful and False if it's not. (See the notes for the function in the code listing for WinAPI.XLS, shown earlier.)

To use this function, pass the four arguments necessary to write an entry in an INI file:

■ The name of the section (for example, an application's name).

■ The name of the entry in that section (for example, "user").

- The particular entry you're writing (for example, the user's name).

- The name of the INI file. (If the INI file doesn't exist, the function creates it.)

The following example uses WinAPI.XLA's PutStringToINI function:

```
Sub WriteToIniFile()
  Dim blnRv As Boolean

'Call custom function.
  blnRv = PutStringToINI("Custom", "User", "Frank Wallner",→
    "Common.INI")
  If Not blnRv Then MsgBox "Couldn't create INI file!"
End Sub
```

Using the GetStringFromINI function

The WinAPI add-in's GetStringFromINI function uses the GetPrivateProfileString API call to read from a private INI file. The GetStringFromINI function returns True if it's successful and False if it's not. (See the notes for the function in the code listing for WinAPI.XLS, shown earlier.)

To use this function, pass a variable to hold the string that you're reading from the INI file, plus the five arguments necessary to identify this string:

- The variable

- The name of the section (for example, an application's name)

- The name of the entry in that section (for example, "user")

- The default value returned if the string can't be found (usually an empty string)

- The name of the INI file

The following example uses WinAPI.XLA's GetStringFromINI function:

```
Sub GetFromINIFile()
  Dim strGetString As String
  Dim blnRv As Boolean

'Call custom function.
  blnRv = GetStringFromINI("Custom", "User", "",→
    strGetString, "Common.INI")
  MsgBox strGetString
End Sub
```

CASE STUDY: Merrill Lynch's Mutual Funds Analysis System

The twofold mission of the mutual funds research department at Merrill Lynch is to analyze *closed-end mutual funds* (funds that have a fixed number of shares and that trade on a major exchange) and to uncover interesting investment opportunities. The department provides the results of its research to more than 10,000 financial consultants (FCs) and their clients, usually in two ways: over the phone and through published reports.

When the department started to consider automating its activities, it determined that the ideal application had to perform three functions:

■ It had to maintain current and historical data on *any* mutual fund.

■ Its data had to be accessible through Excel at the push of a button.

■ It had to enable the department to publish reports directly from Excel.

The solution was an Excel-based application (called the Mutual Funds Analysis System—MFAS for short) that uses the Retrieve engine to get data from closed Excel workbooks. (The Retrieve engine is described in the next section, "SAMPLE APPLICATION: Retrieve.XLS.")

Hold One Second, Please....

Although there are more than 300 closed-end mutual funds, the department used to follow only 34 funds closely. As a result, when FCs called with questions about one of the 266-plus funds that the department *didn't* follow, the analysts didn't always have answers—and the answers they did have took a while to find. MFAS lets analysts easily maintain and retrieve data on *any* closed-end mutual fund on the market—by organizing each fund into an Excel workbook that is updated weekly through an automated batch process.

When FCs call the department for information on particular funds, analysts select the fund and the requested data from a dialog box, and MFAS returns the information in an Excel worksheet. Because each fund's data is stored in a separate workbook, the department can expand the number of funds covered without taking a performance hit. Whether they maintain data for 10 funds or 10,000, the system accesses only a single file at a time. Also, since MFAS doesn't have to open the file to read the data, analysts get the requested data almost instantly.

Some analysts have further improved response time by using MFAS to build templates that retrieve all time-series data on a fund—its daily price over the past 13 weeks, its net asset value, and so on. When FCs call with a question on a fund, analysts need only type the fund symbol into a cell to retrieve all pertinent data.

MFAS enables analysts to deliver, over the phone, complete information on any closed-end mutual fund. Plus, it makes it easier for them to follow more funds more closely. Using MFAS, analysts have nearly tripled the number of funds they track on a regular basis.

Publish or Perish

Before the department had MFAS, it took them two weeks to produce a quarterly report. At that time, they used an MS-DOS–based platform. Analysts stored and crunched numbers in Lotus 1-2-3, wrote text in WordPerfect, and created graphs in GraphWriter. Now, with MFAS (which uses Excel templates for publishing), it takes analysts less than a single day to produce a better-looking version of a quarterly report.

In addition to giving these reports a facelift, MFAS enables the department to use a layout that conserves space. Before MFAS, the average report was 110 pages. But now, due in large part to the template's design, the average report—for more than twice the number of funds—is only 85 pages. Plus, analysts can add one-third more information on each fund, including a second graph.

The new design also provides an introductory "article" at the start of the report in which analysts can write as much as they like. Before MFAS, they had to compress the text into a few lines no matter what was happening in the market.

SAMPLE APPLICATION: Retrieve.XLS

Retrieve.XLS uses "in-cell technology" (see the sidebar titled "In-Cell Technology" later in this chapter) to retrieve data stored in Excel workbooks. I have included four sample workbooks (GE.XLS, IBM.XLS, MM.XLS, and XON.XLS) from which Retrieve reads data (see Figure 9-16).

- Each workbook stores data on a single company. The company is identified by its ticker symbol, which doubles as the workbook's name.

- The first column of the workbook stores the field names, and the second column stores the data.

Figure 9-16. *GE.XLS, one of the four sample workbooks provided with Retrieve.XLS.*

PRODUCT SHEET: Retrieve.XLS

Purpose:

Retrieve.XLS provides an interface for retrieving data from multiple closed Excel workbooks into a single worksheet. This makes it easier for users to analyze data; produce ad hoc reports; and, using the Build Code command, create their own templates. Retrieve.XLS uses two key techniques:

■ It uses custom functions to retrieve data into a single cell or into a range of cells.

■ It organizes Excel workbooks into a database system.

Development tool used:

Excel

How Retrieve works:

Although you can create functions that retrieve data from any database, this version of Retrieve gets data from closed Excel workbooks. The technique of using Excel workbooks as the basis of a database system is important for departments that rely on spreadsheets because it creates a fast, expandable system.

Here's how it works: Each workbook is essentially a single record. Since Retrieve.XLS accesses each record independently of the others, disk capacity is the only limit. No matter how many records (workbooks) you have, there's no deterioration in performance. In addition, since Retrieve can read data from closed Excel workbooks, the system isn't hampered by having to open and close files.

The following diagram illustrates Retrieve's database structure:

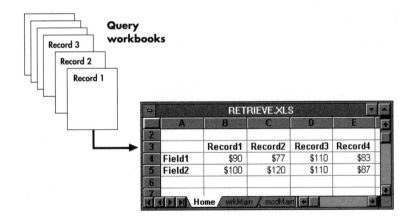

313

In-Cell Technology

Because companies often want to retrieve data from external sources into Excel workbooks, Micro Modeling Associates developed a technique called "in-cell technology" to simplify this process. The term "in-cell" reflects the fact that data is returned by custom functions in cells. The arguments used determine both the data retrieved and the source (see Figure 9-17).

In-cell technology is both flexible and simple. Developers create functions that allow users to specify the arguments relevant to retrieving corporate data—for example, the data source, field, criteria, sort order, and data positioning (vertical or horizontal). Since these functions work on the same principle as Excel's built-in functions, Excel users only have to learn the arguments accepted. Or, to make it easier still, developers can add an interface that hides the functions entirely.

Although the sample application Retrieve.XLS uses in-cell technology to read data from closed Excel sheets, you can use this same technology to read data from most database systems. For example, you can write functions that construct SQL queries, connect to ODBC data sources, or use a proprietary data feed.

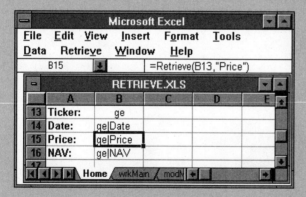

Figure 9-17. *In-cell technology uses functions to return data based on the arguments supplied by users. In this case, the function returns data based on the company in cell B13 (such as GE, which is the stock exchange ticker for General Electric) and on the field of data specified (such as Price).*

Retrieve.XLS Commands

Retrieve.XLS has three custom commands, located on the Retrieve menu:

- The Retrieve Data command opens a dialog box in which you select data. This command calls the RetrieveData procedure, which in turn calls CreateRequestCode and ProcessRequestCode. (See the section titled "The Retrieve Data Command" later in this chapter.)

- The Build Code command opens the same dialog box as Retrieve Data but returns the *function* that retrieves the data rather than the data itself. This command (which calls the CreateRequestCode procedure) lets you build templates. (See the section titled "The Build Code Command" later in this chapter.)

- The Process Code command uses the function created by Build Code to populate a cell with data. This command calls the ProcessRequestCode procedure. (See the section titled "The Process Code Command" later in this chapter.)

The code for Retrieve.XLS follows:

```
Option Explicit
Dim objRDialog As Object, objWMain As Object
Dim strCompany As String, strData As String
Dim objCompany As DropDown, objData As DropDown

'intFlag signals that the user clicked Cancel in
'the Retrieve dialog box.
  Dim intFlag As Integer

'Change this constant to the path to your sheets.
'Sample sheets are IBM.XLS, GE.XLS, MMM.XLS, and XON.XLS.
  Const PATHTOSHEETS = "C:\offsoln\xl_apps\retrieve\"

'Called from menu.
Sub RetrieveData()
  On Error GoTo RetrieveDataError
  Err = 0: intFlag = 0
  Dim strValue As String, intPosition As Integer
  Dim intLength As Integer, intDataPos As Integer
  Application.ScreenUpdating = False
  Application.StatusBar = "Select the data to retrieve..."

'Set objects.
  Set objRDialog = ThisWorkbook.DialogSheets("dlgRetrieve")
```

(continued)

```
  Set objWMain = ThisWorkbook.Worksheets("wrkMain")
  Set objCompany = objRDialog.DropDowns("drpCompany")
  Set objData = objRDialog.DropDowns("drpData")

'Call sub. Build request code in cell.
  CreateRequestCode
  If intFlag = 1 Then GoTo RetrieveDataExit

'Call sub. Get data based on request code in cell.
  ProcessRequestCode

RetrieveDataExit:
  Application.ScreenUpdating = True
  Application.StatusBar = False
  Exit Sub

RetrieveDataError:
  If Err <> 0 Then
    GlobalErrorMsg "Retrieve Data...", Err
    Resume RetrieveDataExit
  End If
End Sub


'Called from menu.
Sub BuildCode()
  On Error GoTo BuildCodeError
  Err = 0: intFlag = 0
  Application.ScreenUpdating = False
  Application.StatusBar = "Select the data for which to build→
    code..."

'Set objects.
  Set objRDialog = ThisWorkbook.DialogSheets("dlgRetrieve")
  Set objWMain = ThisWorkbook.Worksheets("wrkMain")
  Set objCompany = objRDialog.DropDowns("drpCompany")
  Set objData = objRDialog.DropDowns("drpData")

'Call sub. Build request code in cell.
  CreateRequestCode
  If intFlag = 1 Then GoTo BuildCodeExit

BuildCodeExit:
  Application.ScreenUpdating = True
  Application.StatusBar = False
  Exit Sub

BuildCodeError:
```

```
    If Err <> 0 Then
      GlobalErrorMsg "Retrieve Data...", Err
      Resume BuildCodeExit
    End If
End Sub


'Called from menu.
Sub ProcessCode()
  On Error GoTo ProcessCodeError
  Err = 0: intFlag = 0
  Application.ScreenUpdating = False
  Application.StatusBar = "Processing request codes..."

'Set objects.
  Set objWMain = ThisWorkbook.Worksheets("wrkMain")

'Call sub. Get data based on request code in cell.
  ProcessRequestCode
  If intFlag = 1 Then GoTo ProcessCodeExit

ProcessCodeExit:
  Application.ScreenUpdating = True
  Application.StatusBar = False
  Exit Sub

ProcessCodeError:
  If Err <> 0 Then
    GlobalErrorMsg "Retrieve Data...", Err
    Resume ProcessCodeExit
  End If
End Sub


'Builds actual request code in cell.
Sub CreateRequestCode()
'Clear last selections in dialog box.
  objCompany.RemoveAllItems
  objData.RemoveAllItems

'Show dialog box.
  objRDialog.Show

'Call Retrieve function.
  If intFlag <> 1 Then Selection.Formula =⤑
    "=retrieve(""" & strCompany & """,""" & strData & """)"
End Sub
```

(continued)

```
'Initialize dialog box.
Sub Dialog_Show()
'Populate drop-down lists.
  objCompany.ListFillRange = "Companies"
  objData.ListFillRange = "Data"
End Sub


Sub cmdOK_Click()
  strCompany = objWMain.Range("Companies")(objCompany.ListIndex)
  strData = objWMain.Range("Data")(objData.ListIndex)
End Sub


Sub cmdCancel_Click()
  intFlag = 1
End Sub


'Retrieves data based on request code in cell.
Sub ProcessRequestCode()
  If intFlag = 1 Then Exit Sub
  Dim strValue As String, intPosition As Integer
  Dim intLength As Integer, intDataPos As Integer

'Get contents of cell.
  strValue = Selection.Value

'Find pipe in cell.
  intPosition = InStr(strValue, "|")

'Handle case in which there's no code.
  If intPosition = 0 Then
    MsgBox "This cell has no code to process.", 64, "Retrieve"
    Exit Sub
  End If

'Parse cell.
  intLength = Len(strValue)
  strCompany = Left(strValue, intPosition - 1)
  strData = Right(strValue, intLength - intPosition)

'Match is an Excel function that lets you match data in an array.
'Here it returns the position of the data element on wrkMain.
'This position is the same as in the workbooks that store data.
  intDataPos = Application.Match(strData, objWMain.→
    Range("data"), 0)
```

```
'Select closed sheet; return data from column B at the
'specified position; PATHTOSHEETS is a constant defined at the
'start of the module.
  Selection.Formula = "='" & PATHTOSHEETS & "[" & strCompany¬
    & ".XLS]Sheet1'!$B$" & intDataPos

'Change code back into string result.
  Selection.Formula = Selection.Value
End Sub


'In-cell function.
Function Retrieve(Ticker As String, Data As String) As String
  If intFlag = 1 Then Exit Function
  Retrieve = Ticker & "|" & Data
End Function
```

The Retrieve Data command

The Retrieve Data command relies on three main procedures:

- The RetrieveData procedure handles the status bar, screen redraw, error trapping, and so on. It also calls the CreateRequestCodes procedure and the ProcessRequestCode procedure.

- The CreateRequestCodes procedure calls the Retrieve dialog box (see Figure 9-18 on the following page) and the Retrieve function. This version of Retrieve populates the dialog box based on data stored in wrkMain, including the records (workbooks) available (referenced by the defined name "companies") and the data fields available (referenced by the defined name "data"). The data fields must be listed in wrkMain in the same order in which they appear in the data sheets.

  The CreateRequestCodes procedure passes the Retrieve function two arguments: the ticker for the selected company and the name of the data field. The Retrieve function returns code that can be processed by the ProcessRequestCode procedure.

- The ProcessRequestCode procedure processes the code returned by the Retrieve function and then retrieves the requested data. For example, if you select MMM (the stock exchange ticker for 3M Corporation) and Price (price per share) using the sample workbooks provided on the *Office Solutions* disk included with this book, Retrieve returns *$56*.

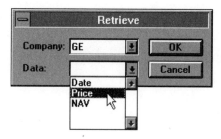

Figure 9-18. *Choose the Retrieve Data command from the Retrieve menu to open this dialog box. Select data items from the drop-down lists.*

The Build Code command

The Build Code command (which relies on the CreateRequestCodes procedure) makes it easy for users to create templates that facilitate both analysis and publishing. (See "CASE STUDY: Merrill Lynch's Mutual Funds Analysis System" earlier in this chapter.) Users can build the request codes to retrieve specific data; format the sheet in any way they like, including adding borders, charts, and so on; and then save the workbook as a template. The key to building these templates is the functions in the worksheet cells.

For example, let's say you build a request code to return the price for General Electric (whose ticker is "GE"). The function in the cell (also referred to as the request code) looks like this:

```
=Retrieve("GE","PRICE")
```

To build a template that returns the price for any company, however, the first argument should be a cell reference:

```
=Retrieve(B13,"PRICE")
```

Now the request code returns data on whatever company users enter into cell B13. All request codes in the template that reference B13 return data on this company.

> **NOTE** To change a string (such as "GE") to a cell reference, simply delete the string and type the reference.

The Process Code command

The Process Code command processes a Retrieve function in a cell and returns the requested data. It parses the cell based on the position of the *pipe character* (ASCII code 124) that returns this symbol: |. (Using the pipe character as a delimiter allows greater flexibility in the types of data returned. For example, if you use commas to delimit data, you can't as easily return data that includes commas.)

As mentioned in the earlier section titled "The Retrieve Data Command," this version of Retrieve reads data stored in wrkMain to handle the companies and data fields available to the system. In addition to using this data to populate the Retrieve dialog box, the system uses it to identify the requested data in the data sheet. It does this through Match—an Excel function that returns the position in an array of matching data. The following line of code (from the ProcessRequestCode procedure) returns the *position* of the requested data field on wrkMain (Date returns *1*, Price returns *2*, and Volume returns *3*).

```
intDataPos = Application.Match(strData, objWMain.⇥
  Range("data"), 0)
```

Since the field's position on wrkMain is identical to its position in the data sheets, the next line of code uses the position to retrieve the data requested. (PATHTOSHEETS is a constant set at the start of the module.

```
Selection.Formula = "='" & PATHTOSHEETS & "[" & strCompany⇥
  & ".XLS]Sheet1'!$B$" & intDataPos
```

Note that this code constructs the following statement, which retrieves data from closed Excel workbooks. (You can rewrite this code to construct statements, such as SQL queries, that retrieve data stored in other database systems.)

```
='C:\OFFSOLN\XL_APPS\RETRIEVE\[IBM.XLS]Sheet1'!$B$2
```

FYI

Developing Applications That Run on Both the Windows and the Macintosh Versions of Excel

Here are some tips (put together by Rick Bullen, a director at Micro Modeling) for developing Excel-based business applications that run on both the Windows and the Macintosh versions of Excel.

Apple File Exchange: When you port .XLM and .XLS files to the Mac through Apple File Exchange, they appear as "document files," not as "Excel documents," so you can't launch Excel by double-clicking them. Open these files using the Open command on the File menu. Once you save them from Excel on the Mac, the Mac recognizes them as Excel documents.

Long filenames: Using long filenames on the Mac causes various problems when porting to PCs running Windows version 3.*x*. Apple File Exchange uses the first 11 nonblank characters of the Mac filename (or the folder name) as the name of the copied file. Thus a folder named "Work in Progress" on the Mac becomes WORKINPR.OGR.

The best way to avoid this problem is to use the lowest common denominator —the MS-DOS standard for filenames. Windows 95 will make it possible to port applications with long filenames between the PC and the Mac.

The Caption property: Use the Window object's Caption property to assign names to workbooks that are similar to long filenames on the Mac. The problem with this method is that Excel occasionally uses the actual filename rather than the window caption when communicating with the user. One case is the "Save changes to *filename.xls*?" message, and another is the status box that the Print command displays. If the window caption appears elsewhere in the application, users won't necessarily recognize the filename.

Filenames and spaces: Filenames on the Mac can contain spaces. You have to "single quote" these in Excel (for example, 'File Name') when you reference them. Applications that reference Macintosh workbooks should therefore use an expression such as:

```
INDIRECT("'["&BookName&"]"&SheetName&"'!DefinedName")
```

Checking the operating system: Use the Application object's Operating-System property to check the environment. On a PC, this property is set to "Windows..." and on a Mac it's set to "Macintosh..." The following code determines the current operating environment:

```
If Left(Application.OperatingSystem, 1, 3) = "Mac" Then
  Mac = True
Else
  Mac = False
End If
```

As soon as you set the Mac variable, you can write platform-independent code, as follows:

```
If Mac Then Action if Mac Else Action if PC
```

SendKeys: The SendKeys method is not available on the Mac.

Keyboard shortcuts: There are differences between keyboard shortcuts on the Mac and on the PC. If you refer to the keyboard shortcuts in your documentation and if your system has to run in both environments, allow extra time to test the keyboard shortcuts for the two environments.

If you disable Excel shortcut keys in your application, you will have to disable a different set of keys, depending on the operating environment. Use two lists of keys, one for the Mac and one for the PC, and then process the appropriate list, as follows:

```
If Running on the PC Then
  Disable the PC Shortcut Keys
Else
  Disable the Mac Shortcut Keys
End If
```

Dates: The Mac defaults to the 1904 date system, and the PC defaults to the 1900 date system. You can move a workbook that contains dates between the PC and the Mac without problems because the date system is encoded in the workbook, but you must beware of the following situation: On a Mac, the user opens a PC workbook, which uses the 1900 date system; the user creates a new workbook, which defaults to the 1904 date system; and the user then copies dates and so forth from the PC workbook to the new Mac workbook.

This situation produces errors because Excel's serial date numbers represent *different dates* in the Mac-based workbook than in the PC workbook. To avoid this problem:

■ Make sure that you carefully track date systems in individual workbooks while you process them.

■ Standardize on either the Mac or the PC date system. (Use the Date System option on the Calculation tab of the Options dialog box, available through the Tools menu.)

NOTE When porting files between any two machines, make sure the date and time are the same.

Add-ins: References to Excel add-ins contain hard-coded paths and are, therefore, de facto links (although they don't appear in the Links dialog box). You have to reestablish references to Excel add-ins when you move a workbook from the PC to the Mac (or vice versa). Or open the add-in at runtime, as follows:

```
Workbooks.Open "Add-InName.XLA"
Run "[Add-InName.XLA]NameOfModule!NameOfProcedure"
```

Another good tool for programming temporary links in worksheets is the INDIRECT function. Use the following line of code to reference a data item without generating a permanent link that has to be changed when you switch machines:

```
INDIRECT("[BookName]SheetName!DefinedName")
```

Path separator: The path separator on the PC is "\", while on the Mac it's ":". When constructing pathnames, use the Application.PathSeparator property instead of the hard-coded character string.

Screen resolution: Because the appearance of dialog boxes varies depending on a monitor's resolution, detect the platform and monitor currently in use and adjust the aspect ratio of the dialog boxes accordingly.

Access keys: Access keys are standard on the PC, but they are user-selectable on the Mac. If you set or reset access keys on the Mac, save and restore the user's selection.

New lines: You can use either Chr(10) or Chr(13) to insert a new line in a message box on the PC. However, since only Chr(13) works on the Mac, you should make that standard for cross-platform applications.

```
MsgBox "The second line starts a new line." & Chr(13) & "New line."
```

10

Developing Business Applications with Access

Unlike word processors and spreadsheets, databases are not end-user tools—they're programmer tools. There are only two reasons to use Microsoft Access: to develop databases to store your data and to build applications to manage that data. Although Access is easier to use than other relational databases, it nonetheless requires that users understand relational databases—and most users don't. Sources at Microsoft estimate that although the company has sold more than 800,000 copies of Access, a large percentage of buyers never open the shrink-wrapped package.

To use Access successfully, you need to understand your data and understand how each data element relates to the others. Building a database application isn't primarily about coding; it's about designing a usable database and organizing it into a series of related tables in such a way that you can answer the questions you have today, as well as those that come up tomorrow. The most common problem with database applications is that the structure of the underlying data prevents people from using the data effectively.

Since Access was first released at the end of 1992, I've seen developers use it to build the following types of business applications (in addition to the more common data-entry systems):

- **Departmental databases.** A department in a major investment bank recently developed an application that lets account managers integrate into an Access database a variety of client data stored on different mainframe systems. Access pulls this data together and adds a handful of new fields not available on the mainframe systems.

- **Accounting systems for small to medium-size organizations.** Because Access is a relational database with solid calculation and reporting features plus the tools necessary to build a good user interface, you can use it to develop easy-to-use accounting applications. (See the section titled "SAMPLE APPLICATION: Time Sheets [TimeNtry.MDB]" later in this chapter.)

- **Decision-support applications.** The marketing department of a major accounting and consulting firm recently developed an Access application that stores data about every company in the world with assets over $1 billion. The goal is to pinpoint those that are current clients and those that are clients of the firm's competitors.

- **Data-consolidation tools.** Access enables you to consolidate desktop data that is stored in Excel workbooks into corporate data that is stored and managed centrally. You can do this using ODBC or through the Import command on the Access File menu. (See "CASE STUDY: From Desktop Data to a Central Database" in Chapter 5.)

- **Business information management systems at the departmental and workgroup levels.** You can develop multiuser databases in Access that store departmental and workgroup-level data. Because end-user development tools such as Microsoft Excel and Microsoft Word can use ODBC to query and retrieve such data, companies use these tools to build front ends that enable businesspeople to use this data productively at their desktops. For example, the sample Word application Business Information Manager (BIM) presented later in this chapter manages address and fax information for business contacts from an Access database.

This chapter presents three sample Access applications. I use them to address some of the programming techniques and practices that can help you develop professional business applications in Access. The sample applications, which can also be found on the *Office Solutions* disk included with this book, are:

- TimeNtry.MDB, an Access application that simplifies the process of entering time sheets and demonstrates how to implement security in Access.

- MenuBldR.MDA, a builder that makes it easier for developers to write Access Basic code that uses built-in menu commands and dialog boxes in Access. This is a handy time-saver because Access Basic does not provide any methods for doing this. Without MenuBldR, you would have to look up the correct arguments in the macro window or in a list of intrinsic constants.

- BIM, a Word front end to a shared Access database that uses ODBC to turn business correspondence into corporate data.

FYI

Access Macros

You can turn Excel and Word macros into powerful BASIC programs that manipulate and extend their host environments. Access macros, however, are nothing more than "scripts" that perform simple tasks by bundling together a sequence of commands into a single instruction. Access even lacks a macro recorder feature. Although you can use Excel and Word macros to develop applications, you should not try to develop applications in Access macros. Instead, use Access Basic modules.

Unlike Excel and Word macros, Access macros are primarily a tool for power users, not developers. Although the 45-plus macro "actions" in Access are a handy way for power users to add automation, macros pose the following problems for developers:

- They offer a limited tool set.

- They don't support traditional control structures, such as loops, case statements, and so on.

- They don't provide any error-trapping capability. When an error occurs, Access displays a vague error message and halts execution.

- They are hard to maintain because the code is essentially "hidden." To read a line of macro code, you have to position the cursor on the macro line itself to see the available arguments. (Access displays these at the bottom of the macro window.) This means that you can read only one line of macro code at a time.

Despite their limitations, macros are required in the following four cases (which Access Basic statements can't handle):

- To run code when users first open their application. (Use the AutoExec macro.)

- To assign accelerator keys. (Use the AutoKeys macro.)

- To create a custom menu.

- To call commands from custom menus and toolbars. (Use the DoMenuItem, RunCode, or RunMacro action.)

One additional way that developers occasionally use Access macros is for prototyping the user interface. When the application goes into production, however, you should *convert the macros to code*.

SAMPLE APPLICATION: Time Sheets (TimeNtry.MDB)

TimeNtry.MDB is an extract from the payroll module of an accounting application built by Mary Chipman (an associate at Micro Modeling Associates) for a medium-size organization (250 people). It demonstrates two things:

- How to develop an Access application that enforces business rules to minimize user error and protect against fraud

- How to develop a security system using Access Basic

PRODUCT SHEET: TimeNtry

Purpose:	The TimeNtry application automates the process of creating time sheets every two weeks for 250 employees. It does this by assuming that all full-time staff (by far the largest segment of the workforce) work standard hours, so time sheet entry becomes a matter of entering two types of data: the exceptions and the hours for part-time staff. This dramatically reduces the time spent on this task.
Development tool used:	Access
How TimeNtry works:	TimeNtry uses a batch process (which you run by clicking the Batch Timesheets button) to create time sheets for all active employees (those who have valid data in both the Employee and Payroll tables). After creating time sheets using the batch process, click the Timesheet Entry button to make changes to the standard time sheets—for example, to add overtime, to record vacation days, and to enter hours for part-time employees.
	TimeNtry also includes a security system (implemented through TimeNtry.MDA) with two groups of users:
	■ Executive users, who have administrative privileges, can handle personnel records and can create batch time sheets
	■ Data entry users, who can enter data for individual time sheets once the batch time sheets are created
	To use TimeNtry, run the Workgroup Administer application from Program Manager to set Time-Ntry.MDA as your system database, and then log on using "Boss" as both the name and the password.
	TimeNtry's main dialog box is shown on the facing page. Note that a label in the center of the dialog box explains key points about each button's functionality.

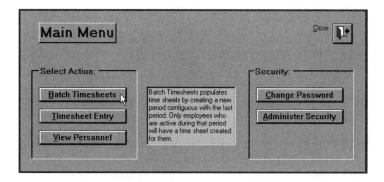

How TimeNtry.MDB Works

The time sheet application includes three main functions:

- Maintenance of basic employee and payroll data, including start date, end date, salary, and so on. (The version of TimeNtry on the *Office Solutions* disk included with this book doesn't let you create new employee records, but you can edit existing records.)

- Creation of time sheets that track each employee's hours during any given (two-week) pay period, including regular hours worked, overtime, sick leave, company holidays, and so on.

- Security, which is implemented through TimeNtry.MDA. (See the section titled "Securing Your Data" later in this chapter.)

The original version of TimeNtry operates within the constraints of several dozen business rules. This version implements only a handful of these rules:

- You can create time sheets for active employees only—in other words, employees whose start date and end date fall *outside* the range of the current two-week period. The application creates partial time sheets for employees whose start date or end date falls *within* the current period. TimeNtry stores this data in two tables—Employees and Payroll—that are used to populate the Personnel form (see Figure 10-1 on the following page).

- The application automatically enters seven hours into the time sheets of full-time employees for every workday and company holiday (as listed in the Calendar table) and stores this data in the Timesheet table. (The original version of TimeNtry stores data until users officially close the period, which triggers a series of reconciliations. Once users close a period, the application locks the records. Users make any further adjustments through journal entries.)

- The application enters zero hours into the time sheets of part-time employees for every day in the pay period.

- The data-entry clerks responsible for entering time sheet data do not have access to personnel or payroll data, and they cannot create time sheets. They can record hours for existing time sheets only, editing the hours worked by part-time employees and entering overtime, vacation days, and so on. (See the section titled "Entering Data into Time Sheets Manually" later in this chapter.)

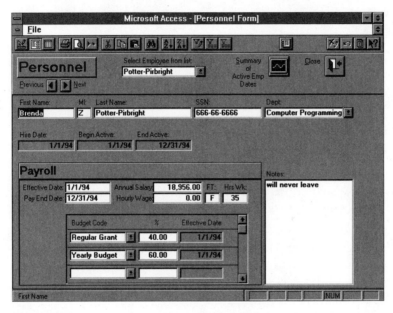

Figure 10-1. *The Personnel form, which is populated from data in the Employee and Payroll tables. Note the custom navigation buttons, which provide greater control than the standard buttons over the records displayed and their order.*

Creating time sheets using the automated batch process

When users click the Batch Timesheets button, TimeNtry creates time sheets for all active employees. It does this by calling the p_NewPeriod function in the Programs module. This function determines the new period by adding 14 days to Latest Period, which is stored in the L_Globals table (see Figure 10-2). It then displays the date of the new period in a message box so that users can verify whether to create time sheets. If they click Yes, p_NewPeriod loops through the days in the period and calls the p_IsWorkday function, which returns *1* if the day is a workday, *2* if it's a weekend day, or *3* if it's a scheduled holiday.

Next, p_NewPeriod calls the p_NewTimesheet function and passes it the dates in the period marked as workdays, weekend days, or scheduled holidays. The p_NewTimesheet function then loops through active employee records and creates a time sheet for each employee (see Figure 10-3).

The following code from p_NewPeriod retrieves information from the p_IsWorkday function and passes it to p_NewTimesheet:

```
'This code loops through the days in the new period,
'checks the kind of day, and then passes it to the
'p_NewTimesheet function. It then loops through all
'active employees and creates a time sheet for each.
    Do Until varWorkDate = varNewPeriod + 14
      intX = p_NewTimesheet(varWorkDate, p_IsWorkday(varWorkDate))
      varWorkDate = varWorkDate + 1
    Loop
```

ID	Latest Period	Earliest Period	Period Length	Last Closed Date
1	11/12/94	11/12/94	14	11/12/94

Figure 10-2. *TimeNtry's L_Globals table.*

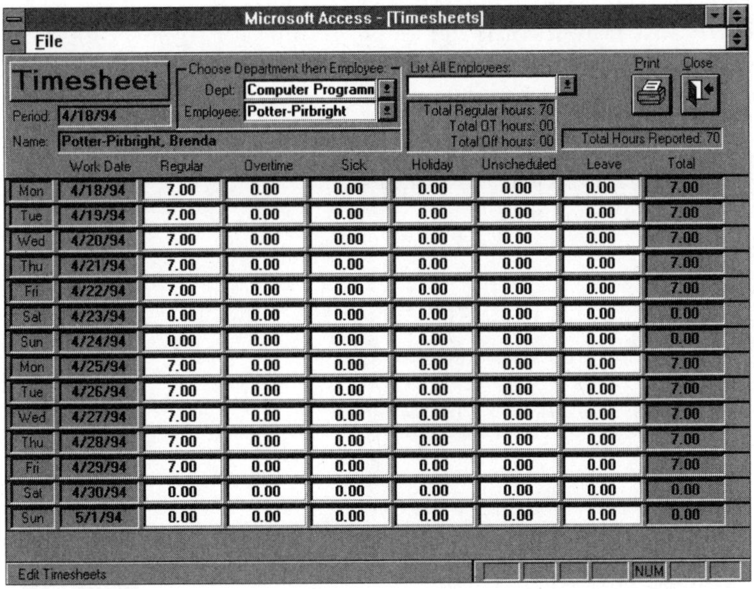

Figure 10-3. *The time sheet created automatically for full-time employees by the Batch Timesheets process. Use the Timesheet Entry process to edit these sheets to reflect information such as an employee's overtime or vacation days.*

The p_NewTimesheet function that actually creates time sheets is shown on the facing page. Note the following:

■ The code *Set db = DBEngine(0)(0)*, which is equivalent to DBEngine.Workspaces(0).Databases(0), references the current database. (*DBEngine(0)* references the current workspace.)

■ This function uses SQL to query the Payroll table to determine which employees are active.

■ The bulk of this function is a Select Case statement that, in each case, calls nearly the same Do...Loop. You can shorten the code by more than one-fifth if you put the Select Case statement inside the Do...Loop. However, if you do this, execution time nearly doubles. One reason for this is that the shorter code selects the case on each pass through the Do...Loop, while the longer code selects the case once and then runs through the loop.

To test this yourself:

1. Remove the comment characters from the u_TimerStart and u_TimerEnd functions.

2. Run p_NewPeriod from the Immediate Window (see Figure 10-4).

The Immediate Window now records the length of time for p_NewTimesheet to execute. Call p_NewTimesheetSlow (which includes the Select Case statement inside the Do...Loop) to compare the speed of these functions.

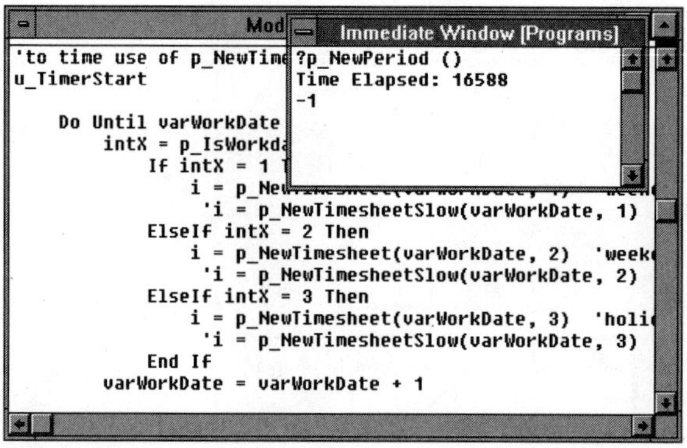

Figure 10-4. *To test the speed of the two versions of the p_NewTimesheet function, type ?p_NewPeriod in the Immediate Window, and then press Enter. Note that p_NewPeriod calls u_TimerStart, a stopwatch utility in the Utilities module.*

```
Function p_NewTimesheet (ByVal WorkDate As Variant, ByVal intType↴
  As Integer) As Integer
  On Error GoTo p_NewTimesheetError

  Dim db As Database, qd As QueryDef, rs As Recordset
  Dim varSSN As Variant, varFT As Variant, intHrs As Integer
  Dim strSQL As String, strSnp As String, strCrit As String
  Dim i As Integer

'Initialize hours to 0.
  intHrs = 0

'Shorthand for DBEngine.Workspaces(0)Databases(0).
  Set db = DBEngine(0)(0)

'SQL string to select all active employees by checking the start
'and end dates in the payroll table.
  strSnp = "SELECT DISTINCTROW EMPLOYEE.*, PAYROLL.PR_FT_IND "
  strSnp = strSnp & "FROM EMPLOYEE INNER JOIN PAYROLL ON "
  strSnp = strSnp & "EMPLOYEE.EP_SSN = PAYROLL.EP_SSN WHERE "
  strSnp = strSnp & "((EMPLOYEE.EP_BEG_ACT_DT<=#"
  strSnp = strSnp & WorkDate & "#) AND "
  strSnp = strSnp & "(EMPLOYEE.EP_END_ACT_DT>=#" & WorkDate
  strSnp = strSnp & "#));"

'Create a temporary QueryDef (using "") and then...
  Set qd = db.CreateQueryDef("", strSnp)

'...open a recordset based on it.
  Set rs = qd.OpenRecordset()

'Case 1, 2, or 3 runs based on what kind of day has been passed
'to the function--regular workday, weekend day, or holiday--and
'whether an employee is full-time.
'Each case loops through the recordset of all active employees.
  Select Case intType

'Add 7 hours for FT employees only.
    Case 1
      Do Until rs.EOF
        varSSN = rs.[EP_SSN]
        varFT = rs.[PR_FT_IND]
        If varFT = "F" Then intHrs = 7
        strSQL = "INSERT INTO TIMESHEET "
        strSQL = strSQL & "(EP_SSN, TS_WRK_DT, "
        strSQL = strSQL & "TS_REG_HR) VALUES (" & varSSN
        strSQL = strSQL & ", #" & WorkDate & "#, "
```

(continued)

```
            strSQL = strSQL & intHrs & ");"
            Set qd = db.CreateQueryDef("", strSQL)
            qd.Execute
            qd.Close
            rs.MoveNext
          Loop

    'For weekend days, insert key fields (no hours).
        Case 2
          Set rs = qd.OpenRecordset()
          Do Until rs.EOF
            varSSN = rs![EP_SSN]
            strSQL = "INSERT INTO TIMESHEET (EP_SSN, "
            strSQL = strSQL & "TS_WRK_DT) VALUES ("
            strSQL = strSQL & varSSN & ", #" & WorkDate
            strSQL = strSQL & "#);"
            Set qd = db.CreateQueryDef("", strSQL)
            qd.Execute
            qd.Close
            rs.MoveNext
          Loop

    'Enter 7 holiday hours for company holidays for FT employees only.
        Case 3
          Set rs = qd.OpenRecordset()
          Do Until rs.eof
            varSSN = rs.[EP_SSN]
            varFT = rs.[PR_FT_IND]
            If varFT = "F" Then intHrs = 7
            strSQL = "INSERT INTO TIMESHEET (EP_SSN, "
            strSQL = strSQL & "TS_WRK_DT, TS_HOL_HR) "
            strSQL = strSQL & "VALUES (" & varSSN
            strSQL = strSQL & ", #" & WorkDate
            strSQL = strSQL & "#, " & intHrs & ");"
            Set qd = db.CreateQueryDef("", strSQL)
            qd.Execute
            qd.Close
            rs.MoveNext
          Loop
      End Select

  p_NewTimesheetDone:
    p_NewTimesheet = True

  p_NewTimesheetExit:
    On Error Resume Next
    qd.Close
    rs.Close
    Exit Function
```

```
p_NewTimesheetError:
  p_NewTimesheet = False
'The constant MB_ICONSTOP (which represents 16) is declared
'in the Globals module.
  MsgBox Err & ": " & Error, MB_ICONSTOP, "p_NewTimesheet"
  Resume p_NewTimesheetExit
End Function
```

Entering data into time sheets manually

TimeNtry uses a single batch process to automatically create time sheets for active employees. Once that is done, users have to edit these time sheets to account for exceptions, such as part-timers, overtime, and vacation days. To keep the time sheet system secure despite editing, the Default Editing property for the time sheet form (frmTimesheet) is set to "Can't Add Records." In other words, users can *edit* data for time sheet records created through the automated batch process, but they can't *create* time sheet records manually. Nor can they delete them, because the time sheet form doesn't have record selectors and the date field is locked.

Also all navigation controls have been removed from the time sheet form so that users can't move through the Timesheet table. Instead, they have to select employees one at a time from combo boxes in the form's header. When users select an employee, TimeNtry changes the Record Source for the entire form and loads only the selected employee's time sheet for the current period. By forcing users to select specific employees to edit (rather than letting them scroll through the table to find an employee), the application minimizes the possibility that users will edit the wrong time sheet.

The Record Source for the time sheet form is a saved query that has as a parameter the value in the combo box in the time sheet's header. TimeNtry hides the detail section of the form until the Record Source query runs and then unhides it and displays the records. Hiding the section before the Record Source changes offers two advantages:

■ It speeds up the process by eliminating screen redraw.

■ It hides the error messages that are displayed whenever bound fields don't have a record source.

The original version of TimeNtry performs additional validation on the time sheet data. For example, the BeforeUpdate property of each control does field-level validation on hours to ensure (among other things) that no one logs overtime on regular workdays until they've worked eight hours.

Access Libraries

An Access *library* is a database that's listed in the [Libraries] section of the Access INI file (MSACC20.INI) so that it's loaded automatically whenever users run Access. (See the sidebar titled "MSACC20.INI" later in this chapter). That's the essential difference between a regular Access database and a library: Access loads libraries at startup.

Wizards, builders, and menu add-ins are all stored in Access libraries (see the section titled "Wizards, Builders, and Menu Add-Ins" later in this chapter), as are two files that are required for Access to run—the system and utility databases. You create a library database just as you do any other database; then you rename it, adding an .MDA extension rather than an .MDB extension.

Debugging Libraries

To view and debug a library's code, add the following line to the [Options] section of the Access INI file:

```
[Options]
DebugLibraries = True
```

With debugging enabled, you can open a library module from the View Procedures dialog box (available through the Procedures command on a module's View menu). The Expression Builder also displays library objects along with database objects. To open a library's forms, type *DoCmd OpenForm NameOf-Form* in the Immediate Window.

One word of caution: The DebugLibraries option can significantly increase the time required to compile code because it forces Access to compile all library code. Once you're satisfied that your library is OK, comment out the line *DebugLibraries = True* by prefacing it with a semicolon (;), or set it to False.

Installing Libraries

Code libraries, which store standard functions and subprocedures, are the simplest libraries to install. Enter the library's name (and the full path if it isn't in the Access program directory) in the [Libraries] section of the Access INI file. For example, the following line loads the code library "CODE-LIB.MDA" read-only (RO):

```
[Libraries]
CODE-LIB.MDA=RO
```

If your library stores users' options, assign it read-write access (RW). Otherwise, set it to read-only because it generally loads faster. (Libraries are always loaded as shared, so Access has fewer multiuser considerations to check with read-only files.) When you use a code library's functions and subprocedures in your applications, make sure the library is always available to your users.

Using System Databases

Access requires both a system database and a utility database to run. The database libraries that ship with Access are SYSTEM.MDA and UTILITY.MDA, but the names themselves aren't important. What's important is that the SystemDB and UtilityDB entries in the [Options] section of the MSACC20.INI file point to valid system and utility databases, as in the following example:

```
[Options]
SystemDB=C:\ACCESS2\SYSTEM.MDA
UtilityDB=C:\ACCESS2\UTILITY.MDA
```

The system database governs who can open Access databases and is therefore the main vehicle for *securing* Access applications. (See the section titled "Securing Your Data" on the following page for more information.) There are two ways to change the system database:

- Use the Access Workgroup Administrator, which appears as an icon in Program Manager and points to the file WRKGADM.EXE. This utility makes it easier for developers to work with multiple applications, many of which probably have their own system database. Use it to change the SystemDB entry in the MSACC20.INI file (shown above) or to create a new system database.

- Edit the MSACC20.INI file directly, and change the entry for SystemDB. For example, the following line changes the system database to the one that comes with TimeNtry (assuming, of course, that you retain the same directory structure used on the *Office Solutions* disk). When you do this, comment out the original so that it's easy to restore in case of error. Remember, you cannot start Access without a valid system database.

  ```
  SystemDB=C:\OFFSOLN\ACCESS\TIMENTRY\TIMENTRY.MDA
  ```

Maintaining Libraries

It's easy to change a library database, as long as it isn't loaded. To uninstall it, comment out references to it in the MSACC20.INI file, or—if the library is a wizard, a builder, or a menu add-in—use the Add-in Manager. When you next start Access, you can load your .MDA file as if it were a regular database. (The Open command on the File menu works fine.) You can't open libraries while they're installed—Access simply displays a "duplicate procedure" error message. (See the sidebar titled "Handling Global vs. Form Modules" later in this chapter for information on preventing such errors.)

Securing Your Data

Access security is generally considered hard to learn and tricky to implement, but if you do it right, you guarantee a secure application. One strategy is to create groups of users and to give these groups the right to access various objects in your database. Then you assign users to appropriate groups. Access has three default groups:

- The Admins group, which has the broadest administrative access and controls basic security

- The Users group, which has full access to database objects (and includes all users except Guests)

- The Guests group, which can view database objects but can't manipulate them

NOTE You can't delete default groups, but you can deny Users and Guests permissions to data objects such as tables.

Security isn't something that you "do" to your Access applications at some point in the development cycle: It's an integral part of Access itself. (You don't notice it because, by default, anyone can log on without a password.) Everyone who uses the system database (SYSTEM.MDA) that's installed when you first install Access technically "logs on" to Access as an Admin user who belongs to the Admins group—and who doesn't have a password.

NOTE The only time you get any hint of this when using the original SYSTEM.MDA is when you use ODBC to connect to an Access database. In this case, you have to type *Admin* as the user ID.

The fact that all new buyers of Access log on as Admin has three important implications as you develop your own Access security system:

- Although Access lets you encrypt databases (which makes it impossible to use text editors to read them), there's no point in encrypting a database that everyone can open using the default Admin logon. To benefit from encryption, you must develop an Access security system.

- When you develop an Access security system, you have to "demote" Admin so that it's no longer a member of the Admins group. If you fail to do this, your database will never be secure because everyone using the SYSTEM.MDA included with the retail version of Access logs on automatically as Admin.

■ When developing an Access security system, you have to 1) create a new database using a user ID (other than Admin) that has membership in the Admins group and 2) import into the new database the database that you want to secure. The user ID in use when you create an Access database is the "owner" of that database and of all objects that it contains. In other words, that user ID has irrevocable permission to access and use the database that it created.

> **NOTE** You can't delete Admin, and although you must remove it from the Admins group as part of implementing security, you can't remove it from the Users group.

To secure your data, you have to create your own system database file, and you have to give "ownership" of the data to a user ID other than Admin (to which all Access users have permissions). This way, no one can use the default Admin ID to access your data.

FYI

Handling Global vs. Form Modules

Access version 2 handles two types of modules: those whose procedures are global in scope (unless you explicitly declare them to be private) and form modules. Form modules (which Microsoft also refers to as "code behind forms," or CBF for short) use Visual Basic's event-handling methodology so that you can attach event-handling procedures to controls. Unlike procedures in global modules, which you can call anywhere in an application, CBF procedures are private to the form or report that contains them and are "invisible" to other forms, reports, and modules. If you create a global procedure, constant, or variable whose name duplicates an existing name in any open module (including library modules), you get a "duplicate procedure" error message.

To avoid this:

■ Make sure that each name—including those in your library databases— is unique. (See the sidebar titled "Access Libraries" earlier in this chapter for more information on libraries.) In fact, use a naming convention in libraries such that names are unlikely to conflict with those in any other database. For example, instead of naming a function that checks to see whether a form is loaded IsFormLoaded, name it zrg_IsFormLoaded.

■ Where feasible, write code in form modules. This avoids naming conflicts completely because such code is private to that form or report. (It's generally a good practice to place procedures used by multiple forms or reports in global modules.)

Access Libraries, Memory, and CBF

Access libraries load global modules on startup, and this code stays in memory until users exit Access. CBF code, on the other hand, loads only when its form or report is opened, and it unloads when that form or report closes. To conserve memory, it often makes sense to put as much library code as possible into CBF containers. Figure 10-5 lists the advantages and disadvantages of using CBF in an Access library.

	Advantages	Disadvantages
CBF	If code isn't used, it isn't loaded into memory.	Access loads and compiles the code every time people use the wizard, builder, or menu add-in.
	Access starts up more quickly because it doesn't load as much code.	Overhead is high when users start the wizard, builder, or menu add-in.
Global module code	Code loads once no matter how many times people use the wizard, builder, or menu add-in.	Code stays in memory until users exit Access.
	The wizard, builder, or menu add-in runs faster.	Access starts up more slowly because it loads more code.

Figure 10-5. *Advantages and disadvantages of using code behind forms and global module code in Access libraries.*

Creating your own security system

This section takes you step-by-step through the process of creating a system database to secure your database. Before trying this, back up both your SYSTEM.MDA (where Access stores Group and User IDs) and the database that you're attempting to secure (where Access stores the actual permissions). It's ridiculously easy to lock yourself out of your own database, and if you do that, you're stuck because Access security really does work. (See Appendix A for other sources of information on Access security.)

To secure a database, take the following steps:

1. Back up both your SYSTEM.MDA and the database that you want to secure.

2. Use the Access Workgroup Administrator to create a new system database, which you can name anything you like. Because it's reasonable to assume that business applications for a particular group of users require similar security, create system databases for *workgroups* rather than for individual applications. This prevents users from having to switch the system database before using an application. Also, use a case-sensitive workgroup ID to ensure that your system database is unique (and make sure you keep a record). The system database for the TimeNtry application is TimeNtry.MDA.

3. Open Access, which now uses the system database that you just created, and then open the database that you want to secure.

4. Use the Change Password command on the Security menu to create a password for Admin. (The Security menu is available only from the database window.) Note that you can change the password only for the ID that you used to log on to Access.

5. Exit Access. When you restart Access, you have to log on as Admin, using the password that you created in the previous step.

6. This time, open the database that you want to secure, and then choose the Users command from the Security menu. Create a new user (for example, Boss), and add that user to *all* groups, including Admins. The Personal ID (PID) is *not* a password, nor does it have to be unique; it's simply another way of identifying users.

> **NOTE** Access uses the PID and the user ID *together* as the unique identifier for users (referred to as the Security ID, or SID). See Chapter 14 in *Building Applications* (which comes with Access) for more information on PIDs and SIDs. Be sure to keep a written record of your PIDs and SIDs in case you need to re-create a corrupt system database. Without the correct system database, you're locked out of your application.

7. Exit and then restart Access. Log on as the new user (Boss in this example) and leave the password blank because you haven't yet assigned one. Open your database.

8. Demote Admin by removing it from the Admins group. Now Admin is a member of only the Users group.

> **NOTE** All users who are in the Admins group when you create a database have full permissions for the objects in that database.

9. Create a new database. If you removed Admin from the Admins group in the previous step, the new user (Boss in this example) is now the sole member of the Admins group and therefore the sole owner of the new database.

10. Use the Import Database add-in (available through the File menu) to import the database that you want to secure into the database you just created with the new user ID.

11. Now you can control access to the database by establishing groups, assigning permissions, and then creating user accounts. To assign permissions, choose the Permissions command from the Security menu, and then click the Groups option. In general, assign permissions by group, not by user, to streamline maintenance.

Note that Access security adheres to a "least restrictive" rule, which provides users with the least restrictive permissions of the groups to which they belong. For example, if a user is a member of two groups, A and B, one of which does not have permissions to an object and the other of which does, the user has permissions.

12. In the Permissions dialog box, select the group for which you want to set permissions (see Figure 10-6). Next, select the type of object for which you want to assign permissions (such as a database or a table). Then select the permissions for that group (such as Read Data or Insert Data). Click the Assign button so that these permissions take effect.

When you're thinking through permissions, remember that Admin is *always* a member of the Users group. To ensure that anyone who opens your database using the original SYSTEM.MDA and an Admin ID can't damage it, remove the Users group's permissions to any object that you want to secure.

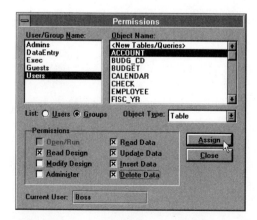

Figure 10-6. *The Permissions dialog box.*

The Access Security Wizard simplifies steps 9 through 12 on the facing page. This wizard is available directly from Microsoft or from CompuServe's MSAccess forum (Library 16). When you download the Security Wizard from CompuServe, it comes with Microsoft's security white paper.

FYI

Security and the Access Object Model

To understand how to use Access Basic to manage security, you have to understand the Access object model. The key point here is that Access has two engines: the *Access engine*, which runs the Access application, and the *Jet engine*, which controls data access (see Figure 10-7 on the following page). Access, Visual Basic, and applications that connect to Access databases through ODBC all use the Jet engine.

When you open an alternate workspace—for example, to manage security in code as described in the next section, "Using Access Basic to Manage Security" —you're in fact running another Jet engine session. Each workspace (or Jet engine session) is completely independent of the other sessions, right down to its user ID. As you can see in Figure 10-7, the Database collection, the User collection, and the Group collection are all children of the Workspace collection. This means that you can have multiple databases open in one workspace; you can have multiple workspaces open that access one database; and you can have multiple users and groups in any workspace. (This is true whether you're using Access Basic or Visual Basic.)

The User and Group collections appear redundant because Access allows two levels of permissions: implicit and explicit. *Implicit permissions* are those that you have by virtue of membership in a group, and *explicit permissions* are those assigned directly to you as a user. Because it's harder to track individual users than groups, it's generally a good practice to assign permissions to groups and then assign users membership in those groups. That way, you can change permissions at the group level without having to do so for each user. Note that the least restrictive rule (described in the previous section) applies to implicit and explicit permissions.

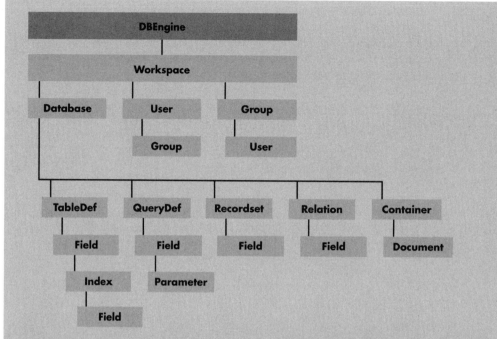

Figure 10-7. *The Access hierarchical object model. At the topmost level, all Access objects are contained in the DBEngine object. All Workspace-related objects are contained in the Workspace object, all Database-related objects are contained in the Database object, and so on. Note that every object in this diagram except DBEngine represents a collection as well as an object. The Workspace, User, and Group collections and objects are integral parts of Access security.*

Using Access Basic to manage security

In addition to managing security through group permissions, you can write Access Basic code to manage security (which is what TimeNtry does). For example, your code can check the objects that the current user has permission to access and then disable menu items and controls that access other objects.

But there's a catch. You can't read permissions unless you're a member of the Admins group, so your code can't check a user's permissions unless the current user is an Admins member. To get around this, open an alternate workspace in code; log on as an Admins user; and then use the system database to check the permissions of the user in the default workspace.

Unfortunately, this solution has two problems:

- It exposes both the user ID *and the password* in your code.
- It makes the application easy to break because any Admins member can delete the user ID or change its password.

You can fix the first problem by denying read access to your modules and encrypting your database, but the second problem is much harder to fix. In fact, the "fix" is to take all users out of the Admins group (except the one whose name you use in code) and then write your own front end for administering security. This solution allows administrative users (who are no longer members of the Admins group but who *are* members of a new group, such as Exec) to create and delete new user IDs and perform other routine security tasks *using your front end*. Naturally, this front end prevents them from even seeing the Admins user ID that you use in code.

There's always a better way

The one drawback of logging on to an alternate workspace and reading the current user's permissions from the system database is that it's relatively time-consuming. You have to use this method when users are performing security tasks in your application, but you can handle most other situations by creating a "permissions" table that stores groups and their user IDs. TimeNtry has such a table, called USysUsrTbl (see Figure 10-8). (The USys prefix ensures that the table is visible only when Show System Objects is turned on. Show System Objects is available through the Options command on the View menu.)

When you set up a "permissions" table, give everyone read permissions and no one write permissions—no one, that is, except the Admins user ID that you use in code. When administrative users use your application's security front end to add or delete users, write this change to the system database and to this "permissions" table, which you can then use to quickly check users' permissions.

User	Exec	DataEntry
Bob	No	Yes
Christine	No	Yes
Eric	No	Yes
Frank	No	Yes
Fred	No	Yes
Patsy	No	Yes
Prunella	No	Yes
Supervisor	Yes	Yes
TimeClerk	No	Yes

Figure 10-8. *TimeNtry's "permissions" table (USysUsrTbl).*

TimeNtry's Security System

TimeNtry has its own security front end so that it can handle security through code. (See Figure 10-9 on the following page for the permissions and the logon IDs that you can use to test the application.)

Group	Members	Permissions	Logon
Admins	Boss	Everything	Name: Boss Password: boss
Exec	High level	All functionality within the application	Name: Christine Password: Christine
DataEntry	Low level	Restricted	Name: Fred Password: Fred
Users	Everyone	Ignored	
Guests	Ignored	Ignored	

Figure 10-9. *Permissions for TimeNtry.*

Below is a brief overview of how TimeNtry's security is structured.

- TimeNtry has five security groups: the three standard groups in Access (Admins, Users, and Guests) and two custom groups (Exec and DataEntry).

- The only user that belongs to the Admins group is "Boss," which is the user ID used in code.

- Users in the DataEntry group can only read and edit time sheets.

- Users in the Exec group can do everything that users in the DataEntry group can do, plus they can read and edit Personnel and Payroll records and create time sheets using the Batch Timesheets process. They also have administrative privileges for the database, but only as defined through the custom security front end. Only Boss has real administrative privileges because it's the only user account in the Admins group, and Exec users must go through Boss via code to perform security chores. Exec users don't have direct access to the code or to the Boss ID and password (which is embedded in the code). The administrative privileges granted to Exec users through the custom front end boil down to three functions:

  - They can create new users and add them to either the Exec group or the DataEntry group. Once new users join a group, they have all the permissions associated with that group, so there's no need to assign explicit permissions to individuals on an object-by-object basis.

  - They can delete users.

  - They can clear passwords—in other words, set them to an empty string. (Anyone who's ever forgotten a password knows how important this function is.)

- All users can manage their own passwords.

The following code lists the Form_Load procedure (from the form module for frmMainMenu) that disables buttons on the main screen for users in the DataEntry group. It does this by using Access Basic's CurrentUser function to get the current user's ID and then checking the USysUsrTbl to determine the group to which the user belongs. If the user isn't a member of the Exec group, this routine disables three buttons: Batch Timesheets, Timesheet Entry, and View Personnel.

> **NOTE** Disabling these buttons is the appropriate way of handling the GUI—it doesn't affect security. Even if you don't disable the buttons, users who aren't in the Exec group get "permission denied" messages when they click them.

```
Sub Form_Load ()
  On Error GoTo Form_LoadError

  Dim db As Database, rs As Recordset
  Dim strUser As String, iExec As Integer

'Generic function that returns who is currently logged on.
  strUser = CurrentUser()

'If Boss (your backdoor user), then exit function; Boss owns
'everything, so we don't need to disable any buttons.
  If strUser = "boss" Then GoTo Form_LoadExit
  strUser = "USER = '" & strUser & "'"

'Shorthand for DBEngine.Workspaces(0).Databases(0).
  Set db = DBEngine(0)(0)
  Set rs = db.OpenRecordset("USysUsrTbl", DB_OPEN_SNAPSHOT)
  rs.FindFirst strUser
  If Not rs.nomatch Then iExec = rs![EXEC]

  If Not iExec Then

'Can't create time sheets.
    Forms!frmMainMenu![btnNewPer].Enabled = False

'Can't access personnel.
    Forms!frmMainMenu![btnPersonnel].Enabled = False

'Can't administer security.
    Forms!frmMainMenu![btnAdmin].Enabled = False
  End If
  DoCmd Restore
```

(continued)

```
Form_LoadExit:
  On Error Resume Next

'Clear status bar.
  u_SysOff
  rs.Close
  Exit Sub

Form_LoadError:
'The constant MB_ICONSTOP (which represents 16) is declared
'in the Globals module.
  MsgBox Error$, MB_ICONSTOP, "Error in Form_Load"
  Resume Form_LoadExit
End Sub
```

FYI

No-Frills Security

If the full-featured Access security system described in this section is too much, you can use no-frills security instead. (This can be handy when you want to keep users out of your code without distributing a custom system database.) The basic principle is the same: You have to create a database owned by a user ID other than Admin, and you have to demote the Admin ID out of the Admins group. To do this, follow the instructions in the section titled "Creating Your Own Security System" earlier in this chapter. Be sure to deny to the Users group read and modify permissions for modules (you can't deny run permissions) and permissions for other objects that you want to secure.

You can now use your application securely with the original SYSTEM.MDA that comes with the shrink-wrapped version of Access. Since everyone using the SYSTEM.MDA "out of the box" is logged on as Admin (and in your application, Admin is a member of the Users group), they will have only the permissions granted to that group. (Be sure to keep a copy of your custom system database for those times when *you* want to get into the database and do something that mere users can't do—such as edit your code.)

Using TimeNtry to create users

When TimeNtry's administrative users create new user IDs, the application displays a dialog box prompting them to type a new user name. The application then validates this name against the other user IDs in the database (including hidden ones) because duplicates aren't allowed. If the name is valid, administrative users assign permissions by selecting either the Executive Level or the Data Entry Level check box (see Figure 10-10).

Selecting either check box triggers a BeforeUpdate event, which calls the s_GroupJoin function. The check boxes are bound to a field in USysUsrTbl. To make sure that USysUsrTbl is perfectly in sync with the system database, TimeNtry doesn't update this field if there's an error while you are assigning user IDs to groups.

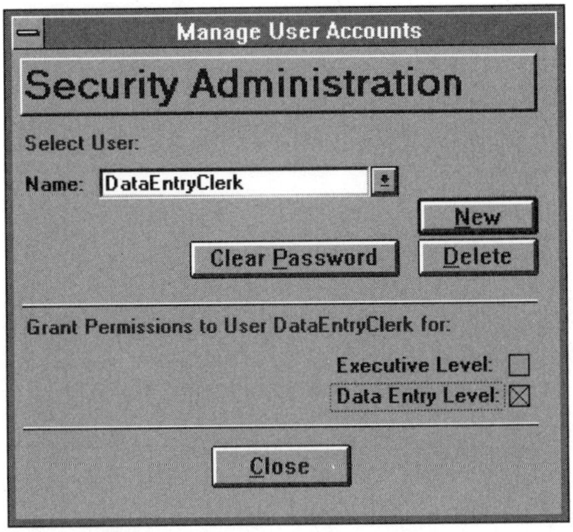

Figure 10-10. *TimeNtry's security front end.*

The following code creates new user IDs. It does all the work in a separate workspace using the Admins user ID and the password "boss" (shown in bold).

> **NOTE** For ease of reading, the → character represents a line break that does not appear in actual code.

```
Function s_NewUser (ByVal varUser As Variant) As Integer
  On Error GoTo s_NewUserError

  Dim db As Database, ws As WorkSpace, usr As User
  Dim qd As QueryDef
  Dim strPID As String, strPW As String, strSQL As String
  Dim frmM As Form

  Set frmM = Forms!frmSecManage

'Predefine a PID, and set the password to be the same as the
'user name.
  strPID = "1234567890"
  strPW = varUser
```

(continued)

```
          If IsNull(varUser) Or IsEmpty(varUser) Or varUser = "" Then

'Handle nulls and blanks.
          s_NewUser = False
          MsgBox "Please type in a name.", 64, "Type New User's Name"
          GoTo s_NewUserExit
       Else
'Shorthand for DBEngine.Workspaces(0).Databases(0).
          Set db = DBEngine(0)(0)

'Log on here with Boss ID and create the new user.
          Set ws = DBEngine.CreateWorkspace("NewWS", "boss", "boss")

'Log on as owner.
          Set usr = ws.CreateUser(varUser, strPID, strPW)

'Create new profile and add to collection.
          ws.users.Append usr
          ws.users.Refresh

'This SQL code adds the new user to the USysUsrTbl.
          strSQL = "INSERT INTO USysUsrTbl ( USER ) VALUES ('"
          strSQL = strSQL & varUser & "');"
          Set qd = db.CreateQueryDef("", strSQL)
          qd.Execute
       End If

s_NewUserDone:
       MsgBox "New User " & varUser & " has been created with a password⏎
          of " & strPW & ".", 64, "User Created"
       s_NewUser = True

'Close user dialog box.
       DoCmd Close

'Sync combo box.
       frmM!cboUser = varUser
       frmM!cboUser.Requery

'Reset form dynaset.
       frmM.RecordSource = "qrySecManage"

'Show controls.
       frmM!ctlUserPerm.visible = True
       frmM!ckEXEC.visible = True
       frmM!ckDATAENTRY.visible = True
       frmM!lblEXEC.visible = True
       frmM!lblDATAENTRY.visible = True
```

```
s_NewUserExit:
  On Error Resume Next

'Close any open objects.
  qd.Close
  ws.Close
  Exit Function

s_NewUserError:
  s_NewUser = False
'The constant MB_ICONSTOP (16) and MB_ICONINFORMATION (64)
'are declared in the Globals module.
  Select Case Err
    Case 3390, 3001, 3030
      MsgBox "Cannot create user " & varUser & ".",↲
        MB_ICONINFORMATION, "Try Another Name"
      Forms!frmSecNewUsr![ctlUser] = ""
      Forms!frmSecNewUsr![ctlUser].SetFocus
    Case 2137
      Resume Next
    Case Else
      MsgBox Err & ": " & Error$, MB_ICONSTOP, "Error in s_NewUser"
  End Select
  Resume s_NewUserExit
End Function
```

Last but not least...ypncrEtion

The final step in implementing security for any application is to encrypt the database. Because Access stores the security in the database (and, in this example, the user ID and the password of an Admins user are listed in module code), encryption not only protects your data from being hacked by a text editor or utility, it prevents your security system from being hacked as well. Encryption does slow performance slightly, but it's the only way to ensure that your data is really secure.

SAMPLE APPLICATION: MenuBldR.MDA

MenuBldR.MDA (written by Mike Gunderloy of Pyramid Computers in Brooklyn, New York) is a custom builder that makes it easier to use Access menu commands and built-in dialog boxes in Access Basic code. To understand MenuBldR, you have to understand these topics:

■ Wizards, builders, and menu add-ins (and how to install them)

■ How to use Access menu commands and display built-in dialog boxes *without* using MenuBldR

PRODUCT SHEET: MenuBldR

Purpose:

MenuBldR is a custom Access builder that makes it easier for developers to write Access Basic code that uses menu commands and built-in dialog boxes. Instead of figuring out the numeric constants for menus and menu items, use MenuBldR to select from drop-down lists the arguments for DoMenuItem (the macro action that lets you use built-in menu commands and dialog boxes in Access).

Development tool used:

Access

How MenuBldR works:

MenuBldR runs in a module when you select Builder from the pop-up menu associated with the right mouse button and then select DoMenuItem Builder. After you choose the arguments for the DoMenuItem action and click OK, MenuBldR returns the full line of Access Basic code required to perform a menu action or display a dialog box.

The following diagram illustrates the steps for building code with MenuBldR:

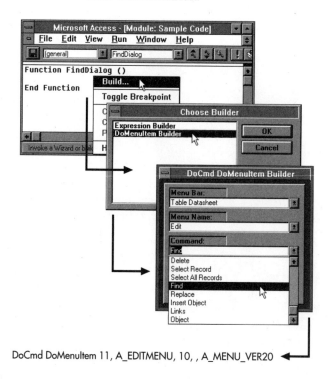

Wizards, Builders, and Menu Add-Ins

Access supports three broad categories of add-ins: wizards, builders, and menu add-ins. All three types are developed in Access Basic, loaded as libraries, and appear as "built-in" elements of the Access interface. (In other words, when you install custom wizards and builders, they appear in dialog boxes along with the standard wizards and builders that ship with Access, and when you install menu add-ins, they appear under the Add-Ins command on the File menu.) Here are the differences among the three types of add-ins that Access uses:

- Wizards (which usually consist of a series of dialog boxes) step users through complex tasks, just as the Form Wizard in Access steps them through the process of creating a form. Access handles the following types of custom wizards as if they were built-in (see Figure 10-11):

    - Table and query wizards

    - Form and report wizards

    - Property wizards

    - Control wizards

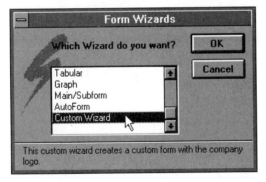

Figure 10-11. *The standard Form Wizards dialog box with a custom wizard added to the list.*

- Builders are mini-wizards. Like the Expression Builder in Access, they generally have a single dialog box with the options available for a specific task. MenuBldR is a builder.

■ Menu add-ins are general-purpose programs that perform tasks (as opposed to guiding users through tasks). Unlike wizards and builders (which are context-sensitive), menu add-ins are listed under the Add-Ins command on the File menu, and users can use them whenever the File menu is available. Four menu add-ins ship with Access:

- ■ Database Documentor

- ■ Attachment Manager

- ■ Import Database

- ■ Menu Builder

Installing add-ins manually

Installing wizards, builders, and menu add-ins requires multiple entries in the Access INI file, which depend on the type of add-in. (See the sidebar titled "MSACC20.INI" later in this chapter and Figure 10-12 on the facing page for more information.) For example, to install a Property Wizard such as MenuBldR, make these two changes to the INI file:

■ Add the filename to the [Libraries] section, and assign read-write access. For example, the following line loads MenuBldR whenever you start Access:

```
[Libraries]
MenuBldR.mda=rw
```

■ Add the following information using the following syntax to the [Property Wizards] section:

```
[Property Wizards]
PyrDoMenuItemBuilder=Module,DoMenuItem─┐
   Builder,fdmi_DoMenuItemBuilder,rw
```

Below is an explanation of the arguments in each case:

- ■ *PyrDoMenuItemBuilder* is a unique name assigned to MenuBldR.

- ■ *Module* is the context in which the builder works. In this case, it works only when you click the right mouse button in a module.

- ■ *DoMenuItem Builder* is the name that Access displays in the Property Wizard selection box.

- ■ *fdmi_DoMenuItemBuilder* is the name of the function that starts the builder.

- ■ *rw* is the code that sets the builder to read-write so it can store the options that users select.

Add-In Type	INI File Changes	Example

All libraries	`[Libraries]`
	`NameOfFile=RWCode`
	
	The RWCode is *rw* (read-write) or *ro* (read-only). All libraries require this change to the INI file. Code libraries require only this one change.
		`[Libraries]`
		`MenuBldR.MDA=rw`

Menu add-ins	`[Menu Add-Ins]`
	`NameOfAddInDisplayed==`↵
	`OnMenuFunctionThat==`↵
	`RunsAddIn`
	
	Precede a letter by an ampersand (&) to provide an access key for your add-in.
		`[Menu Add-Ins]`
		`C&ustom Menu==`↵
		`wizmnuStartCustomMenu()`

Table, Query, Form, and Report Wizards	`[Table Wizards]`, `[Query Wizards]`, `[Form Wizards]`, or `[Report Wizards]` section as appropriate **`NameOfAddInDisplayedIn-`**↵ **`Dialog=FunctionThatRuns-`**↵ **`Wiz,,`** `{Descriptive text`↵ `displayed in dialog box}`
	
	The text in bold is required. The function that launches a Form Wizard or Report Wizard must accept a string argument because Access passes it a string to identify the form's underlying table or the report's underlying query.
		`[Query Wizards]`
		`Sales Wizard=wizqry-`↵
		`StartSalesWiz(),,`↵
		`{This custom Wizard`↵
		`creates a query`↵
		`against the Sales`↵
		`database.}`

Control Wizards	`[Control Wizards]`
	`NameOfWiz=ControlType,`↵
	`NameAsDisplayed,`↵
	`FunctionThatRunsWiz,`↵
	`RWCode`
	
	ControlType is the type of control that your wizard builds, such as ListBox or Command-Button. Set the RWCode to *rw* if the wizard can modify existing controls or to *w* if it creates new controls only.
		`[Control Wizards]`
		`ToggleWizard=Toggle-`↵
		`Button,Toggle Button`↵
		`Builder,wizctlStart-`↵
		`Toggler(),w`

(continued)

Add-In Type	INI File Changes	Example

Property Wizards (builders)	`[Property Wizards]`
	`NameOfAddIn=Property-`↱
	`Name,NameAsDisplayed,`↱
	`FunctionThatRuns-`↱
	`AddIn,RWCode`
		`[Property Wizards]`
		`PyrDoMenuItem-`↱
		`Builder=Module,Do-`↱
		`MenuItemBuilder,`↱
		`fdmi_DoMenuItem-`↱
		`Builder,rw`

	Just as users run Form Wizards and Report Wizards from their respective dialog boxes, they run property builders through the pop-up menu associated with the right mouse button. PropertyName is the "right mouse button" context—such as Module, Picture, FieldName, and so on—in which your builder works. Set the RWCode to *rw* if the builder can modify existing properties or to *w* if it creates new properties only.	

Figure 10-12. *How to install add-ins.*

Installing add-ins automatically

If you want Access to install your add-ins more-or-less automatically so that users don't have to edit their INI files, add a USysAddIns table to your library database (which is what MenuBldR does). The fastest way to create this table is to use the Import command on the File menu to import it from another library database—the Query Wizard (WZQuery.MDA), for example—and then revise it. Don't alter the table's structure, just the information in it. The Add-in Manager (available through the Add-Ins command on the File menu) reads this table and makes changes to the Access INI file based on the information provided.

> **NOTE**   Table names starting with MSys or USys are system tables that are displayed in the Database window only when you set the Show System Objects option to Yes. (To do this, choose Options from the View menu, and then select General.)

Installing MenuBldR automatically   Because MenuBldR handles its installation through the USysAddIns table, you can install MenuBldR through the Add-in Manager after copying MenuBldR.MDA to your Access program directory. Access installs MenuBldR as a Property Wizard, which means that it's available automatically through the right mouse button whenever you're in the appropriate context (a module, in this case).

The USysAddIns table provides a way to link custom add-ins seamlessly to Access. When you choose the Add-in Manager through the Add-Ins command on the File menu, Access scans every file in the program directory with the .MDA extension for a table with this name. It then lists files with such a table in the Add-in Manager dialog box (see Figure 10-13). Click the Install button to install the add-in. Use the Add New button to install add-ins that aren't stored in your Access program directory or that don't have an .MDA extension.

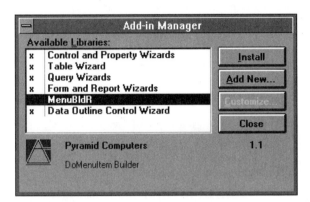

Figure 10-13. *The Access Add-in Manager is available through the Add-Ins command on the File menu.*

MenuBldR's USysAddIns Table The USysAddIns table requires the 10 fields shown below, although some of them appear to be unused. Fields Val1 through Val9 change meaning depending on the value of PropertyName. Figure 10-14 on the following page describes each field.

PropertyName	Text(50)
Val1	Memo
Val2	Memo
Val3	Memo
Val4	Memo
Val5	Memo
Val6	Memo
Val7	Memo
Val8	Memo
Val9	OLE Object

PropertyName	*Value(s)*
AddInVersion	Val1 = Version number of add-in displayed by the Add-in Manager.
CompanyName	Val1 = Company name displayed by the Add-in Manager.
Description	Val1 = Description displayed by the Add-in Manager.
DisplayName	Val1 = Name shown in the Add-in Manager list box.
Logo	Val9 = Logo displayed by the Add-in Manager. You can use any OLE graphics tool to create this logo and then select Change to Picture to minimize its storage requirements.
FunctionToCallOnCustomize	Val1 = Name to display when Customize is chosen. Val2 = Name of function to call, with parentheses.
IniFileEntry	Val1 = Section heading in MSACC20.INI. Val2 = Key name in MSACC20.INI. Val3 = Key value in MSACC20.INI.

Figure 10-14. *Description of fields for the USysAddIns table.*

FYI

MSACC20.INI

The following sections from my Access INI file relate to wizards, builders, and menu add-ins. Whenever I change INI file settings, I comment out the originals using semicolons (which is standard INI syntax for remarks) so I can restore them easily when things go wrong. I also comment the possible values for settings that I'm likely to change and the source of add-ins that I've installed.

Note that MenuBldR requires two entries in the INI file—one in the [Libraries] section and one in the [Property Wizards] section. When you install MenuBldR using the Add-in Manager, MenuBldR makes these entries automatically.

```
[Options]
SystemDB=C:\ACCESS2\FRS.MDA
UtilityDB=C:\ACCESS2\utility.mda
AllowCustomControls=1
AllowOLE1LinkFormat=0
;Debug lets you test libraries (i.e., wizards, builders, and
;menu add-ins).
;DebugLibraries=True
```

```
[Menu Add-Ins]
&Add-in Manager==Wm_Entry()
&Database Documentor==Doc_PrintDataBase()
A&ttachment Manager==Am_Entry()
Im&port Database...==Doc_ImportDatabase()
&Menu Builder==CustomMenuBuilder()

[Libraries]
wzlib.mda=rw
wzTable.mda=rw
wzQuery.mda=rw
wzfrmrpt.mda=rw
wzbldr.mda=rw
;WZOUTL comes with Access Developers Toolkit
WZOUTL.MDA=rw
;MenuBldR is from Mike Gunderloy
MenuBldr.mda=rw

[Table Wizards]
Table=TW_Entry,,{This wizard creates a new table to store data.}

[Table Wizard Data Files]
wztbldat.mdt=Standard MS Sample Fields

[Query Wizards]
;The text in brackets {} appears in the Wizard dialog box as a
;description of the wizard.
Crosstab Query=Xtq_Entry,,{This wizard creates a crosstab query→
  that displays data in a compact, spreadsheet-like format.}
Find Duplicates Query=dup_Entry,,{This wizard creates a query that→
  finds duplicate records (rows) in a single table or query.}
Find Unmatched Query=dwz_Entry,,{This wizard creates a query that→
  finds records (rows) in one table that have no related records in→
  another table.}
Archive Query=arc_Entry,,{This wizard creates a query that copies→
  records from an existing table into a new table.}

[Form Wizards]
Single-Column=zwForm, 1,{This wizard creates a form that displays→
  fields in a single column.}
Tabular=zwForm, 2,{This wizard creates a form that displays each→
  record as a row of fields.}
```

```
Graph=zwGraph,,{This wizard creates a form that displays a graph.}
Main/Subform=zwMainSub,,{This wizard creates a form that contains→
   another form.}
AutoForm=zwAutoForm,,{AutoForm automatically creates a simple form→
   based on the selected table or query.}


[Report Wizards]
Single-Column=zwReport, 3,{This wizard creates a report that→
   displays fields in a single column.}
Groups/Totals=zwReport, 4,{This wizard creates a report that→
   groups records together and displays totals for each group.}
Mailing Label=zwMailingLabel,,{This wizard creates standard Avery→
   mailing labels.}
Summary=zwReport, 12,{This wizard creates a report that displays→
   totals for groups of records.}
Tabular=zwReport, 11,{This wizard creates a report that displays→
   each record as a row of fields.}
AutoReport=zwAutoReport,,{AutoReport automatically creates a→
   simple report based on the selected table or query.}
MS Word Mail Merge=PM_Entry,,{This wizard links your data to a→
   Word document so you can print form letters or address envelopes.}


[Control Wizards]
MSListBoxWizard=ListBox, List Box Builder, LST_ENTRY,w
MSComboBoxWizard=ComboBox, ComboBox Wizard, CMB_ENTRY,w
MSOptionGroupWizard=OptionGroup, OptionGroup Wizard, OGrp_ENTRY,w
MSCommandButtonWizard=CommandButton, CommandButton Wizard, BW_ENTRY,w


[Property Wizards]
MSMenuBarBuilder=Menubar, MenuBar Builder, MB_ENTRY,rw
MSInputMaskWizard=InputMask, Input Mask Builder, IM_ENTRY,rw
MSForeColorBuilder=ForeColor, ForeColor Builder, CP_ENTRY,rw
MSBackColorBuilder=BackColor, BackColor Builder, CP_ENTRY,rw
MSBorderColorBuilder=BorderColor, BorderColor Builder, CP_ENTRY,rw
MSPictureBuilder=Picture, Picture Builder, PP_ENTRY,rw
MSODBCConnectStrBuilder=ODBCConnectStr,ODBC ConnectString→
   Builder,zwBuilderODBCConnectString,rw
MSFieldBuilder=FieldName,Field Builder,tw_FieldEntry,rw
;MenuBldR is from Mike Gunderloy
PyrDoMenuItemBuilder=Module,DoMenuItem→
   Builder,fdmi_DoMenuItemBuilder,rw


[OLE CONTROL WIZARDS]
OutlineWizardEntry=Outl1016Ctrl.COutlCtrl, Data Outline Control→
   Wizard, wz_OutlStartup,w
```

Using Access Menu Commands and Displaying Built-In Dialog Boxes

Although Microsoft added many new data access objects, methods, and properties to Access version 2, you still have to use the DoMenuItem macro action to run standard menu commands and display built-in dialog boxes from Access Basic.

The syntax for the DoMenuItem action requires four arguments, shown below. You can see these arguments when you create a macro action using the macro window.

```
DoCmd DoMenuItem MenuBar, MenuName, Command, SubcommandDoCmd
```

When you use the Access Basic DoCmd statement, you need an additional argument: the version of Access whose menus you're using. A_MENU_VER20 is the intrinsic constant that signals that you're using Access version 2. (The intrinsic constant A_MENU_VER1X signals that you're using a previous version.) For example, the following line of code opens the Toolbars dialog box:

```
DoMenuItem 5, 2, 6, , A_MENU_VER20
```

> **NOTE** Access has a half dozen categories of built-in (or "intrinsic") constants—data access constants, event procedure constants, macro action constants, security constants, variant constants, and miscellaneous constants. Figure 10-15 on the following page shows the intrinsic constants relating to menu commands. Although you should use intrinsic constants by name whenever they're available to ensure compatibility with future versions of Access, you can display an intrinsic constant's actual value by typing *?ConstantName* in the Immediate Window. (For a list of all the Access constants, go to the "Constants" Help topic, which lists the categories of constants, and then go to the topic for each category.)

Before MenuBldR.MDA: Which argument to use when

There are two ways to indicate the arguments for DoCmd DoMenuItem:

- Using numeric constants (which all menus and menu items have)

- Using intrinsic constants (which only a few have)

I use numeric constants in the previous example. Using numeric constants couldn't be simpler—or more time-consuming. It's a matter of switching between windows and counting.

For example, let's say you're coding a module in which you want to display the Find dialog box while users are in the table datasheet. The easiest way to do this (without MenuBldR, anyway) is to open a macro window and select the DoMenuItem action. Next, go to the Menu Bar argument and select the menu bar you want—in this case, Table Datasheet. Now count. The Table Datasheet argument is 12th from the top, so your numeric constant is 11. (The first item is counted as 0.) Switch back to your module, type *DoCmd DoMenuItem 11*, and repeat this process for each of the arguments. Eventually you'll wind up with the following line of code:

```
DoCmd DoMenuItem 11, 1, 10, , A_MENU_VER20
```

Unfortunately, it's not the best line of code. This is because Access Basic uses an intrinsic constant for the Edit menu (A_EDITMENU), and since intrinsic constants help to ensure compatibility with future versions of Access, the best code (which MenuBldR produces automatically) uses it:

```
DoCmd DoMenuItem 11, A_EDITMENU, 10, , A_MENU_VER20
```

ItemName	Symbolic Constant	Argument Type
Form	A_FORMBAR	MenuBar
File	A_FILE	MenuName
Edit	A_EDITMENU	MenuName
Records	A_RECORDSMENU	MenuName
New	A_NEW	Command
Save Form	A_SAVEFORM	Command
Save Form As	A_SAVEFORMAS	Command
Save Record	A_SAVERECORD	Command
Undo	A_UNDO	Command
Undo Current Record	A_UNDOFIELD	Command
Cut	A_CUT	Command
Copy	A_COPY	Subcommand
Paste	A_PASTE	Subcommand
Delete	A_DELETE_V2	Subcommand
Select Record	A_SELECTRECORD_V2	Subcommand
Select All Records	A_SELECTALLRECORDS_V2	Subcommand
Object	A_OBJECT	Subcommand
OLE	A_OBJECTVERB	Subcommand
Refresh	A_REFRESH	Subcommand

Figure 10-15. *Menu items with intrinsic constants (used in MenuBldR).*

How MenuBldR Works

MenuBldR is a "builder" that makes it easier to write Access Basic code that calls built-in menu commands and displays built-in dialog boxes. You can use MenuBldR only when you're in a module. Here's how:

1. Click the right mouse button, and then select Builder. Instead of opening the Expression Builder (which is what Access would have done if you hadn't installed MenuBldR.MDA), Access displays a dialog box that lists both the Expression Builder and the DoMenuItem Builder.

2. Select DoMenuItem Builder. MenuBldR displays a dialog box (see Figure 10-16) from which you can select the arguments required for DoCmd DoMenuItem. This dialog box essentially mimics, in an Access Basic module, the macro window's handling of DoMenuItem.

Figure 10-16. *MenuBldR's main form. Most of MenuBldR's code is in the form module.*

The MenuBldR application consists of the following elements:

- Two modules:
  - bas_awConstants (which declares global constants)
  - basOpenFormBuilder (which contains the function that opens the builder and returns the DoCmd string fdmi_DoMenuItemBuilder)
- A single form, frmDoMenuItemBuilder (see Figure 10-16), and the code behind that form.
- The main table, zstblMenuItems, which is nearly 900 rows long. (I show the first dozen rows in Figure 10-17 on the following page so that you can see its structure.)

■ The USysAddIns table and other system tables. (See the section titled "Installing Add-Ins Automatically" earlier in this chapter for more information.)

ItemID	ItemName	ParentID	SymbolicConstant	NumericConstant
1	Form	0	A_FORMBAR	0
2	File	1	A_FILE	0
3	New	2	A_NEW	0
4	Table	3		0
5	Query	3		1
6	Form	3		2
7	Report	3		3
8	Macro	3		4
9	Module	3		5
10	Close	2		1
11	Save Form	2	A_SAVEFORM	2
12	Save Form As	2	A_SAVEFORMAS	3

Figure 10-17. *zstblMenuItems: the first dozen rows of MenuBldR's main table.*

fdmi_DoMenuItemBuilder

MenuBldR's main function (fdmi_DoMenuItemBuilder) opens the builder, concatenates the string based on the user's dialog box selections, and then returns the DoCmd DoMenuItem string. Access automatically passes the three arguments required by a module builder (such as MenuBldR): module name, procedure name, and null. The code is shown below:

```
Function fdmi_DoMenuItemBuilder (strObjName As String, strControl→
  As String, strCurVal As String) As String

  On Error GoTo fdmi_DoMenuItemBuilder_Err

  Dim strRet As String
  fdmi_fCancel = False

'Opens the form to get user input in dialog mode.
  DoCmd OpenForm "frmDoMenuItemBuilder", , , , , A_DIALOG

'Concatenates the strings from the combo boxes.
  If Not fdmi_fCancel Then
    strRet = "DoCmd DoMenuItem "
    strRet = strRet & fdmi_strMenuBar & ", "
```

```
    strRet = strRet & fdmi_strMenuName & ", "
    strRet = strRet & fdmi_strCommand & ", "
    strRet = strRet & fdmi_strSubCommand & ", A_MENU_VER20"
  End If

'Returns the value to the function.
  fdmi_DoMenuItemBuilder = strRet

fdmi_DoMenuItemBuilder_Exit:
  Exit Function

fdmi_DoMenuItemBuilder_Err:
  MsgBox "Error " & Err & ": " & Error$, 16, "fdmi_DoMenuItemBuilder"
  Resume fdmi_DoMenuItemBuilder_Exit

End Function
```

frmDoMenuItemBuilder

MenuBldR's main form (frmDoMenuItemBuilder) has two main features:

■ It uses SQL queries as the RowSource property for its four combo boxes.

■ It contains two important chunks of code behind forms: one attached to the AfterUpdate event and the second attached to the OK button.

FYI

Don't Know SQL? No Problem...

You can use Access to construct SQL code:

1. Create a new query. (Don't use the wizard.)

2. From the Query menu, choose the type of query you want to create. The default is Select, but you can choose any query listed—Make Table, Update, Append, or Delete. (Note: An insert query is referred to as "append.")

3. After creating a query, test it using the Datasheet command on the View menu. This command doesn't run the query, but it shows the results so you can verify that it's correct. Choosing the Run command from the Query menu actually executes the query.

4. Use the SQL command on the View menu to copy the SQL code into Access Basic, VBA for Excel, or WordBasic.

To use Access to test a SQL query that you've written, follow these steps:

1. Create a new query. (Don't use the wizard.)

2. Use the SQL command on the View menu to enter the query. (Either type it or paste it from the Clipboard.)

3. Use the Datasheet command on the View menu to test the query.

RowSource property Each of the main form's combo boxes uses a variation on the following SQL query as its RowSource property. (The query is actually a single, unbroken string—I've broken it out here so that it's easier to read. See the sidebar above for more information on SQL.)

```
SELECT DISTINCTROW zstblMenuItems.NumericConstant,→
   zstblMenuItems.ItemName, zstblMenuItems.ParentID,→
   zstblMenuItems.SymbolicConstant, zstblMenuItems.ItemID→
   FROM zstblMenuItems→
   WHERE ((zstblMenuItems.ParentID=0))→
   ORDER BY zstblMenuItems.NumericConstant;
```

The only element that differs among the queries for each of the four combo boxes is the ParentID field targeted by the WHERE statement. This field (which is in the zstblMenuItems table) identifies the types of arguments required for the DoMenuItem macro action, and it populates the combo boxes accordingly. The RowSource query populates the Menu Bar combo box with items with ParentID = 0; the Menu Name combo box with items with ParentID = 1; the Command box with items with ParentID = 2; and the Subcommand box with items with ParentID = 3.

Because menus are structured hierarchically, the combo boxes are populated hierarchically. In other words, the choices available in the Menu Name combo box depend on the choice you make in the Menu Bar combo box, and the choice you make for Menu Name determines the choices available for the Command combo box. The AfterUpdate events attached to the Menu Bar, Menu Name, and Command combo boxes repopulate the dependent combo boxes based on the user's selection.

Code behind forms The following code lists the AfterUpdate event for the Menu Bar combo box, which repopulates the dependent combo boxes (Menu Name, Command, and Subcommand) based on the ParentIDs and the user's selection. The AfterUpdate events for the Menu Name and Command combo boxes are virtually identical.

```
Sub cboMenuBar_AfterUpdate ()
'This SQL statement updates the Menu Name combo box.
'Note that SQL statements used by Access Basic end
'with a semicolon.
  Me![cboMenuName].RowSource = "SELECT DISTINCTROW→
    zstblMenuItems.NumericConstant, zstblMenuItems.ItemName,→
    zstblMenuItems.ParentID, zstblMenuItems.SymbolicConstant,→
    zstblMenuItems.ItemID FROM zstblMenuItems WHERE→
    ((zstblMenuItems.ParentID=" & Me![cboMenuBar].Column(4) & "))→
    ORDER BY zstblMenuItems.NumericConstant;"
  Me![cboMenuName].Requery

'Update the Command combo box.
  Me![cboCommand].RowSource = "SELECT DISTINCTROW→
    zstblMenuItems.NumericConstant, zstblMenuItems.ItemName,→
    zstblMenuItems.ParentID, zstblMenuItems.SymbolicConstant,→
    zstblMenuItems.ItemID FROM zstblMenuItems WHERE→
    ((zstblMenuItems.ParentID=" & Me![cboMenuName].Column(4) & "))→
    ORDER BY zstblMenuItems.NumericConstant;"
  Me![cboCommand].Requery

'Update the Subcommand combo box.
  Me![cboSubcommand].RowSource = "SELECT DISTINCTROW→
    zstblMenuItems.NumericConstant, zstblMenuItems.ItemName,→
    zstblMenuItems.ParentID, zstblMenuItems.SymbolicConstant,→
    zstblMenuItems.ItemID FROM zstblMenuItems WHERE→
    ((zstblMenuItems.ParentID=" & Me![cboCommand].Column(4) & "))→
    ORDER BY zstblMenuItems.NumericConstant;"
  Me![cboSubcommand].Requery
End Sub
```

The following code lists the OK event, which assigns the user's combo box selections to global variables:

```
Sub cmdOK_Click ()
'Assign global variables for the Menu Bar combo box.
  If Not IsNull(Me![cboMenuBar]) Then

'Check whether there's an intrinsic constant.
    If Me![cboMenuBar].Column(3) <> "" Then
      fdmi_strMenuBar = Me![cboMenuBar].Column(3)
    Else
      fdmi_strMenuBar = CStr(Me![cboMenuBar])
    End If
  Else
    fdmi_strMenuBar = ""
  End If
```

(continued)

```
'Assign global variables for the Menu Name combo box.
  If Not IsNull(Me![cboMenuName]) Then

'Check whether there's an intrinsic constant.
    If Me![cboMenuName].Column(3) <> "" Then
       fdmi_strMenuName = Me![cboMenuName].Column(3)
    Else
       fdmi_strMenuName = CStr(Me![cboMenuName])
    End If
  Else
    fdmi_strMenuName = ""
  End If

'Assign global variables for the Command combo box.
  If Not IsNull(Me![cboCommand]) Then

'Check whether there's an intrinsic constant.
    If Me![cboCommand].Column(3) <> "" Then
       fdmi_strCommand = Me![cboCommand].Column(3)
    Else
       fdmi_strCommand = CStr(Me![cboCommand])
    End If
  Else
    fdmi_strCommand = ""
  End If

'Assign global variables for the Subcommand combo box.
  If Not IsNull(Me![cboSubcommand]) Then

'Check whether there's an intrinsic constant.
    If Me![cboSubcommand].Column(3) <> "" Then
       fdmi_strSubcommand = Me![cboSubcommand].Column(3)
    Else
       fdmi_strSubcommand = CStr(Me![cboSubcommand])
    End If
  Else
    fdmi_strSubcommand = ""
  End If
  DoCmd Close
End Sub
```

FYI

Designing Relational Data

Eighty percent of a database application is the data itself and the structure of that data; you might say that the data *is* the application. What users call "the application" is nothing more than a tool for using the database. That being the case, it's crucial to separate how data is used from how it is structured. No matter what tools you build for using the data, the database structure should remain the same. To achieve this, you must structure and design the data correctly at the outset. The following introduction to database design (written with Adrian Baer of Baer & Associates, a New York City firm that specializes in database design and client-server consulting) will help you turn raw data into a usable database.

Designing for the Future

You must design data in such a way that it can survive change with minimal adjustment. To do this, store data in a form that is as independent of specific applications' requirements as possible. For example, even if an application needs an account summary, there's no reason to include a field for that summary in the database. Instead, the application should compute the summary.

Normalization is the process of structuring a database (i.e., defining the tables and the fields included in those tables) in such a way that it stores every piece of data in the correct context but requires that the data be entered only once. An efficient way to normalize data is to identify the *objects* that define your business and the *rules* that define their behavior. For example, a mail order business is generally defined by its products and its customers. Both exist independently. In other words, you can have products without customers, and you can have customers who haven't bought products. (These people are referred to as "prospects.") In the database, represent each of these two business objects as a table. You might also need tables for orders and the items (quantities of products) sold to customers in the context of these orders. The following rules of thumb will help you design tables and table structure:

Rule 1: Identify data that stands alone, such as customers or products. Test the independence of this data by determining whether it can meaningfully exist in your database without a relationship to other data. If so, it requires a *kernel table*—a table used to model stand-alone business data.

Rule 2: Identify data that *characterizes* stand-alone data, such as branch offices or client contacts. Test the independence of such data by determining whether it would need to be deleted if the parent data (the kernel table that it characterizes) is deleted. For example, would branch offices be meaningful without a parent company? If not, the data requires a characteristic table—a table used to model a set of detail data that characterizes a single kernel table. Note that part of maintaining *referential integrity* is ensuring that deleted parent records do not result in orphan records in dependent tables. In today's client-server environment, this task can be programmed either into each business application or, preferably, into the database as a stored procedure or a database trigger. Such a program is often called a *deletion constraint.*

Rule 3: Identify data that involves more than one existing table, such as orders. Orders can't exist without both a customer and a product. And, if a customer or product is deleted, the orders associated with that customer or product are likely to be meaningless and must be deleted as well. Such data requires an *associative table*—a table used to model data that exists only as an association between other data.

Practical Database Design

The following example shows how to parlay the three rules mentioned above into a practical database design. Say you're building a database to track billings for a consulting firm. The first task is to identify the data that must be stored in the database: clients, consultants, projects, client contacts, and hours worked. The next task is to structure the tables.

Clients, consultants, and projects are, arguably, the data that define the consulting business. Now, apply rule 1 to determine whether each data group should be a kernel table. Clearly, clients can stand alone (as prospects), and consultants can stand alone (they might be between projects). What about projects then? Although projects can exist without having a specific consultant assigned, they cannot exist without a client. Therefore, projects are not a candidate for a kernel table. The following diagram represents the two kernel tables:

Client   **Consultant**

Applying rule 2, it becomes obvious that projects characterize clients; therefore they belong in a characteristic table. If you delete a client from the database, the client's projects are orphaned and must be deleted as well. However, removing a consultant from the project means only that you have to assign another consultant. Applying the same reasoning, you should also model client contacts as a characteristic table. The following diagram represents the two kernel tables plus the client table's two characteristic tables:

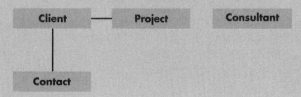

You now have to fit the remaining data (hours worked) into the database model. Clearly, hours worked cannot stand alone. The question comes immediately to mind: Hours *by* whom *for* whom? Hours worked is dependent on two other tables: Consultant and Project. Applying rule 3, you determine that hours worked belongs in an associative table because it can't survive meaningfully without either of its parents. The following diagram represents the required data tables:

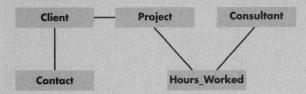

The "Relations" in Relational Databases

At this point, we need to define the relationships among the data tables (from which relational databases get their name). These relationships are *rules of correspondence* between the records of one table and the records of another. For example, one relationship in the billing system is that any given client might have one associated project, many projects, or none.

Needless to say, such a formulation is very powerful because it incorporates *rules about the behavior of the data*—or, more specifically, rules about the behavior of records. Generally, relationships link exactly two tables and can have these properties:

- A relationship has *cardinalities.* For example, one client can have zero or more projects. This relationship is expressed in a diagram of a data model as a line between the two tables, with a crow's foot at the "many" end.

- A relationship has *optionalities.* For example, while a client can have zero or more projects, a project must have exactly one client. This is expressed in a diagram by a bar (meaning 1) at one end and a circle (meaning 0 or optional) at the other.

The following diagram represents the data model:

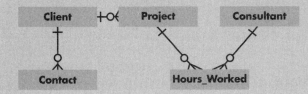

Keys for Relational Databases

Each table requires a unique *key*, which is a field or group of fields uniquely identifying each record stored in the table. Because duplicate names occur, consecutive numbering schemes provide more effective keys. With this in mind, Client_ID and Staff_ID are logical keys for the two kernel tables, clients and consultants.

A simple way to determine the keys of dependent tables is to let them *inherit* keys through relationships. Such keys are referred to as *foreign* keys (primary keys in other tables). For example, to identify the client to which a client contact belongs, the contact table can inherit the Client_ID through its relationship to the client table.

Here's a hint for inheriting keys: Start from the independent tables in the data model, and pass keys toward the dependent tables. If you do this across the entire data model, the project table will use as its key Project_ID plus the inherited Client_ID. The hours worked table will use Work_Date plus three foreign keys: Client_ID and Project_ID (inherited from the client table) and Staff_ID (inherited from the consultant table).

The following diagram represents the data model for the billing system, complete with fields and keys. (Key fields are enclosed in the top box, and FK designates a foreign key.)

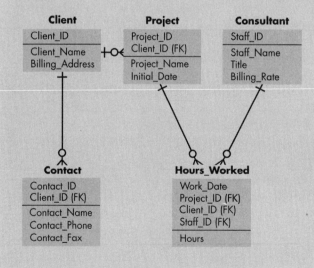

SAMPLE APPLICATION:
Business Information Manager (BIM)

Computer Reseller News recently published an article on how expensive "information mismanagement" is for companies. The article referred to a report by Forrester Research (of Cambridge, Massachusetts) that noted how hard it is for companies to manage what I call "desktop data"—corporate data stored in spreadsheets and word processing files. Desktop data includes faxes, budget forecasts, report drafts, and other such information that individuals accumulate in the course of getting their jobs done.

The cost of mismanaging (or, in most cases, *not* managing) desktop data is lower productivity—people continuously reinvent the wheel for one of two reasons:

- They don't know that someone down the hall has the wheel.

- No one can find the wheel.

Although document management systems certainly help manage desktop data, relatively few companies are willing to invest the sums needed to install such a system. Several companies I work with have decided to try "thinking small" about this problem and are experimenting with solutions that turn desktop data into workgroup and departmental data rather than into centralized corporate data.

There are several advantages to this approach:

- It's direct. In many cases, people who need the same data work in the same areas.

- It's relatively easy to do and is less costly than centralized document management systems.

- It lets companies "grow" an appropriate set of applications for managing and sharing desktop data.

BIM is a business information manager (as opposed to a "personal" information manager) that turns desktop data into departmental data. BIM consists of a shared Access database (BIM.MDB) and a Word template (BIM.DOT). The database stores the following information on business contacts: name, title, company, address, fax and phone numbers, and a salutation for use in letters. (Although the BIM database provided on the *Office Solutions* disk included with this book is a single table, you can structure a more complex, relational database to make this data more broadly useful.)

The Word template, which serves as a front end for the database, simplifies business correspondence by providing a list of business contacts from which users can select. It also enables users to add new contacts, delete contacts, or edit them. Although the version of BIM provided on the *Office Solutions* disk handles only faxes, you can easily expand the application to include business letters or other correspondence.

Not only does BIM turn desktop data into departmental data, it incorporates a key principle of reengineering: the enter-once-use-frequently principle. Once this data is available on a shared database, others can use it for mass mailings and a variety of vertical applications—from sales tracking to account management—in addition to correspondence (see Figure 10-18).

"Vertical" applications built off of BIM:

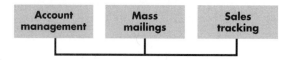

Word front end

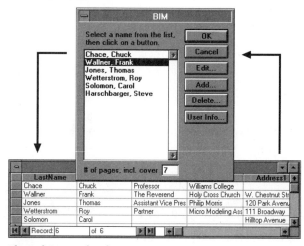

Shared Access database

Figure 10-18. *BIM applies the "enter-once-use-frequently" principle. It collects data once as a by-product of work (in this case, correspondence), rather than as a business activity in its own right, and then shares that data with everyone who can use it. You can adapt the system easily to feed vertical applications (such as sales tracking) by expanding the database.*

How BIM Works

The BIM.MDB database consists of a single table (called "BIM") with the following fields: LastName, FirstName, Title, Company, Address1, Address2, City, State, Zip, Telephone, Fax, and Salutation. The primary key combines LastName and FirstName fields.

The Word template (BIM.DOT) runs the application. When users create a new fax based on BIM.DOT, they either select an existing contact from the list or type data for a new contact. BIM.DOT's EditBIM macro, called from AutoNew, controls interaction with the database. The principal procedures are the Main subroutine and the SelectName and EditEntry functions.

SelectName and EditEntry are written as functions because they open dialog boxes that users might call repeatedly. For example, users might add or edit several contacts, one after the other. Because of this, these functions return a value of −1 to indicate that users have dismissed the dialog box by clicking OK or Cancel; otherwise, they return 1. The procedure that calls the function (Main calls SelectName, and SelectName calls EditEntry) contains a loop that calls the function again if it returns 1. This is the loop from Main, which calls the SelectName function:

```
'Display the Select Name dialog box until users click OK or Cancel.
  iContinue = 1
  While iContinue = 1
    iContinue = SelectName(connectID)
  Wend
```

PRODUCT SHEET: Business Information Manager (BIM)

Purpose:	BIM simplifies the process of transforming desktop data (in this case, faxes and letters sent to business contacts) into shared departmental data. It does this by turning Word (the tool used for creating faxes) into a database front end.
	With BIM, users enter information into the database and update that information in the course of corresponding with business contacts. Because "data entry" takes place when users are about to send a fax, it's folded naturally into the business process.
Development tools used:	Access; Word; SQL; ODBC
How BIM works:	BIM creates fax cover sheets from a shared database of business contacts. If information for a contact already exists, people use it. Otherwise, they type data for the contact, which then appears on the fax. Users can also update the information on a contact or delete the contact from the list.
	The diagram on the next page shows how BIM works.

BIM's main dialog box

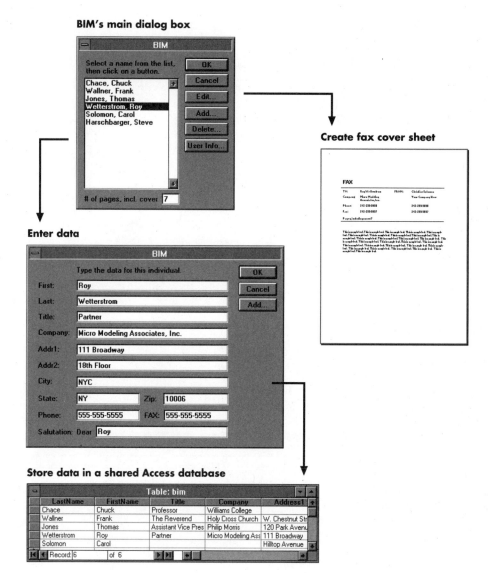

Create fax cover sheet

Enter data

Store data in a shared Access database

An overview of BIM.DOT's three main procedures follows.

■ Sub Main: Connects to the BIM database and disconnects when users
finish. An important feature of ODBC is that it opens database files
without opening the application that owns those files (in this case,
Access), so there's little decrease in performance. The Main subroutine
calls the SelectName function (which opens BIM's main dialog box)
until users click OK or Cancel.

■ Function SelectName: Opens BIM's main dialog box (see Figure 10-19
on the following page), reads the database (using the SQL functions
available in WBODBC.WLL), and then fills the list box with the contacts
in the database. BIM's main dialog box has six command buttons,
which work as follows:

Button	Result
OK	Generates a fax cover sheet.
Cancel	Closes BIM.
Edit	Calls the EditEntry function and passes it the name of the contact that users selected in the main dialog box.
Add	Calls the EditEntry function but doesn't pass it a name. This lets users type data for a new contact.
Delete	Prompts users to make sure that they want to delete the record for the selected contact, and if they do, removes that record from the database.
User Info	Calls the EditUserInfo subroutine, which lets users change the default user info (their name, title, phone number, and so forth).

■ Function EditEntry: Opens a dialog box that lets users enter data into
the database. When users click the Edit button in the main dialog box,
this function displays data for the selected contact so that users can edit
it (see Figure 10-19). When users click the Add button, it opens a blank
dialog box so that users can enter information for a new business contact. This dialog box has three command buttons, which work as shown
on the following page.

Button	Result
OK	After users edit a record, clicking OK updates it. After users add a record, clicking OK inserts it into the database. In both cases, clicking OK returns the user to the main dialog box.
Cancel	Returns the user to the main dialog box.
Add	Calls the EditEntry function but doesn't pass it a name. This lets users type data for a new business contact. If they have just typed data for a new contact, clicking Add inserts that record into the database and then calls the EditEntry function again.

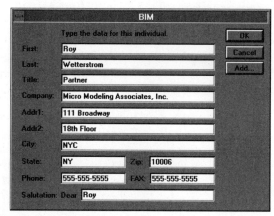

Figure 10-19. *BIM's main dialog box, shown at left, contains the list of business contacts stored in the Access database. Users can then select the contact they want to send a fax to, update data for the selected contact (right), or enter data for a new contact.*

Managing Data from Word Using ODBC and SQL

The Word add-in library (WBODBC.WLL, on the *Office Solutions* disk included with this book) contains WordBasic functions that let you use SQL to manage data in ODBC databases. I provide an overview of these functions in Chapter 5. (You can use the same set of functions in Excel by installing the ODBC add-in, XLODBC.XLA.)

Before using BIM (indeed, before developing or using any application that calls WordBasic's SQL functions), you have to load WBODBC.WLL. BIM's AutoNew macro takes care of this automatically as long as WBODBC.WLL is in

Word's template directory. It does this by using CountAddIns, GetAddInName$, and AddInState to check whether the library is loaded already. If it isn't, AutoNew uses AddAddIn to load it. AutoNew then calls SetDocumentVariable to set a flag (ODBC State) indicating whether the library was loaded already. AutoClose uses GetDocumentVar$ to read this flag, and if WBODBC.WLL wasn't loaded when users started BIM, AutoClose uses AddInState to unload it.

I declare WordBasic's SQL functions at the beginning of BIM.DOT's EditBIM macro. These functions fall into three categories:

- Database connections (SQLOpen and SQLClose)

- Queries (SQLExecQuery, SQLRetrieveRows, SQLRetrieveColumns, and SQLRetrieveItem$)

- Error handling (SQLCountErrors, SQLErrorClass, SQLErrorCode, and SQLErrorText$)

Although I don't use them here, the library also contains "mapping" functions for getting the structure of the database. (For complete information on WordBasic's SQL functions, see Appendix B of the *Microsoft Word Developer's Kit*.)

Opening and closing the database: SQLOpen and SQLClose

To connect to an ODBC database from any application, you have to register that database with the ODBC Driver Manager. (See the sidebar titled "Making ODBC Work for You" in Chapter 5 for instructions.) After you register BIM.MDB with the ODBC Driver Manager, the Main subroutine in the EditBIM macro uses the SQLOpen and SQLClose functions to handle connections to this database. The SQLOpen function returns a value with the numeric identifier for the database connection. Virtually all other SQL functions require this value.

The following code from EditBIM's Main subroutine attempts to connect to the BIM database; if the connect attempt fails, the code prompts the user for the correct location of BIM.MDB:

```
'Connect to database; read connection string from INI file.
  Connect$ = GetPrivateProfileString$("ODBC", "ConnectString",⇥
    "BIM.INI")

'Call SQLOpen function.
  ConnectID = SQLOpen(Connect$,, 4)
```

(continued)

```
'If ConnectID = 0, the connection failed, so connect by
'calling SQLOpen again, with the last argument = 3. This opens
'the ODBC dialog box so users can select the BIM database.
'Write the connect string (now stored in WholeConnect$) to
'the BIM.INI file.
  If ConnectID = 0 Then
    ConnectID = SQLOpen(Connect$, WholeConnect$, 3)
    SetPrivateProfileString "ODBC", "ConnectString",⤏
      WholeConnect$, "BIM.INI"
  End If
```

When users click OK in BIM's main dialog box to create a fax cover sheet, EditBIM's Main subroutine uses the following code to disconnect from the database:

```
'Close connection to database.
  SQLClose(connectID)
```

Querying the database

The EditBIM macro includes two functions (SelectName and EditEntry) that use SQL statements to perform four types of queries:

- SELECT
- UPDATE
- DELETE
- INSERT

> **NOTE** Access uses its own flavor of SQL, which is similar but by no means identical to ANSI SQL (the approved standard). Also, UPDATE, DELETE, and INSERT are SQL statements that perform "action queries" (in other words, *actions*) on a database. See the sidebar titled "Don't Know SQL? No Problem…" earlier in this chapter for more information on using SQL with Access.

SELECT Selecting data from an ODBC-compliant database management system is a three-step process:

1. Use SQLExecQuery to query the database. No matter what type of query you perform, always use this function. The syntax is:

   ```
   ReturnValue = SQLExecQuery(ConnectID, QueryToBePerformed)
   ```

SQLExecQuery uses the following arguments:

- ConnectID: The number returned by the SQLOpen function that identifies the database to which you're connected.

- QueryToBePerformed: The query that you're executing.

The value that the SQLExecQuery function returns depends on the type of query executed. For example, when you execute a SELECT query, it returns the number of columns in the result set. When you execute an UPDATE, DELETE, or INSERT query, it returns the number of rows affected by the query. If the SQLExecQuery function cannot perform the query, it returns an error.

2. Use the SELECT statement to select the data that you want from the database. The syntax is as follows:

```
SELECT NameOfFields FROM NameOfTable WHERE ListOfCriteria
```

The SELECT statement uses the following arguments:

- NameOfFields: The fields from which you want data. Use * to get all fields; otherwise, type a list of fields and separate them by commas.

- NameOfTable: The name of the table from which you want to get data.

- ListOfCriteria: The criteria you use to select data.

3. Use the SQL "retrieve" functions to get the data. For example, SQLRetrieveItem$ returns the data from a specified row and column. The syntax is as follows:

```
ReturnString$ = SQLRetrieveItem$(ConnectID, ColNumber,→
  RowNumber)
```

SQLRetrieveItem$ uses the following arguments:

- ConnectID: The number returned by the SQLOpen function that identifies the database to which you're connected.

- ColNumber: The column number in the database from which you want data.

- RowNumber: The row number in the database from which you want data.

NOTE Word treats all data it retrieves as a string. You must use other Word-Basic functions (for example, Val) to convert strings to numeric data.

The following code from the SelectName function uses SQLExecQuery and the SELECT statement to get the first and last names of all the contacts listed in the database:

```
'Execute query to get list of names and tell user whether the
'query failed.
  QuerySel$ = "SELECT LastName, FirstName FROM BIM"
  iQueryRet = SQLExecQuery(connID, querySel$)
```

The SelectName function uses the SQLRetrieveRows and the SQLRetrieveItem$ functions to retrieve the names of all the contacts listed in the database. It then stores them in an array. The value returned by SQLExecQuery indicates whether any errors have occurred. If an error has occurred, SelectName calls the ParseErrors procedure to alert users.

```
  Dim Names$(0)

  If iQueryRet <= 0 Then

'Call sub.
  ParseErrors
  Else

'Read results of query into Name$().
  iNumNames = SQLRetrieveRows(connID)
  If iNumNames = 0 Then
    MsgBox "There are no names in the BIM database. Click the→
      Add button to add names or the Cancel button to close the→
      dialog box.", "BIM", 64

'Store the names retrieved in an array.
  Else
    Redim Names$(iNumNames - 1)
    For i = 0 To iNumNames - 1
      Names$(i) = SQLRetrieveItem$(connID, 1, i + 1)
      Names$(i) = Names$(i) + ", " + \
        SQLRetrieveItem$(connID, 2, i + 1)
    Next i
  End If
  End If
```

UPDATE To update data in the BIM database, use SQLExecQuery and the SQL UPDATE statement. The syntax for the UPDATE statement is as follows:

```
UPDATE NameOfTable SET NameOfField1 = 'Data1', NameOfField2 =⮞
  'Data2', ... WHERE ListOfCriteria
```

The arguments are essentially the same ones used for the SELECT statement. Note, however, that you have to enclose the data that you're updating in single quotation marks.

The following code from EditBIM's EditEntry function uses SQLExecQuery and the UPDATE statement to update data for the selected contact (technically, the record whose FirstName and LastName fields are specified by the firstName$ and lastName$ variables). The Update dialog box stores the edited data. (The query is actually a single, unbroken string—I've broken it out here so that it's easier to read.)

```
'SQL query to update an existing record with info from dialog box.
  QueryEdit$ = "UPDATE BIM⮞
    SET LastName = '" + dlgEntry.LastName + "', FirstName = '" +⮞
    dlgEntry.FirstName + "', Title = '" + dlgEntry.Title + "',⮞
    Company = '" + dlgEntry.Company + "', Address1 = '" +⮞
    dlgEntry.Address1 + "', Address2 = '" + dlgEntry.Address2 +⮞
    "', City = '" + dlgEntry.City + "', State = '" + dlgEntry.State⮞
    + "', Zip = '" + dlgEntry.Zip + "', Telephone = '" +⮞
    dlgEntry.Telephone + "', Fax = '" + dlgEntry.Fax + "',⮞
    Salutation = '" + dlgEntry.Salutation + "' WHERE LastName =⮞
    '" + LastName$ + "' And FirstName = '" + FirstName$ + "'"

'Execute query.
  iQueryRet = SQLExecQuery(connID, queryEdit$)
```

DELETE To delete data from the BIM database, use SQLExecQuery and the SQL DELETE statement. (The arguments are the same ones used for the SELECT statement.) The syntax for the DELETE statement is:

```
DELETE FROM NameOfTable WHERE ListOfCriteria
```

The following code from EditBIM's SelectName function uses SQLExecQuery and the DELETE statement to delete the selected contact from the database:

```
'When users click Delete, prompt to make sure they're sure.
  iDelete = MsgBox("Are you sure you want to delete " +⮞
    Names$(dlgNames.lstNames) + "?", " BIM ", 36)
```

(continued)

```
'If so...
  If iDelete = -1 Then

'Initialize strings to receive first and last names.
    FirstName$ = "" : LastName$ = ""

'Call BreakUpNames to get first name and last name of selected
'contact.
    BreakUpNames(Names$(dlgNames.lstNames),→
      FirstName$, LastName$)

'Create SQL delete query.
    queryDel$ = "DELETE FROM BIM WHERE FirstName = '" + FirstName$→
    + "' And LastName = '" + lastName$ + "'"

'Execute query and notify user of errors.
    iQueryRet = SQLExecQuery(connID, queryDel$)
    If iQueryRet <= 0 Then ParseErrors
  End If
```

INSERT To add records to the BIM database, use SQLExecQuery and the SQL INSERT statement. (The arguments are the same ones used for the UPDATE statement.) The syntax for the INSERT statement is:

```
INSERT INTO NameOfTable(NameOfField1, NameOfField2, ...) SELECT→
  'Data1', 'Data2', ...
```

The following code from EditBIM's EditEntry function inserts a record in the BIM database whenever users add contacts. The Update dialog box stores the new record. (The query is actually a single, unbroken string—I've broken it out here so that it's easier to read.)

```
'SQL query to add a new record using info from dialog box.
  queryAdd$ = "INSERT INTO BIM(LastName, FirstName, Title, Company,→
    Address1, Address2, City, State, Zip, Telephone, Fax,→
    Salutation) SELECT '" + dlgEntry.LastName + "','" +→
    dlgEntry.FirstName + "','" + dlgEntry.Title + "','" +→
    dlgEntry.Company + "','" + dlgEntry.Address1 + "','" +→
    dlgEntry.Address2 + "','" + dlgEntry.City + "','" +→
    dlgEntry.State + "','" + dlgEntry.Zip + "','" +→
    dlgEntry.Telephone + "','" + dlgEntry.Fax + "','" +→
    dlgEntry.Salutation + "'"
'Execute query.
  iQueryRet = SQLExecQuery(connID, queryAdd$)
```

FYI

Who Are You, and How Much Money Is in Your Checking Account?

In the early 1980s, as relational databases entered the mainstream, businesses began to change how they viewed and managed data. Before that time, attention was primarily focused more on the processing applied to data. With the development of relational databases, people began to focus on the data itself. Glenn Shimamoto, a vice president at Bankers Trust, explained how this notion changed the way companies do business and the kind of business that they *can* do:

> You have to remember that in the early to mid-1980s, people heard, for the first time, about the importance of data. James Martin (who was the main proponent of the "enterprise data model," as it was called) was the big man on campus. His seminars were just great— he was like Mick Jagger strutting on stage with multiple slide machines and a wireless mike. And he pounded home the centrality of data: the importance of rationalizing a company's data into a relational model, the importance of knowing all the data in an enterprise, the importance of organizing data and normalizing it to get rid of duplicates, and the importance of creating a central repository of data and then developing consistent front-end applications to enter and retrieve it.

> Unfortunately, for most of us this was the Impossible Dream. It turns out that it's very difficult to rationalize data across an organization. For example, in a large organization it's a major ordeal to define a single customer number because there are dozens of applications that use this number, and each one's different. Some have a "Cust Num" field, others call it "Cust ID," or "ID," or "CID." Some applications define the customer number as 12 characters, and others use 8. Some applications have numerical customer IDs, and some include characters. The customer number is the classic bugaboo in every big organization, particularly in banks.

> Today, the best banks are the ones that can identify who their customers are. They know whether Jane Q. Smith and Jane Smith are the same person. They know every occurrence of these Smiths—their CD accounts, their savings accounts, their car loans.

> And you can see why this is so important. Let's say that Company A (which seems like a good credit risk) wants to borrow $1 million. However, this company has a subsidiary that's in hock to you and to 50 other banks. You would have no way of knowing this unless you

could relate Company A to this other organization. The banks that can do this—the ones that know who they're doing business with—can identify risks and cross-sell products.

For example, they can tell which customers keep lots of money in a checking account and then give them a break on loans. (Banks love customers who keep money in their checking accounts because it gives them cheap money to lend out at night when no one's looking for it.) But to do this, you have to be able to store, organize, cross-reference, and retrieve massive amounts of data.

11

Integrating Office Applications with OLE

OLE lets users create compound documents and lets developers create "compound applications." Just as compound documents include materials created using a variety of applications—such as charts from Microsoft Excel, illustrations from CorelDRAW!, and sound from Sound Recorder—compound applications include both custom objects and objects from shrink-wrapped products. For example, a Microsoft Access–based application might use Excel's worksheet object as a financial calculation engine, or an Excel-based application might use Microsoft Word's WordBasic object to create a text processor. The ability to create compound applications—sometimes called *inter-application programmability*—provides developers with a new set of tools that leverages a company's investment in shrink-wrapped products.

That's the good news. The bad news is that the observation attributed to Gandhi regarding Western civilization—that it would be a good idea—also applies to OLE. Although you can certainly deliver OLE automation applications that incorporate *two* shrink-wrapped products, such applications often generate "out of memory" messages if users have other products open while running the custom application. Also, OLE automation applications that use shrink-wrapped products tend to perform slowly even on 486 PCs. On the other hand, OLE automation enables you to build applications that use custom business objects (built in C/C++ or Visual Basic version 4) in which the speed is such that performance is a nonissue.

There's also more good news. The latest release of Microsoft Windows NT and the next release of Microsoft Windows (called Windows 95) should, by and large, alleviate the problems that occur when using OLE automation with shrink-wrapped products.

Dynamic Data Exchange (DDE) is still the most widely supported method of exchanging information among applications, because all applications that support OLE automation (and many that don't yet support it) support DDE. Chapter 12 explains how OLE automation and DDE differ.

This chapter begins with an explanation of what OLE is. It then presents two applications that use OLE automation. I use these applications to address some of the programming techniques and practices that can help you develop professional business applications that integrate functionality from more than one shrink-wrapped product. These applications, which are also on the *Office Solutions* disk included with this book, are:

- PIVOT, an Access application that creates a pivot table in Excel

- BulkMail, an Excel application that simplifies the process of managing an Excel mailing list and lets you do a mail merge with Word

> **NOTE** In this chapter, I discuss OLE automation as it relates to four products: Access, Excel, Word, and Visual Basic. Other products support OLE automation, but I don't address them here.

What's All This About Objects?

The term "object," which was once a fairly well defined technical term, has recently turned into a catchall word to describe anything from a programming construct to a button in a dialog box. When object-oriented programming came up in a conversation recently, a personnel manager with little computer experience asked me, "What's an object?" I answered, almost without thinking, "A thing. Any thing." The key to understanding computer objects is to understand how they compare with tangible objects in the real world.

One aspect of real-world objects is that the tasks they perform are inherent in the objects themselves. For example, you can use a teacup only for tasks physically suited to a small, open container with a flat bottom and a handle; you can drink liquid from a cup or use it to scoop sugar. Likewise, the tasks that users can perform with a computer object must be inherent in the object itself. Computer objects should also represent real-world things that contain information—such as charts, worksheets, customer lists, or sales reports.

Technically, a computer object combines data with functions for using the data. (See the sidebar titled "That Obscure Object of Desire" later in this chapter for more information.) It used to be that data was stored in one place (for example, in a database) and the means of accessing the data was stored elsewhere (for example, in a particular business application). Object-oriented programming languages such as Smalltalk and C++ let you bundle the data and the mechanism for accessing it into a single object. You can then build applications with these objects. For example, you can use Excel's objects to build spreadsheet-based business applications.

Microsoft has expanded the notion of objects to include "programmable objects," which you can control through OLE automation. This increases usability *and* reusability by making it possible to build an application that controls another application's objects. For example, any application that supports OLE automation can use Excel's objects. In fact, when you write VBA code to control Excel, you're actually manipulating Excel's objects through OLE automation.

Making OLE Work for You

OLE is a published specification that defines how applications handle objects. Applications that adhere to this spec can share objects with other applications. This sharing can take place in two ways:

- Users can link or embed these objects in their files. This lets them create compound documents whose data originates in different applications.

- Developers can build applications that use objects that are *exposed* (made public) by other applications. This lets developers integrate functionality that exists in shrink-wrapped products or integrate custom applications into new business applications.

OLE from a user's perspective

OLE lets users create compound documents by associating two types of data with an object: *presentation data* (which displays the object) and *native data* (which is all the information necessary to edit the object). Users can link or embed objects created in other applications into their files.

When users link objects to a file, they're really adding two things to the file: 1) the object's display data and 2) a pointer to the object's source file (the file that created the object and that includes everything necessary to edit it). When someone updates the object's source file, the object in the document is updated as well. The tricky thing about working with linked files is that moving the source file from its original location or moving the compound document to a location where it can't access the source breaks the link.

When users embed objects in a file, they include both the object's presentation data and all the data necessary to edit it from within the compound document they're creating. This naturally makes files that contain embedded documents quite a bit larger. Figure 11-1 on the next two pages compares linking and embedding.

NOTE From a user's perspective, some applications are OLE clients (they can contain linked or embedded objects) and others are OLE servers (they let users link or embed their data into other applications).

Task	Linking	Embedding
Number of files	You have to maintain at least two separate documents: the source document for the linked object (such as an Excel worksheet) and the destination document (such as a Word document) that uses the linked object. You can set up a link so that when you change the source document it's updated automatically in the destination document.	You have to maintain only one document—the one that contains the embedded object.
Creating objects	You create a linked object by copying it from the source document and paste-linking it into the destination document.	You create an embedded object either by pasting it or by dragging and dropping it into the destination document.
Updating objects	More than one destination document can use the same source document. When you change the source document, all the destination documents are updated automatically.	You have to change the embedded object for each document.
Destination format	Depending on the nature of the object itself and the capabilities of the OLE client, you can link it in several different formats. For example, you can link worksheet data from Excel to Word as an object that appears as a graphic, as formatted text, as unformatted text, as a picture, or as a bitmap.	All embedded objects appear as graphics in the destination document.
Maintaining objects	You have to keep track of separate files and maintain links between the source document and the destination document.	Everything you need is bundled with the document that contains the embedded object.
Object size	Because the source document exists as a separate file, the destination document isn't affected by the size of the source document.	Because the embedded object and all the information necessary to create it are stored in the destination document, that file can get quite large.

Task	Linking	Embedding
Managing objects	In some applications, you can use the Links command (which is usually on the Edit menu) to manage linked objects. For example, you can set a link so that you can update it manually or automatically, lock it temporarily, change it, or break it. You can relink data easily.	You can *un*embed most embedded objects; they then exist as a picture. You can't re-embed them in their native format. To reduce the size of the destination document, save it under a different name.

Figure 11-1. *A comparison of linking and embedding.*

FYI

What Price Convenience?

It can be convenient to bundle all the data created in various applications into a single document, but you pay a price for that convenience—files grow large very quickly. These large files suffer decreased performance, to the extent that several companies I work with discourage the use of embedded objects. In fact, their attitude can be summed up as "If you embed objects and your documents blow up, you're out of luck."

The following table shows how quickly files with embedded objects can grow. Note that a Word document containing a single embedded chart is nearly twice the size of a document with the same chart linked and is more than three times the size of a page of text.

Document Type	File Size
Empty Word document	7 KB
Word document with only a linked Excel chart object	20 KB
Word document with only an embedded Excel chart object	38 KB
Word document with a page of text (900 words)	12 KB

OLE from a developer's perspective

The OLE specification includes a feature called *OLE automation*, which lets developers do three things:

- Control, through code, objects exposed by another application

- Create and expose custom business objects that are OLE compliant
- Control, through code, linked and embedded objects (see the sidebar tilted "Controlling Linked and Embedded Objects Through Code" later in this chapter)

Applications that can control another application's exposed objects are called *OLE automation clients,* and applications that expose objects are called *OLE automation servers.*

You need Visual Basic version 4—or, for greater control and speed, C/C++—to create objects, but you can use the objects that you create (or that are exposed by shrink-wrapped products) with any programming language that provides "client support" for OLE automation. Exposed objects are considered to be objects only by a programming language that can manipulate them. For example, to a language that includes OLE automation capabilities, WordBasic is an object, the Excel application itself is an object, and so are Excel worksheets. People who use integrated business applications, however, may never know that another application is involved behind the scene. Figure 11-2 shows the extent to which the Microsoft BASICs support OLE automation.

	Access version 2	Excel version 5	Visual Basic version 3	Visual Basic version 4	Word version 6
OLE client (end user's perspective)	X	X			X
OLE server (end user's perspective)		X			X
OLE automation client (developer's perspective)	X	X	X	X	
OLE automation server (developer's perspective)		X		X	X
Implement DDE	X	X	X	X	X

Figure 11-2. *How the Microsoft BASICs implement OLE. Note that Excel version 5 has 127 exposed objects (objects that can be used by another application via OLE automation), and Word version 6 has one—WordBasic, which gives you complete control over Word. Despite the fact that WordBasic is an exposed object, it doesn't let you use exposed objects in other applications. (In other words, it isn't an OLE automation client.)*

Where am I now? One issue that comes up in the design of an integrated application is how to organize the application. There are three main organizational models:

- **The app-centric model.** In this model, one Microsoft Office application controls the others. BulkMail, a sample application in this chapter, uses this model. The application is written in VBA for Excel and uses OLE automation to control Word.

- **The .EXE model.** In this model, all component Office applications are controlled from a stand-alone .EXE file—such as one built in Visual Basic.

- **The to-each-its-own model.** In this model, each Office application and/or .EXE file does its share of the processing. Two sample applications in this book, PIVOT (in this chapter) and PublshXL (in Chapter 12), use this model, which requires that you write code in the component applications as well as in the startup application. This model is useful when you can't control processing in component applications through OLE automation. This might be because the client application doesn't support OLE automation (as in the sample application PublshXL) or because the client application doesn't support a particular data type or method used by the server application (as in the sample application PIVOT). This model also increases efficiency. For example, VBA for Excel code always runs faster from within Excel than from a remote application via OLE automation.

Who's in control? Another issue that comes up when you design integrated applications is how much users should see of component applications. Here are a few rules of thumb, which depend on the nature of the integrated business application you're developing:

- When you develop integrated applications that use a particular Office product to deliver data to users, you should generally leave users in that product. For example, if you build an Access application that generates a pivot table or a report in Excel, leave users in Excel. (See the section titled "SAMPLE APPLICATION: PIVOT" later in this chapter.)

- When you develop integrated applications that use only the *functionality* of a shrink-wrapped product, users should never see that product. For example, if you build an application in Access, Word, or Visual Basic that uses Excel to perform a series of calculations and return a number, users don't need to (and shouldn't) see Excel. This model improves both the speed of applications and their integrity because it prevents users from interfering with the application's execution.

- Unless you're automating the process of building compound documents that require users to edit or update the source data, there's no reason to link or embed data from one application into another.

■ When you develop integrated applications that take data from one application and integrate it into another, try to do it in such a way that you don't have to launch another shrink-wrapped product. This provides the best performance. For example, don't copy data from Access to Excel or Word—instead, use ODBC. Launching Office applications is one of the most time-consuming things you can do, so it's worthwhile to explore alternatives.

Minimizing problems for users When you build an application that opens more than one Office product simultaneously, you can minimize the possibility that users will get an "out of memory" message (or "hang") by testing to determine the percentage of free resources a particular inter-application operation needs to complete successfully. Once you've determined this, whenever users execute the command, check in code to see whether the application to be launched is already open. If it's not, make sure that this minimum is available.

For example, use the IsAppOpen function (shown below) in Access Basic, VBA for Excel, or Visual Basic to determine whether an Office product (in this case, Excel) is already open. If it's not, the function CheckResources (also shown below) verifies whether there are sufficient free resources to open the product and continue processing. You can find the following code in Solution.MDB on the *Office Solutions* disk included with this book. (See Chapter 6 for more information on the Windows API, including the FindWindow function.)

When using OLE automation, you can also trap the error generated by the GetObject function when the object (such as the Excel application) isn't open. See the section titled "The CreatePIVOTTable Function" later in this chapter for an example. Also, remember that you may need to alias API functions.

```
Declare Function FindWindow Lib "User" (ByVal lpClassName→
    As Any, ByVal lpWindowName As Any) As Integer
Declare Function GetFreeSystemResources Lib "User" (ByVal→
    fuSysResource As Integer) As Integer

Function IsAppOpen()
    Dim hExcel As Integer, hPrevActive As Integer
    Dim intGo As Integer

'The API function FindWindow requires a class name argument
'(such as XLMAIN) and a window title argument. ByVal 0&
```

```
'causes the function to search by class name only.
  hExcel = FindWindow("XLMAIN", ByVal 0&)
  If hExcel <> 0 Then

'If Excel is open, call SetActiveWindow to switch to Excel.
'hPrevActive stores the handle for the currently active
'window so that you can easily switch back.
    hPrevActive = SetActiveWindow(hExcel)
  Else

'If Excel isn't open, check the free resources before
'continuing by calling the CheckResources custom function.
    intGo = CheckResources()
  End If
End Function


Function CheckResources ()
  Dim intFree As Integer

'Specify the go-ahead threshold.
  Const THRESHOLD = 65

'The argument 0 specifies system resources; 1 specifies
'graphics resources (GDI); and 2 specifies user resources.
  intFree = GetFreeSystemResources(0)
  If intFree > THRESHOLD Then
    MsgBox "It's a GO!", 64, "Check Resources"
  Else
    MsgBox "NO GO. Resources only " & intFree & "% free.",¬
      16, "Check Resources"
  End If

End Function
```

Although Word isn't an OLE automation client, it can control other applications through DDE. Use code similar to that shown above to determine whether an Office product is open and to launch it or warn users depending on the resources available. Use the following WordBasic code to check free system resources.

```
Sub MAIN
'The argument 25 specifies the system resources.
  FreeResources$ = GetSystemInfo$(25)
  MsgBox "Available resources: " + FreeResources$ + " %."
End Sub
```

FYI

Controlling Linked and Embedded Objects Through Code

You can write code that controls linked and embedded objects. For example, you can establish links to materials created in other applications programmatically, lock links, edit them so that they point to a different source, or update them. You can also create embedded objects, edit them, and so on. In Excel, you handle linked or embedded objects in code in much the same way that you handle chart and drawing objects. For example, the following code activates a chart so users can edit it. The chart's name (as listed in the name box of the formula bar) is "Chart 1." (All of the code in this sidebar is in Solution.XLS on the *Office Solutions* disk included with this book.)

```
Sub EditChart
  Dim objChart As ChartObject
  Set objChart = ActiveSheet.ChartObjects("Chart 1")
  objChart.Select
  objChart.Activate
End Sub
```

The following code activates an embedded OLE object named "Picture 1." Note that this code works for any type of object embedded on the sheet that's active when users run this macro—a Word object, an Excel object, a WordArt object, and so on.

```
Sub EditOLEObject
  Dim objOLE As OLEObject
  Set objOLE = ActiveSheet.OLEObjects("Picture 1")
  objOLE.Select
  objOLE.Activate
End Sub
```

The Activate method used in both of the examples above opens objects for in-place editing. When you work with objects embedded from other applications (in other words, objects of the type OLEObject), VBA supports the Verb method in addition to the Activate method for editing objects. The Verb method supports actions defined by the object's source application.

VBA for Excel has two Verb constants that most objects support: xlOpen and xlPrimary. The constant xlPrimary, which represents the default action, often activates the object for in-place editing (just as the Activate method does). The constant xlOpen generally opens the object in its own window. Access Basic has a Verb property that is similar to VBA for Excel's Verb method.

The following code links an existing object (a file) to an Excel sheet:

```
Sub InsertLinkedObject()
'Change PATH to point to the full path for the file to link.
  Const PATH = "c:\book\disk\xl_apps\solution\OLETest.BMP"
  Worksheets("wrkMiscOLE").OLEObjects.Add FileName:=PATH,→
    Link:=True
End Sub
```

You can also use OLE automation to control embedded or linked objects in other applications.

Using OLE Automation

No matter which Microsoft BASIC you use to start OLE automation (Access Basic, VBA for Excel, or Visual Basic), you start it with one of two functions:

- CreateObject
- GetObject

Once you start OLE automation, you can think of it as a superset of all programming languages that support OLE automation as servers, such as Excel and Word. For example, when you build an integrated business application in Access that uses Excel as an OLE automation server, you use Excel's objects, properties, and methods in your Access Basic code.

Since the Microsoft BASICs are so similar, you can often write code for the OLE automation server in the client just as you would if you were writing it in the server. If you're not comfortable with the server's macro language, start with code from the macro recorder, and then copy it into the client. (See the sidebar below for an overview of how to port code between server and client.)

FYI

From One BASIC to Another

This sidebar provides examples of the changes you have to make to port code from one BASIC to another. (See Chapter 2 for a more detailed comparison of the Microsoft BASICs.)

There are four main reasons to change to code from OLE automation clients when you use it in servers:

- All code used in OLE automation must be preceded by the OLE automation object.

- Enclose in square brackets ([]) keywords used in clients that conflict with those used by the server.

- VBA for Excel version 5 has a number of features that Access Basic version 2 and Visual Basic version 3 don't support.

- WordBasic version 6 doesn't use the object-centric syntax used by Access Basic, VBA for Excel, and Visual Basic.

Handling Features Used Only by VBA for Excel

You can use VBA for Excel code wholesale in Access Basic and Visual Basic *unless* you use a VBA feature that Access Basic or Visual Basic version 3 doesn't support, such as For Each...Next, With...End With, named arguments, and variant data types containing arrays. For example, you can generate the following code using Excel's macro recorder. (This code creates a new workbook, titles the first sheet "Sales Summary," creates column headings labeled from 1992 through 1997, and activates the first cell in which users should type information.)

```
Sub NewXLBook()
  Workbooks.Add
  ActiveCell.FormulaR1C1 = "Sales Summary"
  Range("B3").Select
  ActiveCell.FormulaR1C1 = "1992"
  Selection.AutoFill Destination:=Range("B3:G3"),↪
    Type:=xlFillSeries
  Range("B3:G3").Select
  Range("A4").Select
End Sub
```

To run this code under Access Basic or Visual Basic version 3, you must make four changes:

- Precede each command with the Excel object that the OLE automation code creates.

- Rewrite the AutoFill method to use positional arguments rather than named arguments.

- Rewrite the Range argument for the AutoFill method to reference the OLE automation object (in this case, objXL).

- Rewrite the Type argument for the AutoFill method and substitute the numeric value (2) for the xlFillSeries constant. One way to determine the value for an Excel constant is to use the following line of code: MsgBox str$(*NameOfConstant*).

The following code shows the previous example rewritten for use in an Access Basic or Visual Basic OLE automation procedure. (See the section titled "Creating Objects" on the following page for more information on using Excel as an OLE automation server.) Note that since the last line of code sets the Excel object's Visible property to True, this function leaves you in Excel.

```
Function NewXLBook ()
  Dim objXL As Object
  Set objXL = CreateObject("Excel.Application")
  objXL.Workbooks.Add
  objXL.ActiveCell.FormulaR1C1 = "Sales Summary"
  objXL.Range("B3").Select
  objXL.ActiveCell.FormulaR1C1 = "1992"
  objXL.Selection.AutoFill objXL.Range("B3:G3"), 2
  objXL.Range("B3:G3").Select
  objXL.Range("A4").Select
  objXL.Visible = True
End Function
```

Handling WordBasic Code from the Other BASICs

WordBasic doesn't have the object-centric syntax used by Microsoft's other BASICs. However, under OLE automation, you treat WordBasic statements and functions as if they use object-centric syntax. This means that you precede WordBasic statements with a reference to the OLE automation object and a dot (.). For example, you can generate the following code using Word's macro recorder. This code creates a new document based on the Normal template, inserts the words "Sales Summary," styles these words as Heading 1, and inserts a paragraph where users can start typing.

```
Sub MAIN
  FileNew .Template = "Normal", .NewTemplate = 0
  Insert "Sales Summary"
  Style "Heading 1"
  InsertPara
End Sub
```

To run this code under Access Basic, VBA for Excel, or Visual Basic, you must make two changes. (See the section titled "Word as an OLE Automation Server" later in this chapter for more information.)

■ Precede each command with the Word object that the OLE automation code creates. By doing this, you treat WordBasic statements as methods of the WordBasic object.

■ Rewrite the FileNew statement to use positional arguments. This means dropping references to the arguments .Template = and .NewTemplate = and ensuring that each argument is positioned correctly with commas marking unused arguments. (See the section titled "Positional vs. Named Arguments" in Chapter 2 for more information.) The best way of getting the correct position for arguments is to use the macro recorder. (The positions listed in the WordBasic Help file aren't always correct.)

The following code shows the previous example rewritten for use in an OLE automation procedure in Access Basic, VBA for Excel, or Visual Basic. Note that since objWord is a global variable, this function leaves you in Word.

```
Function MakeWordObject ()
   Set objWord = CreateObject("Word.Basic")
   objWord.FileNew "Normal", 0
   objWord.Insert "Sales Summary"
   objWord.Style "Heading 1"
   objWord.InsertPara
End Function
```

Creating objects

You can use CreateObject to start an application as an OLE automation server and create an *instance* of that application object's class. An object is an instance, or an example, of a particular class. (See the sidebar titled "That Obscure Object of Desire" later in this chapter for more information on classes.) The syntax for the CreateObject function is as follows:

```
Dim objVariable As Object
Set objVariable = CreateObject("ApplicationName.ObjectType")
```

ApplicationName.ObjectType is the *class* of object that you're creating. For example, the following code creates an Excel application object (another instance of Excel running) in Access Basic, VBA for Excel, or Visual Basic:

```
Function MakeAnotherXL()
   Dim objXL As Object
   Set objXL = CreateObject("Excel.Application")
   objXL.Visible = True
End Function
```

In this example, the line *objXL.Visible = True* unhides the instance of Excel launched by the CreateObject function and leaves users there. Unless you're using OLE automation to deliver data to users in Excel—for example, by generating a report in Excel—you should leave the Excel object hidden (its normal state) and close the Excel object when you're done with it. Not only will your integrated business applications run faster, but closing OLE automation objects frees up system resources. (See the section titled "Where Am I Now?" earlier in this chapter for more information.)

The following Access Basic code creates a Word application object. To leave users in Word, declare the object variable (in this case, objWord) as a global variable. (When you declare variables local to a procedure, they're no longer valid at the procedure's end.) The following code, which declares objWord in the declarations section, leaves users in Word.

```
Function MakeWordAppObject()
  Set objWord = CreateObject("Word.Basic")
End Function
```

Figure 11-3 shows the application names and object types for the two OLE automation clients included with Office—Excel and Word. Although Word exposes only one class of objects to OLE automation (the Word.Basic class), Excel exposes three—Excel.Application, Excel.Sheet, and Excel.Chart.

Application	Object Type
Excel	Application
	Sheet
	Chart
Word	Basic

Figure 11-3. *Application names and object types for OLE automation servers.*

Each of these classes behaves somewhat differently, and each is suited to particular purposes. Here's a brief summary of when to use each of the classes that Excel exposes to OLE automation:

- Use the Excel.Application class when you want to present data in Excel and leave users there. If you set the Excel application object's property to Visible, you can exit the application that created the Excel object, such as Access, *without exiting Excel*. When you use Excel's other two classes, the object persists only as long as the creating application remains open. When you use the Excel.Application class, you can use VBA for Excel's methods and properties to create and populate sheets. (See the section titled "SAMPLE APPLICATION: PIVOT" later in this chapter for an example of this.)

- Use the Excel.Sheet class when you want to calculate data in Excel behind the scenes or populate a sheet with data for later use. Even if you make this object visible, it closes when you exit the application that created it (such as Access). (See the MakeXLObject and the ComputeVDB functions in the following sections for sample code.)

■ Use the Excel.Chart class when you want to create a chart for later use. Even if you make this object visible, it closes when you exit the application that created it (such as Access).

Sample code: The MakeXLObject function The following MakeXLObject function uses the Excel.Sheet class to create an instance of an Excel worksheet. It then populates it with data from an Access database and saves the sheet for later use. "Later use" can be use by the Access application that created it or by users themselves. This function, written in Access Basic, saves the worksheet as a standard Excel workbook (CSTMRPT.XLS) that contains a single sheet. The code is in Solution.MDB on the *Office Solutions* disk included with this book. Here are a few things worth noting about the code on the facing page:

■ All VBA for Excel code is in bold, so it's easy to spot.

■ When you launch Excel through OLE automation, it's completely invisible. In fact, it doesn't even appear in the Task List. But if you monitor your free resources, it's obvious that it *is* open. To close Excel, use the following code:

```
objVariable.Application.[Quit]
Set objVariable = Nothing
```

■ Put *Quit* in square brackets so that the OLE automation client that's creating the Excel object, such as Access, associates it with Excel and not with the client's own application object. Also, although it's not strictly necessary to use the second line (and the keyword *Nothing* is undocumented in Access Basic), it's good practice. You'll see why when you experiment with making the various classes of Excel objects visible. For example, to make the Excel.Sheet class visible, you have to declare the object variable as a global variable. Of course, if you do this, the object variable remains in memory at the end of the function— unless you set it to Nothing.

■ The MakeXLObject function declares the variable objXL globally by putting it in the declarations section. To leave users in the newly created worksheet, comment out the two lines that close the object (see Figure 11-4) and then add the following line:

```
objXL.Application.Visible = True
```

■ When you test this, notice that the title of the sheet isn't "CSTMRPT.XLS," but "Object." When you close Access, this object closes too, although the Excel application itself remains open. (See the section titled "Opening Objects" later in this chapter for more information.)

- The following line of code prevents Excel from prompting users if the filename used for this report already exists; if it does exist, it will be overwritten:

```
If Dir$(strSavedReport) <> "" Then Kill strSavedReport
```

You need this line because the usual method for suppressing such prompts—*Application.DisplayAlerts = False*—doesn't work under OLE automation, and the SendKeys statement works only when Excel is visible.

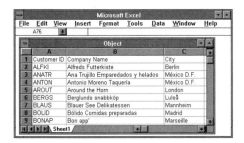 

Figure 11-4. *If you add the line* objXL.Application.Visible = True *and you comment out the two lines of code that close the object, the MakeXLObject function leaves users in the worksheet on the left (named "Object"). Use the GetObject function to leave users in the worksheet on the right (named "CSTMRPT.XLS"), which is saved by the MakeXLObject function.*

```
Function MakeXLObject ()
  On Error GoTo ErrorMakeXLObject

  Dim dbSolution As Database
  Dim tdfCustomers As TableDef
  Dim rstCustomers As Recordset
  Dim intRow As Integer
  Dim intColumn As Integer
  Dim strSavedReport As String

  Set dbSolution = DBEngine(0)(0)
  Set tdfCustomers = dbSolution.TableDefs("Customers")
  Set rstCustomers = dbSolution.OpenRecordset("Customer")

'Set full path and name for saved Excel object (i.e., report).
  strSavedReport = "C:\ACCESS2\CSTMRPT.XLS"

'objXL is declared in [Declarations] section because otherwise
'you can't display the Sheet object and leave users in it.
```

(continued)

```
'Create an Excel worksheet object.
  Set objXL = CreateObject("Excel.Sheet")

'Display hourglass.
  DoCmd Hourglass True

'Add column headings from table.
  intRow = 1
  For intColumn = 1 To tdfCustomers.Fields.Count
    objXL.Cells(intRow, intColumn).Value =⮑
      tdfCustomers.Fields(intColumn - 1).Name
  Next intColumn

'Select first record.
  intRow = 2
  rstCustomers.MoveFirst
  Do Until rstCustomers.EOF
    For intColumn = 1 To rstCustomers.Fields.Count
      objXL.Cells(intRow, intColumn).Value =⮑
        rstCustomers.Fields(intColumn - 1)
    Next intColumn

'Select other records and increment row counter.
    rstCustomers.MoveNext
    intRow = intRow + 1
  Loop

'Check whether CSTMRPT.XLS exists and kill it if it does;
'this prevents prompt to users to overwrite existing file.
'Excel's usual method, Application.DisplayAlerts = False,
'doesn't work under OLE automation. Also, SendKeys works only
'when Excel's application object is visible.
  If Dir$(strSavedReport) <> "" Then Kill strSavedReport

'Best-fit Excel columns and save sheet.
  objXL.Cells(1, 1).CurrentRegion.EntireColumn.AutoFit
  objXL.SaveAs strSavedReport

'Exit Excel and clear object variable.
  objXL.application.[Quit]
  Set objXL = Nothing

ExitMakeXLObject:
    MsgBox "Saved Excel object as C:\CSTMRPT.XLS.", 64,⮑
      "MakeXLObject"
'Turn off hourglass.
  DoCmd Hourglass False
  Exit Function
```

```
ErrorMakeXLObject:
  If Err <> 0 Then
    MsgBox "An unidentified error occurred. " & Chr$(13) &¬
      "ERROR =" & Str$(Err), 48, "MakeObject"
  End If
    Resume ExitMakeXLObject
End Function
```

Sample code: The ComputeVDB function The ComputeVDB function, shown below, uses Excel to compute variable declining balance depreciation on assets tracked in an Access database. (This calculation isn't available in Access.) Although the function displays the depreciation in a message box, you can just as easily add this number to a report. Note that the basic idea for populating an Excel sheet with Access data is essentially the same as in the MakeXLObject function described above. You can use this same idea to populate a sheet for charting Access data with an Excel chart.

The code for ComputeVDB is in Solution.MDB on the *Office Solutions* disk included with this book. Once again, the VBA for Excel code is in bold, so it's easy to spot.

```
Function ComputeVDB ()
  On Error GoTo DepreciationError

  Dim dbSolution As Database
  Dim rstAsset As Recordset
  Dim intNumFields As Integer
  Dim i As Integer
  Dim strMsg As String

  Set dbSolution = DBEngine(0)(0)
  Set rstAsset = dbSolution.OpenRecordset("Assets")

'objXL is declared in the [Declarations] so that you can display the
'Sheet object and leave users in it. Create worksheet object.
  Set objXL = CreateObject("Excel.Sheet")

'Display hourglass.
  DoCmd Hourglass True

'Read values from the Assets table into the Excel worksheet.
  rstAsset.MoveFirst
  For i = 2 To rstAsset.Fields.count - 1
    objXL.Cells(i - 1, 1).Value = rstAsset.Fields(i)
  Next i
```

(continued)

```
'Set the year for which to compute depreciation.
  objXL.Cells(1, 2).Value = 3

'Compute the depreciation and display it.
  objXL.Cells(3, 2).Formula = "=VDB(A1, A2, A3, B1-1, B1, A4)"
  strMsg = "The third year depreciation on the first asset "
  strMsg = strMsg & "recorded in the table ""Assets"" is "
  strMsg = strMsg & Format$(objXL.Cells(3, 2).Value, "Currency")
  MsgBox strMsg, 64, "Compute Depreciation"

'Exit Excel and clear object variable.
  objXL.Application.[Quit]
  Set objXL = Nothing

DepreciationExit:
'Turn off hourglass.
  DoCmd Hourglass False
  Exit Function

DepreciationError:
  If Err <> 0 Then
    MsgBox "An unidentified error occurred. " & Chr$(13) &→
      "ERROR = " & Str$(Err), 48, "Compute Depreciation"
  End If
  Resume DepreciationExit
End Function
```

FYI

OLE vs. ODBC

The fastest way to get data into Excel or Word is through ODBC. The ODBCReport subroutine (written in VBA for Excel), shown on the facing page, uses ODBC to create the same report that the MakeXLObject function creates through OLE automation. At startup, it runs two-and-a-half times faster than MakeXLObject; after startup, it runs about six times faster. Figure 11-5 shows the time it takes to run each procedure immediately after starting Windows.

	MakeXLObject	*ODBCReport*
1st try	14,061 milliseconds	5,822 milliseconds
2nd try	11,590 milliseconds	3,351 milliseconds
3rd try	11,754 milliseconds	1,922 milliseconds

Figure 11-5. *MakeXLObject vs. ODBCReport. I ran the tests on a Dell Dimension XPS 466V with 16 MB of RAM and a math coprocessor.*

One reason that ODBC is faster than OLE automation is that it uses SQL to read and write directly to the database file without launching the database management system. However, despite its relative speed, ODBC has a few drawbacks. Weigh the following when deciding between building an Excel-based application using ODBC to retrieve data from Access and an Access-based application using OLE automation to provide data to Excel:

- ODBC stores queries in SQL strings, which are not as easy to maintain as Access QueryDef objects.

- ODBC implemented from add-ins (such as XLODBC.XLA) is harder to debug than OLE automation.

- ODBC returns data in a contiguous block, while OLE automation lets you position data anywhere.

The code for ODBCReport is in Solution.XLS on the *Office Solutions* disk included with this book. (See Chapter 5 for more information.)

```
Option Explicit
Declare Function GetTickCount Lib "USER" () As Long

Sub ODBCReport()
  On Error GoTo ODBCError

'lngRetVal holds return value of GetTickCount function.
'ConnectID is the unique connection ID returned by SQLOpen.
'Query 1 holds SQL string.
  Dim lngRetVal As Long, ConnectID As Integer, Qry1 As String
  Dim blnConnectTried As Boolean
  Application.ScreenUpdating = False

  Qry1 = "SELECT Customers.`Customer ID`, "
  Qry1 = Qry1 & "Customers.`Company Name`,Customers.City FROM "
  Qry1 = Qry1 & "Customers Customers"

'Select sheet in which to write data.
  Sheets("wrkODBCvsOLE").Select

'Select any existing data and delete it.
  Selection.CurrentRegion.Select
  Selection.Delete
  Range("A1").Select

'Connect to data source.
  blnConnectTried = False
  ConnectID = SQLOpen("DSN=Solution Database")
```

```
'If SQLOpen fails, it generates error 13. The error trap sets
'blnConnectTried to True, resumes at this line, and displays
'data sources. If users click Cancel, it generates error 13 again.
  If blnConnectTried Then ConnectID = SQLOpen("")

'Query, retrieve data, close data source.
  SQLExecQuery ConnectID, Qry1
  SQLRetrieve ConnectID, Sheets("wrkODBCvsOLE").Cells(1, 1)
  SQLClose ConnectID

'Best-fit selected range.
  ActiveSheet.Range("A1").CurrentRegion.EntireColumn.AutoFit

ODBCReportExit:
'Go home.
  Range("A1").Select
  Application.ScreenUpdating = True
  Exit Sub

ODBCError:
'If unable to connect to data source...
  If Err = 13 Then

'...the first time, prompt user with list of registered data
'sources.
    If Not blnConnectTried Then
      MsgBox "Select the data source for Solution.MDB", 64,→
        "ODBC Report"
      blnConnectTried = True
      Resume Next

'If users click Cancel in data source list, clean up and exit.
    Else
      MsgBox "This procedure automatically uses a data source→
        named Solution Database for Solution.MDB.", 64,→
        "ODBC Report"
      Resume ODBCReportExit
    End If

'Otherwise, notify user of error and exit.
  ElseIf Err <> 0 Then
    If Err <> 0 Then MsgBox "An unidentified error occurred.→
      Error code is" & Err, 48, "ODBC Report"
    Resume ODBCReportExit
  End If
End Sub
```

Opening objects

Use the GetObject function to open an existing object. For example, you can use this function to open Excel workbooks but not Word documents. The syntax for the GetObject function is as follows:

```
Dim objXL As Object
Set objXL = GetObject("PathOfFile", "ApplicationName.ObjectType")
```

When you use GetObject to open a file, the second argument, *Application-Name.ObjectType,* is optional. But if you use the second argument, use either Excel.Sheet or Excel.Chart—you can't open a file with the Excel.Application class. You can, however, use this class to determine whether Excel is already open. (See the section titled "The CreatePIVOTTable Function" later in this chapter for more information.) For example, the following Access Basic code (from Solution.MDB) opens the workbook created by the MakeXLObject function.

> **NOTE** If you run GetXLObject with the Immediate Window open, it displays the first five rows of data from this sheet.

```
Function GetXLObject ()
  Dim objXLOpen As Object
  Dim intRow As Integer
  Dim intColumn As Integer

'Open CSTMRPT.XLS in its normal, hidden state.
  Set objXLOpen = GetObject("C:\CSTMRPT.XLS", "Excel.Sheet")
  For intRow = 1 To 5
    For intColumn = 1 To 3
      Debug.Print objXL.Cells(intRow, intColumn).Value
    Next intColumn
  Next intRow
  objXLOpen.Parent.Saved = True
  objXLOpen.Application.[Quit]
  Set objXLOpen = Nothing
End Function
```

To open a workbook and make it visible, put the workbook's name in square brackets, and declare the object variable globally. For example, the following code opens CSTMRPT.XLS and leaves users there. However, when you close Access, the Excel.Sheet object closes, too.

```
Function OpenXLObject()

'Open CSTMRPT.XLS in its normal, hidden state.
  Set objXL = GetObject("C:\[CSTMRPT.XLS]", "Excel.Sheet")
  objXL.Application.Visible = True
End Function
```

The previous code sample is quite similar to that shown below. However, when you close Access, the following code leaves you in CSTMRPT.XLS.

```
Function OpenXLSheet()
   Set objXL = CreateObject("Excel.Application")
   objXL.Workbooks.Open "C:\CSTMRPT.XLS"
   objXL.Application.Visible = True
End Function
```

Word as an OLE automation server

You can't use the GetObject function to open a Word document. Instead, use the CreateObject function and then open the file using the FileOpen statement, as shown in the following code:

```
Function OpenWordDoc()
   Dim objWordDoc As Object
   Set objWordDoc = CreateObject("Word.Basic")
   objWordDoc.FileOpen "C:\WORD6\MEMBER.DOC"
   Set objWordDoc = Nothing
End Function
```

Here are a few things worth noting about this code:

- Although OLE automation creates and opens new instances of Excel, it doesn't create or open new instances of Word.

- If Word *isn't* running, this code starts it, opens the document specified (you'll see it flash by on screen), and then closes both the document and Word. If Word *is* running, this code merely opens the document, not another instance of Word. It doesn't close either Word or the document. To close the document, add the following line of code before Set objWord = Nothing:

  ```
  objWordDoc.FileClose
  ```

- Adding the last line (Set objWordDoc = Nothing) is good programming practice and mimics the handling of Excel objects, but it's not necessary. Note that Word doesn't require (and doesn't support) code to formally quit the application.

- To leave users in Word, declare the object variable globally and comment out the last line.

FYI

That Obscure Object of Desire

The essence of object-oriented programming is *encapsulation*—that is, the combination of two things: data and functions to use that data. You could say that an object is the *capsule* with the data on the "inside," and the functions that control access to that data serve as the "outside" interface. Objects provide two important benefits—reusability and data protection.

Reusability

To understand how objects work, you have to understand *classes*. Classes are to objects as data types are to variables. For example, in Access Basic, VBA for Excel, or Visual Basic, you might write one of the following lines of code:

```
Dim intCounter as Integer
```

or

```
Dim DB as Database
```

In the first line of code, the variable intCounter is of type Integer, while in the second, DB is an object of the Database class. To understand how data types and classes relate, consider the following example.

Most programming languages let you create new data types by combining existing ones. For example, in Access Basic, VBA for Excel, and Visual Basic you can define a data type for a date as follows:

```
Type DateInfo
   Month as String
   Day as Integer
   Year as Integer
End Type
```

After you define this data type, you can declare variables of the type DateInfo, which is great—unless you decide to change the type definition. Let's say you decide to store months as integers rather than strings. This is easy enough to do in the type definition itself: Simply replace the line *Month as String* with *Month as Integer*. Unfortunately, you then have to change every line of code that refers to the month component of DateInfo-type variables to accommodate integers rather than strings. If you used this type widely, you could be in for a bit of work.

At one level, you can think of classes as the solution to this problem. Classes contain data members (just like user-defined types) as well as a set of functions that handle the data. The data (and often some of the functions) is *private*, so you can't access it directly from outside the class.

The remaining functions are *public*. Any code outside of the class has to use public functions to access the data. The public members of a class form its *interface*. The data and private functions are its *implementation*.

Continuing the comparison of data types and classes, suppose you have a DateInfo class whose data members are the same as the user-defined type shown on the previous page. Suppose, too, that this class has a public function named GetMonth, which returns the Month component as a string. If you later decide to store months as integers, simply rewrite the GetMonth function so that it manipulates the integer data internally and still returns a string. You don't have to change any code that uses the DateInfo class.

This is how a class provides *reusability* in object-oriented applications. It's like subcontracting: When you hire another company to make widgets, you focus on the quality of the widgets, the timeliness of delivery, and the price—not on the manufacturing process. In fact, the subcontractor can change the manufacturing process as long as the quality, delivery, and price don't suffer.

A class is a data subcontractor. The code that uses it doesn't care how the class handles the data internally, as long as it returns the data in the right form. You can change the implementation of the class all you want, and as long as the interface doesn't change (in other words, as long as the public functions take the same types of arguments and return the same types of data), you don't have to change a single line of code outside the class.

To get a feeling for how important reusability can be, count the number of Word documents on your PC. No matter what's in the document, it uses the same code—that of the Word document class. Similarly, every Excel spreadsheet uses the code for the spreadsheet class. In fact, every window in Windows uses the code for the Window class—in other words, every window is an *instance* of the Window class.

Data Protection

In addition to reusability, classes provide *data protection*. Here's an analogy that shows how data protection works. You could say that jewelry stores are more object-oriented than grocery stores. In grocery stores, the goods are generally well organized, but occasionally you'll find a can of peas in the cookie section. This is because anyone in a grocery store can pick up something and put it somewhere else.

In jewelry stores, on the other hand, everything is locked up. Salespeople personally hand you a ring or a watch to try on. These salespeople provide an interface that protects the jewelry while giving others access to it.

Interfaces for computer objects work in the same way. For example, the user-defined type in the DateInfo example is analogous to the grocery store. Since anyone can put anything (of the correct data type) into any of the data components, you can end up with a date like *Hamburger 37, -973*. When you use a DateInfo *class*, however, you have to call the appropriate public functions to enter the month, day, and year, and these functions check to see whether the input makes sense.

SAMPLE APPLICATION: PIVOT

PIVOT drafts Excel's pivot table feature into serving as a reporting engine for Access. Many companies that I work with use Excel as a database reporting engine because doing so prevents data from running into a dead end on the paper trail. Instead of (or in addition to) delivering paper reports, these companies deliver "live" reports in Excel. This allows users who are more familiar with spreadsheets than databases to analyze data, roll it up into summary form or expand it into full detail, chart it, link it to Word for publishing purposes, and generally extend and expand the data's useful business life.

PRODUCT SHEET: PIVOT

Purpose:	PIVOT uses an Excel pivot table to summarize inventory data stored in an Access database. It demonstrates how to use OLE automation and ODBC to turn Excel into a reporting engine for database applications. Such applications generally include a front end for entering data and a set of tools for reporting that data. PIVOT uses Excel as one of those tools.
Development tools used:	Access; Excel; Windows API; OLE automation; ODBC
How PIVOT works:	To run PIVOT:
	1. Place Pivot.MDB and Pivot.XLA in the same directory, and then register Pivot.MDB with the ODBC driver manager.
	2. When you open Pivot.MDB, specify *shared,* not *exclusive,* access. If Pivot.MDB isn't shared, Excel can't use ODBC to query the database and get data for the pivot table.
	3. To create the pivot table, click the Show button on the Pivot toolbar.

(continued)

---

4. Use the Close button on the Pivot toolbar to close the pivot table. This command closes Excel if it wasn't open when you first created the pivot table; otherwise, it closes only the workbook used for the pivot table. This command also restores Excel's original display settings.

The following diagram illustrates PIVOT's overall structure:

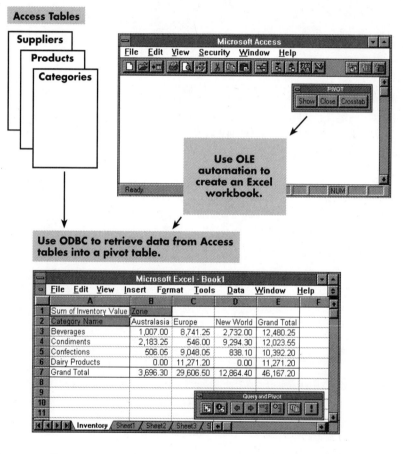

PIVOT has two components:

- An Access database, Pivot.MDB, which serves as the main application controlling Excel

- An Excel add-in, Pivot.XLA, which controls creation of the pivot table

The database, Pivot.MDB, contains three related tables that store data on inventory: Categories, Products, and Suppliers. It also contains functions that summarize the inventory data in an Excel pivot table by product category and by the supplier's geographic zone. For example, the pivot table lets you see at a glance the value of your inventory in beverages or the dollar amount that comes from European suppliers. Even though the Access crosstab query summarizes data in much the same way, it doesn't let you manipulate that data in *any* way—which is why it's worthwhile to use an Excel pivot table (see Figure 11-6).

Figure 11-6. *Although the Access crosstab query summarizes essentially the same data as does Excel's pivot table, very few businesspeople know how to use database systems productively. Because of this, you can extend the data's useful life by delivering it in an Excel pivot table that lets users chart it, roll it up into summary form, link it to a Word report, and so on.*

When you open Pivot.MDB, the application uses an AutoExec macro to display the Pivot toolbar, which has three buttons: Show, Close, and Crosstab. Click the Show button to create a pivot table, click Close to close the pivot table (and Excel too, if it wasn't running when you created the pivot table), and click Crosstab to run the crosstab query so that you can compare it with the pivot table.

PIVOT has three main routines, which I explain in the following sections:

■ The CreatePIVOTTable function uses OLE automation to launch Excel (if necessary), record current display settings, and then use Pivot.XLA to create a pivot table.

■ Pivot.XLA uses ODBC to retrieve data from Access into the PivotTableWizard method.

■ The ClosePIVOTTable function closes the pivot table. It also closes Excel if it wasn't running when the user created the pivot table.

The CreatePIVOTTable Function

When you click the Show button on the Pivot toolbar, the application runs the CreatePIVOTTable function, which creates an Excel pivot table. The Create-PIVOTTable function (shown below) performs six main tasks:

- It performs typical startup tasks, such as checking to see whether Pivot.MDB is open for shared access and declaring variables.

- It calls the CheckConnect subroutine, which ensures that the ODBC connection string points to Pivot.MDB's current path. (This routine uses the Windows API GetPrivateProfileString and WritePrivateProfileString functions; see Chapter 6 for more information.)

- It checks to see whether Excel is open and if it is, it creates a workbook for the pivot table using the existing instance of Excel. Otherwise, it launches Excel. (This prevents users from opening two copies of Excel simultaneously.) One way to do this is to use the IsAppOpen function described earlier in this chapter, and another is to use the GetObject function. When using the GetObject function, specify the Excel.Application class rather than a filename, as shown here:

```
Set objExcelApp = GetObject(, "Excel.Application")
```

If Excel *isn't* open, the preceding code returns error message #2713. The CreatePIVOTTable function then traps this error and launches a new copy of Excel using the CreateObject function.

- The CreatePIVOTTable function uses OLE automation to save Excel's existing screen position and then reposition Excel to display the pivot table on top of the Access window.

- The CreatePIVOTTable function creates a new Excel workbook with a sheet named "Inventory."

- The CreatePIVOTTable function opens Pivot.XLA (an Excel add-in), which actually creates the pivot table. (See the next section, "Pivot.XLA," for more information.) It uses the following code to open the add-in, run the add-in's MakePivotTable subroutine, and then close the add-in:

```
objExcelApp.Workbooks.Open strAddInPath
objExcelApp.Run "MakePivotTable"
objExcelApp.Workbooks("PIVOT.XLA").[Close] False
```

```
Function CreatePIVOTTable ()
  On Error GoTo PIVOTError
```

```
'Return value of IsCurDBExclusive function.
  Dim intIsExclusive As Integer

'Message for message box.
  Dim msg As String

'Is Pivot.MDB open for shared access?
'Call IsCurDBExclusive function to find out...
  intIsExclusive = IsCurDBExclusive()
  Select Case intIsExclusive
    Case 0
      'Do nothing.
    Case -1
      msg = "This database is open for exclusive access. To "
      msg = msg & "create a pivot table, close the database, "
      msg = msg & "and then reopen it for shared access."
      MsgBox msg, 48, "PIVOT"
      Exit Function
    Case Else
      Error intIsExclusive
  End Select

'Note that this function uses Excel intrinsic constants
'(declared globally) to manage the window state. You must
'declare all such constants to use them via OLE automation.

'Object variable for Pivot.MDB.
  Dim DB As Database

'Full path for Pivot.MDB.
  Dim strAppPath As String

'Full path for Pivot.XLA.
  Dim strAddInPath As String

'Excel worksheet containing pivot table.
  Dim objPIVOTSheet As Object

'Status indicator form and label control.
  Dim frmInvStatus As Form, lblWhatGoesOn As Control

'Path for Pivot.XLA.
  Dim strAddInName As String

'Get the full path for Pivot.MDB.
  Set DB = DBEngine(0)(0)
  strAppPath = DB.Name
```

(continued)

```
'Call sub to verify database path in connection string.
  CheckConnect strAppPath

'Verify that Pivot.XLA is in the same directory as Pivot.MDB.
'If it isn't, the Dir$ function returns an empty string and
'the application displays a message box with instructions.
  strAddInPath = ExtractPath(strAppPath) & "PIVOT.XLA"
  Do
    strAddInName = Dir$(strAddInPath)
    If strAddInName <> "" Then
      Exit Do
    Else
      If MsgBox("Can't find Pivot.XLA. To continue, switch→
        to File Manager and move Pivot.XLA to " &→
        ExtractPath(strAppPath) & ", and then return and→
        click OK. Otherwise, click Cancel.", 49, "PIVOT")→
        = 2 Then
        Exit Function
      End If
    End If
  Loop

'Handles status indicator form.
  DoCmd OpenForm "Inventory Status", A_NORMAL, , , A_READONLY,→
    A_NORMAL
  Set frmInvStatus = Forms("Inventory Status")
  Set lblWhatGoesOn = frmInvStatus!StatusInfo

'Get an Excel application object.
  lblWhatGoesOn.Caption = "Opening Excel..."
  frmInvStatus.Repaint

'If Excel isn't open, this generates error 2713.
  Set objExcelApp = GetObject(, "Excel.Application")
  fCloseExcel = False

ExcelOpened:
'Record Excel's display settings. ClosePIVOTTable restores
'these settings. If Excel is minimized, it will be restored
'to its state prior to minimization.
  ExcelAppState = objExcelApp.WindowState
  fMinimized = False
  If ExcelAppState = xlMinimized Then
    fMinimized = True
    objExcelApp.WindowState = xlNormal
    ExcelAppState = objExcelApp.WindowState
  End If
  ExcelLeft = objExcelApp.Left
```

```
  ExcelTop = objExcelApp.Top
  ExcelWidth = objExcelApp.Width
  ExcelHeight = objExcelApp.Height
  PIVOTToolbarState = objExcelApp.Toolbars("Query and→
    PIVOT").Visible

'Set the size and position of Excel's application window.
  objExcelApp.WindowState = xlNormal
  objExcelApp.Left = 46
  objExcelApp.Top = 90
  objExcelApp.Width = 398
  objExcelApp.Height = 203
  objExcelApp.Toolbars("Query and PIVOT").Visible = True

'Create a new workbook.
  lblWhatGoesOn.Caption = "Creating new workbook..."
  frmInvStatus.Repaint
  objExcelApp.ScreenUpdating = False
  objExcelApp.Workbooks.Add
  Set objWorkbook = objExcelApp.ActiveWorkbook

'Add a new worksheet to the workbook.
  lblWhatGoesOn.Caption = "Adding new worksheet..."
  frmInvStatus.Repaint
  Set objPIVOTSheet = objWorkbook.ActiveSheet
  objPIVOTSheet.Name = "Inventory"

'Record current window state, and then maximize it.
  ExcelCurrWindowState = objExcelApp.ActiveWindow.WindowState
  objExcelApp.ActiveWindow.WindowState = xlMaximized

'Open Pivot.XLA.
  lblWhatGoesOn.Caption = "Opening Pivot.XLA..."
  frmInvStatus.Repaint
  objExcelApp.Workbooks.Open strAddInPath

'Call the MakePIVOTTable macro in Pivot.XLA.
  lblWhatGoesOn.Caption = "Creating pivot table (this can→
    take a while)..."
  frmInvStatus.Repaint
  objExcelApp.Run "MakePIVOTTable"

'Close Pivot.XLA.
  objExcelApp.Workbooks("PIVOT.XLA").[Close] False

'Display worksheet with the pivot table.
  lblWhatGoesOn.Caption = "Displaying Excel..."
```

(continued)

```
frmInvStatus.Repaint
  objExcelApp.ScreenUpdating = True
  objExcelApp.Visible = True

'Set the focus to Excel.
  hExcel = FindWindow("XLMAIN", ByVal 0&)
  hAccess = SetFocusAPI(hExcel)

PIVOTExit:
'Close the status indicator form.
  DoCmd Close A_FORM, "Inventory Status"
  Exit Function

PIVOTError:
'If Excel isn't open when the GetObject function is called,
'this error occurs. Launch Excel, and then resume execution.
  If Err = 2713 Then
    Set objExcelApp = CreateObject("Excel.Application")
    Err = 0
    fCloseExcel = True
    Resume ExcelOpened

'Notify users, clear object variables, and then exit.
  Else
    Select Case Err

'This error occurs if Excel returns an error.
    Case 2763
      MsgBox "Error in Excel: " & Error$
    Case Else
      MsgBox Str$(Err) & ": " & Error$
    End Select

    Set objPIVOTSheet = Nothing
    Set objWorkbook = Nothing
    Set objExcelApp = Nothing

    DoCmd Close A_FORM, "Inventory Status"
    Exit Function
  End If
  Resume PIVOTExit
End Function
```

Pivot.XLA

OLE automation can only control one application from another if both applications "speak" the same language. (See the sidebar titled "From One BASIC to Another" earlier in this chapter.) PIVOT needs an Excel add-in to supplement

OLE automation because Excel's PivotTableWizard method requires an argument of the Variant data type containing an array. Since Access Basic doesn't support this, you can't invoke Excel's PivotTableWizard method from Access.

My workaround for this problem was to create an Excel add-in (Pivot.XLA). I explained in the previous section how to open the add-in from Access Basic. Here I cover how to create the add-in. (See the section titled "SAMPLE APPLICATION: The WinAPI Add-In" in Chapter 9 for more information on Excel add-ins.)

The easiest way to generate code for pivot tables is to start Excel's macro recorder. Before trying this with *any* external (non-Excel) database, register that database with the ODBC driver manager.

1. After registering the database with the ODBC driver manager, start the macro recorder by choosing Record Macro from the Tools menu. Then choose Record New Macro.

2. Choose PivotTable from the Data menu. Excel opens the PivotTable Wizard, which walks you through most of the steps below.

3. In step 1 of the PivotTable Wizard, select the type of data source. (PIVOT uses an external data source.)

4. Step 2 of the wizard launches Microsoft Query when you click the Get Data button. Select the ODBC data source that you want to query (I selected the PIVOT data source) and then click the Use button.

5. Add Pivot.MDB's three tables (Categories, Products, and Suppliers) to the Query window, and then perform the query. I used three fields in PIVOT: Category Name from the Categories table, Zone from the Suppliers table, and a calculated field that multiplies the two fields—Unit Price and Units in Stock—from the Products Table (see Figure 11-7 on the next page). Type the following into a field in the Query window (or in the Add Column dialog box) to perform this calculation:

```
[Unit Price]*[Units In Stock]
```

> **NOTE** You should put these field names in square brackets ([]) because they use spaces, which the ODBC version of SQL doesn't support.

6. Click the Return Data button to close MS Query and return to Excel. In step 3 of the PivotTable Wizard, drag the fields to the place you want them to appear in the pivot table. I positioned Category as the Row, Zone as the Column, and Sum of Expr1002 as Data. (Sum of Expr1002 is the calculated field, which I double-clicked and then renamed "Inventory Value.")

7. In the last step of the wizard, name the pivot table and indicate where to position it on the worksheet.

8. Click the Stop Macro button to stop recording.

Excel records the following code:

```
Sub RecordPivotTable()
  ActiveSheet.PivotTableWizard SourceType:=xlExternal,
    SourceData:=Array("DSN=PIVOT;DBQ=C:\BOOK\DISK\OLE&DDE\PIVOT\PIVOT.MDB;
    DefaultDir=C:\BOOK\DISK\OLE&DDE\PIVOT;Description=
    for Access-Excel pivot table example;FIL=MS Access;
    JetIniPath=MSACC20.INI;SystemDB=C:\ACCESS\SYSTEM.MDA;
    UID=Admin;", "SELECT Categories.`Category Name`, Suppliers.Zone,
    `Unit Price`*`Units In Stock` FROM Categories
    Categories, Products Products, Suppliers Suppliers
    WHERE Products.`Category ID` = Categories.`Category ID` AND
    Suppliers.`Supplier ID` = Products.`Supplier
    ID`"), TableDestination:="R1C1", TableName:="PivotTable3"
    ActiveSheet.PivotTables("PivotTable3").AddFields
    RowFields:="Category Name", ColumnFields:="Zone" ActiveSheet.
    PivotTables("PivotTable3").PivotFields("Inventory
    Value").Orientation = xlDataField
End Sub
```

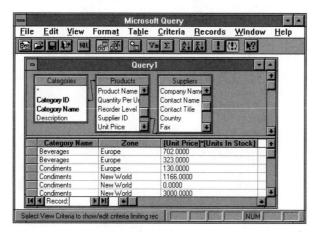

Figure 11-7. *The query used for the pivot table. To create a calculated field in MS Query, type the calculation.*

From macro recorder to finished product

Pivot.XLA's MakePivotTable subroutine, shown below, is similar to the recorded macro. I made three main changes:

- The subroutine now reads the ODBC connection string from the Pivot.INI file. This works as follows: Pivot.MDB's CheckConnect routine reads the connection string from the INI file and determines whether it has the correct path for the database. If not, it deletes the connection string. If Pivot.XLA's MakePivotTable routine doesn't find a connection string in the INI file, it calls the SQLOpen function and passes an empty string for the first argument and 3 for the last argument, which prompts users to select a database. Once users select a database, the routine records the connection string in the INI file for future use.

- The SourceData argument for the PivotTableWizard method is now packaged as a string array (ArrayConnect) so that it's easier to read and manage.

- I added an error trap.

> **NOTE** Remember that you have to use the References command on the Tools menu to open XLODBC.XLA in order to use Excel's ODBC functions.

```
Option Explicit
Declare Function GetPrivateProfileString Lib "KERNEL" (ByVal→
  lpSectionName As String, ByVal lpEntryName As String, ByVal→
  lpDefault As String, ByVal lpReturnedString As String, ByVal→
  nSize As Integer, ByVal lpFileName As String) As Integer
Declare Function WritePrivateProfileString Lib "KERNEL" (ByVal→
  lpSectionName As String, ByVal lpEntryName As String, ByVal→
  lpString As String, ByVal lpFileName As String) As Integer

Sub MakePivotTable()
'ODBC connection string for Pivot.MDB.
  Dim strConnect As String

'Cell to receive whole connection string from SQLOpen function.
  Dim objDummyCell As Object

'Connection ID returned by SQLOpen function.
  Dim iConnID As Integer

'All-purpose integer variable to receive return values from
```

(continued)

```
'add-in and API functions.
  Dim iRet As Integer

'Return value of GetPrivateProfileString.
  Dim iLength As Integer

'Array argument for PivotTableWizard method.
  Dim ArrayConnect() As String

'Name of INI file.
  Const strINIFile = "PIVOT.INI"

'Turn off screen updating.
  Application.ScreenUpdating = False

'Get ODBC connection string from INI file.
  strConnect = String$(256, 0)
  iLength = GetPrivateProfileString("PivotTableWizardInfo",→
    "ConnectionString", "", strConnect, Len(strConnect), strINIFile)

GetConnection:
  If iLength <> 0 Then
    strConnect = Left$(strConnect, iLength)

'If there's no connection string in the INI file, get one by calling
'the SQLOpen function with an empty string as its first argument and
'the number 3 as its final argument. This function prompts users to
'select a database and records the connection string in a cell. (The
'function doesn't let you store it in a variable directly.) Read the
'connection string from the cell into strConnect, clear the cell,
'close the database connection via SQLClose, and record the
'connection string in the INI file for future use.
  Else
    Set objDummyCell = ActiveSheet.Range("A1")
    iConnID = SQLOpen("", objDummyCell, 3)
    strConnect = objDummyCell.Value
    objDummyCell.Clear
    iRet = SQLClose(iConnID)
    iRet = WritePrivateProfileString("PivotTableWizardInfo",→
      "ConnectionString", strConnect, strINIFile)
  End If

  On Error GoTo PivotProblem

'Invoke the PivotTableWizard method for the active sheet. The
'SourceType argument constant xlExternal indicates an external
'database. The SourceData argument is an array--its first element
'is the ODBC connection string and the remaining elements are
```

```
'the query for the pivot table data broken into chunks no longer
'than 200 characters (which is what the PivotTableWizard method
'requires). The Table Destination argument R1C1 places the
'pivot table at the upper left corner of the active sheet. The
'TableName argument assigns a name to the pivot table.
ReDim ArrayConnect(1 To 8)
ArrayConnect(1) = strConnect
ArrayConnect(2) = "SELECT DISTINCTROW Categories.➛
  [Category Name], "
ArrayConnect(3) = "Suppliers.Zone, [Products]![Unit Price]*"
ArrayConnect(4) = "[Products]![Units In Stock] AS➛
  [Inventory Value] "
ArrayConnect(5) = "FROM Categories INNER JOIN (Suppliers➛
  INNER JOIN "
ArrayConnect(6) = "Products ON Suppliers.[Supplier ID] = "
ArrayConnect(7) = "Products.[Supplier ID]) ON Categories.➛
  [Category ID]"
ArrayConnect(8) = " = Products.[Category ID];"

  ActiveSheet.PivotTableWizard SourceType:=xlExternal,➛
    SourceData:=ArrayConnect(), TableDestination:="R1C1",➛
    TableName:="Inventory"

'Add fields to the pivot table. This table has a single row field,
'"Category Name", and a single column field, "Zone".
  ActiveSheet.PivotTables("Inventory").AddFields RowFields:=➛
    "Category Name", ColumnFields:="Zone"

'Designate "Inventory Value" as the data field and display its
'entries with the specified number format.
  With ActiveSheet.PivotTables("Inventory").PivotFields("Inventory➛
    Value")
    .Orientation = xlDataField
    .NumberFormat = "#,##0.00_);[Red](#,##0.00)"
  End With

ExitPivot:
'Turn on screen updating.
  Application.ScreenUpdating = True
  Exit Sub

PivotProblem:
'If the PivotTableWizard method fails (Err = 1004),
'the connection string might be bad. Create a new one.
  If Err = 1004 Then
    Err = 0
    iLength = 0
```

(continued)

425

```
      Resume GetConnection
    Else
      MsgBox Str$(Err) & ": " & Error$()
      Exit Sub
    End If
    Resume ExitPivot
End Sub
```

The ClosePIVOTTable Function

Click the Close button on the Pivot toolbar to run the ClosePIVOTTable function. This function does one of two things, depending on the value of fCloseExcel, a global variable set by the CreatePIVOTTable function:

- If fCloseExcel = False, Excel was already open when the user created the pivot table, so ClosePIVOTTable doesn't close Excel.

- If fCloseExcel = True, Excel wasn't open before the user created the pivot table, so ClosePIVOTTable closes Excel.

In either case, the ClosePIVOTTable function calls the RestoreExcel subroutine, which restores Excel's screen position to its original settings. These settings are global variables stored by the CreatePIVOTTable function. The code for the ClosePIVOTTable function follows.

```
Function ClosePIVOTTable ()
  On Error GoTo CloseProblem
  Dim iTest As Integer

'Check the visible property of the Excel application object to see
'if the object variable is set. If not, it generates an error that
'is trapped below.
  iTest = objExcelApp.Visible

'Set the focus to Excel.
  hExcel = FindWindow("XLMAIN", ByVal 0&)
  hAccess = SetFocusAPI(hExcel)

'If the flag fCloseExcel is true, Excel wasn't running before.
'In this case, close Excel.
  If fCloseExcel Then
    RestoreExcel
    objExcelApp.[Quit]

'Otherwise, close the workbook and reset the focus in Access.
'("OMain" is the class name of Access's main window.)
  Else
```

```
    objWorkbook.[Close]
    RestoreExcel
    hAccess = FindWindow("OMain", ByVal 0&)
    hExcel = SetFocusAPI(hAccess)
  End If

ExitClosePIVOTTable:
'Free the application object variable.
  Set objWorkbook = Nothing
  Set objExcelApp = Nothing
  Exit Function

CloseProblem:
'If the user has closed the table already, an error occurs.
'Error 91 occurs if the user closed the table using the
'Inventory toolbar, and error 2731 occurs if the user closed
'Excel using Excel's own File Exit command.
  If (Err = 91) Or (Err = 2731) Then
    MsgBox "The PIVOT table is not open."
  ElseIf Err <> 0 Then
    MsgBox "Error " & Str$(Err) & ": " & Error$
  End If
  Resume ExitClosePIVOTTable
End Function
```

The code for the RestoreExcel subroutine follows.

```
Sub RestoreExcel ()

'Restore Excel's display settings as recorded in the
'CreatePIVOTTable function.
  objExcelApp.WindowState = ExcelAppState
  objExcelApp.ActiveWindow.WindowState = ExcelCurrWindowState
  objExcelApp.Toolbars("Query and PIVOT").Visible = PIVOTToolbarState

  If ExcelAppState = xlNormal Then
    objExcelApp.Left = ExcelLeft
    objExcelApp.Top = ExcelTop
    objExcelApp.Width = ExcelWidth
    objExcelApp.Height = ExcelHeight
  End If

  If fMinimized Then objExcelApp.WindowState = xlMinimized
End Sub
```

SAMPLE APPLICATION: BulkMail

BulkMail is an Excel-based application designed to make it easier to manage mailing-list data in Excel. Microsoft estimates that more than 70 percent of the people who use Excel use it as a database—and why not? Anyone who can use a spreadsheet can organize data into a simple but effective flat-file format. There's no need for relational database theory and no need to figure out how to construct a query that returns the data you need. Excel version 5's list feature (which treats any contiguous range as a database) makes this especially easy.

PRODUCT SHEET: BulkMail

Purpose:	BulkMail demonstrates how to build an Excel database application for managing mailing lists. It is structured so that users enter, edit, and delete data through a custom Excel dialog box and perform mail merges in Word through OLE automation. Although this version of BulkMail focuses on performing the mail merge with a letter already written in Word, you can expand the application to enable users to control Word through OLE automation to *write* the letter as well.
Development tools used:	Excel; Word; Windows API; OLE automation
How BulkMail works:	To run BulkMail:
	1. Use BulkLttr.DOT to create the new letter you want to merge. This template (which uses Header.DOC as the data source) already has merge fields.
	2. In Excel, choose the Mail Merge command from the BulkMail menu.
	3. In the BulkMail dialog box, select the Word document you want to use as the letter. Next, select the criterion for selecting the letter's recipients—for example, All or Companies.
	4. Click OK when you're ready to do the mail merge.
	The diagram on the facing page illustrates BulkMail's overall structure.

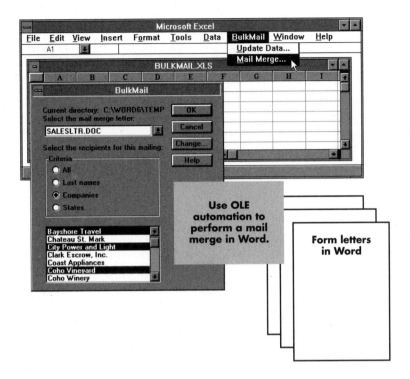

BulkMail has two components:

- BulkMail.XLS, an Excel database and mail merge interface that serves as the main application controlling Word
- BulkLttr.DOT, a Word template for creating the mail merge letter

BulkMail.XLS contains the Excel database, which stores standard address information for contacts, and a custom menu with two commands: Update Data and Mail Merge. The Update Data command is a placeholder for a custom dialog box (not included in this sample application) that lets users add new records, edit existing records, and delete unwanted records. Whenever you deal with applications for *any* database (from Access to Excel to Oracle), you should provide an interface that hides the actual data from users and strictly controls the type and format of data entered in the database. This prevents mistakes from corrupting the data.

The Mail Merge command opens a dialog box that lets users select the recipients of the mailing, and then uses OLE automation to perform the mail merge in Word.

BulkMail has four main routines (stored in the module modMailMerge), which I explain in the following sections.

- ListDocFiles uses the Files function to list the Word .DOC files in the current directory.

- The cmdChange_Click subroutine lets users select a mail merge letter in a directory other than the default directory.

- The ListDistinctEntries subroutine lets users select the recipients of the mail merge letters.

- The cmdOK_Click subroutine performs the query that users specified regarding letter recipients, and then performs the mail merge with Word.

Which Letter?

To do a mail merge, users write a letter using the BulkLttr.DOT template. This template includes standard merge fields for letters and uses Header.DOC, a table with the column headings from the BulkMail database. Using BulkLttr.DOT, users can write new text without bothering with fields.

Once users write the form letter for the mail merge, they can perform the merge by choosing the Mail Merge command from the BulkMail menu. The application opens a dialog box (see Figure 11-8) that lets users select the form letter and its recipients.

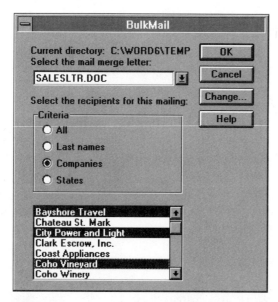

Figure 11-8. *The BulkMail dialog box lets users select both the Word document that contains the form letter and the form letter's recipients. The drop-down list displays the .DOC files in the last directory used. Click the Change button to select a letter in another directory.*

When the BulkMail dialog box first opens, the drop-down list displays the .DOC files in the current directory. (The current directory is stored in the label above the drop-down list; if this label is empty, the current directory is the Word program directory.) Users can select from this list or click the Change button to select a .DOC file in a different directory.

Most of the code for handling this list is in the ListDocFiles subroutine in modMailMerge. This routine calls the Files function in modMain to retrieve a list of .DOC files in the current directory. The Files function uses the Dir$ function to retrieve files that meet a given specification (such as *.DOC), stores their names in a string array provided by the calling procedure (ListDocFiles), and returns the number of filenames retrieved.

The Files function follows.

```
Function Files(ByVal strPath As String, strFiles() As String) As→
   Integer
   Dim counter As Integer
   Dim strTemp As String
   ReDim strFiles(1 To 1)
   On Error GoTo FilesProblem

   strFiles(1) = Dir$(strPath)
   If strFiles(1) <> "" Then
     counter = 1
     Do
       strTemp = Dir$()
       If strTemp <> "" Then
         counter = counter + 1
         ReDim Preserve strFiles(1 To counter)
         strFiles(counter) = strTemp
       End If
     Loop Until strTemp = ""
   End If
   Files = counter
   Exit Function

FilesProblem:
'If the path doesn't exist, return -1.
   If Err = 76 Then
     Files = -1
     Exit Function

'With any other error, notify user and return -2.
   ElseIf Err <> 0 Then
     GlobalErrorMsg "Files", Err
     Files = -2
     Exit Function
   End If
End Function
```

The Change button

When users click the Change button, BulkMail calls the cmdChange_Click subroutine in modMailMerge. CmdChange_Click uses the GetOpenFilename method to open the standard File Open dialog box—with a twist. Rather than opening the selected file, this method returns the file's full path. The selected directory becomes the current directory, and its .DOC files are displayed in the drop-down list. The code follows.

```
Sub cmdChange_Click()
    On Error GoTo ChangeError

    Dim strCurDir As String
    Dim strDocDirectory As String
    Dim strFullPath As String
    Dim strPath As String
    Dim strFileName As String

'Store the current directory in strCurDir, and make the
'directory displayed in the dialog box the current directory.
    strCurDir = CurDir()
    strDocDirectory = objDocDirectory.Caption
    ChDir Left$(strDocDirectory, Len(strDocDirectory) - 1)

'Open the File Open dialog box to allow the user to
'select a mail merge document. (The GetOpenFilename method
'makes it possible to get the full path for the selected
'document from the File Open dialog box without actually
'opening the document.)
    strFullPath = Application.GetOpenFilename→
        (fileFilter:="Word Docs (*.doc),*.doc",→
        Title:="Select Mail Merge Document")

'When the user clicks the OK button...
    If strFullPath <> "False" Then

'...extract the path and filename from the full path for
'the document chosen by the user.
        strPath = Extract(strFullPath, 0)
        strFileName = Extract(strFullPath, 1)

'Write the path in the current directory label in the dialog box,
'and call ListDocFiles to fill the document list box.
        objDocDirectory.Caption = strPath
        ListDocFiles strPath
        objDocList.Text = strFileName
    End If
```

```
RestoreDirectory:
'Restore the original directory.
  ChDir strCurDir
  Exit Sub

ChangeError:
'If the directory displayed in the dialog box isn't a valid
'directory, leave the current directory at its original setting.
  If Err = 76 Then
    Resume Next
  ElseIf Err <> 0 Then
    GlobalErrorMsg "cmdChange_Click", Err
    Resume RestoreDirectory
  End If
End Sub
```

Who Gets Letters?

In addition to letting users select a form letter, the BulkMail dialog box lets them select the letter's recipients by clicking one of four option buttons:

- All (everyone in the database)

- Last Names

- Companies

- States

When users select Last Names, Companies, or States, they can further target the mailing by clicking particular names, companies, or states. For example, if users select the States option button, they can then select California, Texas, and New York from the multiselect list box.

The BulkMail Database worksheet contains the contact data in a range named Database. ("Database" is an Excel reserved name that you must use to manipulate data *as a database* through code.) When users select an option such as Companies or States, the ListDistinctEntries subroutine uses the Advanced-Filter method in the following code to query the database and select the data specified.

```
objDatabase.Range("Database").Columns(iField).AdvancedFilter→
  Action:=xlFilterCopy, CopyToRange:=.Cells(2, 10), Unique:=True
```

The variable objDatabase in this code represents the Database range on the BulkMail Database worksheet: iField is the number of the column that users select (1 is Last Name, 3 is Company, and 6 is State), and strField is the column heading (Last Name, Company, or State). The Unique argument is set to True to return only nonduplicate entries in the selected column. Also, setting the Action argument to xlFilterCopy copies the entries to the location specified by the CopyToRange argument.

The ListDistinctEntries routine then fills the multiselect list box in the BulkMail dialog box with the entries selected. From here, users can further target recipients. The code for ListDistinctEntries follows.

```
Sub ListDistinctEntries(iField As Integer)
  On Error GoTo ListError

  Dim objCriteriaRange As Object

'Run an advanced filter to get a list of the distinct entries
'in the column specified by the argument iField.
  With objDatabase
    strField = .Cells(1, iField).Value
    .Range("Database").Columns(iField).AdvancedFilter→
      Action:=xlFilterCopy, CopyToRange:=.Cells(2, 10), Unique:=True
    Set objCriteriaRange = .Cells(2, 10).CurrentRegion
  End With

'Trim off the column heading and sort the list.
  With objCriteriaRange
    .Rows(1).Delete
    .Sort Key1:=.Cells(1, 1)
  End With

'Fill the criteria list box with the extracted data.
  Dim i As Integer
  objCriteriaList.RemoveAllItems
  For i = 1 To objCriteriaRange.Rows.Count
    objCriteriaList.AddItem objCriteriaRange.Rows(i).Value
  Next i

'Clear the extracted data range.
  objCriteriaRange.ClearContents
  Set objCriteriaRange = Nothing
  Exit Sub

ListError:
  If Err <> 0 Then
    GlobalErrorMsg "ListDistinctEntries", Err
    Exit Sub
  End If
End Sub
```

Performing the Mail Merge

After users select the form letter and its recipients, they click the OK button to retrieve the records specified and to merge them with the Word document. The code that handles this is in the cmdOK_Click subroutine.

This subroutine uses the AdvancedFilter method to retrieve the specified records. The code is nearly identical to that used in the previous section, except that it requires a CriteriaRange argument, which contains the criteria for selecting records.

BulkMail's criteria range is a single column whose first entry indicates the selected option button—Last Names, Companies, or States. (If users select All, there's no need for a criteria range; the application selects all records.) The remaining entries indicate the items that users selected from the list box (see Figure 11-9). The AdvancedFilter method retrieves records that match these criteria and copies them into a separate range on the worksheet.

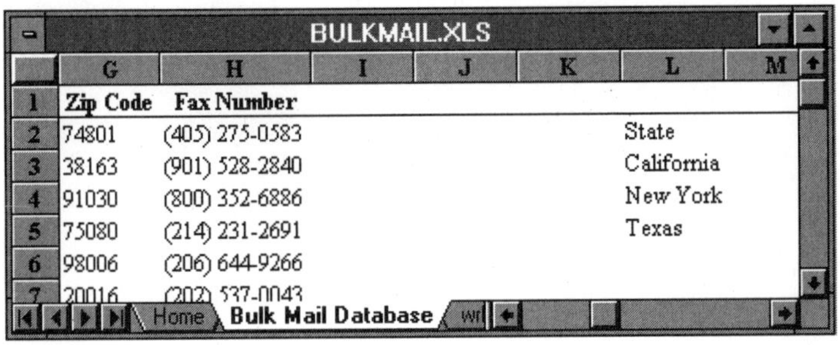

Figure 11-9. *This sheet shows the criteria range (right) that BulkMail creates when users select State and then specify California, New York, and Texas. The application uses these criteria to select records for form-letter recipients.*

After selecting the recipients' records, BulkMail uses OLE automation to perform a mail merge in Word. Although Word normally lets you use an Excel database as the data source for a mail merge, it doesn't let you do this under OLE automation. Why? Because Word itself uses DDE to communicate with Excel during a mail merge, and you can't DDE Excel from inside an OLE automation operation controlled by Excel.

As a workaround, BulkMail creates a temporary Word document (TMP.DOC), pastes the selected records from Excel into this document, performs the mail merge, and then deletes the temporary file.

The code for cmdOK_Click is shown on the following page.

```
Sub cmdOK_Click()
On Error GoTo OKError

  Dim i As Integer
  Dim iRow As Integer
  Dim strDocDirectory As String
  Dim strFormLetter As String
  Dim objAddresses As Object

'Read selected names from the list box, and use these as
'criteria for the AdvancedFilter method.
  iRow = 2
  objDatabase.Cells(iRow, 12).Value = strField
  With objCriteriaList
    For i = 1 To .ListCount
      If .Selected(i) Then
        iRow = iRow + 1
        objDatabase.Cells(iRow, 12).Value = .List(i)
      End If
    Next i
  End With

'Run advanced filter.
  With objDatabase
    .Range("Database").AdvancedFilter Action:=xlFilterCopy,⬎
      CriteriaRange:=.Cells(2, 12).CurrentRegion,⬎
      CopyToRange:=.Cells(2, 14),Unique:=False

'Set object variable to extracted data range and trim off
'column headings.
    Set objAddresses = .Cells(2, 14).CurrentRegion
    objAddresses.Rows(1).Delete

'Clear criteria range.
    .Cells(2, 12).CurrentRegion.ClearContents
  End With

'Do mail merge with extracted data.
'Get path and name of mail merge letter.
  strDocDirectory = objDocDirectory.Caption
  strFormLetter = objDocList.Text

'Copy extracted data to the Clipboard.
  objAddresses.Copy

  Set objWord = CreateObject("Word.Basic")
  With objWord
    .ScreenUpdating 0
```

```
'Create a temporary document, and paste mail merge data in it.
    .FileNew Template:="Normal"
    .EditPaste
    .FileSaveAs Name:=strDocDirectory & "tmp.doc"

'Open the mail merge letter.
    .FileOpen Name:=strDocDirectory & strFormLetter

'Perform the mail merge.
    .MailMergeOpenDataSource Name:=strDocDirectory & "tmp.doc"
    .MailMerge CheckErrors:=2, Destination:=0, MergeRecords:=0,→
      Suppression:=0, MailMerge:=True

'Close the mail merge letter.
    .Activate strFormLetter
    .FileClose 2

'Close the temporary document.
    .Activate "tmp.doc"
    .FileClose 2
    .ScreenUpdating 1
  End With

'Delete the temporary document.
  Kill strDocDirectory & "tmp.doc"

'Clear the range containing the extracted data.
  Application.CutCopyMode = False
  objAddresses.ClearContents
  Set objAddresses = Nothing

CleanUp:
  ClearObjectVariables
  Exit Sub

OKError:
  If Err <> 0 Then
    GlobalErrorMsg "cmdOK_Click", Err
    Resume CleanUp
  End If
End Sub
```

12

DDE: It's Not Dead Yet

Dynamic Data Exchange (DDE) is one of Microsoft's core technologies for enabling applications to share data. It's been around since Word for Windows version 1 and Excel version 3; Microsoft has been gradually replacing it with newer data-exchange technology such as OLE automation.

You can think of DDE as OLE automation without the OLE—in other words, without the objects. Both OLE automation and DDE let you share data between applications, and both let you control another application. Their means for doing this, however, are fundamentally different. When you use OLE automation (described in Chapter 11), you create an instance of another application (the OLE automation server application) and control it directly with the server's own macro programming language; when the server processes commands in its macro language, the client application transfers control temporarily to the server application.

With DDE, the client application is in control throughout the DDE session. Figure 12-1 on the next page summarizes the DDE commands available for Access Basic, VBA for Excel, WordBasic, and Visual Basic. Since all of these languages support DDE as both clients and servers, DDE is a more universal method than OLE automation for sharing data between applications.

Although many implementations of DDE have only five commands, you can use one of these commands (DDEExecute) to simulate the level of control that OLE automation provides by running a macro in the DDE server application. (See the next section, "SAMPLE APPLICATION: PublshXL," for an example of how this works.)

Task	Command	Syntax

Start the DDE "conversation"	DDEInitiate	`ChannelNumber =↴`
		`DDEInitiate(ApplicationName,↴`
		`TopicName)`

Retrieve data (in the form of text) from another application	DDERequest	`VariableName =↴` `DDERequest(ChannelNumber, Item)`
Send data (in the form of text) to another application	DDEPoke	`DDEPoke ChannelNumber, Item,↴` `Data`
Execute a command in another application	DDEExecute	`DDEExecute ChannelNumber,↴` `DDECommand`
End the DDE "conversation"	DDETerminate	`DDETerminate ChannelNumber`

Figure 12-1. *The most common DDE commands for Access Basic, VBA for Excel, WordBasic, and Visual Basic.*

SAMPLE APPLICATION: PublshXL

PublshXL is a Word-based utility that lets users paste information from named Excel ranges without the fuss of wading through worksheets to find and copy these ranges. This utility makes it easier for Word publications to use data that is stored in multiple Excel workbooks. The original version of this utility is used by a financial publishing group that incorporates large amounts of Excel data into its publications. They use this utility in two ways:

- They have a number of Excel applications that pull data off of the mainframe, format it, and assign range names. Editors then use a version of the PublshXL utility to bring the Excel data into Word.

- Analysts can give editors a list of files and their named ranges, and editors can quickly add these to publications.

PublshXL has two components:

- PublshXL.DOT, a Word template that serves as the main application

- PublshXL.XLA, an Excel add-in that lists the ranges available in whatever Excel workbook users select

NOTE You can find these files—PublshXL.DOT and PublshXL.XLA—on the *Office Solutions* disk included with this book. I also provide PublshXL.XLS so that you can edit the VBA for Excel code.

PRODUCT SHEET: PublshXL

Purpose:
PublshXL uses DDE to eliminate traditional copy-and-paste and to quickly retrieve data marked by named ranges from Excel workbooks into Word.

Development tools used:
Word; Excel; DDE

How PublshXL works:
To use PublshXL:

1. Put both PublshXL.DOT and PublshXL.XLA into the same directory.

2. Assign named ranges in Excel to mark data for use in Word.

3. Start a new document based on PublshXL.DOT. Position the cursor where you want to paste the Excel data, and then run the PublishExcelData macro by clicking its toolbar button.

4. Word launches Excel (if it isn't running already), opens the PublshXL add-in, lets users select an Excel workbook and range name, and then pastes this range into Word.

The following diagram illustrates PublshXL's overall structure:

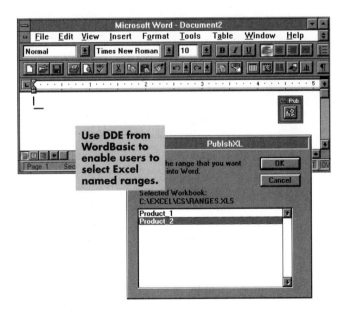

PublshXL.DOT contains the WordBasic macro PublishExcelData, which initiates the DDE conversation with Excel. Word then opens PublshXL.XLA (the Excel add-in) and uses a DDEExecute command to run the add-in's main subroutine, PublishR. This routine controls everything that happens in Excel.

When it's finished, PublishExcelData terminates the DDE conversation, pastes the range that users selected into Word, and then closes Excel.

How PublshXL.DOT Uses DDE to Retrieve Data from Excel

The main difficulty you face with any DDE operation is to provide users with as much freedom as possible while keeping the DDE client in at least nominal control of the process. One aspect of "control" in DDE is that the DDE client has to initiate *everything*. For example, if Word starts a DDE conversation with Excel, Word can execute commands in Excel. It can use the DDEPoke command to send data to Excel, and it can use the DDERequest command to retrieve data from Excel. Because the conversation is so one-sided, you have to carefully structure business applications that use DDE.

At one level, Excel can't do anything but respond to Word's initiatives. On the other hand, that response can be fairly expansive. The response can be an entire Excel application, as long as Word starts it and as long as Word gets the data it needs when the application is done. Excel can't initiate any contact with Word—not through DDE commands or OLE automation—until Word officially terminates the conversation with the DDETerminate command.

When you use DDE, it's not always obvious how best to transfer data from Excel to Word. Here are two options that I use:

■ In Excel, write data (including data that users select) to a range in an Excel sheet, and then have Word request that data.

■ Use Excel to copy data to the Clipboard, and then use Word to paste it. This is an especially good method for transferring charts and tables from Excel to Word. (DDERequest and DDEPoke can handle text only—no graphics.) I use this method in PublshXL.

Using DDE Between Word and Excel

Word's PublishExcelData macro performs four tasks:

■ It starts a DDE conversation with Excel.

■ It opens the PublshXL.XLA add-in and then runs the PublshR macro that it contains.

■ It ends the DDE conversation with Excel.

■ It pastes the data that users select (and that Excel copies to the Clipboard) into the Word document.

The syntax for DDE commands is fairly standard across DDE client applications. What differs most is the functionality provided by the DDE servers. For example, although Excel responds to DDEExecute commands, those commands have to be written in the Excel version 4 macro language. Most DDE conversations, however, start in the same way.

Initiating a DDE conversation with Excel Before starting a DDE conversation, determine whether the server application is already running, and then set a flag indicating whether to close the server application at the end of the DDE session. The following code from PublshXL.DOT's PublishExcelData macro does this.

```
IsXLRunning = AppIsRunning("Microsoft Excel")
If IsXLRunning = 0 Then
   Shell "Excel.EXE", 1
   AppActivate "Microsoft Word", 1
   XLFlag = 1
End If
```

Once Excel is running, say "hello," which looks like this in DDE-speak:

```
ChannelNumber = DDEInitiate("Excel", "System")
```

The variable ChannelNumber is an integer that uniquely identifies this conversation. (ChannelNumber is very much like the ODBC ConnectionString.) Each DDE server defines its own application name (see Figure 12-2 for a list of names used by Microsoft products), and each supports a variety of different topics. The one topic that nearly all DDE servers support is the general topic "System," which I use here. (Another popular topic is a particular filename.)

Application	DDE Application
Access	MSAccess
Excel	Excel
Word	WinWord
Project	Project
Windows Program Manager	ProgMan

Figure 12-2. *Application names for use with DDE.*

Executing DDE commands in Excel Once you use the code shown above to establish a DDE connection, you can execute commands using DDEExecute and the Excel version 4 macro language. If you're not familiar with this language, you can record the code by selecting Options in the Record New Macro dialog box and then selecting Microsoft Excel 4.0 Macro as the language. Also, remember the rules shown on the next page.

■ Enclose Excel's commands in square brackets ([]) so that WordBasic doesn't try to read them as its own.

■ Since Excel doesn't recognize Word's double quotes ("), use ASCII character 34 instead.

■ Activate Excel before you execute commands so that users can respond to Excel's dialog boxes.

Although you can send only Excel version 4 macro language commands to Excel using the DDEExecute command, you can use this macro language to launch VBA code, which is what I do in Word's PublishExcelData macro. The variable PublshXLDirectory$ stores the full path for the Publsh.XLA add-in, and Macro$ stores the name of the macro in that add-in to run (PublishR). The variable XLAll$ stores the full Excel version 4 macro language command to open the add-in and run the PublishR macro, which enables users to select a named range from an Excel workbook.

The following code runs the PublishR macro:

```
Q$ = Chr$(34)
Macro$ = "PublishR"
XLcmd1$ = "[OPEN(" + Q$ + PublshXLDirectory$ + Q$ + ")]"
XLcmd2$ = "[RUN(" + Q$ + Macro$ + Q$ + ")]"
XLAll$ = XLcmd1$ + XLcmd2$
AppActivate "Microsoft Excel", 1
DDEExecute ChannelNumber, XLAll$
```

Terminating a DDE conversation with Excel After Excel's PublishR macro ends, Word's PublishExcelData macro activates Word, "hangs up" on Excel, and then closes Excel if it wasn't open when you started. The following code does this:

```
AppActivate "Microsoft Word", 1
DDETerminate ChannelNumber
If XLFlag = 1 Then
  AppClose "Microsoft Excel"
End If
```

The code for the PublishExcelData macro follows. Note that Main controls the DDE conversion. It also calls the Extract$ function to parse the directory in which PublshXL.DOT is stored. (This function is similar to the one used in Excel's PublishR macro.)

```
Sub Main
  On Error Goto ErrorTrap
  ScreenUpdating 0
```

```
'Copy dummy text to the Clipboard in case users don't select
'anything in Excel.
  EditBookmark .Name = "BackToHere"

'Go to end of document and insert an empty space; this
'prevents cutting the BackToHere bookmark in an empty document.
  EndOfDocument : Insert Chr$(32)
  EditBookmark .Name = "StartDummyText"
  Insert "You didn't copy an Excel range to the Clipboard..."
  EditGoTo "StartDummyText" : EndOfLine 1 : EditCut
  EditGoTo "BackToHere"
  EditBookmark .Name = "BackToHere", .Delete
  EditBookmark .Name = "StartDummyText", .Delete

'Current directory so you can return at end of macro.
  WhereAmI$ = Files$(".")

'Excel add-in--PublshXL.XLA--has to be in same directory as template;
'check whether it is. Note that this code gets whatever directory
'PublshXL.DOT is in, which might not be the official Word \Template
'directory.
  Dim dlg As FileSummaryInfo
  GetCurValues dlg
  PublshXLDirectory$ = Extract$(dlg.Template, 0)

'Is Excel add-in in this directory?
  ChDir PublshXLDirectory$
  WW2_FileFind .Title = "", .Subject = "", .Author = "",→
    .Keywords = "", .SearchPath = Directory$, .Text =→
    "", .SavedBy = "", .DateCreatedFrom = "",→
    .DateCreatedTo = "", .DateSavedFrom = "", .DateSavedTo→
    = "", .Name = "PublshXL.XLA", .Location = "Path Only",→
    .MatchCase = 0, .Options = 0, .SortBy = 4, .View =→
    1, .SelectedFile = 1

'If Excel add-in isn't in the same directory as PublshXL.DOT...
  a = CountFoundFiles()
  If a <> 0 Then
    MsgBox "You must have PublshXL.XLA in the same directory as→
      PublshXL.DOT.", "PublshXL", 16
    Goto BYE
  End If

'Is Excel running?
  IsXLRunning = AppIsRunning("Microsoft Excel")
```

(continued)

```
'No...
  If IsXLRunning = 0 Then
    Shell "Excel.EXE", 1
    AppActivate "Microsoft Word", 1
    XLFlag = 1
  End If

'Yes and No...
  ChannelNumber = DDEInitiate("Excel", "System")
  Q$ = Chr$(34)
  Macro$ = "PublishR"

'Excel commands must be in the Excel version 4 macro language.
'Command to open Excel add-in.
  XLcmd1$ = "[OPEN(" + Q$ + PublshXLDirectory$ + Q$ + ")]"

'Command to run the PublishR subroutine in the add-in.
  XLcmd2$ = "[RUN(" + Q$ + Macro$ + Q$ +  ")]"

'Put both commands into a single string so you can run them through
'a single DDEExecute command.
  XLAll$ = XLcmd1$ + XLcmd2$

'Activate Excel.
  AppActivate "Microsoft Excel", 1

'Execute Excel commands.
  DDEExecute ChannelNumber, XLAll$

'At the end of the Excel PublishR subroutine, switch back to Word.
  AppActivate "Microsoft Word", 1

'End DDE.
  DDETerminate ChannelNumber

'Paste Excel range into Word; the Excel PublishR subroutine pasted
'it to the Clipboard.
  EditPaste

'Restore Excel to the way Word found it.
  If XLFlag = 1 Then
    AppClose "Microsoft Excel"
  End If

  Goto BYE

ErrorTrap:
  If Err > 0 Then MsgBox "An error occurred in PublishExcelData.→
```

```
      Check to see whether it did what you expected, and if not, try↵
      selecting the command again. ERROR = " + Str$(Err),↵
      "PublishExcelData", 48

BYE:
  ChDir WhereAmI$
  ScreenUpdating 1
End Sub



Function Extract$(strFullPath$, fPathOrFile)
'Find the place of the last backslash. If there is no backslash,
'find the place of the colon.
  If InStr(strFullPath$, "\") = 0 Then
    iPlace = InStr(strFullPath$, ":")
  Else
    iPlace = 0
    While 1 = 1
      iNewPlace = InStr(iPlace + 1, strFullPath$, "\")
      If iNewPlace = 0 Then Goto ExitWhile
      iPlace = iNewPlace
    Wend
  End If

ExitWhile:
'Return path if second argument is 0.
  If fPathOrFile = 0 Then
    Extract$ = Left$(strFullPath$, iPlace)

'Return filename if second argument is 1.
  ElseIf fPathOrFile = 1 Then
    Extract$ = Right$(strFullPath$, Len(strFullPath$) - iPlace)
  End If
End Function
```

The Publsh.XLA Add-In

As described above, Word's PublishExcelData macro calls Excel's PublishR macro in the Publsh.XLA add-in. PublishR, in turn, calls the SelectXLBook subroutine to open a dialog box for users to select an Excel workbook. It then opens another dialog box for selecting the named range to paste into Word.

The VBA for Excel code for the Publsh.XLA add-in follows.

```
Option Explicit
Dim objPublishR As Object
Dim blnCancel As Boolean
```

(continued)

```
'Path of selected Excel workbook.
  Dim strSelectedFile As String

'Name of selected Excel workbook.
  Dim strFileName As String


Sub PublishR()
  On Error Resume Next

'Name of range to copy to the Clipboard.
  Dim ImportRange As String

'Index of item selected from list box.
  Dim intSelected As Integer

  Set objPublishR = ThisWorkbook.DialogSheets("dlgPublishR")
  Application.ScreenUpdating = False
  Application.DisplayAlerts = False

'Call sub to display the File Open dialog box to allow
'users to select a workbook.
SelectWorkbook:
  SelectXLBook

'If user cancels the File Open dialog box...
  If blnCancel = True Then

'Close active workbook without saving it and close PublishXL.XLA.
    ActiveWorkbook.Close(False)
    Workbooks("PublishXL.XLA").Close
    Exit Sub
  End If

'Show the dialog box dlgPublishR.
  blnCancel = False
  objPublishR.[RangeNames].RemoveAllItems
  objPublishR.Show

'If user clicks the Cancel button in dlgPublishR, it calls the
'cmdCancel_Click procedure, which sets the flag blnCancel to True,
'and then returns to this line, which returns to the first
'dialog box.
  If blnCancel Then GoTo SelectWorkbook

'If the user clicks OK, the following code runs.
'The reason this isn't in a "cmdOK_Click" procedure is that
```

```
'the Goto method used in the CopyToClipboard procedure doesn't
'work if the dialog box is still active. (The dialog box would be
'active if a cmdOK_Click procedure were running.)

  intSelected = objPublishR.[RangeNames].ListIndex
  If intSelected = 0 Then intSelected = 1
  ImportRange = objPublishR.[RangeNames].List(intSelected)

  Application.ScreenUpdating = True
  CopyToClipboard ImportRange

End Sub


'User cancels dlgPublishR...
Sub cmdCancel_Click()
  blnCancel = True
  ActiveWorkbook.Close
End Sub


'Displays File Open dialog box for user to select an Excel workbook.
Sub SelectXLBook()
'Prompt user to select a file.
  blnCancel = False
  strSelectedFile = Application.GetOpenFilename("Excel workbooks→
    (*.xls),*.xls", , "Select an Excel File")
  If strSelectedFile = False Then
    blnCancel = True
    Exit Sub
  End If
  Workbooks.Open filename:=strSelectedFile
  strFileName = Extract(strSelectedFile, 1)
End Sub


'Initialize dlgPublishR dialog box.
Sub Dialog_Show()
  Dim objDefinedName As Object

  objPublishR.[WorkbookName].Caption = strSelectedFile
  For Each objDefinedName In ActiveWorkbook.Names
    objPublishR.[RangeNames].AddItem Text:=objDefinedName.Name
  Next objDefinedName
End Sub
```

(continued)

```
'Copies range to the Clipboard.
Sub CopyToClipboard(ByVal strRange As String)
  Workbooks(strFileName).Activate
  Application.Goto Reference:=strRange
  ActiveSheet.Range(strRange).Copy

'Close active workbook without saving it and close PublishXL.XLA.
  ActiveWorkbook.Close(False)
  Workbooks("PublishXL.XLA").Close
End Sub


'Extracts the path or the filename from a full path string.
Function Extract(ByVal sFullPath As String, ByVal fPathOrFile→
  As Integer) As String
  Dim iPlace As Integer
  Dim iNewPlace As Integer

'Find the place of the last backslash. If there is no backslash,
'find the place of the colon.
  If InStr(sFullPath, "\") = 0 Then
    iPlace = InStr(sFullPath, ":")
  Else
    iPlace = 0
    Do
      iNewPlace = InStr(iPlace + 1, sFullPath, "\")
      If iNewPlace = 0 Then Exit Do
      iPlace = iNewPlace
    Loop
  End If

'Depending on the value of the argument fPathOrFile, return
'the path or the filename.
  If fPathOrFile = 0 Then        'return path
    Extract = Left$(sFullPath, iPlace)
  ElseIf fPathOrFile = 1 Then    'return filename
    Extract = Right$(sFullPath, Len(sFullPath) - iPlace)
  End If
End Function
```

PART

THREE

The Professional's
Handbook

The last part of this book addresses the last part of the development process—the finishing touches, if you will, for delivering custom business applications to end users:

- Windows Help, which you can use to add context-sensitive Help to business applications and which lets you create online publications and presentations

- Documentation, training, and support, which are key elements for ensuring that the development process produces applications that are, in fact, used productively

- Tips for successfully managing application rollouts of both shrink-wrapped products and custom business applications

My colleagues frequently repeat the adage that the last 10 percent of a project requires 90 percent of the effort. In many ways, context-sensitive Help, training, documentation, and a well-managed rollout make up that last 10 percent. They might not require 90 percent of your effort, but they can play a disproportionate role in determining how users (and management) rate the overall application development process and your final product.

13

Building Publication and Presentation Systems with Windows Help

When PCs first made their way onto our desktops, computer evangelists trumpeted the advent of the paperless office. Well, they trumpeted too soon. Rather than encouraging people to read on line, PCs have made it easier to create more paper. In fact, most people I've talked to about online publications admit to not really liking to read on line because of eyestrain. So lately I've been thinking about ways to make online reading more appealing.

One obvious way is to spruce up online publications so that people *want* to read them—by adding a dash of color, bigger fonts, wider margins, and a catchy graphic or two. Bigger fonts and wider margins, by the way, are more than cosmetic. They make online text easier to read. Graphics and color are also more than "Windows-dressing" because they capture attention in a way that a space crammed with words does not.

The next question is: What tools make it easy to *create* appealing online publications? One answer is Microsoft Windows Help.

Windows Help is more than a tool for creating context-sensitive documentation for your latest business application. You can use it to create policy manuals, newsletters, presentations, hypertext slide shows—you name it. Windows Help is a giant step toward the paperless office.

One reason that Windows Help is such an effective publishing tool is its market presence: Everyone who has Windows has Help. WINHELP.EXE (the "viewer") is installed automatically in the Windows system directory when you install Windows 3.*x*. If you create a Help-based publication or presentation with the standard TrueType fonts and the 16 standard colors available on VGA monitors, you can distribute it to virtually everyone with Windows. Since everyone who has used Help will know how to handle your Help-based publication, you have a potential audience of 50 million or so.

NOTE	To launch Help files by double-clicking an icon in Program Manager or a .HLP file in File Manager, use the Associate command on File Manager's File menu to associate the .HLP extension with WinHelp.EXE.

To start building online publications and presentations with Windows Help, you need to understand the following issues, which are covered in this chapter:

- How to obtain the tools you need to create Help files. (See the section titled "Tools for Creating Help-Based Publications and Presentations.")

- How to structure hypertext files. (See the section titled "Building Help Files: The Big Picture.")

- How to use the WHAT6 template for Microsoft Word to create .RTF (Rich Text Format) files. (You can't use standard Word .DOC files to create Help; see the section titled "Using WHAT.")

- How to create hot-spotted graphics with SHED.EXE. You can click hot-spotted graphics to do such things as display additional information and run animations. (See the section titled "Using Graphics in Help-Based Publications and Presentations.")

- How to create .HPJ (Help project) files. These files (which are in ASCII text format) provide structural information about your Help file. (See the section titled "Using Help Project Files.")

- How to create context-sensitive Help. (See the section titled "Creating Context-Sensitive Help.")

FYI

Business Uses for Windows Help

Companies are beginning to use Windows Help in a number of nontraditional ways:

■ **For online publications of all sorts.** Because anyone running Windows can launch Help, some companies are starting to distribute corporate policy manuals and related materials as online Help files. This method provides important control, distribution, and security benefits:

  ■ Since Help files are compiled, online publications are tamperproof.

  ■ Because you can distribute Help files from the network, online publications can be secured so that only a certain group of people (for example, managers) can access them.

  ■ Online publications are relatively easy and inexpensive to update because there's no need to reprint or redistribute the document. Simply upload the latest version to the network, and send out e-mail alerting everyone to the fact.

  ■ People who use online publications can take advantage of Help's built-in features—for example, the ability to bookmark topics of particular interest, annotate topics, and print out specific information.

■ **For marketing and sales presentations.** Although it's not as easy to create a Windows Help file as it is to create a Microsoft PowerPoint slide show, Help-based presentations offer several important advantages:

  ■ They're "hyper" rather than linear. You can show ancillary bits of information in secondary windows without leaving the main screen. This creates a quasi-multimedia feel and a potentially exciting presentation.

  ■ Because they're compiled and can be greatly compressed, highly graphical Help files run faster than highly graphical PowerPoint presentations.

  ■ You can distribute them to anyone who has Windows (which has a built-in viewer).

> ■ **For training materials.** One company I work with decided to use Help to present information from training seminars that they hold several times a year. They built an easy-to-use, interesting-to-view "encyclopedia" of information that people can use for both training and reference purposes. They designed a highly graphical format with a quasi-multimedia feel that doesn't require extra hardware—it runs on all Windows PCs that use a VGA monitor, including laptops.

Tools for Creating Help-Based Publications and Presentations

The Help compiler (which comes in three versions—HCP.EXE, HC.EXE, and HC31.EXE) is distributed with Visual Basic, Visual C++, and the Word for Windows 6.0 Help Authoring Toolkit (available as an unsupported product on the Microsoft Developer Network CD). The Help compiler, a word processor, and some know-how are all you really need to create Help files. But you can simplify the process further by using the Help Authoring Toolkit. The most essential tools from this kit are on the *Office Solutions* disk included with this book. They include the following:

■ The Help compiler (HC.EXE) and an error log (HC.ERR). Copy these files to your Windows directory. Note that the Help compiler runs under MS-DOS, not Windows.

■ A slightly modified version of the WHAT6 template (WHAT6.DOT), which simplifies the process of creating Help files. Copy this template to your Word template directory.

■ WHAT6.INI, which you should copy to your Windows directory.

■ SHED.EXE, an application that lets you add *hot spots* (pops, jumps, and macros) to graphics and compresses these graphics. Copy this file to its own directory, and attach it to an icon.

This chapter focuses on how to build Help files using the modified version of the WHAT6 template provided on the *Office Solutions* disk. (See Appendix A for other tools for creating Help.)

Building Help Files: The Big Picture

To create Help files from scratch—without using a tool such as the WHAT6 template—follow these three general steps:

- Include codes in .RTF (Rich Text Format) files to format the Help file, including popping up text, jumping to new topics, and running macros; creating a Search capability; and creating a browse sequence.

- Create an .HPJ (Help project) file that contains the code that establishes the Help file's structure, including which .RTF files to compile, whether to compress the Help file, and use of secondary windows.

- Compile the .HPJ file using the Help compiler (HC.EXE). The compiler reads the .HPJ file; calls the .RTF files listed; reads the codes in the .RTF files to create pops, jumps, and macros; and creates a Help file with a .HLP extension).

The WHAT6 template features built-in commands for each of these steps. Because these commands are written in WordBasic, you can modify them to better suit your particular needs. For example, I changed the version of the template provided with the *Office Solutions* disk to simplify the process of turning existing documents into Help files.

Structuring Hypertext

Help files are the now-classic example of Windows hypertext, just as HyperCard, the first hypertext application available for the desktop, is the classic example of hypertext for the Macintosh. Help files let people use information in an organized but seemingly random fashion—*organized* because someone planned and built the bridges that lead from one concept to another, and *random* because users can cross whatever bridges they need.

Written documents are sequential: They have a beginning, a middle, and an end. Hypertext publications, however, let users jump directly to the topic that most interests them, drill down further into that topic, and jump to related topics or to entirely new topics. Because of this, Help authors must structure Help files carefully, building bridges between related topics and providing mechanisms for users to take up new threads.

One common way to organize Help files is to provide a table of contents from which users can jump into the publication's main topics. If you think of these main topics as first-level, second-level, and perhaps third-level headings (which Word users would style as Heading 1, 2, and 3), the file's basic organization falls into place quickly.

The "Hyper" in Hypertext

Jumps and *pops* put the "hyper" into hypertext. Jumps are live (clickable) text or graphics (also called *hot spots*) that let you jump directly from one topic to another. Pops are hot spots that display additional information (such as definitions) on top of the current screen. To understand how to create jumps and pops, you have to understand two concepts: topics and context strings. Organize the document that serves as the basis of your Help file (which must be saved, before compiling, as an .RTF file) into a series of discrete *topics* (technically, text that users can jump to or pop up). Each Help file topic is sandwiched between hard page breaks. *Context strings* tie the Help file's clickable text and graphics to the various topics (see Figure 13-1).

This is the basic idea: First you name topics by assigning them a context string. (Use the Topic command on WHAT6's Insert menu.) Next you create jumps and pops by indicating which topic to jump to or pop up when users click the text or graphic marked as a jump or a pop.

To mark text as a jump or a pop, use special formatting (recognized by the Help compiler) in the document that serves as the basis of your Help file.

- To turn text into a jump, format it with a *double* underline and follow it immediately with a context string formatted as hidden text. (Use Word's Format Font command.)

- To turn text into a pop, format it with a *single* underline and follow it immediately with a context string formatted as hidden text.

When you create jumps and pops using the WHAT6 template, it applies this formatting automatically when you choose Jump or Popup Hotspot from the Insert menu.

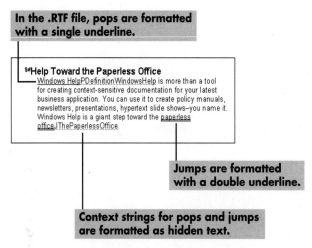

Figure 13-1. *Jumps and pops put the "hyper" into hypertext. Context strings associate jumps and pops with the various topics in the Help file.*

Hypertext macros

In addition to jumps and pops, which are the most common, Windows Help provides a third type of hot spot: the *macro* hot spot. The Help language includes 55 macros (and 20 abbreviated commands that duplicate the main language). You can use these commands to create buttons for the Help file, to launch applications, and generally to make your Help files more sophisticated.

The Macro Hotspot command on the WHAT6 Insert menu lists these macros and provides sample syntax. (See "Creating Hot-Spotted Graphics" later in this chapter for an example of how to use macros.)

Context strings: The very short story of a very powerful tool

As I mentioned before, Help files are both organized and random. They are organized by their creator and are random to users, who can click any hot spot.

Context strings (the internal names that you assign to each Help topic) are the organizing principle behind Help files. When you create a jump or a pop, you specify how you want users to be able to access a particular topic. Although you can jump to a topic at one point and pop it up at another, in most cases you won't do this because pops have to be short enough to fit within a screen, whereas jumps can be quite long.

Here's the rule: Every topic you want to jump to or pop up must be named with a context string (no spaces or punctuation marks allowed). When you create hot spots on text or graphics, reference the context string of the topic that users jump to or pop up.

Name that context string Since context strings literally hold your Help file together, the choice of a naming convention is one of the most important decisions you'll make. As the weeks pass, as your Help file gets bigger and as you remember less and less of what you did the week before, you'll bless your naming convention because it will be your only clue as to what goes where. I use the following conventions:

- Every context string that marks a topic users can jump to starts with a J.

- Every context string that marks a topic users can pop up starts with a P.

- After that, every context string contains the title I use for that topic, minus spaces and punctuation marks. For example, if the topic title is "Help Toward a Paperless Office," I might assign it the context string *JHelpTowardAPaperlessOffice*. (Note that context strings are not case sensitive.) To enable users to pop up the definition of Windows Help, I might create a topic titled "Definition: Windows Help" and assign it the context string *PDefinitionWindowsHelp*.

The Raw Ingredients of Help-Based Publications and Presentations

The following are the ingredients for Help files. (You don't need WHAT6, but I generally use it as a starting point.)

- WINHELP.EXE (which comes with Windows 3.1).

- HC.EXE.

- One .HPJ file, which you can create in one of two ways: 1) You can use the WHAT6 View File command to create one automatically, or 2) you can create one manually. (See the section titled "Creating Custom .HPJ Files" later in this chapter for more information on how to create .HPJ files that add color and secondary windows to Help files.) The .HPJ file contains directions for building the Help file, including the path for the .RTF file or files containing the text, the path for the graphics, the background color, which buttons appear, and so on. This file is in standard ASCII (text-only) format.

- As many .RTF files as you like. You can create these with the WHAT6 template, with Word alone (use the Save As command on the File menu), or with any word processor that lets you save files in Rich Text Format. The .RTF files contain the text for the Help file, the graphics (or references to graphics, if you use SHED.EXE), codes marking the text that's clickable, codes marking the text to pop up or where to jump when users click clickable text, codes marking the text that appears in the Search dialog box, and so on.

- SHED.EXE (a.k.a. the "hot-spot editor"), which lets you create *hypergraphics* (add multiple pops, jumps, and macros to graphics). See the section titled "Using SHED.EXE" later in this chapter for more information on this tool. You can use any program (including PowerPoint, Paintbrush, or CorelDRAW!) to create hypergraphics and then paste them into the hot-spot editor. (By the way, great graphics are a key ingredient of dynamic online publications and presentations.)

Using WHAT

This section steps you through the process of creating a Help file using the WHAT6 template. I've included the finished .RTF file in the sidebar titled "A Sample .RTF File (Including Footnotes)" later in this chapter.

> **NOTE** The Help compiler can't interpret "smart quotes" (curly quotes and apostrophes), so you should turn off this feature (using the AutoCorrect command on the Tools menu) when you use WHAT6.

1. After you install the WHAT6 template, create a new document based on it by choosing New from the File menu. (To use an existing document, open it and attach it to WHAT6 using the Template command on the File menu.)

2. WHAT6 uses Arial as its Normal font. To use another font, redefine Normal. Remember to use only TrueType fonts or built-in fonts in Windows, such as MS Sans Serif or MS Serif, that most users have installed.

3. Type your table of contents. The Help compiler recognizes the first topic as the table of contents (which users can return to easily by clicking the Help file's Contents button). Format the title "Table of Contents" with the Heading 1 style. Type two or three topic titles to get started.

> **NOTE** If you prefer, you can type your topics before typing the table of contents and then generate the table of contents using the Table of Contents command on the Insert menu.

4. Now you're ready to create topics for your Help file. Position the cursor in a blank paragraph after the table of contents, and then choose Topic from the Insert menu. WHAT6 pops up the Insert Topic dialog box (see Figure 13-2 on the next page). Type a title and a context string—the other features (summarized in Figure 13-3 on pages 465–66) are optional. In general, you'll want to ensure that the End Of File option at the bottom of the dialog box is selected. Click OK when you're done.

   WHAT6 adds a hard page break above the title (which it formats in the Heading 1 style) and a string of characters in front of it (the more information you entered in the dialog box, the longer the string). These characters are footnote references that the Help compiler uses to build your Help file (see Figure 13-3). Choose Footnotes from the View menu to see them in detail.

   Choose the Topic command from the Edit menu (or choose the Footnotes command from the View menu) to change the features for a particular topic. If you're working from an existing file rather than creating a new one, highlight the heading for a topic, and then choose the Topic command from the Insert menu. WHAT6 provides a context string automatically by eliminating the spaces and punctuation marks from the heading.

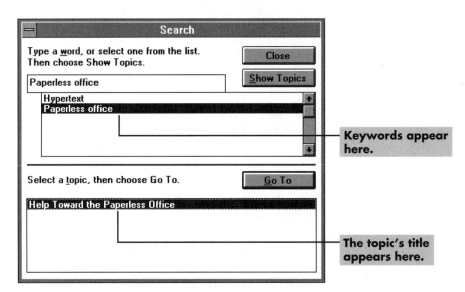

Figure 13-2. *The Insert Topic dialog box (top) enables you to specify a context string as well as the other features associated with Help topics. For example, use keywords to create list topics in the Help File's Search dialog box (bottom).*

Option	General Information	Footnote Symbol
Title	Here are some guidelines for creating topic titles: ■ The title should be identical to the topic's heading. ■ Every topic that users can jump to and that is accessible through the Search dialog box must start with a title. Topics displayed only as pops do not have to have a title. ■ Titles can be up to 127 characters long (including spaces). ■ Help uses the following rules to sort titles for the Search capability: Short titles precede long titles; punctuation precedes numbers; numbers precede letters.	$
Context string	Every topic must have at least one unique context string. No spaces or punctuation marks are allowed, except for periods (.) and underscores (_).	#
Keywords	The Help compiler lists the keywords in the Search dialog box (which users access by clicking the Search button). To list more than one keyword or phrase, separate them with semicolons.	K
Browse sequence	Browse sequences enable users to read topics sequentially. When you use this feature, the system adds Browse buttons to the Help file. (They look like fast-forward and rewind buttons on a VCR.) Browse sequences are the only topics that should appear in sequential order in the .RTF file. The reason? The browse sequence is determined by both the code used (+) and the topics' sequence in the .RTF file.	+

(continued)

465

Option	General Information	Footnote Symbol
Build tag	You can share a single .RTF file among several Help projects by using build tags to mark the topics you want to compile. In addition to adding a tag (such as "User") to all topics that belong in a particular version of Help, you have to add a [BUILDTAGS] section to the .HPJ file.	*
Entry macro	When you add entry macros to a topic, Help runs them whenever users open that topic by jumping to it, using the Browse buttons, or using the Search dialog box.	!
Comment	Anything goes! Since the Help compiler ignores comments, you can write whatever you want.	@

Figure 13-3. *Summary of the footnote codes that the Help compiler uses to turn an .RTF file into a Help file.*

5. As you type the text for your Help topics, keep in mind the following formatting tips (see Figure 13-4):

   ■ **Bullets.** Most bullets that appear in your document don't translate into Help. To create round bullets for your Help file, select the TrueType Symbol font, and with NumLock on, press Alt+0183 on the numeric keypad.

   ■ **Hanging indents.** To create hanging indents that translate from Word into the final Help file, you must add a tab stop at the indent.

   ■ **Nonscrolling headings.** When you have a long Help topic that users have to scroll through, keep the title on screen at all times so users don't get lost. To do this, format the headings with the Keep With Next option (available through the Text Flow tab of the Paragraph dialog box).

   ■ **Margins.** I generally narrow the width of paragraphs to 3 inches or less in topics that I use for pops, because they look better.

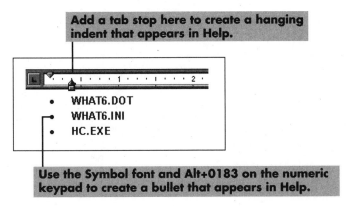

Figure 13-4. *To create a hanging indent, add a tab stop at the indent. To create a bullet, use the TrueType Symbol font and press Alt+0183 on the numeric keypad. (Make sure that NumLock is on.)*

6. After entering a table of contents and a few topics, you're ready to create hot spots. First, create jumps from the table of contents into the Help file. You might also want to create a jump from a particular word or phrase into a topic that discusses that word or phrase more extensively.

   To create a jump, highlight the word or phrase for users to click, and then choose Jump or Popup Hotspot from the Insert menu. WHAT6 opens a dialog box with the highlighted text marked as the hot spot (see Figure 13-5 on the next page).

   Type the context string. If you want the hot spot to look like the standard Windows hot spots (green underlined text for jumps and green dotted text for pops), leave the Unformatted check box unchecked. If you turn on the Unformatted feature, the hot spot will appear in the Help file just as you formatted it in the document.

   Use the File Name option to jump to a topic in another Help file. (Type that file's name in the File Name text box.) Use the Window Name option to make the topic that users jump to appear in a secondary window. (See the section titled "Referencing Secondary Windows" later in this chapter for more information.)

   You create pops in the same way that you create jumps, except that you select the Pop option.

NOTE To make jumps and pops easier to distinguish in the Word document, WHAT6 colors the hidden text for jumps dark red and the hidden text for pops dark cyan. This coloring has no effect on the resulting Help file.

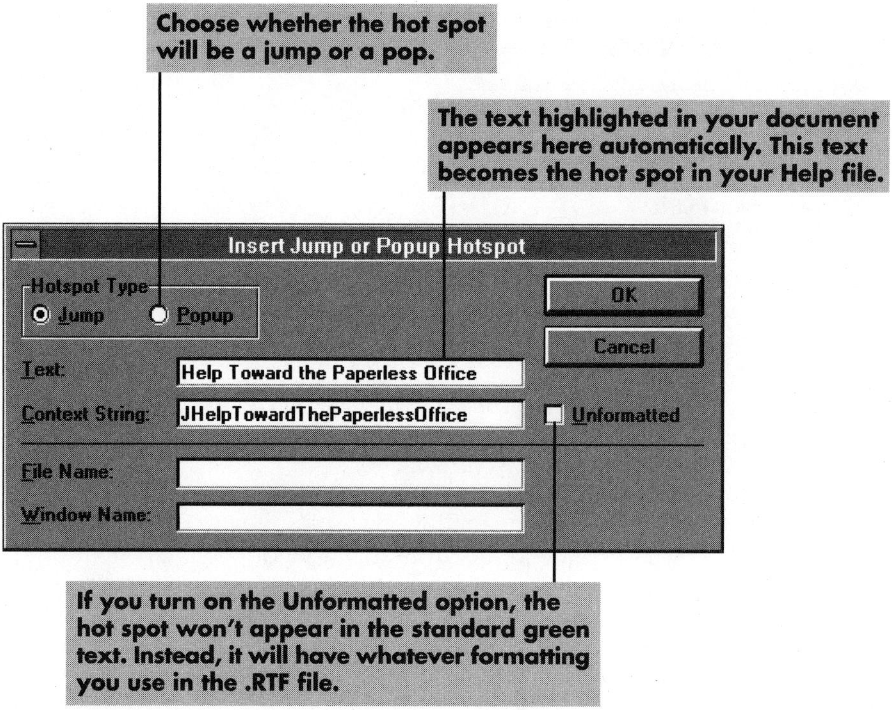

Choose whether the hot spot
will be a jump or a pop.

The text highlighted in your document
appears here automatically. This text
becomes the hot spot in your Help file.

Insert Jump or Popup Hotspot

Hotspot Type

◉ Jump   ○ Popup

OK

Cancel

Text: Help Toward the Paperless Office

Context String: JHelpTowardThePaperlessOffice   ☐ Unformatted

File Name:

Window Name:

If you turn on the Unformatted option, the
hot spot won't appear in the standard green
text. Instead, it will have whatever formatting
you use in the .RTF file.

Figure 13-5. *To format text as a hot spot, highlight it and then choose Jump or Popup Hotspot from the Insert menu. The highlighted text appears in the first text box. Enter the context string, and select either the Jump or the Pop option.*

7. To turn your document into a Help file, choose File from the View menu. WHAT6 opens a dialog box in which you enter the path for the graphics you've referenced. If you haven't referenced any graphics, click OK to continue. WHAT6 performs the following tasks:

- It saves an .RTF file named ~WHAT~.RTF in either the directory specified by the TMP environment variable or the root directory (for example, C:\).

- It saves an .HPJ file named ~WHAT~.HPJ in the TMP or the root directory.

- It saves an error log named ~WHAT~.ERR in the TMP or the root directory.

- It compiles the .RTF file and the .HPJ file into a Help file named ~WHAT~.HLP and saves it in the TMP or the root directory.

If you want to save any of these files for future use, use File Manager to rename them. The following is the .HPJ file that WHAT6 creates automatically for the .RTF file shown earlier in the sidebar titled "A Sample .RTF File (Including Footnotes)."

```
[options]
errorlog = ~what~.err

[files]
~what~.rtf

[config]
BrowseButtons()
```

FYI

A Sample .RTF File (Including Footnotes)

The following document, HelpDoc.DOC, is on the *Office Solutions* disk included with this book. I use angled brackets (< >) to denote elements such as hard page breaks that appear in the document but are difficult to represent in print.

Table of Contents

Help Toward the Paperless Office⌡HelpTowardThePaperlessOffice

The Raw Ingredients⌡TheRawIngredients

<HARD PAGE BREAK>

$#K**Help Toward the Paperless Office**

Windows HelpPDefinitionWindowsHelp is more than a tool for creating context-sensitive documentation for your latest business application. You can use it to create policy manuals, newsletters, presentations, hypertext slide shows—you name it. Windows Help is a giant step toward the paperless office.

One reason that Windows Help is such an effective publishing tool is that everyone who has Windows has Help. WINHELP.EXE (the "viewer") is installed automatically in the Windows system directory. If you create a Help-based publication or presentation with the standard TrueType fonts and the 16 standard colors available on VGA monitors, you can distribute it to virtually everyone with Windows.

<HARD PAGE BREAK>

#$**The Raw Ingredients**

- **WHAT6.DOT,** a Word for Windows template that includes a dozen or so commands that make it easier to build Help files

- **WHAT6.INI,** an INI file that stores WHAT6 settings, including the name of the Help compiler that you use

- **HC.EXE,** the Help compiler

- **HC.ERR,** an error log that records any errors that occur when Help compiles

- **SHED.EXE,** a program that lets you compress graphics and add "hot spots"—pops, jumps, and macros

<HARD PAGE BREAK>

$^{$\#}$**Definition: Windows Help**

Windows Help is the Windows hypertext system. Hypertext lets users jump directly to the topic that most interests them, drill down further into that topic, and jump to related topics or to entirely new topics.

<FOOTNOTES FOLLOW>

$^{$}$ Help Toward the Paperless Office

$^{\#}$ JHelpTowardThePaperlessOffice

^{K} Paperless office; Hypertext

$^{$}$ The Raw Ingredients

$^{\#}$ JTheRawIngredients

$^{$}$ Definition: Windows Help

$^{\#}$ PDefinitionWindowsHelp

FYI

How Help-Based Publications Fit onto Standard Desktops

Many firms are increasingly reluctant to add more software to desktops that are already hard to maintain. So instead of adding new software as needs arise, they're focusing on creating a standard desktop (including, perhaps, Microsoft Excel, Word, and even Windows Help) and then using that desktop as the starting point for developing new business applications.

Philip Morris is one such firm. The company's commitment to a standard desktop was one of the main reasons that the Philip Morris human resources department decided to produce online policy manuals using Windows Help rather than another hypertext package or Adobe Acrobat. Not only was the Help engine on all Windows desktops already, but it also worked on Macintosh desktops through a simple Excel macro.

To that end, Philip Morris developed a Word application that automatically converts documents into a fully formatted Help file (complete with jumps and pops). Even though they had to spend the money to develop this application, the solution was still a fraction of the cost of purchasing another site license, installing the software, and doing the inevitable customization.

Using Graphics in Help-Based Publications and Presentations

Help files support four types of graphics: bitmaps (.BMP), device independent bitmaps (.DIB), Windows metafiles (.WMF), and SHED.EXE files (.SHG). There are two ways to add these graphics to Help files:

- By adding them physically to documents
- By referencing the graphics files by name

Although I focus primarily on the second technique (because it's the more powerful of the two—see "Using SHED.EXE" on the next page), the following section provides a brief description of how to *add* graphics to .RTF files.

> **NOTE** You can find the sample files described in the following sections (HelpGrfx.DOC, HelpDemo.DOC, HelpMain.BMP, HelpGraf.EXE, and HelpDemo.HLP) on the *Office Solutions* disk included with this book.

Adding Graphics to .RTF Files

You add graphics to documents that serve as the basis for Help files just as you add them to any Word document—by pasting them from the Clipboard or by using the Picture command on the Insert menu. After they appear in your document, turn them into hot spots just as you would text. First, select the graphic. Next, choose Jump or Popup Hotspot from the Insert menu. Select the type—Jump or Popup—and then type the context string (see Figure 13-6 on the next page). After you compile the Help file, click the graphic to jump to or pop up topics.

> **NOTE** When you insert a graphic, use the Paragraph command on the Format menu to change WHAT6's line spacing to Single to accommodate the graphic's height.

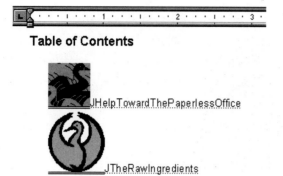

Figure 13-6. *Graphics formatted as jumps. Use HelpGrfx.DOC on the* Office Solutions *disk to test how this works.*

Using SHED.EXE

SHED.EXE (the "hot-spot editor") lets you create *hypergraphics*—in other words, it lets you add multiple jumps and pops to a single graphic. You can create graphics that serve as the basis for hypergraphics by using any graphics package—from Paintbrush to CorelDRAW! You can get these graphics into SHED.EXE by opening them directly (if they're saved as .BMP, .DIB, or .WMF) or by pasting them from the Clipboard.

SHED.EXE also compresses graphics files. For example, HelpMain.BMP (used for the main Help screen in the example in this section) is 31,262 bytes. I reduced the file to one-fifth of its original size (6686 bytes) by using SHED.EXE to save it as a .SHG file (pronounced "shag").

Creating hot-spotted graphics

Although you can turn a graphic that you physically added to a document into a hot spot, SHED.EXE lets you go further and hot-spot specific parts of graphics. For example, you can hot-spot one area (such as a button) to jump to a particular topic, and you can hot-spot another button (or, indeed, any portion of a graphic) to run a macro.

There are four steps to creating hot-spotted graphics:

1. After launching SHED.EXE, open a graphics file (.BMP, .DIB, .WMF, or .SHG) or paste one from the Clipboard.

2. The only thing that SHED.EXE can do is draw hot spots, so to draw one, simply click the graphic and then drag the mouse.

3. After drawing a hot spot, double-click it to open its Attributes dialog box. Select a type of hot spot (jump, pop, or macro), specify whether you want it to be visible (invisible generally looks more professional),

and then type the context string (for jumps and pops) or a macro (see Figure 13-7).

For example, the following macro runs HelpGraf.EXE (from the *Office Solutions* disk) as long as it's in either the same directory as the Help file or the Windows directory:

```
ExecProgram("HelpGraf.EXE", 0 )
```

The second argument specifies the window state of the executing program: 0 = Normal; 1 = Minimized; 2 = Maximized.

NOTE To run this macro from hot-spotted text in a document, use the same code, but precede the macro with a bang (!). When you use the Macro Hotspot command on WHAT6's Insert menu, it does this for you automatically. In a document, macros (like context strings) must be formatted as hidden text.

4. Save the file as a .SHG file.

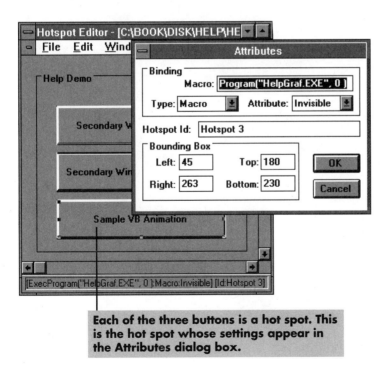

Each of the three buttons is a hot spot. This is the hot spot whose settings appear in the Attributes dialog box.

Figure 13-7. *In SHED.EXE, simply click and drag to draw a hot spot on a graphic. Double-click a hot spot to open its Attributes dialog box, and then specify the action for a hot spot to perform when users click it.*

Using .SHG files in .RTF files

When using hot-spotted graphics, you must *reference* those graphics from the document—you can't add them to the document directly. To reference them, follow these steps:

1. Create hot-spotted graphics as described in the previous section.

2. Choose the Graphic command from WHAT6's Insert menu (see Figure 13-8), and then type the filename. (Type the full path if your graphics aren't in a single directory.)

3. To center the graphics, keep the As Character option as the default (and center the resulting code); otherwise, select Left Aligned or Right Aligned.

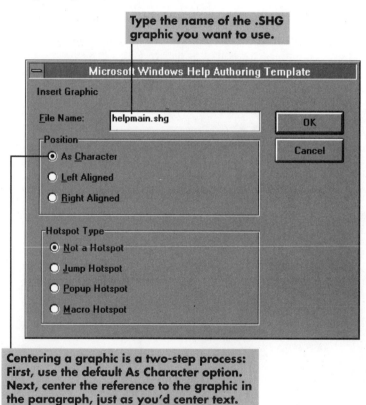

Figure 13-8. *When you use hot-spotted graphics, you must reference them in your document. To do this, choose Graphic from WHAT6's Insert menu.*

4. When you click OK, WHAT6 inserts the following into your document, where *bmX* = bmc (As Character), bml (Left Aligned), or bmr (Right Aligned):

```
{bmX NameOfFile}
```

5. When you choose File from the View menu, WHAT6 opens a dialog box prompting you to type a path for the graphics directory. Although you do not need to do this if you've referenced the graphics' full paths when you inserted them, it's generally easier to store all graphics in one directory and reference that directory in this dialog box.

After the Help file compiles, test the hot-spotted graphics by clicking them.

Using Help Project Files

The Help project file provides essential information on the overall structure of your Help file: for example, whether to compress it; what the copyright notice should be; which .RTF files to include; and the position, size, and colors of any *secondary windows*. (Secondary windows appear on top of the main Help window.) The table below summarizes several common commands for the structural elements of Help files that you can specify in .HPJ files.

Section	General Information
[OPTIONS]	This section is optional. If you use it, it must be the .HPJ file's first section. Here are some common options:
	BMROOT: Lists the path for bitmaps referenced by your .RTF file.
	COMPRESS: Indicates the level of compression. Use 0 for none, 1 for high, and "Medium" for medium.
	COPYRIGHT: Lets you post a copyright notice in your Help file's About box.
	ROOT: Specifies the directory for your .RTF files (and your graphics, if they're the same). This way, you don't have to type the files' full path in the [FILES] section. For example, this [OPTIONS] section sets a number of common options:

```
[OPTIONS]
errorlog = HelpDemo.ERR
title = Help Demo
compress = 0
copyright = Copyright 1994, Christine Solomon
warning = 3
; Don't need a separate bmroot command
; because it's the same as root.
root = c:\offsoln\help
```

(continued)

Section	General Information

[FILES]	This section, which is required, lists all the .RTF files you want to use to build the Help file. For example, this [FILES] section compiles two files into the Help file:
	
	`[FILES]`
	`c:\solution\help1.rtf`
	`c:\solution\help2.rtf`

[CONFIG]	Use this section to create custom buttons, to enable browse buttons, and to register DLLs and DLL functions. For example, the following [CONFIG] section uses the CreateButton macro to add a button named Index to the Help file Demo.HLP. Users click this button to jump to the Index topic, which has the context string JIndex. Note that btn_Index is the button's internal name assigned by the developer and that JumpID is a macro that jumps to the specified topic.
	
	`[CONFIG]`
	`CreateButton("btn_Index", "&Index",`↱
	`   "JumpID(` `demo.hlp', ` `JIndex')")`

[MAP]	Use this section to create context-sensitive Help by "mapping" context strings to context numbers. (See the section titled "Creating Context-Sensitive Help" later in this chapter.)
[WINDOWS]	Use this section to create secondary windows for Help files. You can have up to five secondary windows in addition to the main window, and you can define each window with its own colors, size, and location. (See the section titled "Creating Secondary Windows" below.)

Figure 13-9. *Commands available for use in .HPJ files. (.HPJ files are similar to INI files. For example, use text in square brackets to indicate sections and use semicolons to comment out lines.)*

Creating Custom .HPJ Files

The easiest way to create a custom .HPJ file is to start with the one that WHAT6 creates: ~WHAT~.HPJ. Open it in Word, and then save it as Text Only under another name and in a directory other than the root directory. (I always use the Windows directory because that's where the Help compiler, HC.EXE, is stored.) Type additional commands to structure and enhance your Help file.

Creating secondary windows

As you can see in Figure 13-9, the .HPJ file gives you a significant amount of control over Help files, even to the point of letting you create your own windows. A Help file can have up to six windows—the main Help window (always called "main") and five others—each with its own screen position, size, and colors. You never have to create a main window—unless you want its appearance to deviate from the Windows default.

To create a window in your Help file, enter the following information in the [WINDOWS] section of your .HPJ file:

- A name for the window, such as "main" or "Text."

- A caption for the window's title bar, such as "Help Demo" or "Sample Text Window."

- A size and position for the window, specified in pixels and enclosed in parentheses, as follows:

  ```
  (Left,Top,Width,Height)
  ```

  Windows Help always assumes that the screen is 1024 pixels wide, regardless of resolution.

- An argument indicating whether to use the size and position specified in the previous argument (if set to 0 or left blank) or to maximize the window (if set to 1).

- The background color of the window, specified in RGB values. (One of the easiest ways to get RGB values is from the Edit Colors command on Paintbrush's Options menu.)

- The background color of any nonscrolling area at the top of the window (where the topic title is).

I used the following [WINDOWS] section for HelpDemo.HPJ:

```
[WINDOWS]

main = "Help Demo", (200,200,570,700),, (192,192,192), (192,192,192)
Text = "Sample Text Window", (520,150,400,800),,,
Graphic = "Sample Graphic Window", (150,175,720,720),,⤳
  (255,255,128), (255,255,128)
```

Referencing secondary windows

It's easy to display text in a secondary window when you use WHAT6. When you hot-spot text as a jump, type the secondary window's name in the Insert Jump or Popup Hotspot dialog box. The hidden text associated with that jump looks similar to the following:

HotspotsJSecondaryWindowWithText>Text

The code to the left of the angled bracket (>) is the context string, and the code to right is the name of the secondary window (in this case, "Text"). When you use a hot spot in a .SHG file to jump to a secondary window, use exactly the same code.

Figure 13-10 shows HelpDemo.HLP's main and secondary windows.

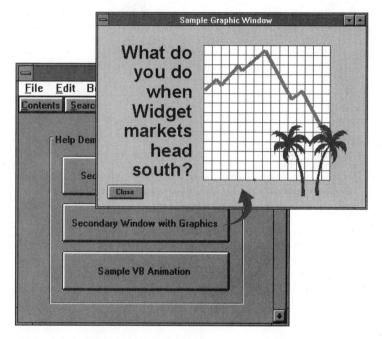

Figure 13-10. *The main window for the Help file HelpDemo.HLP. When you click the middle button, the "heading south" window opens. Click the Close button to close this window. The Close button runs the macro CloseWindow("Graphic"), where "Graphic" is the name of the secondary window.*

Compiling Custom .HPJ Files

To use a custom .HPJ file to provide the structure for your Help-based publication or presentation, you must compile your Help file manually. Follow the steps below:

1. Choose Save As from the File menu to save the document that serves as the basis for the Help file as an .RTF file. In the Save As dialog box, select Rich Text Format from the Save File As Type drop-down list.

2. Switch to an MS-DOS window. The first command listed below uses the HC.EXE Help compiler to compile the .HPJ file Demo.HPJ located

in the Windows directory. The second command compiles the same file located in the C:\HELP directory:

```
HC Demo.HPJ

HC C:\HELP\Demo.HPJ
```

3. The Help compiler lists errors that occur on screen. In general, these errors aren't fatal, so you can launch the Help file even if the pops, jumps, and macros don't all operate correctly. In some cases, you might need to exit Windows to run the Help compiler.

4. Return to Windows and launch File Manager. The Help file you compiled is in the same directory as the .HPJ file used to create it. You can double-click the Help file to launch Help as long as the .HLP extension is associated with WinHelp.EXE.

FYI

A Sample Presentation's .RTF and .HPJ Files

The following document shows HelpDemo.RTF, which served as the basis for the HelpDemo.HLP file on the *Office Solutions* disk. This file differs in a few important respects from the .RTF file shown in the sidebar titled "A Sample .RTF File (Including Footnotes)" earlier in this chapter:

■ This file uses a hot-spotted graphic rather than an explicit table of contents.

■ Both .SHG graphics are centered in the .RTF file in such a way that they appear centered in their respective Help windows.

■ The second graphic has a context string but no title. You don't need a title unless you add keywords for the Search capability.

I use angled brackets (< >) to describe elements such as hard page breaks that appear in the document but are difficult to represent in print.

{bmc helpmain.shg}

<HARD PAGE BREAK>

$^{\$\#K}$**Secondary Window with Text**

SHED.EXEPDefinitionOfSHEDEXE lets you create *hypergraphics*—in other words, it lets you add multiple jumps and pops to a single graphic. You can create graphics that serve as the basis for hypergraphics by using any graphics package—from Paintbrush to CorelDRAW! You can get these graphics into SHED.EXE by opening them directly (if they're saved as .BMP, .DIB, or .WMF) or by pasting them from the Clipboard.

SHED. EXE also compresses graphics files. For example, HelpMain.BMP (used for the main Help screen in the example in this section) is 31,262 bytes. I reduced the file to one-fifth of its original size (6686 bytes) by using SHED.EXE to save it as a .SHG file (pronounced "shag").

When using hot-spotted graphics using SHED.EXE, you must *reference* those graphics from the document—you can't add them to the document directly.

\<HARD PAGE BREAK>

$^{S\#}$Definition of SHED.EXE
SHED.EXE is also known as the "hot-spot editor." Hotspots include jumps, pops, and macros!ExecProgram("HelpGraf.EXE", 0).

$^{\#}$Go south, too!

\<HARD PAGE BREAK>

$^{\#}${bmc helpwndw.shg}

\<FOOTNOTES FOLLOW>

---

^{S} Secondary Window with Text
$^{\#}$ JSecondaryWindowWithText
^{K} Secondary window; Text
^{S} Definition of SHED.EXE
$^{\#}$ PDefinitionOfSHEDEXE
$^{\#}$ PSouth
$^{\#}$ JSecondaryWindowWithGraphics

HelpDemo's .HPJ File

The following document shows HelpDemo.HPJ, the Help project file for HelpDemo.HLP:

```
; This help project requires HC.EXE.
[OPTIONS]
errorlog = helpdemo.err
title = Help Demo
compress = 0
copyright = Copyright 1994, Christine Solomon
```

```
warning = 3
; don't need a separate bmroot command because it's the same
; as root.
root = c:\offsoln\help

[FILES]
helpdemo.rtf

[WINDOWS]
main = "Help Demo", (200,200,570,700),, (192,192,192), (192,192,192)
Text = "Sample Text Window", (520,150,400,800),,,
Graphic = "Sample Graphic Window", (150,175,720,720),,↵
   (255,255,128), (255,255,128)
```

Creating Context-Sensitive Help

To create context-sensitive Help for a custom business application, follow these steps:

1. Create an .RTF file (as described in this chapter).

2. Create a custom .HPJ file with a [MAP] section that associates a topic's context string with a context number. (See the next section.)

3. Call the context number from the business application. (See the section titled "Adding Context-Sensitive Help to Custom Business Applications" on the next page.)

Creating the [MAP] Section for an .HPJ File

You need to assign context numbers only to topics for which you provide context-sensitive Help. The syntax for the [MAP] section follows:

```
[MAP]
ContextString ContextNumber
```

ContextString must be the full context string for the topic; *ContextNumber* can be any unique number in either decimal or hexadecimal format. For example, the following [MAP] section provides context numbers for topics that users can access directly by clicking the Help button in custom dialog boxes:

```
[MAP]
JMainCustomDialog 1
JPrintCustomReportsDialog 2
JAddCustomersDialog 3
JMailMergeDialog 4
JEditCustomerDialog 5
```

Once you assign context numbers and compile a Help file, you can provide context-sensitive Help by calling those context numbers from custom business applications.

Adding Context-Sensitive Help to Custom Business Applications

The method for calling context-sensitive Help depends on which Microsoft BASIC you use. The following sections provide instructions for calling Help from Access, Excel, and Word.

Calling Help from Access

To call context-sensitive Help from an Access form or report, you must provide information for two properties: the Help File property (enter the full path for the Help file) and the Help Context ID property (enter the context number). For example, the properties for the sample Access form shown in Figure 13-11 call the topic identified by the context number 8 in the Help file C:\WINDOWS\HelpDemo.HLP when users press F1. You can add context-sensitive Help to individual controls by assigning a unique Help Context ID property.

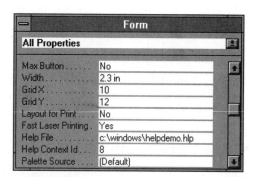

Figure 13-11. *Set the Help File property and the Help Context ID property to provide context-sensitive Help from Access forms and reports when users press the F1 key. Use the WinHelp API function to provide context-sensitive Help from a custom Help button.*

Using WinHelp with Access

To call a context-sensitive Help topic when users click a custom Help button in an Access-based application, use the WinHelp API function. (Use this same technique in Word.) The following Access Basic code opens a custom Help file to the topic identified by the context number 5:

```
Declare Function WinHelp Lib "User" (ByVal hWnd As Integer, ByVal↘
   lpHelpFile As String, ByVal wCommand As Integer, ByVal dwData As↘
   Long) As Integer

Function CustomHelp ()
  Dim Ret As Integer, HelpFileName As String

  HelpFileName$ = "c:\windows\helpdem2.hlp"
  Ret = WinHelp(Screen.ActiveForm.hWnd, HelpFileName$, 1, 5)
End Function
```

Calling Help from Excel

VBA for Excel has a method for calling Help from a button in a custom dialog box: the Help method. The following code opens the custom Help file C:\WINDOWS\HelpDemo.HLP to the topic identified by the context number 1:

```
Sub DisplayHelp()
'The first argument is the full path to the Help file.
'The second is the context number.
  Application.Help "C:\WINDOWS\HelpDemo.HLP", 1
End Sub
```

Calling Help from Word

Like Access, Word uses the WinHelp API function to call context-sensitive Help from a button in a dialog box. Unlike Access, however, Word requires that you use the GetActiveWindow API function to retrieve the handle for the current Word window. The following code opens the custom Help file C:\WINDOWS\HelpDemo.HLP to the topic identified by the context number 6:

```
Declare Function WinHelp Lib "User"(hWnd As Integer, lpHelpFile$,↘
   wCommand As Integer, dwData As Long) As Integer
Declare Function GetActiveWindow Lib "User"() As Integer

Sub MAIN
  hWnd = GetActiveWindow
  HelpFileName$ = "C:\WINDOWS\HelpDemo.HLP"
  iRet = WinHelp(hWnd, HelpFileName$, 1, 6)
End Sub
```

14

Documentation, Training, and Support (Or, Are We Happy Yet?)

It's not enough to develop solid business applications. You have to *deliver* solid business applications. As with a good joke, there's as much riding on the delivery as on the punch line. Because the perceived quality of business applications depends in large part on how quickly and productively people can start using them, a solid application development process should take into account documentation, training, and support.

I learned this lesson when I headed a project to develop a series of highly automated Microsoft Word templates for a top investment bank. The templates had a user population of more than 150 people, about a third of whom were professional word processors. I assumed initially that these people would require less training than others because they knew Word better, but in fact they required more training. Because each of them had developed certain tricks and work-arounds for common problems, they all needed explicit instruction on the best way to approach these problems when working with the new templates. Similarly, the documentation for the word processing staff had to reinforce these general, non-template-specific practices. In the end, documentation, training, and support accounted for nearly half the cost of the project.

Documentation, training, and support are features of business applications, just as commands for batch-printing reports and an easy-to-use GUI are. This chapter addresses how to create documentation and how to provide training and support that help users work more productively with your business applications.

Successful Documentation

Although many people routinely belittle documentation (and, of course, some of it deserves this treatment because it's done poorly), documentation is more than a necessary evil. It's an important feature of successful business applications. Here are four arguments for the value of documentation—both online and printed:

- The documentation process provides one last testing opportunity. As writers document the steps required for each feature to work properly, they test to see whether the feature does, in fact, work. (Note that since it isn't the job of documentation writers to test the application per se, systematic testing should precede documentation.)

- Complete documentation makes training and support easier because the necessary materials and information exist in one place. (As described later in this chapter, good documentation and training go hand-in-hand: Trainers use the documentation to prepare classes, and classes teach people to use the documentation.)

- Complete documentation (including technical documentation) makes the next phase of development easier.

- Good documentation ensures that the key to productive use of custom business applications stays with the application, even when employees leave the job.

How to Document Applications

During the documentation process, documentation writers must do the following:

- Learn to use the business application and understand its business purpose

- Collect, organize, store, and maintain a complete record of the application and its associated documents

- Obtain technical documentation from developers and work with them to include additional information

A *complete* documentation package includes the following elements:

- A copy of the application and its source code.

- Technical documentation. (See the next section.)

- An end-user manual, ideally provided as online help as well as in printed form.

- A copy of the context-sensitive online help and its source files, and a printout of both the .RTF file and the .HPJ file. (See Chapter 13.)

Technical documentation

As discussed in the section titled "Step #3. Analyze the Threads" in Chapter 3, developers should "document as they code," writing comments and noting design decisions to provide an accurate record of the development effort.

A complete technical documentation package includes the following:

- The application's specs, plus changes made to these specs and the reasons for the changes.

- A list of the application's files.

- Installation instructions.

- An overview (including a diagram) of how the program is structured and why it's structured that way. (In the case of a database, this should include the data model.)

- A description of the application's inputs and outputs.

- A list of the application's modules and what they do.

- A list of the application's main procedures and functions and what they do.

- A list of revisions to the original application, the developers involved, and the subsequent release dates.

- A list of the changes made with each revision.

- A printout of commented code (in landscape orientation).

Although this seems like a long list, you can usually pull these elements together in two or three days (for a fair-sized Office development project) if the developers have been commenting code and keeping notes on the evolving spec.

End-user documentation

At seminars on software development, I've heard speakers say that good documentation is the key ingredient of successful software. This gives me hope because too often business-application development units refuse to spend money on documentation. The conventional wisdom is that users don't read it and therefore don't need it.

Although many people who use an application don't read its documentation, *all* users of an application need to learn how it works. They can do this in the following ways:

- They can read the documentation.

- They can ask someone for guidance—someone who has been working with the application longer and presumably knows more about it, or someone who has read the documentation.

- They can fiddle with the application until they figure it out.

Good documentation minimizes reliance on the most expensive method of learning business applications—fiddling.

> **NOTE** Context-sensitive help is ideal for end-user documentation because there's no danger of someone misplacing it. Also, if you construct online help with a printed manual in mind, you can often print the help file and add a cover for situations that require hard copy.

FYI

Tips for Writing Readable Documentation

A few years ago, some colleagues who wanted to create professional documents without resorting to *The Chicago Manual of Style* or Strunk and White asked me to provide tips for writing readable documentation. Like most people, they were interested enough to read only a single piece of paper, so here's what I gave them:

- Use the active voice.

  NO: "This system was designed to…"

  YES: "Company Name designed this system to…"

  NO: "A dialog box is opened…"

  YES: "The application opens a dialog box…"

- Address the reader.

  NO: "This can also be done by…"

  YES: "You can do this by…"

  NO: "The user clicks…"

  YES: "Click…"

- Be consistent. Here are some stock phrases that come in handy:

    "(See XXX for more information.)"

    "Click the OK button" or "Click the Calculate Interest option."

    "Press the <ESCAPE> key." Notice that the key name is in small caps.

- Tell readers *why* they might use a particular option. The documentation form (see Figure 14-1 on page 491) helps you do this.

- Use the plural form to avoid using "he/she," "his or her," and so on.

    NO: "The supervisor can check the records entered by a particular data entry clerk by clicking the Review button in the Supervisory Options dialog box. He or she can then…"

    YES: "Supervisors can check the records entered by a particular data entry clerk by clicking the Review button in the Supervisory Options dialog box. They can then…"

    NO: "Enter the employee's personnel information, including his/her social security number."

    YES: "Enter employees' personnel information, including their social security numbers."

Finding what you're looking for Few people read documentation from cover to cover. Instead, they find the material they need by looking in the index, and then they skim through it. Or, more precisely, if they can find the material they need, they skim through it. The crux of the problem is *finding the relevant material*. People sitting at their PCs using a new business application have specific questions, such as "What happens if I select this option rather than that one?" If there's anyone to ask, that's the quickest way to get an answer. If there isn't anyone to ask, users generally turn to the documentation. If the options in question are listed in alphabetical order in the index, the user will probably find the answer. If the options aren't listed, however, the user may not find the relevant information. One key to usable documentation is an index that includes every menu item and every dialog box control in the application.

Making documentation easy to use Usable documentation includes the following features:

- Labeled screen shots of dialog boxes with brief explanations (up to two sentences) of when to use each option and how the option affects the results. Note that users are more likely to read headings, labels, and captions on figures than solid paragraphs of text.

- Two versions: the *short* version and the *complete* version (the "bible"). The short version provides concise, step-by-step instructions for specific tasks. For example, I've created a "short sheet"—a single, laminated sheet—that describes how to perform a fairly complex and relatively infrequent task, such as a targeted mailing. Users can post the sheet on the bulletin board for easy access.

- Answers to common questions such as "Why should I use this option?" or "What business function does it perform?" Step-by-step instructions serve an important purpose, but they don't provide an explanation of how business applications relate to real-world jobs.

A complete end-user documentation package includes the following:

- A one-page introduction to the application. (Why does the application exist, and how does it simplify and otherwise change the user's job?)
- Complete, step-by-step instructions for using the application.
- The business rationale for using particular menu items and options.
- Pitfalls of certain approaches.
- Answers to obvious questions.
- Descriptions of how to undo common mistakes.
- Troubleshooting tips.
- An exhaustive index.
- A screen shot of every dialog box.

Many users may never know that all this information is available, but anyone who needs this information—whether it's someone on the help desk or a developer working on the next release—will have it in the documentation.

Figure 14-1 shows a sample form that I developed to simplify the documentation process. Use one form for each dialog box; when you're done, you'll have the essential information you need to document the application.

NOTE Whenever a task requires that one person interview another (for example, when documentation writers have to interview developers), I recommend using a tape recorder. Subjects that seem clear and obvious when you hear them explained can seem confusing and illogical when you're sitting in front of the application trying to remember what to do next. Tape recorders help bridge that gap, plus they can prevent you from having to pester the developer.

System name _____

Screen/dialog box title _____

General purpose of this screen _____

How did I get here? _____

What can I do here? *Fill in the following table.*

Tool used and its label (*Circle one and type its name*)	**Why should people use this tool?**	**What happens when people use this tool?**
1 Button, menu, option box, radio button, other Label:		
2 Button, menu, option box, radio button, other Label:		
3 Button, menu, option box, radio button, other Label:		
4 Button, menu, option box, radio button, other Label:		
5 Button, menu, option box, radio button, other Label:		
6 Button, menu, option box, radio button, other Label:		
7 Button, menu, option box, radio button, other Label:		
8 Button, menu, option box, radio button, other Label:		
9 Button, menu, option box, radio button, other Label:		

Figure 14-1. *A sample form for documenting applications.*

Successful Training and Support

I occasionally meet people who think that training is no more worthwhile than documentation. It's easy to understand this point of view, especially at a time when many educators are rethinking reliance on lecture-oriented classroom teaching and embracing experiential learning.

People who grow up with computer games, for example, learn to play those games simply by playing them a thousand times. They don't read manuals to learn how to kill the monsters. Rather, they play the game repeatedly until they can kill all the monsters every time. Computer games make people learn by *doing*.

In our culture, computer games have become a learning model, and fast-paced corporate schedules allow little time for classroom training. Experiential learning is becoming a practical necessity. Kurt Lewin, an early twentieth-century psychologist and educator, conceived the notion of an ideal learning loop that starts with experiential learning:

1. People do something.
2. They observe what happens.
3. They reflect on this.
4. They abstract principles that they can use the next time they do the same thing.

A colleague of mine observed that different occupations have different learning loops. For example, the stereotypical loop in corporate culture is trial and error, which translates into either "do, observe, do, observe" or, in the worst case, into "do, do, do, do." The stereotypical loop in academia is just the opposite: "reflect, abstract, reflect, abstract." The point is, both cases result in too little learning.

The trick is to find techniques and methods that foster the *ideal* learning loop. The method that I've found most worthwhile for computer-oriented training (including training for users of Office products generally and business applications specifically) is the workshop.

Learning in Workshops

The problem with most computer-oriented teaching is that it focuses on what the instructor does, says, and shows, when it should focus on how participants *learn*. The following learning techniques work well for business applications (and computer-oriented training generally).

- Participants must immerse themselves in the application, hands-on, as if they're already using it to do their jobs.

- As part of this immersion, participants should engage in a variety of activities.

  - They should read relevant information from the whiteboard.

  - They should take a break from hands-on learning to discuss their jobs and ask questions.

  - They should encounter problems and then solve them.

  - They should practice using the documentation to find answers to their questions.

- Participants should understand that the workshop is an extension of their everyday work at the office. They should work on their own as well as help each other, just as they will when they return to their desks. By the end of the workshop, participants should be asking the instructor specific questions, just as they will when they work with floor support staff.

- Participants should focus on a single topic, and everything the instructor does, says, writes, and hands out must address this topic: *How does this business application help people do their jobs better?*

NOTE Good documentation is a feature, and training and support should emphasize how to use this feature.

FYI

Learning Office

One challenge of developing business applications with end-user development tools and then training people to use them is that not all users know how to use Microsoft Excel and Word effectively. Just as developers should incorporate best practices for using Excel and Word when automating tasks, users need to follow these best practices when learning to use the resulting business application. Don't assume that users know these practices. *Show* them these practices in the context of using the business application to do their jobs.

Also, when possible, have developers conduct the training or assist in the training. This helps them understand how users work with both business applications and the underlying Office product.

Short courses

Training, like documentation, should come in a short version as well as a complete version. For years I've been teaching short, job-specific courses on big topics. For example, I teach an intensive short course (two hours maximum) on performing financial analysis with Excel. Although most people would consider the topics covered (such as views, reports, scenario manager, and functions) "advanced," I frequently teach this course to people who know only the rudiments of Excel, and they've had no problem learning the material. They aren't bored because the workshop is fast-paced, and they know that the material is absolutely relevant to their jobs.

Naturally, during this workshop, people who know little about Excel learn the basics because I show them how to perform a task correctly when I see them doing it wrong. This helps them immediately associate the best practice with the everyday tasks that they perform in their jobs.

Another notable consideration about the "short course" method is that even busy people see its value. In fact, two clients made the short course on financial analysis with Excel mandatory when they switched from Lotus 1-2-3 to Excel. A third client made this class mandatory—even though employees had been using Excel for nearly a year—because the class helped people become more productive. This client also offered a series of related short courses on such topics as how to create business presentations in Excel and how to write simple macros.

These key elements make short courses successful:

- Short courses are workshops. All participants have a PC to work on.

- There are no slide shows and no lectures. The instructor stands *behind* the participants to see who needs assistance. (I always start the class by explaining to participants why I'm standing at the back, because it might seem odd. At first, people will turn around when I speak, but soon they don't bother because they're too busy.)

- Participants complete a series of carefully crafted, job-relevant exercises using samples of materials and analyses that they work with on the job.

- Before each exercise, the instructor describes the business purpose of using a particular feature or technique, as well as the general steps for doing so. The instructor then leads participants step by step through the exercise, prefacing each step with an explanation of why it's necessary.

- Class size is small. The ideal number of participants is four, and the maximum number is six. Participants should have a similar level of experience with the software, and all must perform the same job. It doesn't make sense to teach clerical staff and financial analysts the same material or to present that material in the same way.

■ Instructors must be experts in using the software so they can field nearly any question that might arise. If they are stumped by a question, instructors should admit it and promise to get back to the participant with an answer—preferably the next day. (Such calls provide a great opportunity for getting feedback on the workshop.)

Support

In some business environments, *support* (which I define as one-on-one training) is the only mechanism for training. If you can't get people into the classroom, go to their desks. This is similar to the door-to-door salesperson's approach—get your foot in the door, and if you can show people clearly and concisely how to work with a new business application, they'll learn it. Ask for five minutes, and if your pitch is good enough they'll let you stay for twenty.

Because technical support staff provide information to users within the context of solving problems on the job, support can be a valuable training vehicle. Although I work with only a few companies that rely heavily on this type of support, more companies could benefit from this approach. Unfortunately, support staff sometimes know too little about the applications they support to provide training. Also, certain support staff cultures prefer to "get it fixed and move on" rather than help users learn better practices.

NOTE   Of course, there are times when all you need to do is get it fixed and move on. One-on-one training clearly isn't the *only* reason for support, but it's a natural addition to the support function.

CASE STUDY: Learning Should Be as Much Fun as Doom

Because the amount of learning required of employees has outstripped what traditional classroom training can provide, Bankers Trust (BT) uses a variety of alternative learning techniques, including workshops, brown baggers (lunchtime seminars on important topics), and computer games.

BT is turning to computer games for three reasons:

■ The fast-paced corporate "cowboy" or "pinball" culture leaves little time for structured learning.

■ That same culture requires that people understand a constantly changing array of complex products and processes.

■ Computers and television are changing the way people learn.

Marc Prensky, a vice president at BT, is trying to refocus corporate learning by turning formal training into informal, computer-based gaming. Games are becoming an important learning medium not only because computer games are staples of the computer age, but because hectic corporate environments often cannot accommodate formal training. Instead, learning occurs increasingly during commuting time or "personal" time. Of course, people won't spend their off-hours on job-oriented learning without incentives:

- First, the "learning material" must be absolutely useful. People have to *want* the material presented.

- Second, the material must be presented in a way that is so absorbing that people are willing to persist until they master it.

Games provide these incentives.

Games also provide corporations with a flexible approach to teaching a variety of subjects: Developers can create a standard "game shell" and then plug content into that shell. Although all content is clearly not appropriate for the same game, some significant percentage of it is—*if* the game is well designed.

Prensky has built several game-based learning tools. One is a humorous computer game that throws challenging situations at receptionists and clerical staff so they learn how to manage the impossible. The game is organized so that losers have to stay late to fix the mess, and winners get an immediate promotion with a new barrage of challenges. Another is a *Jeopardy*-style trivia game (played against the company's chairman, Charlie Sanford) about Bankers Trust as a business.

Prensky points out that since we know which types of computer-based activities engage people's interest—for example, screen savers and games such as Solitaire and Doom—we should build *learning* versions of these programs. The trick is to transform activities that people like into activities that are useful and still engaging.

At the moment, Prensky is finishing a multimedia learning series based on flash cards to teach BT employees about the bank and about complex banking products such as equity swaps (see Figure 14-2). Just as people used flash cards as children to learn arithmetic, they can use BT Flashcards to learn about derivatives, to get instructions on how to order office supplies, and to "get acquainted" with management through photographs and biographical sketches.

Users of BT Flashcards can maintain a personal list of information for quick reference, mark information for self-testing, and use the extensive search capability.

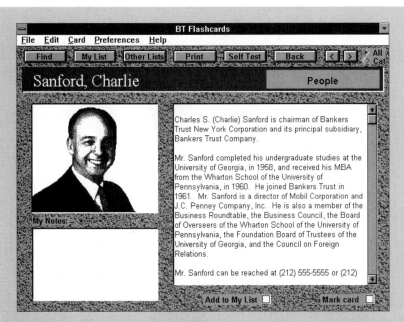

Figure 14-2. *A screen from Bankers Trust's multimedia flash cards—a fun tool for learning about the bank's personnel, procedures, and products.*

But Does Computer-Based Learning Work?

Game-based learning is too new to have much statistical evidence measuring its value, but evidence suggests that computer-based training results in more learning than traditional classroom training. For example, one study on how people learn to prepare income tax returns found that students who were taught with computers scored higher on average and had a narrower distribution around the mean than those taught in traditional classroom settings. In addition, students who were taught with computers typically completed the learning in half the time required by those taught in classrooms.

15

Roll Out the Barrel

I overheard the following conversation at a client's office early one Monday morning:

Banker: What happened to OIS? [OIS stands for Office Information System, an e-mail system on the VAX.]

Secretary: As far as I can tell, it doesn't exist anymore. Now we're on Lotus Notes.

Banker: Well, that's pretty interesting because I don't know how to use Lotus Notes. How am I going to get in?

Secretary: I don't know.

Banker: [*Pause*] Do I even have Lotus Notes on my machine? [*They go off together to check.*]

Some IS departments manage application rollouts in this manner because if they warn people in advance, those people will mobilize to prevent change, and political wrangling will ensue. (A *rollout* is the process of introducing an application to users and incorporating it into the business.) To avoid such unpleasantness, some IS departments operate according to the tried-and-true principle that it's easier to obtain forgiveness than permission. Although I have never seen rollouts scrapped due to political mobilization, only delayed, the process is distasteful to all involved, and I have seen many an IS department implement rollouts in the dead of night as a result.

This approach is understandable—except to the users who come in one morning to find their work lives reorganized. The story above ends with the banker calling IS and learning that he doesn't have Lotus Notes on his machine and won't get it until later that afternoon—at the earliest. But he needs to get into OIS. IS, unsympathetic, tells him that he can't get into OIS until he has Lotus Notes and then suggests two alternatives: 1) He can write information by hand

and give it to his secretary to type, or 2) he can type it in Microsoft Word and give his secretary the disk, and she can transfer it into OIS. The banker fumes and starts phoning higher-ups.

This is how *not* to manage a rollout.

This chapter provides some tips for managing application rollouts correctly— from large-scale rollouts of Microsoft Excel, Word, or Lotus Notes (involving several thousand people) to small-scale rollouts of departmental applications built with end-user development tools. It provides sample materials that I have seen used successfully in such rollouts, which you can adapt for your own use.

To Switch or Not to Switch?

It's very instructive to witness large-scale mobilization within a company for or against a given software package (or, on a smaller scale, for or against development of a particular business application). Here's an eyewitness account by a senior IS professional in a leading bank:

> We had to fight hard, uphill battles to get both Excel and Word. The 1-2-3 vs. Excel battle was harder than the WordPerfect vs. Word battle because every single associate all the way up to the vice presidents and managing directors who used 1-2-3 fought Excel.

> The WordPerfect vs. Word battle was more focused. The document preparation center vigorously said, "We don't want to touch this," and groups of developers and secretarial staff said the same, but the political clout was used on behalf of 1-2-3.

I've seen several strategies in various combinations employed in the process of deciding whether to switch. The least disruptive processes have been those in which people are prepared for differences of opinion and implement a process (with a clearly stated, not-too-distant end) for voicing opinions and resolving differences. This process might include the following:

- Presentations by external experts, internal user groups, members of IS, and/or software companies

- A survey of the business lines and the user populations, followed up by a public report on the results

- A computing needs analysis, possibly conducted by an outside firm

- Tests in which individuals use the competing products to perform specific tasks and then complete a questionnaire evaluating each product

- A public report containing the results of independent research, vendor analyses, and/or industry analyses

Because of my experience with Microsoft products, people often ask me to make a case for these products when deciding which off-the-shelf products to buy. To date, all skirmishes but one have been decided in Microsoft's favor (and the jury is still out on that one).

Here are five points (and a general strategy) that have proven effective in converting fans of competing products to Microsoft products. (With a little modification, you can use the same strategy to argue the case for building an application using end-user development tools or for building a new business application.)

- Remember that the opponents are likely to arm themselves with the latest bug reports culled from CompuServe and Internet forums to corroborate their objections. Admit up front that the tools are not perfect. Note bugs in the features that your company is likely to use heavily and, if possible, provide information from Microsoft regarding scheduled fixes.

- Admit any limitations that these tools have regarding the types of tasks that users in your company perform.

- Demonstrate the power of these tools, particularly as development tools.

- Demonstrate that these tools make it easier to share data and—through ODBC, DDE, and OLE automation—easier to build custom applications that share data.

- Admit that there are reasons to go with the other choice. Know the other choice, respect it, and acknowledge its strengths, but make clear that if the company needs a tool that will help automate everyday processes relatively inexpensively, Microsoft's end-user development tools are the best choice.

NOTE This last point is extremely important because it starts the process by managing expectations. It's so easy to oversell—the computer industry practically hoodwinks us into doing so—but if you win with an oversell, you'll have to beat a hasty retreat and essentially *unsell* before the project is done. This can take a big bite out of your credibility.

Ten Good Reasons Why Users Hate to Convert— and Ten Good Responses

Here are the 10 best arguments I've heard for why a company should *not* switch to Excel or Word (or why it should not upgrade to the latest versions of Excel or Word, or even why it should not build a new business application)— along with the best responses. (Companies backed up these responses with well-wrought plans, manpower, muscle, and budget.)

- **We have materials and information for the past 10 years in Brand X format.** Before announcing a new platform, test the conversion process. Provide users with the results of this test, including a list of known problems, solutions to these problems, and an estimate of the percentage of materials that should convert smoothly.

- **We're too busy to learn a new application.** Provide training at convenient times for users. If necessary, offer daytime, lunch-hour, evening, and weekend classes as well as one-on-one, "at-your-desk" sessions. Provide floor support for an appropriate period of time. (Calculate "appropriate" according to the number of users, the general amount of use, and crunch periods when use may be heavier than normal and/or require more sophisticated support.) Be prepared to modify floor support on the fly as the rollout proceeds.

- **We're productive using Brand X, but sometimes we have more work than we can handle. Since the workload isn't likely to decrease, how can we keep up with our work while learning the new application?** Some business areas, such as word processing, can benefit from temporary assistance. When developing a rollout plan, factor in such assistance where appropriate.

- **We already have macros, formulas, and styles set up in Brand X.** The goal in rolling out a new application is not to duplicate the old application, so you need to take a couple of tacks to answer this objection:

  - Show that some of the functionality provided by macros in the old application is built into the new application.

  - In the cases where the functionality is not built into the new application, determine those user processes that most need automating and then investigate the feasibility of developing this functionality for the new application in-house. (You may need to hire the expertise necessary to do this development.)

- **Brand X has an upgrade coming out that will be just as good as the new application that IS is advocating, plus it will be easier to learn.** Demonstrate the new application's *existing* capabilities. Provide information, if available, on the relative ease of use of the two applications. Let key users test the new application to verify ease of use.

- **Our clients use Brand X, too, which makes it easier to produce materials jointly.** Provide a mechanism for translating documents from the new application into Brand X format. This capability is often built into the new product or can be obtained through a filter sold by a third party. In some cases, you'll want to augment filters with custom macros.

- **Ten years ago we switched from Brand Y to Brand X. Do you remember the nightmare?** If you don't, in fact, remember the nightmare, imagine it. Prepare summary planning documents for public consumption describing the rollout. Include all major elements of the rollout, such as training, floor support, conversion services, and temporary assistance. Accept feedback, make changes, and get "buy-in" from users.

- **Although we've had Brand X for 10 years, IS has just integrated it with our major corporate systems. If we switch to a new application, it will take a long time to integrate the new application with these systems.** Point out two advantages of the new application: It's programmable, and it includes features to simplify integration with existing systems. Explain the types of custom applications that IS will build with the new application, and provide a worst-case schedule for doing so. (Don't provide a best-case schedule because people will hold you to it.)

- **It's too expensive.** Address cost issues in terms of reducing manual labor and increasing productivity by using the new application to automate business tasks. Explicitly allay the fear that the goal is to eliminate existing jobs—unless that's actually the goal.

- **It's not *necessary*.** Address the need to reengineer the business to grow the business, and describe the contribution that the new application can make to this end—for example, streamlining the publishing process, providing "live" reports to management, and storing desktop data centrally.

Plan, Plan, Plan, Plan, Plan.... (Need I Say More?)

The company I work for, Micro Modeling Associates, has helped dozens of Fortune 1000 companies make the transition to Microsoft Windows and Office products. In addition, Micro Modeling is regularly involved in rolling out custom business applications to sizable user populations. The key to managing these rollouts is understanding that they require behavioral and cultural changes as well as technical changes.

Micro Modeling structures application rollouts according to the following principles:

- **Ensure that the intended hardware platform is suitable for the new applications.** It isn't realistic to install Office products and Office-based business applications on low-end PCs or on PCs with limited disk space. Users will complain if the new applications aren't at least as fast as the old ones.

- **Roll out software by workgroup.** Install new applications for small groups of people who work together on a daily basis. Roll out applications to carefully selected workgroups that serve as pilot programs for testing and correcting the rollout plan.

- **Designate a member of each workgroup as project coordinator for that group.** Project coordinators are responsible for overseeing the rollout in their areas, including collecting files for conversion, coordinating training and scheduling, and working with technical staff. Coordinators should be senior personnel who command the respect of workgroup members. They may assign junior staff members to perform the actual tasks.

- **Management should ensure that all users are aware of the rollout before they are affected by it.** Use executive briefings to communicate overall goals, introduce and demo the new technology, and manage expectations. These briefings should focus on the solutions the new technology provides for the problems users face, rather than praising individual features. In addition, use workgroup kickoff meetings to introduce technical personnel, explain the role of the project coordinator, and address any concerns workgroup members may have. Such meetings help to get user buy-in and to identify potential problems.

- **Install new applications first for the workgroups that are either the most willing to convert or the easiest to convert.** This ensures a positive beginning for the project. In addition, these users can provide assistance to workgroups converted later.

- **Identify influential end users who can help to promote the effort.** The buy-in and approval of respected power users will help build support for the project throughout the organization.

- **Software and hardware installations must coincide with training.** Users must have access to the new applications as soon as they finish training. If you install new applications prior to training, you risk support problems, discouraged users, and bad press. If you install new applications too long after training, users will have forgotten what they learned.

- **Provide sufficient training for all staff.** This is absolutely critical to the success of the project. The most successful training programs address users by function and skill level. (See Chapter 14 for more information on training.)

- **Provide sufficient support.** Again, this is absolutely critical to the success of the project. Frustrated users will spread the word that "this new software doesn't work" and are likely to return to their old way of doing things. (See Chapter 14 for more information on support.)

- **Carefully assess existing files to determine how to convert them most effectively.** You can waste a great deal of time and money converting all files. Old files that are needed solely for reference can remain in their current form and can be accessed using old software if necessary. Remember that end users can often convert simple files themselves.

- **Ensure that existing mission-critical applications operate smoothly with the new applications.** Companies can't stop doing business while installing new applications. If you ensure that mission-critical applications work with the new applications, users are less likely to return to their old ways.

- **Reengineer applications whenever possible.** It doesn't make sense to port inefficient or ineffective applications to new platforms, so plan your suite of custom business applications according to the features and capabilities offered by the new platform rather than the existing list of applications.

- **Management must communicate commitment to the rollout.** In addition to providing sufficient resources, support, and training, managers can demonstrate their commitment to the new applications by using these applications themselves. (One way to encourage the use of e-mail is to have the head of the company send messages that require a response.)

Planning Documents

Every rollout should begin with a written plan. The following issues must be covered in the plan:

- Number of users to be converted.

- Definition of workgroups.

- Hardware and infrastructure issues: Are existing PCs fast enough? Will software reside locally or on a network? Is there enough disk space?

- Identification of mission-critical applications and files that need to be reengineered or converted, and a plan for doing so.

- Training for rollout support staff, staffing requirements, and so on.

- Clearly defined "escalation" procedures that detail under which circumstances rollout support staff should report unforeseen problems, and to whom.

- End-user training: one-on-one, classroom, onsite/offsite, special topics to be covered.

- Hardware purchasing plan for companies upgrading hardware in tandem with a rollout.

- Schedule for the rollout: installation, conversion, training, new application development.

In the plan, name names. The discipline of attaching actual names to schedules and responsibilities helps to identify areas in which there aren't enough resources. It also directly links individuals to the generic tasks of training and installation of new applications, which helps ensure that execution of these tasks stays in sync.

You should tweak the plan to keep it current as the rollout proceeds.

I've included in this chapter sample planning documents from an Excel version 5 rollout to several thousand users. You can easily adapt these documents to the application that you're rolling out (including custom business applications).

- Figure 15-1 shows a sample project plan for a rollout. It contains a checklist of nearly 50 items common to most rollouts, including converting existing business applications; converting existing materials; evaluating the effect of the new application on workflow and on existing applications; creating a pilot program; developing appropriate training; evaluating the pilot program and then revising the general rollout based on the pilot's evaluation.

NOTE You can use this checklist as the basis for every rollout, no matter how small. Most rollouts involve conversion and connectivity issues, so you should always conduct a pilot program (even if it only involves two people) because you'll inevitably learn something that improves the general rollout.

- Figure 15-2 is a questionnaire used to *quantify* the size and scope of the rollout. Once respondents return the questionnaire (or when you tire of waiting and simply phone them for the information), create a master list that summarizes the number of people affected by the rollout, and then make more definite plans for providing support (from training to temporary assistance).

- Figure 15-3 is a checklist for staff charged with converting documents from Lotus 1-2-3 to Excel. To simplify file conversion from one platform to another, always provide instructions. Creating the list—which, in essence, codifies the expertise necessary to convert materials—is key to successful conversions. Staff at Micro Modeling Associates created the checklist in Figure 15-3 after converting dozens of complex 1-2-3 spreadsheets to Excel.

Start Date	End Date	Task	Leader	Comments
		Preliminary Evaluation of Excel Version 5		
		Compile Excel version 5 evaluation criteria		
		Ensure compatibility with current workstation hardware		
		Ensure compatibility with current workstation applications and data feeds		
		Finalize new workstation configuration and determine ready date of new configuration (include effects of equipment delivery dates)		
		Determine if configuration changes will be done before or with Excel rollout		
		Ensure compatibility with new workstation hardware		
		Ensure compatibility with new workstation applications and data feeds		
		Evaluate system resource demands		
		Determine effects of DLL changes on other Microsoft applications		
		Ensure compatibility with custom utilities/DLLs		
		Compile bug list		
		Evaluate all of the above and make Go/No Go decision		
		Installation, Configuration, and Excel Version 4/5 Coexistence Requirements		
		Inventory pilot group for new configuration and determine equipment needs		
		Determine manpower requirements for pilot installations		
		Determine required configuration for Excel version 5		
		Develop installation instructions		
		Develop Excel version 4/5 coexistence guidelines		
		Develop fallback plan to revert to Excel version 4		
		Training Support Personnel		
		Identify personnel to be trained and their training requirements: installers, help desk, and application support		
		Develop training materials		
		Train support personnel		
		Converting Excel-Based Applications		
		Convert applications to Excel version 5		
		Conduct parallel run/test of versions 4 and 5 of Excel-based applications		

Figure 15-1. *Sample project plan for Excel version 5 rollout.* *(continued)*

Start Date	End Date	Task	Leader	Comments
		Training Application Programmers to Assist in Conversions		
		Prepare conversion guidelines document		
		Develop training materials		
		Train lead programmers		
		Train other programmers		
		Planning End-User Training for Pilot		
		Develop initial training materials		
		Finalize number of users to be trained by skill set or title		
		Schedule classes and reserve training facilities if necessary		
		Converting Pilot Group		
		Develop handouts/cheat sheets		
		Train pilot group		
		Install Excel version 5/new workstation configuration		
		Provide on-site support for pilot		
		Conducting Pilot		
		Inventory pilot group for new configuration and determine equipment needs		
		Determine manpower requirements for pilot installs		
		Identify pilot user group and pilot application for conversion		
		Convert application		
		Parallel-run application		
		Train pilot group		
		Install Excel version 5/new workstation configuration		
		Provide on-site support for pilot		
		Evaluating Pilot and Implementing Changes		
		(to be determined)		
		Planning End-User Training for General Rollout		
		Determine training capacity—trainers, space, and so on		
		Finalize number of users to be trained by business line, skill set, or title		
		Develop training schedule to fit rollout schedule		
		Prepare updated training materials		
		Train the trainers		

SURVEY OF PROJECT MANAGERS

OBJECTIVE: QUANTIFY REQUIREMENTS FOR EXCEL VERSION 5 ROLLOUTS

PROJECT PLAN ISSUES

- Does the project plan seem relevant to your area? _____
- Are there steps missing that you would like to see added? _____

NUMBER OF SPREADSHEET APPLICATIONS AND CONVERSIONS

- Symphony applications/sheets _____
- 1-2-3 applications/sheets _____
- Excel version 4 applications/sheets _____
- Critical production applications vs. stand-alone sheets _____
- What resources do you think you will need to convert these applications? Can you convert these applications with training/guidance? Will your users do it themselves? Do you need outside assistance? If so, how many people and for how long?

  _____

  _____

  _____

Note: Try to identify different types of applications and spreadsheets. For example, 250 deal sheets that have the same structure but contain different data are easier to manage than 250 deal sheets of varying structure. Try to identify production applications (such as spreadsheets that feed the accounting and control process) vs. stand-alone sheets.

NUMBER OF USERS

- Symphony _____
- 1-2-3 _____
- Excel version 4 _____
- Total users for conversion _____

Figure 15-2. *Sample survey of project managers for Excel version 5 rollout.* *(continued)*

TRAINING

- What kind of training will your users need?

    one-on-one   classroom

- What times are best?

    early   late   weekends   after hours   other _____

- Do your users have specific training needs such as charting, database functions, and macro development?

    _____

    _____

SUPPORT

- What kind of support will your users need during and after training?

    _____

- Who do you envision providing this support?

    your department   IS   other _____

- Who currently provides spreadsheet support (for example, who answers questions such as "Why can't I print?" or "How do I...")?

    _____

- Who currently provides spreadsheet *application* support (for example, who fixes financial models when they're not working)?

    _____

- Identify any periods where use of Excel and/or overall workload traditionally peaks (for example, at the end of the month). Will you need temporary assistance during those periods?

    _____

HARDWARE AND CONFIGURATION

- How many PCs in your area may not be powerful enough to run Excel version 5 (assuming that 486/25 with 8 MB is baseline)? _____

- Is there enough disk space to have both Excel version 4 and Excel version 5 on your users' PCs? _____

- Do you need assistance with hardware configuration in your area?

    _____

Lotus ➡ Excel Conversion Checklist

Date converted: _____   Converter: _____

Filename: _____   File owner: _____

_____ Load Excel version 5, and choose File Open.

_____ In the List Files of Type drop-down list, change selection to **Lotus 1-2-3 (*.wk*)**. Click OK.

_____ Click **Yes** to record cells with errors. (Note cell references for review.)

_____ Check cell formats. (Lotus formats should convert OK in Excel version 5, but it's worth checking!)

_____ Check column widths, number formats, and links.

_____ **Save As** a Microsoft Excel Workbook.

_____ Delete unused cells. (Lotus files will become larger when converted to Excel because of formatting differences.)

_____ **Microsoft Excel Menus** will be the default under **Tools Options Transition**, unless one of two conditions is true: Global options have been preset to read Lotus Help, or this is not the first Lotus file opened during this work session. Check the option you prefer.

_____ The options **Transition Formula Evaluation** and **Transition Formula Entry** are checked automatically. These options allow the sheet to behave as a Lotus file. Deselect these options for Excel characteristics.

_____ Any cell formulas that did not convert need to be re-created in Excel. (Errors convert as Notes.) Use the **Edit Goto Special** command, and then select **Notes** for assistance.

_____ Review any macros. Most will run by pressing **CTRL+Letter**, except for print macros.

_____ Use **Views** and **Reports** as an alternative to rewriting Lotus print macros that no longer work.

_____ Use **Tools Auditing Precedents** and **Dependents** to track problem cells and circular references.

_____ Determine the mission-critical files to be converted first.

_____ Evaluate the advantages and disadvantages of doing straight conversions vs. reengineering a sheet.

Figure 15-3. *Lotus 1-2-3 to Excel conversion checklist.*

Managing Expectations

Managing expectations is an important part of planning for a rollout. I've seen IS departments sell users on a new application too enthusiastically (not unlike how the computer industry sells its products) and then flop on the rollout because users believed that there wouldn't be any pain. No matter how small the rollout, it's painful for the users who have to change. As Don Tapscott and Art Caston note in *Paradigm Shift*:

> The most overlooked and, ironically, the largest components of system costs are the human costs of change. These are so poorly understood that they often do not appear at all on the cost side of a systems cost-benefit analysis. Overlooking these costs is a significant oversight by any organization trying to become profitable in a highly competitive market.

After a *successful* rollout of a successful application to approximately 40 people, one of them publicly accused me of ruining her life. Although she later apologized, it was a good lesson. Change is stressful, and in times of change people's abilities come under close scrutiny when, perhaps, they can least bear scrutiny. Some people don't survive rollouts because they don't adjust to the new application. Although I've seen this occur most often with clerical and word processing staff, I've also seen management deliver an ultimatum to a senior employee who refused to use Excel two years after the rollout. He decided to use Excel.

By managing expectations, you take pressure off everyone involved in the rollout, including IS.

Appendix A: Resources

This appendix includes additional sources of information on developing business applications with Microsoft Office and Visual Basic.

General Information

- *Encyclopedia of Computer Science,* Third Edition, edited by Anthony Ralston and Edwin D. Reilly (Van Nostrand Reinhold).

- *How to Program: The Skill That Will Sharpen Your Thinking* by Chris Crawford (Storm King Press).

Office

- *Microsoft Office Developer's Kit*, a CD-ROM title published by Microsoft—the best reference available for the Office developer. It includes Object Model reference charts for Microsoft Access and Microsoft Excel; reference materials on how to design and program integrated solutions with Microsoft Office; sample applications; the *Microsoft Word 6 Developer's Kit*; and reference materials for Access Basic, VBA for Excel, WordBasic, and Visual Basic. The *Microsoft Office Developer's Kit* is available on the Microsoft Developer Network CD and can be ordered separately through Microsoft Sales (800-426-9400).

Methodology

- *Code Complete: A Practical Handbook of Software Construction* by Steve McConnell (Microsoft Press).

- *MSF/Solution Development Discipline Version 1.0*—a CD-ROM title authored by Microsoft Consulting Services and published by Microsoft.

- *Object-Oriented Software Engineering: A Use Case Driven Approach* by Ivar Jacobson (Addison-Wesley)—the seminal reference on use case analysis.

ODBC

- Microsoft provides a set of ODBC drivers with Access, Excel, and Microsoft Word. Unfortunately, this set doesn't include a driver for Excel. You can purchase a separate package, called Microsoft ODBC drivers, which includes ODBC drivers for Excel and text files.

- To connect to the ODBC forum on CompuServe, sign on to the MS Access Support forum (type *GO MSACCESS*), and then change to the ODBC/Client/Server library.

- *Microsoft ODBC 2.0 Programmer's Reference and SDK Guide* (Microsoft Press)—the complete reference for using the ODBC API.

Windows API

- Help files available with the professional edition of Visual Basic:

  - WIN31WH.HLP, which describes the API functions.

  - WIN31API.HLP, which provides Visual Basic–style declare statements for Windows API functions. These work seamlessly with AccessBasic, VBA for Excel, and Visual Basic, but they need some modification to work with Word.

- *Microsoft Windows 3.1 Programmer's Reference Library* (Microsoft Press).

- *Visual Basic Programmer's Guide to the Windows API* by Daniel Appleman (Ziff-Davis Press)—a must-have Windows API reference no matter which Microsoft BASIC you use.

- *Windows 3.1 Programming for Mere Mortals* by Woody Leonhard (Addison-Wesley)—an excellent introduction to Windows programming, from the Microsoft BASICs to the Windows API.

Access

- *Creating Professional Applications with Microsoft Access* by Mike Gunderloy (Pinnacle Publishing).

- *Microsoft Access 2 Developer's Handbook* by Ken Getz, Paul Liwin, and Greg Reddick (Sybex).

- The Access Security Whitepaper and the Security Wizard—two invaluable security-related tools available from Microsoft. Both are available in SECWZ2.ZIP in the Security library of CompuServe's MS Access Support forum (type *GO MSACCESS*) and as \SOFTLIB\MSLFILES\WX1051.EXE on ftp.microsoft.com.

- The Access Developer's Toolkit (from Microsoft)—includes, among other things, a runtime version of Access and SETWIZ.MDB, which helps to create installation disks for your Access applications.

Excel

- *Microsoft Excel 5 Developer's Kit* (Microsoft Press)—provides some useful information on Excel (including Excel C-API documentation, Excel file format documentation, Excel's Apple Events/Apple Script reference, EXCEL5.INI information, and documentation for creating Excel file converters) but is not nearly as useful day-to-day as its Word counterpart.

Word

- *Microsoft Word 6 Developer's Kit* (Microsoft Press)—an indispensable book for anyone who wants to develop Word-based applications.

OLE

- *OLE 2 Programmer's Reference*, Volumes I and II (Microsoft Press)—the complete reference for using OLE.

- You'll find the correct listing of the argument positions for WordBasic statements and functions in POSITION.HLP, a Help file available from Microsoft through the Microsoft Software Library forum on CompuServe (type *GO MSL*) and as \SOFTLIB\MSLFILES\POSITION.EXE on ftp.microsoft.com.

Help

The complete version of WHAT6 is available from the "Unsupported Tools and Utilities" section of the Microsoft Developer Network CD, through the Microsoft Software Library forum on CompuServe (type *GO MSL*), and as \SOFTLIB\MSLFILES\WHAT6.EXE on ftp.microsoft.com. Although you can't get support for these tools from Microsoft, you can check out these titles:

- *Windows Help Authoring Guide* (Microsoft Developer Network CD).

- *Microsoft Windows 3.1 Programmer's Reference Library* (Microsoft Press).

- *Microsoft Visual Basic Version 3.0, Professional Features Book 1* (Microsoft).

Electronic Information Services

All Microsoft customers have 24-hour, seven-day-a-week access to Microsoft's free or low-cost Electronic Information Services:

- **Microsoft FastTips.** Toll-free access to common questions and answers and technical notes about key Microsoft products.

    Advanced Systems: (800) 936-4400
    Desktop Applications: (800) 936-4100
    Development: (800) 936-4300
    Personal Operating Systems: (800) 936-4200

- **Microsoft Knowledge Base.** A database of more than 40,000 detailed articles on Microsoft products, bug lists, fix lists, and more.

    CompuServe: At any ! prompt, type *GO MSKB*.
    Internet: Log on as anonymous@ftp.microsoft.com.

- **Microsoft Forums on CompuServe.** A variety of forums facilitated by Microsoft that provide an interactive dialog with a worldwide community of Microsoft customers. CompuServe connect charges apply. At any ! prompt, type *GO MICROSOFT*. (For an introductory CompuServe membership kit, call (800) 848-8199, operator 524.)

- **Microsoft Driver Library.** An archive of drivers for Microsoft products.

    Internet: Log on as anonymous@ftp.microsoft.com.
    Microsoft Download Service: (206) 936-6735. Use a 1200-, 2400-, or 9600-baud modem, no parity, 8 data bits, and 1 stop bit.

Appendix B:
A BASIC Primer

When you program a computer, you're providing, in essence, a cyborg version of a Miss Manners guide to appropriate behavior. For example, you can program a computer to display "Hello" on startup or "Bye" on exit.

Computer programs (including VBA for Excel and WordBasic macros) are a series of instructions that control the hardware to produce certain results such as displaying text, graphics, or color on the screen. Of course, not all programming languages can control the hardware directly. BASIC, for example, which seems quite English-like to programmers, requires an interpreter to translate the programmer's instructions into the machine code necessary to control the hardware.

To program computers, you must understand the following:

- The techniques for organizing and structuring how programs perform tasks
- The programming language itself, including the keywords and symbols used to control the computer

This appendix introduces key programming techniques used in the Microsoft BASICs and in the core BASIC language. Beginners should read this appendix before reading Chapter 2, which compares the Microsoft BASICs.

This appendix introduces the following topics:

- How to structure a BASIC program
- Variables vs. constants
- Core BASIC statements, functions, and syntax
- How to use the macro recorder

Structuring BASIC Programs

The most basic organizational unit for writing BASIC programs is the subroutine. (Traditionally, *subroutines* are defined as instructions that perform specific tasks but don't return a value, while *functions* always return a value, whether or not they perform tasks.) In WordBasic, you must launch programs from a subroutine called MAIN. Access Basic, VBA for Excel, and Visual Basic, however, let you launch programs from any subroutine. All subroutines start with the keyword *Sub* followed by the name of the subroutine, and they end with the phrase *End Sub*, as follows:

WordBasic

```
Sub MAIN
   Code
End Sub
```

Access Basic, VBA for Excel, and Visual Basic

```
Sub NameThisSub()
   Code
End Sub
```

Notice that in Access Basic, VBA for Excel, and Visual Basic parentheses follow the subroutine's name. These parentheses enclose a subroutine's arguments. (An *argument* is information that a subroutine or function uses to perform a task or process a result.) In Access Basic, VBA for Excel, and Visual Basic, an empty set of parentheses means that the subroutine doesn't require arguments. Add the parentheses to WordBasic subroutines only when they require arguments.

BASIC programs usually consist of multiple subroutines and/or functions. The structure of functions is similar to that of subroutines, except that they start and end with the keyword *Function* rather than *Sub*. You can use the value returned by functions in a variety of ways—for example, as a flag to indicate a certain state or as the result of a calculation. To have a function return a value, set it equal to an expression, as shown below. (An *expression* is any part of a program statement that resolves to a value. For example, 1 + 1 and 1 − x are both expressions.)

```
Function NameOfFunction()
   Code
   NameOfFunction = Expression
End Function
```

FYI

Introducing Variables

Suppose television sets were hardwired to receive a single channel. You'd have to own three TVs just to watch the major networks. (Don't even *think* about cable.) Code that doesn't use variables is as inefficient as a TV that gets only one channel.

Variables are single-word names that store a particular type of data. The data might come from users, from another subroutine or function, or from an initialization (INI) file. Every programming language enables you to work with two general types of data—string data (text) and numeric data (numbers). Some languages, such as Access Basic, VBA for Excel, and Visual Basic, support a variety of other types of data (known as *data types*) as well. (See the section titled "Data Types" later in this appendix for more information.)

It's generally a good practice to *declare* variables—in other words, to list at the start of the program the variables used and the type of data each variable represents. You declare variables using the keyword *Dim*. For example, the following code specifies that the variable MyName is a string, sets the variable equal to "Christine," and then displays that variable in a message box.

```
Sub MyName()
  Dim MyName As String
  MyName = "Christine"
  MsgBox MyName
End Sub
```

In general, you're not required by the Microsoft BASICs to declare variables unless you've specified Option Explicit in Access Basic, VBA for Excel, or Visual Basic. However, it makes code easier to maintain. Because WordBasic supports only two types of variables (string and numeric) and requires use of the type declaration character $ to identify strings, it isn't nearly as useful to declare variables in WordBasic, except in the three cases in which WordBasic requires you to do so: 1) to share variables across subroutines, 2) to create an array, or 3) to create a "dialog record" variable for a Microsoft Word dialog box (explained in Chapter 8). Throughout this book, I declare variables for Access Basic, VBA for Excel, and Visual Basic but not for WordBasic.

Calling Subroutines and Functions

You can call subroutines and functions from within a subroutine or a function. To do this, type the name of the subroutine or function that you're calling. For example, the first of the following subroutines calls the second, which displays a message box that says "Hello, World!" Note that BASIC requires that text be enclosed within double quotation marks.

```
Sub MainSub()
  SecondSub
End Sub

Sub SecondSub
  Msgbox "Hello, World!"
End Sub
```

When you call a subroutine or a function (for example, from a macro command), control switches to that subroutine or function. The program statements execute sequentially and then control switches back to the original procedure.

Control Structures

Control structures determine the order in which code executes. Generally, subroutines and functions execute one line at a time, from beginning to end, unless this sequential flow is altered by events or control structures that cause the program either to execute code repeatedly or to execute code out of sequence. (*Events* are "outside" elements that affect the computer program, such as a given amount of time passing, the user clicking a certain button, or the user opening a certain file. *Control structures* are techniques for processing "decisions" within the computer program itself.) The Microsoft BASICs generally use these four control structures:

- If...Then...Else
- Select Case
- For...Next
- Do...Loop/While...Wend

If...Then...Else

If...Then...Else may be the most basic of the BASICs' control structures. It's certainly the most intuitive—it means exactly what it says. The simplest form of this control structure executes code based on whether a certain condition exists. Here's the syntax:

```
If Condition1 Then
  Code1
End If
```

When a program executes this control structure, it first evaluates *Condition1*. If *Condition1* evaluates to True, program execution continues with the first statement in *Code1*. If *Condition1* evaluates to False, *Code1* is skipped and execution continues with the first statement following End If. For example, the code shown below works as follows: *If* x = 1 (which is the case), *then* the computer beeps. If x doesn't equal 1, nothing happens.

```
Sub ExampleI()
  Dim x As Integer
  x = 1
  If x = 1 Then
    Beep
  End If
End Sub
```

Two clauses, ElseIf and Else, allow you to add more tests to your If…Then…Else control structures. Use these optional clauses to enable your code to take different actions depending on current conditions. The conditions can be quite complex, including logical operators such as And (see the section titled "Logical Operators" later in this appendix) and comparison operators such as = (see the section titled "Comparison Operators" later in this appendix). In fact, the condition can be any expression that evaluates to either True or False. The basic syntax follows. (Note that square brackets enclose optional parts of the control structure.)

```
 If Condition1 Then
    Code1
[ElseIf Condition2 Then
    Code2]
[ElseIf Condition3 Then
    Code3]
 .
 .
 .
[ElseIf ConditionN Then
    CodeN]
[Else
    CodeElse]
 End If
```

When a program executes this control structure, it evaluates *Condition1* first. If *Condition1* evaluates to True, *Code1* executes. When *Code1* finishes, the program skips to the first statement following End If. If *Condition1* evaluates to False, however, the program skips to the next ElseIf clause and evaluates *Condition2*. If *Condition2* evaluates to True, *Code2* executes and the program continues with the first statement following End If. If *Condition2* evaluates to False, the program skips to the next ElseIf clause. The same process continues until one of three things happens: An ElseIf condition evaluates to True (in which case its block of code executes); the program reaches the end of the control structure; or the program encounters an Else clause. An If...Then...Else control structure can have only one Else, which always appears as the last clause. Else clauses don't have conditions; they execute when all of the other conditions fail.

Here's a more complicated example using If...Then...Else. The code shown below works as follows: *If* x = −1 and y = −1, *then* the computer beeps; *else if* y = 0, *then* the computer does nothing; *else if* x or y equals any other number, the computer displays a message box with the word "Hi!"

```
Sub ExampleII()
  Dim x As Integer
  Dim y As Integer
  x = -1
  y = 0
  If x = -1 And y = -1 Then
    Beep
  ElseIf y = 0 Then
  Else
    MsgBox "Hi!"
  End If
End Sub
```

Select Case

The Select Case control structure, like If...Then...Else, enables your code to perform different actions depending on the current conditions. However, while If...Then...Else can evaluate any condition, Select Case can evaluate only a single expression. In situations where only a single expression needs to be evaluated, Select Case is generally better than If...Then...Else because it requires less typing and is easier to read.

Here's the syntax for the Select Case control structure:

```
Select Case ExpressionCase
  Case Expression1
    Code1
 [Case Expression2
    Code2]
     .
     .
     .
 [Case ExpressionN
    CodeN]
 [Case Else
    CodeElse]
End Select
```

When a program executes this control structure, it evaluates *ExpressionCase* and then skips directly to the first Case expression that matches *ExpressionCase* and executes its block of code. If none of the Case expressions matches *ExpressionCase* and the Select Case has a Case Else, *CodeElse* executes; otherwise, the program skips the entire control structure.

The code shown below is similar to the previous If...Then...Else example, but it can evaluate only one variable. It works as follows: If x = 1, the computer beeps; if x = 0, nothing happens; and if x equals any other number, the computer displays a message box with the word "Hi!"

```
Sub ExampleIII()
  Select Case x
  Case 1
    Beep
  Case 0
  Case Else
    MsgBox "Hi!"
  End Select
End Sub
```

Loops

PCs are dumb. Because of this, they can perform the same task repeatedly. In fact, repetitive tasks are arguably the tasks for which PCs are best suited. In programming languages, control structures that perform repetitive tasks are called *loops*. A loop repeats the same lines of code until you tell it to stop. If you don't tell it when to stop, you'll experience the computer equivalent of what happened to the sorcerer's apprentice: the infinite loop.

Loops come in two flavors:

- Those that run a prescribed number of times. The Microsoft BASICs use the For...Next structure to control this type of loop.

- Those that run until a specified condition (other than the number of repetitions) is met. The Microsoft BASICs use the Do...Loop structure—or, in the case of WordBasic, While...Wend—to control this type of loop.

For...Next The For...Next control structure enables you to loop through code a specific number of times. Here's the syntax for the For...Next control structure:

```
For LoopCounter = StartValue To EndValue
  Code
Next LoopCounter
```

When a program executes this control structure, it assigns *StartValue* to the variable *LoopCounter*. The program then executes *Code*. The Next statement adds 1 to the value of *LoopCounter* and then compares this new value with *EndValue*. If the value in *LoopCounter* is less than or equal to *EndValue*, *Code* executes again; otherwise, the program continues execution with the first statement following Next. The code shown below runs the For...Next loop three times. Here's how it works. When the variable Counter equals a value from 1 through 3, the For...Next loop displays a message box with Counter's value and then increments that value to the *next* value. When Counter is greater than 3, the loop ends. So the first time through the loop, the message box displays 1; the second time, it displays 2; and the third and final time, it displays 3.

Note that message boxes display only text. Because of this, in Access Basic and WordBasic you must convert numbers to text using the Str$ function. Although VBA for Excel and Visual Basic perform this conversion automatically, I use the Str$ function when displaying numbers in message boxes for portability with every Microsoft BASIC. (See the section titled "Common Statements and Functions" later in this appendix for more information on the Str$ function.)

```
Sub ExampleIV()
  Dim Counter As Integer
  For Counter = 1 To 3
    MsgBox Str$(Counter)
  Next Counter
End Sub
```

Do...Loop and While...Wend The Do...Loop control structure in Access Basic, VBA for Excel, and Visual Basic (and WordBasic's While...Wend structure) enables you to loop through code until a specified condition is met. As with the If...Then...Else control structure, the condition can be any expression that evaluates to either True or False.

Here's the syntax for the While...Wend control structure:

```
While Expression
  Code
Wend
```

A program encountering this control structure first evaluates *Expression*. If *Expression* is False, the program skips the entire control structure; otherwise, the program executes *Code*. Each time the program reaches Wend, it reevaluates *Expression*. If *Expression* is still True, *Code* executes again; otherwise, the program skips to the first statement following Wend.

The WordBasic subroutine shown on the facing page illustrates how to use the While...Wend control structure. When the variable Counter equals a value greater than 0, the loop displays a message box with Counter's value. The expression Counter = Counter − 1 decreases the value. The last loop runs when Counter = 1. So the first time through the loop, the message box displays 3; the second time, it displays 2; and the third and final time, it displays 1.

Because this is a WordBasic subroutine, it's called MAIN, and there's no need to declare the Counter variable. Again, since message boxes display only text, convert the integer to text using the Str$ function.

```
Sub MAIN
  Counter = 3
  While Counter > 0
    MsgBox Str$(Counter)
    Counter = Counter - 1
  Wend
End Sub
```

The Do...Loop structure is a more recent addition to BASIC than While...Wend and is more flexible.

The syntax for Do...Loop follows:

```
Do While Condition
  Code
Loop
```

or

```
Do Until Condition
  Code
Loop
```

When a program encounters the Do While...Loop control structure, it first evaluates *Condition*. If *Condition* is True, *Code* executes. Each time the program reaches Loop, it reevaluates *Condition* and reexecutes *Code* for as long as *Condition* remains True. The Do Until...Loop control structure executes in a similar way, except that *Code* executes for as long as *Condition* evaluates to False.

The following subroutines are functionally equivalent: The first time through the loop, the message box displays 1; the second and final time, it displays 2.

```
Sub ExampleV()
  Dim Counter As Integer
  Counter = 1
  Do While Counter < 3
    MsgBox Str$(Counter)
    Counter = Counter + 1
  Loop
End Sub
```

(continued)

```
Sub ExampleVI()
  Dim Counter As Integer
  Counter = 1
  Do Until Counter = 3
    MsgBox Str$(Counter)
    Counter = Counter + 1
  Loop
End Sub
```

Do...Loop also lets you specify whether to check the condition at the beginning or at the end of the loop. This difference is subtle but important: If the code checks the condition at the end of the loop, it must run the loop at least once. For example, the following loops are identical except for the placement of the condition, but the loop in the first example never executes. It displays a message box with the Counter value of 0, while the second loop displays a message box with the Counter value of 101.

```
Sub ExampleVII()
  Dim Counter As Integer
  Counter = 0
  Do While Counter > 0 And Counter <= 100
    Counter = Counter + 1
  Loop
  MsgBox Str$(Counter)
End Sub
```

```
Sub ExampleVIII()
  Dim Counter As Integer
  Counter = 0
  Do
    Counter = Counter + 1
  Loop While Counter > 0 And Counter <= 100
  MsgBox Str$(Counter)
End Sub
```

Core BASIC Statements, Functions, and Syntax

This section provides an overview and examples of the essential features in the Microsoft BASICs' core language that are used to develop applications:

- Common statements and functions
- Arithmetic operators
- Logical operators
- Comparison operators
- Concatenation

- Data types
- Type declaration characters
- Declaring variables

Common Statements and Functions

Figure B-1 below lists roughly 60 statements and functions that are common to traditional BASIC and to the Microsoft BASICs. (Refer to online Help for more detailed information on how these commands work in Access Basic, VBA for Excel, WordBasic, and Visual Basic.)

NOTE Items within brackets ([]) are optional for Access Basic, Visual Basic, and VBA for Excel. The $ indicates that the function returns a string; otherwise the function returns a variant data type (the least efficient). Because WordBasic has no variant data type, it requires a $. (The asterisk indicates functions that WordBasic doesn't use.)

Statement or Function	Purpose/Description
Abs()	Returns the absolute value.
Asc()	Although Asc is short for ASCII, this function returns the ANSI code for a character.
Beep	Beep. (What more can I say?)
Call	This statement, which calls a Sub procedure, is never required. To call a subroutine or a function, type the procedure's name.
Chr[$]()	Returns the character for the specified ANSI code.
Close	Closes a text file.
Date[$] or Date[$]()	In its statement form, it sets the current system date. As a function, it returns the current system date. Note that WordBasic uses only the function form.
Declare	Declares functions to be called from DLLs.
Def *type* statements, including DefInt and DefStr*	Sets the default data type.
Dim	Used to declare variables.
Err	Returns the error code after a trappable error occurs.
Error or Error()	In its statement form, it uses an application-defined error code to generate an error. As a function, it returns a string describing the error.
For...Next	Control structure for looping through a series of statements a specific number of times.

(continued)

Statement or Function	Purpose/Description
GoSub…Return*	You should never use this statement (which branches off to execute a subroutine within a procedure and then resumes execution from the branch point) because it isn't good programming practice. Instead, make all subroutines and functions discrete entities.
Goto	Moves to a specified line.
Hex[$]()*	Returns the hexadecimal form of a number.
If…ElseIf…Else…End If	Control structure that executes specific Code based on whether a certain condition occurs.
Input #	Reads data from a text file and stores it in variables.
InStr()	Returns the position of the first occurrence of one string in another.
Int() or Fix()*	Returns the integer part of a number.
Kill	Deletes a file.
Left[$]()	Returns the leftmost part of a string.
Len()	Returns the length of a string.
Let (not required)	This statement, which is used to assign a value to a variable, is never required. Instead, assign variables to values as follows: x = 1.
Math functions, including Atn()*, Cos()*, Exp()*, Log()*, Sin()*, Sqr()*, and Tan()*	Arctangent, cosine, exponential, natural logarithm, sine, square root, and tangent functions (just the way you knew and loved them in high school math class).
Mid[$] or Mid[$]()	In its statement form, it replaces part of a specified string. As a function, it returns part of a specified string.
Mod	Returns the remainder of a division operation.
On Error	Resumes execution after a trappable error has occurred.
On…GoTo/On…GoSub*	You should never use this structure, which branches to one of several specified lines, depending on an expression's value. Instead use Select Case, which is more structured and flexible.
Open	Opens a text file.
Print #	Writes data to a text file.
Randomize*	Seeds a random number generator.
Read	Reads data from a text file. Note that only WordBasic uses this statement.
Rem	Indicates a comment line. (A *comment* is text that isn't executed.) In general, use a single quote rather than the Rem statement to indicate comments. This method provides greater readability and requires less typing.
Right[$]()	Returns the rightmost part of a string.

Statement or Function	Purpose/Description
Rnd()	Returns a random number.
Sgn()	Returns 1, −1, or 0, depending on the sign of the given number.
Stop	Stops execution (used in debugging).
Str[$]()	Returns a string representation of a number.
String[$]()	Returns a string of specified length, all of whose characters are set to the function's character argument.
Sub…End Sub	Designates the beginning and end of a Sub procedure.
Tab()*	Moves to a specified column (used with Print #).
Time or Time[$]()	In its statement form, it sets the current system time. As a function, it returns the current system time.
UCase[$]()	Returns a specified string with all characters converted to uppercase.
Val()	Returns the numeric value of a string (essentially the opposite of the Str[$]() function).
While…Wend	The original BASIC control structure for looping through a series of statements until a specified condition is met. The newer, more flexible Do…Loop is the preferred method of looping, except in WordBasic, which doesn't support it.
Write #	Writes data to a text file.

Figure B-1. *Still standard after all these years.*

Standard Operators and Variables

In addition to the standard BASIC statements and functions that form the common core of Access Basic, VBA for Excel, WordBasic, and Visual Basic, these programming languages use standard arithmetic, logical, and comparison operators. (*Operators* are symbols that instruct the program to perform operations, such as addition, on the expressions on either side of the symbol.) These languages also handle variables in similar ways.

Arithmetic Operators

Arithmetic operators perform calculations:

- * (multiply)
- \+ (add)
- − (subtract)
- / (divide and return decimal)

- \ (divide and return integer)
- ^ (raise to exponent)
- ( ) (define the order for evaluating expressions)

> **NOTE** Integer arithmetic is always faster than floating-point (decimal) arithmetic, so use integers for calculations whenever possible. WordBasic, which performs only floating-point arithmetic, doesn't support integer division or exponents.

The following example performs a calculation and displays a message box with the result (693.3333). Use parentheses to define the order in which calculations occur, just as you would in arithmetic. Again, since message boxes display only text, convert numbers to text using the Str$ function.

```
Sub SampleCalculation()
  MsgBox Str$((130 + 130) * 8 / 3)
End Sub
```

Logical Operators

Logical operators combine Boolean expressions (expressions that evaluate to either True or False) to produce a Boolean (True/False) result:

- And
- Not
- Or
- Eqv (logical equivalence)
- Imp (logical implication)
- Xor (logical exclusion)

Figure B-2 shows how these logical operators evaluate to either True or False depending on whether the individual expressions evaluate to either True or False. Note that True has the integer value of -1 and False has the integer value of 0. This means that the expression x = 1 Eqv 1 (which is True) evaluates to -1.

> **NOTE** WordBasic supports only the first three logical operators.

Logical Operator	Individual Expressions	Result
And	True And True	True
	True And False	False
	False And True	False
	False And False	False
Not	Not True	False
	Not False	True
Or	True Or True	True
	True Or False	True
	False Or True	True
	False Or False	False
Eqv (logical equivalence)	True Eqv True	True
	True Eqv False	False
	False Eqv True	False
	False Eqv False	True
Imp (logical implication)	True Imp True	True
	True Imp False	False
	False Imp True	True
	False Imp False	True
Xor (logical exclusion)	True Xor True	False
	True Xor False	True
	False Xor True	True
	False Xor False	False

Figure B-2. *Results of logical operations on expressions, based on whether the individual expressions evaluate to True or False.*

The following example uses the InputBox function (which is a standard part of the Microsoft BASICs) to get input from users and an If...Then...Else control structure to evaluate this input and respond accordingly. (See Chapter 2 for more information on input boxes.) If users type *clothing* and *NJ*, the program displays a message box indicating that the purchased items aren't taxable. If users type *food* and the abbreviation for any state, the program displays the same message. (Note that the UCase$ function eliminates the need to require that users enter the information in either uppercase or lowercase.) If users type anything else, the program displays a message box indicating that the purchased items *are* taxable.

Remember that the Microsoft BASICs treat text that begins with an apostrophe (') as a comment.

```
Sub IsItTaxable()
  Dim Purchase As String
  Dim Taxable As Integer

'Use input boxes to get input from users.
  Purchase = InputBox$("Enter your purchase:")
  State = InputBox$("Enter the state where you made the purchase:")

'Evaluate the input from users and set Taxable accordingly.
  If UCase$(Purchase) = "CLOTHING" And UCase$(State) = "NJ" Then
    Taxable = False
  ElseIf UCase$(Purchase) = "FOOD" Then
    Taxable = False
  Else
    Taxable = True
  End If

'Display a message box based on whether Taxable is True or False.
  If Taxable = True Then
    MsgBox "Taxable!"
  Else
    MsgBox "Not Taxable!"
  End If
End Sub
```

Comparison Operators

Comparison operators allow you to compare expressions. The result is always Boolean—in other words, either True or False:

- = (equal to)

- <> (not equal to)

- < (less than)

- > (greater than)

- <= (less than or equal to)

- >= (greater than or equal to)

The following example uses an input box and an If...Then...Else control structure to compare the age entered to the legal drinking age in New York. The program responds with an encouraging word if the age entered is "legal," and a beep if it's not. Note that since the InputBox function returns a string and the "greater than or equal to" operator requires a number, you must use the Val function to represent that string as a number.

```
Sub SampleCompare()
  Dim Age As String
  Age = InputBox$("Enter your age:")
  If Val(Age) >= 21 Then
    MsgBox "Have a beer!"
  Else
    Beep
  End If
End Sub
```

Concatenation

All concatenation in WordBasic is done using the plus sign (+). While the other BASICs also support this syntax, for clarity's sake it's generally better to use the ampersand (&) for concatenation and to reserve + for addition. The following example uses an If...Then...Else control structure to determine whether users entered a valid number (stored in the variable Answer) in the input box. If users entered a valid number, the program concatenates that number with other text and displays a message box. Otherwise, it beeps and displays a message box alerting users to the fact that they entered an invalid number.

```
Sub ShowAnswer()
  Dim Answer As String
  Answer = InputBox$("Enter a number from 1 through 101:")
  If Val(Answer) <= 101 And Val(Answer) >= 1 Then
    MsgBox "The answer is: " & Answer & "."
  Else
    Beep
    MsgBox "You entered an invalid number."
  End If
End Sub
```

Data Types

Visual Basic and Access Basic have eight data types: Integer, Long, Single, Double, Currency, String, Variant, and Object. VBA for Excel has these plus two more: Boolean and Date. WordBasic (which is beginning to remind me of the ugly duckling) has only four data types—String, Number (any number, with or without decimals), Integer, and Long—and it uses Integer and Long only to communicate with DLLs.

Variant is the default data type in Access Basic, Visual Basic, and VBA for Excel (unless you use the Def *type* statement to set a different default). Although you must use a variant if you don't know the type of data that a variable will receive, variants are the least efficient data type and the largest (16 bytes or more—compared to 2 bytes for an integer and 4 bytes for a long).

An Example Illustrating How to Use Subroutines and Functions

The sample subroutine below calls the function GetLastName, which accepts as an argument a full name in the form *LastName, FirstName*. The subroutine passes it the name "Kemeny, John," and the function uses the BASIC functions InStr and Left$ to return only the last name.

```
Sub DisplayLastName ()
  Dim LastName As String

'Call the function GetLastName.
  LastName = GetLastName("Kemeny, John")
  MsgBox LastName
End Sub

Function GetLastName (FullName As String) As String
  Dim i As Integer
  i = InStr(FullName, ",")
  GetLastName = Left$(FullName, i - 1)
End Function
```

Type-Declaration Characters

As in traditional BASIC, the Microsoft BASICs let you use type-declaration characters for data types instead of keywords (such as Integer, String, and so on). Although developers tend to have strong opinions about whether to use these, type-declaration characters are certainly quicker to type than keywords are. The complete list of type-declaration characters is as follows: % (Integer), & (Long), ! (Single), # (Double), @ (Currency), and $ (String).

Developers who don't like to use type-declaration characters tend to argue along two lines: 1) the characters make code harder to read (which is true only if the reader doesn't know what the symbols mean), and 2) they make variable names asymmetrical because not all data types have a type-declaration character.

In WordBasic, always use the $ sign to identify string variables; otherwise, the language treats the variable as a number.

Using the Macro Recorder

The purpose of macro languages is to automate tasks that users perform with the host application and to enhance the functionality of that application. Both Microsoft Word and Microsoft Excel (but not Microsoft Access) provide a macro recorder, which lets you record the code necessary to execute the task from a macro while you perform the task manually. Although it's rarely a good idea to use macro-recorded code wholesale, this code is often a good starting point for automating specific tasks.

Recording Word Macros

To use the macro recorder in Word:

1. Choose Macro from the Tools menu.

2. Click the Record button in the Macro dialog box.

3. In the Record Macro dialog box, you can:

- Name the macro.

- Assign it to a toolbar, a menu, or a keyboard command.

- Select the template in which to store the macro.

- Enter a brief description of the macro. (This description appears in the status bar when you run the macro from a menu item or a toolbar.)

When you click OK, Word closes the dialog box and displays the Macro Recorder toolbar, which has two buttons: Stop and Pause.

4. Perform the task. Use the Pause button to perform any actions that you don't want to record.

5. After you finish, click the Stop button.

6. To view the recorded macro, choose Macro from the Tools menu, and then select the macro from the list and click the Edit button.

As a sample, I recorded the following code for opening a file. To do this, I chose Open from the File menu, switched to the directory C:\MYDIR\MYDOCS, selected the file EXAMPLE.DOC, and then clicked OK.

```
Sub MAIN
ChDefaul  ", 0
FileOpen .Name = "EXAMPLE.DOC", .ConfirmConversions = 0,
  .ReadOnly = 0, .AddToMru = 0, .PasswordDoc = "",
  .PasswordDot = "", .Revert = 1, .WritePasswordDoc = "",
  .WritePasswordDot = ""
End Sub
```

Recording Excel Macros

Using Excel's macro recorder is similar to using Word's macro recorder:

1. Choose Record Macro from the Tools menu, and then select Record New Macro.

2. Type a name and a brief description of the macro you are recording. Click the Options button to:

   - Assign the macro to a menu item or a shortcut key
   - Specify a location other than the current workbook for the recorded macro
   - Record your macro in the Excel version 4 macro language

   When you click OK, Excel closes the dialog box and displays the Stop Recording toolbar, which has one button: Stop.

3. Perform the task.

4. After you finish, click the Stop button.

5. To view the recorded macro, scan through the sheets until you see a new module, called Module1. (If you already have a Module1, the recorded macro will be in Module*N*, where *N* is the next number.) All macros that you record in the current session with the current workbook appear in this module.

As a sample, I recorded the following code for selecting a range of cells. To do this, I selected Sheet3, and then I selected the cells from A1 through C13.

```
Sub TestMacro()
  Sheets("Sheet3").Select
  Range("A1:C13").Select
End Sub
```

Turning Macro-Recorded Code into Solid Code that Won't Break

The problem with macro-recorded code is that it's hard-coded—in other words, it performs only the *specific* actions that you record. For example, the WordBasic code recorded in the previous section can open only one file, EXAMPLE.DOC, when this file is located in the directory C:\MYDIR\MYDOCS. Similarly, the VBA for Excel code recorded above can select only the range A1 through C13 on the worksheet named Sheet3. The way to turn hard-coded code into reusable code is to use variables.

Using Variables in WordBasic

Let's say you want to rewrite the WordBasic example shown earlier (in the section titled "Recording Word Macros") so that it uses a variable. There are four steps:

1. Delete the reference to changing the default directory, because that's not the directory you always want to use.

2. Create a variable, such as FileToOpen$, to store the path and name of the file to open. For example, the following code sets the variable FileToOpen$ to C:\MYDIR\MYDOCS\EXAMPLE.DOC:

```
FileToOpen$ = "C:\MYDIR\MYDOCS\EXAMPLE.DOC"
```

3. Clean up the code. Macro-recorded code lists all the arguments for Word's FileOpen statement (which corresponds to options in the File Open dialog box), even if you didn't select those options. In the example I recorded, I specified only one option—the file to open—but the macro-recorded code nonetheless includes values for all options. *Delete extra options.* If you don't, the macro will use these options rather than the options last used by the user.

The first example below shows the original macro-recorded code, and the second shows the new code produced by following steps 1 through 3.

Macro-Recorded WordBasic Code

```
Sub MAIN
ChDefaultDir "C:\MYDIR\MYDOCS\", 0
FileOpen .Name = "EXAMPLE.DOC", .ConfirmConversions = 0,→
    .ReadOnly = 0, .AddToMru = 0, .PasswordDoc = "",→
    .PasswordDot = "", .Revert = 1, .WritePasswordDoc = "",→
    .WritePasswordDot = ""
End Sub
```

WordBasic Code that Uses a Variable

```
Sub MAIN
  FileToOpen$ = "C:\MYDIR\MYDOCS\EXAMPLE.DOC"
  FileOpen .Name = FileToOpen$
End Sub
```

4. Although the second subroutine is cleaner than the first, it's still hard-coded. The only way to specify the file to open is for the developer to type *as part of the code itself* a new path and filename for the FileToOpen$ variable. However, the user (not the developer) should choose the file to open.

One way to handle this is to display an input box in which users can type the path and name of the file to open. The following subroutine uses WordBasic's InputBox function to do this. This subroutine opens any file for which users type a full path:

```
Sub MAIN
  FileToOpen$ = InputBox$("Type the path of the file to open:")
  FileOpen .Name = FileToOpen$
End Sub
```

Using Variables in VBA for Excel

Let's say you rewrite the VBA for Excel example shown earlier (in the section titled "Recording Excel Macros") so that it uses a variable. The idea is the same as in the WordBasic example above.

1. Create a variable, such as WhichSheet, to store the name of the sheet to select.

2. To avoid hard-coding the sheet name, provide a mechanism (such as an input box) for getting information from the user.

   The first example below shows the original macro-recorded code, and the second shows the new code produced by following steps 1 and 2.

Macro-Recorded VBA for Excel Code

```
Sub TestMacro()
  Sheets("Sheet3").Select
  Range("A1:C13").Select
End Sub
```

VBA for Excel Code that Uses a Variable

```
Sub TestMacro()
  Dim WhichSheet As String
  WhichSheet = InputBox$("Type the name of the sheet to use:")
  Sheets(WhichSheet).Select
  Range("A1:C13").Select
End Sub
```

GLOSSARY

access keys Access keys are represented by underlined letters on menus and in dialog box labels. Press Alt plus the key for the underlined letter to access the command or control.

active window The window of the application that has the focus.

add-ins Custom applications built with end-user development tools that you can "add in" to that tool. Add-ins are a handy way to distribute business applications because their code is typically protected so that users can use, but not change, the application. This feature also makes add-ins good vehicles for delivering code libraries. Microsoft Access, Microsoft Excel, and Microsoft Word all let you create and use add-ins.

ANSI American National Standards Institute, which provides hardware standards and programming language standards. For example, C, BASIC, and SQL each have ANSI-developed standards.

API Application programming interface. A set of routines that an application uses to request lower-level services. An "open" API (as opposed to a "proprietary" API) is one whose specifications are made available for everyone to use. Windows has an open API.

architecture A term used to describe how the components of a computer system (such as PCs, file servers, and minicomputers) work together.

argument Information that a subroutine or function requires to perform a task or to process a result.

bookmark A feature of Word that lets you return to a particular spot in a template, paragraph, table, or field code. Bookmarks are similar to named ranges in Excel. Recordset objects in Access also have a Bookmark property that lets you return to specific records easily. *See also* named range.

child window A child window belongs to another window, called, of course, the *parent*. For example, a Word document window is a child of the Word application window in which it is displayed. *Siblings* are children of the same parent window. *See also* parent window.

class Classes contain data members, plus a set of functions to handle the data. The data itself, and possibly some of the functions, are *private* so that you can't access them directly from outside the class. The remaining functions are *public* and form the interface for the class. Any code outside the class must use these public functions to access the data. An object is an example of a class. *See also* object.

client Generally, an application that receives data from other applications. *See also* server.

client-server model Client-server is the latest network computing model. In the simplest sense, any PC that gets data from a network (which supplies data) is a client. Technically, however, client-server architecture takes things a step further. It actually splits client-server applications into a *front end* (the client), which runs on the PC, and a *back end* (the server), which runs on a remote computer. The goal of the client-server architecture is to structure appropriately the amount of processing that each end of an application does. *See also* file server; peer-to-peer computing.

code library A collection of procedures that you can call from an application. You can use libraries to store routines that you use often. Access, Excel, and Word all support use of code libraries. In Access, such a library might be presented as a library database or a wizard; in Excel, as an add-in or a workbook; and in Word, as a macro-editing window or a global template.

collection A collection (or *collection object*) is a list of the current members that a given type of object contains. For example, in VBA for Excel, the Workbooks collection is a list of Workbook objects; in Access Basic, the Forms collection is a list of Access forms.

compiled programming language Languages such as C++ that require you to translate a program's source code into a machine executable form (a process called *compiling*) as a separate step before running the program. *See also* interpreted programming language.

compound document A document that includes data and materials created in more than one application—for example, a Word document that includes charts created in Excel and reports generated from Access.

container Another term for an OLE client application. *See also* OLE client.

control A user interface object (such as a command button or a list box) that lets users control the application.

custom control A user interface object built by a third-party vendor. Visual Basic version 3 uses custom controls in VBX format, and Visual Basic version 4 uses custom controls in both VBX and OCX formats. (OCX stands for OLE Custom Controls, which are OLE automation objects.) Access Basic lets you use OLE Custom Controls.

data type A type of data that a programming language recognizes—for example, strings (text data) and integers (whole numbers).

DDE Dynamic Data Exchange, one of Microsoft's core technologies for enabling applications to share data. DDE has been around since Word for Windows version 1 and Excel version 3; Microsoft is replacing it gradually with newer data-exchange technology such as OLE automation.

DDE client An application that requests data from other DDE applications.

DDE server An application that supplies data via DDE to other applications.

dialog box A special type of window used to present data to users and to get data from them. *See also* form.

dialog record A special data structure that lets developers retrieve and change the settings for Word's built-in dialog boxes. All the settings possible for a dialog box make up the dialog record. Once you create a dialog record, you can manipulate each setting individually.

DLL Dynamic link library of procedures. "Dynamic" refers to the fact that applications use these procedures dynamically at runtime, as opposed to compile time. This means that dynamic link libraries can be updated independently of the applications that use their procedures. *See also* WLL; XLL.

enabled window A window that can receive mouse or keyboard input. *See also* active window; focus.

end-user development tool A shrink-wrapped application such as Excel or Word that includes programmable macro languages that let you turn the product into a custom business application.

event-driven application In an event-driven application, the user—not the program—is in control. Users control the application by clicking a certain button (which runs one procedure) or pressing a certain key (which runs another). An event-driven application also responds to system events (such as timer functions) and to events triggered indirectly by the code (such as Load events, which occur whenever Access Basic or Visual Basic opens a form).

exposed object An object that other applications can use through OLE automation.

field code Field codes (or *fields*) are instructions that tell Word where to find data, what to do with it when it's found, and how to format it. You can view field codes in two different ways: as results (formatted text or graphics) or as the field codes or instructions themselves.

file server A computer that provides centralized control over files on a network. Traditional PC networks use central file servers to enable PCs to share data by sending files to the server. The server then routes these files to PCs according to address, or it stores them on a network drive. Traditional file-server applications (which support multiple users) are generally structured in one of two ways: either they run entirely from the file server or, in the case of some database applications, entirely from the PC, which accesses data from the server. *See also* client-server model; peer-to-peer computing.

flat-file database A database that is nonrelational—i.e., that does not establish relationships between multiple files or tables. Excel is a flat-file database, while Access is a relational database.

focus The properties of an object (window, dialog box, or control) that determine whether it receives the current mouse or keyboard input. Only one object at a time receives mouse or keyboard input. For example, an Access dialog box might have several controls, all of which are enabled, but only one has the focus. *See also* enabled window.

form In business applications, a form is a special type of dialog box in which users can enter, edit, and view data stored in a database. In Access Basic and Visual Basic, forms are the windows and dialog boxes that make up the application's interface.

function A group of related instructions with a single name that might perform a task but always returns a value. *See also* subroutine.

GUI (Pronounced "gooey.") Graphical user interface.

handle A reference number that Windows uses to identify an object (such as a window or a task). Just about everything in Windows has a handle, and a large proportion of Windows API functions either require a handle as an argument or return a handle. Some do both.

help *See* Windows Help.

hypertext Documents with special links added that let users move through the document's information in an organized but seemingly random fashion—*organized* because someone planned and built the links that lead from one topic to another, and *random* because users can follow whatever links they want.

INI files Initialization files used by Windows applications to store information such as user preferences or application settings. INI files are standard text files.

interpreted programming language A language (such as Visual Basic) that translates (or compiles) code into a machine executable form line by line as it executes the program. Such languages essentially compile a line of code, run it, compile the next line, run it, and so on. *See also* compiled programming language.

LAN Local area networks connect PCs and let them communicate via e-mail and share files, printers, modems, and so on.

legacy application Any application that runs on "old" technology. Also called *legacy system*.

library *See* code library.

links A pointer connecting a client application that displays certain data to the server application that actually stores the data. In Office applications such as Excel and Word, you manage linked data (which can be updated) through the Links command on the Edit menu. There are two types of links: *cold links*, in which the client application (or container) must explicitly request data from the server to update that data (set the linked item to "Manual"), and *hot links*, in which the server sends updated data to the server every time the data changes (set the linked item to "Automatic").

macro A sequence of frequently used commands bundled into a single instruction.

macro language A programming language built into an application that lets you combine a series of tasks into a single command.

MDI Multiple Document Interface is the standard for applications that use multiple documents or forms.

metacollection A collection of objects of different types. For example, in VBA for Excel, DrawingObjects is a metacollection. For any given worksheet, this metacollection contains all of the graphical and user-interface objects, from Rectangles to Buttons.

method The specific functions you can use on an object, such as Clear, Drag, and Hide. *See also* property.

named range A feature of Excel that lets you return easily to a particular group of cells. Named ranges are similar to bookmarks in Word. *See also* bookmark.

object The term *object*, which was once a fairly well-defined technical term, has recently become a catchall phrase referring to everything from a programming construct to a button in a dialog box. As programming constructs, computer objects combine data with functions for using the data. Microsoft has expanded the notion of objects to include *programmable objects*, which you can control through OLE automation. Technically, an object is an example of a class. *See also* class.

ODBC Open Database Connectivity, Microsoft's standard interface for accessing data.

ODBC data source The data source includes three pieces of information: the ODBC driver; a unique, descriptive name; and the full path and the name of the database. You set up ODBC data sources using the ODBC driver manager. *See also* ODBC driver manager.

ODBC driver A DLL that an ODBC-enabled application uses to access a particular database. Each database or database management system (DBMS), such as Oracle, Paradox, or Access, requires a specialized driver.

ODBC driver manager A Control Panel application that lets you set up ODBC data sources, install drivers, and otherwise manage ODBC.

OLE A Microsoft specification for how applications handle objects. OLE handles two categories of objects: objects that represent data to users and objects that developers manipulate through OLE automation.

OLE automation A feature of OLE2 that lets a programming language use another application's exposed objects.

OLE automation client An application that can manipulate another application's exposed objects.

OLE automation server An application that exposes objects that programming languages can manipulate.

OLE client An application that provides "containers" for storing and displaying data (or "objects") created in other applications. OLE clients let you create compound documents.

OLE server An application that creates objects and lets you embed or link those objects in OLE client applications.

open systems architecture A technology infrastructure that emphasizes standards to which all vendors adhere. Such standards enable businesses to select products from multiple vendors rather than limiting businesses to a particular vendor's product line.

operator A symbol that performs a task. Programming languages have three basic types of operators: arithmetic (for example, + adds and / divides); comparison (for example, = is "equal to" and <> is "not equal to"); and logical (for example, Not).

parent window A window that has children—in other words, it "owns" other windows. For example, a Word application window can have several document windows, which are its children. *See also* child window.

peer-to-peer computing Peer-to-peer networks (such as Windows for Workgroups) turn every PC into a potential server as well as a client. PCs that share their resources with others act as de facto servers, and PCs that borrow resources act as clients. *See also* client-server model; file server.

pointer A memory address. Although pointers are used widely in programming, none of the BASICs uses them. Since many Windows API functions take pointers as arguments, use a variable of the type indicated by the pointer when you call these functions from one of the BASICs. For example, if one of the arguments to an API function is a pointer to a string, use a string variable.

procedural application An application in which the program is in control. The program—not the end user—determines what happens next, and when it needs user input it displays a dialog box.

procedure A general term encompassing both subroutines and functions.

property A characteristic or an attribute that belongs to an object, such as color, size, and position and whether the object is visible. *See also* method.

reengineering The analysis and redesign of business systems at every level, including workflow, information flow, and so on.

relational database Databases that establish relationships between multiple files or tables. Access is a relational database, while Excel is a flat-file database.

rollout The process of introducing an application to users and making it a useful business tool.

screen redraw A feature that updates the screen so users see files opening and data appearing as code executes. Also called *screen updating*.

secondary window In Windows Help, a subsidiary window that appears on top of the main Help window. Secondary windows can have various positions, sizes, and colors. (Limit: five secondary windows per Help file.)

server Generally, an application that supplies data to other applications. *See also* client.

.SHG The standard extension for *hot-spotted* graphics created using SHED.EXE, an application that's also known as the *hot-spot editor*. The .SHG extension is an acronym for Segmented HyperGraphics, which is a highly compressed bitmap format. Since Microsoft has not made the spec for this graphics format public, the only application that supports it is Windows Help.

SQL (Pronounced "sequel.") An acronym for Structured Query Language. This language (which comes in a variety of flavors) is the standard for communicating with relational databases. For example, ODBC uses SQL commands to communicate with databases.

SQL Server Microsoft's multiuser relational database management system (RDBMS) that runs on local area networks (LANS).

statement An instruction to a computer defined by the programming language.

subroutine A group of related instructions with a single name that performs a task but doesn't return a value. *See also* function.

system resources The fixed amount of memory available to two of Window's three main DLLs—USER.EXE (which stores information about all open windows) and GDI.EXE (which stores information about graphical objects). When you get "out of memory" messages in Windows version 3.*x*, you're really getting "out of system resources" messages. Installing additional memory doesn't help because GDI.EXE can use a maximum of 64 KB.

task Any application that is running under Windows at a given time.

template A model—for example, a sheet on which you model other sheets or a document on which you model other documents. Templates make it easy to create standard documents, workbooks, charts, and so on.

twip One twip = $\frac{1}{20}$ of a point. There are approximately 1440 twips per inch.

VBA Visual Basic for Applications. Eventually this will be the common macro language for Office products, including Access, Excel (where it exists already), and Word.

WAN Wide area networks connect PCs long-distance and let them communicate via e-mail and share files, printers, modems, and so on. Today, WANs are often connected through fast, dedicated data-switching centers known as *frame relay clouds*.

Windows Help Help is the native hypertext tool in Windows. It is built into WINHELP.EXE, a Help viewer installed automatically when you install Windows version 3.1.

wizard A series of dialog boxes that leads users through the steps necessary to perform a complex task, such as creating and formatting a report.

WLL A DLL that can execute WordBasic commands, built specifically for use by Word. *See also* DLL; XLL.

WOSA Windows Open Services Architecture—a published specification that enables hardware and software manufacturers to build Windows-compatible products. The open architecture approach helped to move the PC industry away from the proprietary model toward standardization. Now businesses essentially build their own systems. They choose from a wide variety of computer vendors, printer manufacturers, monitor manufacturers, and software developers to put together highly customized solutions.

wrapper An interface that makes it easier to use an API function (or a series of API functions). Visual Basic custom controls are often wrappers for Windows API functions. You can also create Access Basic, VBA for Excel, or WordBasic functions that make it easier to use API calls with these programming languages.

XLL A DLL that can execute VBA for Excel commands, built specifically for use by Excel. *See also* DLL; WLL.

INDEX

Numbers in italics refer to figures or tables.

Ctrl+Shift+F9 key combination, 97
curly brackets ({}), denoting field characters, 97
custom DLLs. *See* DLLs (dynamic link libraries)

D

databases
  Access (*see* Microsoft Access)
  back ends, 82–86, 87
  connectivity (*see* DDE [Dynamic Data
    Exchange]; ODBC [Open Database
    Connectivity])
  departmental, 325
  encryption, *176*, 351
  front ends, 83, 87, 96–109, 265
  querying (*see* SQL [Structured Query
    Language])
  relational (*see* relational databases)
  retrieving external, into Excel workbooks,
    312–24
  security, 338–51
  security, objects, and, 412–13
data-consolidation applications, 326
data protection, OLE, 412–13
data sources, ODBC, 88–89
data structures, API functions and, 116
data types
  Microsoft BASICs, 519, 533–34
  type-declaration characters, 30, 534
  VBA for Excel, *270–71*
dates, Windows vs. Macintosh, 323
DDE (Dynamic Data Exchange), 439–50
  commands, *440*
  Excel add-in, 447–50
  executing DDE commands, 443–44
  initiating DDE conversations, 443
  OLE vs., 439 (*see also* OLE)
  retrieving data from Excel, 442–47
  sample Word and Excel utility, 440–53
  terminating DDE conversations, 444–47
DDEExecute command, *440*
DDEInitiate command, *440*
DDEPoke command, *440*
DDERequest command, *440*
DDETerminate command, *440*
debugging Access libraries, 336
decision-support applications, 326

Declare statement, 116
Define Names sample utility, 294–300
DELETE statement (SQL), 383–84
deletion constraint programs, 370
deliveries, application, 47–48. *See also*
    rollouts, application
Del key, 97
design. *See* development methodologies and
    issues
desktop integration, 5–7. *See also* ODBC
    (Open Database Connectivity)
desktop publishing
  case study, 234–36
  sample application, 237–49
development methodologies and issues
  acting as end user, 45
  analyzing threads, 47
  beta testing threads, 48
  different operating systems, 321–24
  different PC configurations, 168–70
  documentation (*see* documentation)
  end-user (*see* end-user development tools)
  grouping threads into deliverables, 47–48
  GUI development vs., 44 (*see also* GUI
    [graphical user interface] development)
  Help (*see* applications, Windows Help–based)
  identifying tasks, 45
  identifying threads of functionality, 46–47
  importance of, 41–42
  as iterative processes, 48
  measuring productivity gains, 49
  PC-based, 42–43
  preventing failed projects, 43
  productivity and, 48–51
  resources, 513
  rollout planning (*see* rollouts, application)
  sample data-entry task scenario, 46
  six development steps, 44–48
  software and hardware hype, 51
  support, 495
  template-based development, 267
  traditional, 42
  training (*see* training)
DevelopR.XLS sample application, 294–304
  AppMakeR vs., 295
  Book Browser utility, 300–304
  defined names, 296

X

Christine Solomon is a director at Micro Modeling Associates, Inc., a consulting firm that provides Microsoft Windows–based solutions to Fortune 500 companies and financial institutions. In this capacity, she established the firm's Microsoft Word development group and has pioneered new techniques for creating Microsoft Office–based publishing and presentation systems using such tools as Microsoft Excel, Word, Visual Basic, and Windows Help.

Solomon, who developed her first Excel-based application in 1989, was responsible for designing and developing the original version of one of the two applications featured in Microsoft's Office Launch (kicked off by Bill Gates in New York City in October 1993). She is the author of the *Print and Presentation Kit* series published by Addison-Wesley. She speaks frequently at seminars and conferences.

A licensed scuba diver, Solomon lives in New York City with her husband and a Russian Blue named Boris.

097-000-680